The Dynamics of Population Policy in Latin America

The Dynamics of Population Policy in Latin America

Terry L. McCoy, Editor
The Ohio State University

Ballinger Publishing Company • Cambridge, Mass.
A Subsidiary of J.B. Lippincott Company

Copyright © 1974 by Ballinger Publishing Company. All rights reserved. No part of this publication may be reproduced, stored in a retrieval system, or transmitted in any form or by any means, electronic mechanical photocopy, recording or otherwise, without the prior written consent of the publisher.

International Standard Book Number: 0-88410-350-1

Library of Congress Catalog Card Number: 73-16353

Printed in the United States of America

Library of Congress Cataloging in Publication Data

McCoy, Terry L   1940-   comp.
    The dynamics of population policy in Latin America.

Includes bibliographical references.
    1. Birth control—Latin America—Addresses, essays, lectures.
2. Latin America—Population—Addresses, essays, lectures. I. Title.
HQ766.5.L3M3   301.32'1   73-16353
ISBN 0-88410-350-1

Contents

List of Figures	xi
List of Tables	xiii
Acknowledgements	xv
Introduction, *Terry L. McCoy*	xvii
Latin America in Demographic Transition	xvii
Approach and Selections	xxii
The Dynamics of Population Policy in Latin America	xxvi
Notes to Introduction	xxvii
Part I: **An Overview of the Politics of Population in Latin America**	1
Chapter One **Politics and Population Control in Latin America** *J. Mayone Stycos*	3
Latin American Attention to Population Problems	3
Nationalism	5
Marxism	7
Marxist Influence on Latin American Thought	9
The United States and Population Control	12
Conclusions	14
Notes to Chapter 1	16

Chapter Two
The Relationship Between Population Planning and Belief Systems: The Catholic Church in Latin America
Thomas G. Sanders — 19

Notes to Chapter 2 — 33

Chapter Three
Factors Affecting the Population Attitudes of Latin American Elites
Axel Mundigo — 37

Introduction — 37
Honduras: A Case Study — 38
Elite Attitudes — 40
Conclusions — 55
Notes to Chapter 3 — 57

Chapter Four
Linkage Politics and Latin American Population Policies
Terry L. McCoy — 59

Introduction — 59
External Linkage Groups — 61
Internal Linkage Groups — 77
Conclusions — 80
Notes to Chapter 4 — 87

Part II:
Perspectives on Population Control — 95

Chapter Five
The Population Explosion
Benjamin Viel — 97

Notes to Chapter 5 — 105

Chapter Six
The World Bank Perspective on Population Growth
Robert S. McNamara — 107

Chapter Seven
On the Regulation of Birth: *Humanae Vitae*
Pope Paul VI — 123

I. New Aspects of the Problem and Competency of the Magisterium	123
II. Doctrinal Principles	125
III. Pastoral Directives	130

Chapter Eight
The Population Explosion Myth
Jorge Iván Hubner Gallo — 137

The Inopportune Return of Malthus	137
Family Planning	142
The Natural Self-Regulation of Populations	152
Notes to Chapter 8	160

Chapter Nine
Birth Control as a Weapon of Imperialism
José Consuegra — 163

The Rationale of the Antinatalist Thesis	163
Economic Thought and Population Growth	173
Natural Resources and Population	177
Notes to Chapter 9	180

Chapter Ten
The Demographic Problems of Mexico and Latin America
Gilberto Loyo — 183

Part III:
National Policies — 203

Chapter Eleven
Family Planning Programs and the Dynamics of Agenda-Building in Costa Rica and Chile
Vivian Epstein-Orlowski — 205

Introduction	205
Costa Rica	208
Chile	228
Conclusions	243
Notes to Chapter 11	251

Chapter Twelve
National Planning and Population Policy in Colombia
Germán Bravo — 265

Evolution of Concern with Population   265
The Institutional Framework   274
Government Population Policy   280
Conclusion   284
Notes to Chapter 12   288

Chapter Thirteen
The Politics of Family Planning in the Dominican Republic: Public Policy and the Political Process
Howard J. Wiarda   293

The Dominican Context   294
Toward A Family-Planning Program   299
The Politics of Family Planning   308
An Assessment   315
Notes to Chapter 13   318

Chapter Fourteen
Approaches and Strategies of Population Policy-Making in a Democratic Context: The Case of Venezuela
Iêda Siqueira Wiarda   323

The General Context of Policy-Making in Venezuela   324
Approaches and Strategies toward Population Policy
   Formulation   326
The Search for Political Allies and Sponsors in the Policy Process 333
Some Impliciations for Population Policy-Making in a
   Democratic Context   341
Notes to Chapter 14   345

Chapter Fifteen
The Context of Population Policy Formation in Peru
Richard Lee Clinton   353

Current Status of Population Activities   354
Conclusions   367
Notes to Chapter 15   370

Chapter Sixteen
A Paradigmatic Analysis of Mexican Population Policy
Terry L. McCoy   377

Environment, Policy, and Process	377
The Interest Group Subsystem	382
Policy-Making within the Regime	394
Conclusions	399
Notes to Chapter 16	401

Bibliographical Notes on Contributing Authors   409

About the Editor   411

List of Figures

4-1	External Linkage Group Network for Latin American Population Assistance	71
4-2	Linkage Network for Latin American Population Policies	80
11-1	Principle Sources of Costa Rican Family-Planning Program Financing, 1970 [in U.S. dollars]	222
12-1	Colombian Planning Process	277
12-2	Population Policy-Making and National Planning in Colombia	279

List of Tables

I-1	Latin American Population Growth: A Summary Profile	xix
I-2	Selected Indicators of Demographic Pressure (1970)	xx
3-1	Religiosity and Political Ideology (Percentages)	41
3-2	Political Ideology by Religiosity (Percentages)	42
3-3	Attitudes Toward Birth Control and Population (Percentages)	43
3-4	Attitudes Toward Birth Control by Religiosity and Political Ideology (Percentages)	45
3-5	Opposition to Birth Control by Religiosity and Political Ideology (Percentages)	47
3-6	Correlations of Four Variables Used for Population Score	49
3-7	Population Score and Modernism Scales: Rotated Factors	50
3-8	Elite Rejection of Birth Control by Type of Education (Percentages)	51
3-9	Selected Population Knowledge and Attitude Items by Religiosity of Elites (Percentages)	52
3-10	Selected Population Knowledge and Attitude Items by Political Ideology of Elites (Percentages)	54
4-1	USAID Grants to IPPF ($1,000's)	70
4-2	External Population Policy Inputs in Latin America	73
4-3	Latin American Population Policies and External Inputs	82
11-1	Principal Organizations Active in Family-Planning Programs or Population Research in Costa Rica and Chile, 1970	209
11-2	1970 Calendar of Family-Planning and Population Conferences in Costa Rica	224
12-1	Coercion and Population Policy Types	285
16-1	External Assistance for Population-Related Activities in Mexico (Cumulative, January, 1973)	389

xiii

Acknowledgments

The overall preparation of this book was made possible by a grant from the Population Council (administered by the Ohio State University Research Foundation) and the generous assistance of the Mershon Center at The Ohio State University. Personal thanks go to Charles Lininger and David Sills of the Population Council and to Mary Ellen Caldwell, Richard Snyder, and James Robinson of the Mershon Center. Their encouragement, given throughout the all-too-long history of this project, is deeply appreciated. J. Mayone Stycos and Parker Marden graciously opened the considerable resources of the International Population Program at Cornell University to me during the summer of 1972. A number of other individuals assisted in this project. They include: Debi Harper, Jennie Lincoln, Kitty Bernick, Richard Stoddard, Philip Choate, Ron Jones, Jolane Poling, and Wendy Howard. Finally, I must thank the contributors to this volume, especially those who prepared original pieces.

Terry L. McCoy

Introduction

Terry L. McCoy

Population has become a political issue in Latin America. With the highest regional rate of population growth in the world, demands that public action be taken to defuse the Latin American "population explosion" are increasingly heard throughout the region and throughout the world. This book presents a comprehensive analysis of contemporary Latin American population policies, specifically those dealing with fertility and growth. Composed of original pieces, translated excerpts from works by Latin Americans, and reprinted articles, speeches, and documents, it explores the political dimensions of population and examines, what, if anything, governments are doing to control growth.

The book was designed with three audiences in mind: demographers, sociologists, and policy-makers who are familiar with population dynamics but not with policy analysis; political scientists and other students of politics who have some feeling for public policy-making in Latin America but little background in demography; and informed laymen who are experts in neither but interested in the governmental response to what appears to be a significant problem. In order to make the population-public policy interface comprehensible to all three, the Introduction will first review the nature of the population explosion, its significance, and the role of government in defusing it. Then, the 16 selections contained in the book are previewed. Finally, the Introduction concludes with some generalizations about the dyamics of Latin American population policies.

LATIN AMERICA IN DEMOGRAPHIC TRANSITION

The popular image of Latin America is that of an area in constant ferment, a land of perpetual revolution. While these stereotypes, usually applied to politics, are often inaccurate, there is a dimension of Latin American reality which is today undergoing great change—perhaps even revolutionary change.

In the early decades of this century, Latin America began a dramatic demographic transition that is yet to be completed in most of the 20 countries. The most publicized aspect of current demographic ferment is a population explosion or rapid increase in population growth rates and total size. Another dimension is a "population implosion"—massive rural-to-urban migration—which we will not deal with here largely because it has yet to attract the political attention of rapid population growth, even though in the long run it may prove more troublesome. The population explosion, also sometimes referred to as the "vital revolution," is caused by a significant drop in mortality rates—particularly infant mortality rates—which means more people live longer. In 1930, for instance, the average life expectancy at birth for Latin America was less than 40 years. By 1960 it had risen to between 50 and 60 years, and a baby had more than a 50 percent chance of surviving to age 60 compared with less than a 50 percent probability of living to 30 years of age in 1930.[1] Decline in Latin American death rates began in the more advanced countries in about 1910 and spread to the less developed countries where the rate of decline accelerated after 1930. According to Arriaga, ". . . the speed of mortality decline seems to follow a general pattern: the later the date of decline, the faster its rate."[2] This rule reflects the fact that recently declining mortality is due largely to the importation of advanced medical and sanitary practices through international public health programs. Because it occurs independently of local socio-economic modernization, death control has thus arrived in varying degrees in all Latin American countries, even the most backward.

Declining mortality represents the first phase in the "demographic transition." The second is a decline in fertility rates that eventually brings them into rough balance with death rates. This, at least, is the sequence that the developed countries went through in arriving at their currently low levels of population growth. With few exceptions Latin America has not yet entered the second stage of the demographic transition. Only in Argentina, Cuba, and Uruguay have crude fertility rates fallen below 30 births per 1,000 population to levels approaching those of the developing world (see Table I-1). In all but Chile, which seems to be approaching 30, of the other 17 countries, they remain at pre-twentieth century levels—above 40 per 1,000.[3] The result of this severe fertility-mortality imbalance is rapid population growth in most, but not all, Latin American countries. From Table I-1, it is clear that Bolivia and Haiti have relatively low overall growth rates because of continued high mortality. This means that their growth rates will probably accelerate before they drop. To further grasp the consequences of the imbalance, compare the 1950 and 1970 populations of the Dominican Republic with those of Uruguay in Table I-1. In 1950 the two countries had virtually the same number of

Table I-1. Latin American Population Growth: A Summary Profile

Country	Population 1950 (thousands)	Fertility 1970 (births/1,000)	Mortality 1970 (deaths/1,000)	Annual Growth Rate, 1970 (% increase)	Population 1970 (thousands)
Argentina	17,085	23	9	1.5	24,352
Bolivia	3,019	44	19	2.4	4,931
Brazil	51,976	38	10	2.8	93,549
Chile	6,062	33	10	2.3	9,780
Colombia	11,331	45	11	3.4	21,117
Costa Rica	859	45	7	3.8	1,798
Cuba	5,516	27	7	2.0	8,341
Dominican Republic	2,129	49	15	3.4	4,348
Ecuador	3,231	45	11	3.4	6,028
El Salvador	1,859	47	13	3.3	3,441
Guatemala	2,805	43	15	2.8	5,179
Haiti	3,353	44	20	2.4	4,867
Honduras	1,389	49	17	3.4	2,583
Mexico	26,282	43	9	3.4	50,718
Nicaragua	2,052	46	17	2.9	2,021
Panama	795	40	8	3.2	1,463
Paraguay	1,397	45	11	3.4	2,418
Peru	7,969	42	11	3.1	13,586
Uruguay	2,196	21	9	1.2	2,889
Venezuela	4,962	41	8	3.3	10,399

Sources: Organización de Estados Americanos, Departamento de Asuntos Sociales, *Datos básicos de población en América Latina,* 1970 (Washington, D.C.: OAS, 1971). 1950 Population from UN, ECLA, *Statistical Bulletin for Latin America,* VIII, No. 1 (March 1971), p. 19.

people, but by 1970, under the influence of a 3.4 percent growth rate, there were almost 1.5 million more Dominicans than Uruguayans. (The direct influence of external migration on current population growth is negligible. If anything, it accounts for some flow out of Latin America, especially Middle America, to the United States. There is also some intra-regional migration.)

The Costs of Rapid Population Growth

When exposed to the sheer magnitude of population growth in Latin America, the almost automatic reaction is to conclude that it must be harmful. But it was not too long ago that population growth was widely perceived as a healthy phenomenon for a nation. After all, consider the experience of the United States during the nineteenth century throwing open its doors to millions of immigrants while it grew from a small rural country to a modern industrial power. The fact is that many informed Latin Americans still view population growth in positive terms.

Table I-2. Selected Indicators of Demographic Pressure (1970)

Country	1970 Population (thousands)	Density (Inhabitants/Sq. Km. of Arable Land	Percent Urban	No. of Years To Double	Dependency (% of Population under 15)
Argentina	24,352	17	78.8	47	29
Bolivia	4,931	32	35.4	29	43
Brazil	93,549	56	47.6	25	42
Chile	9,780	75	70.4	30	39
Colombia	21,117	113	57.6	21	47
Costa Rica	1,798	116	33.5	18	48
Cuba	8,341	142	53.4	35	34
Dominican Republic	4,348	345	36.8	21	48
Ecuador	6,028	118	45.7	21	47
El Salvador	3,441	315	37.9	21	46
Guatemala	5,179	252	30.7	25	46
Haiti	4,867	333	17.3	29	42
Honduras	2,583	61	27.7	21	47
Mexico	50,718	44	62.2	21	46
Nicaragua	20,021	59	39.9	24	47
Panama	1,463	105	50.1	22	45
Paraguay	2,418	22	36.0	21	46
Peru	13,586	68	49.2	23	44
Uruguay	2,889	18	79.8	58	28
Venezuela	10,399	51	71.9	21	46

Source: OEA, *Datos básicos.*

A brief review of many of the arguments for population control reveals that they are not very meaningful in the Latin American context; take total population (see Table I-2), for example only Brazil is large in world terms. A more accurate notion of overpopulation is density. Rapid population growth conjures up images of masses of humanity crowded into small areas. Once again, in terms of persons per unit of national surface, the Latin American countries are not densely populated when compared to Asia, Europe, or even the United States. Brazil's approximately 100 million people live in country larger than continental United States while El Salvador and Haiti have far fewer persons per square kilometer of national territory than does the Netherlands or Japan.[4] Two other measures of concentration—persons per square kilometer of arable land and percent urban—put the question of density into more meaningful perspective. The fact that large numbers of people cannot live in the Amazon Basin, Atacama Desert, or rugged mountain chains spread throughout Latin America shows up in the measure of relative density used in Table I-2. Yet even taking these limitations into consideration, most Latin American countries are not overpopulated, and others, such as Argentina and Uruguay, could support considerably more people. Percent urban of the total population taps another dimension of crowding.

As with the rest of the world, Latin America is steadily becoming more urbanized, although, notwithstanding the ugly slums surrounding large Latin cities, it still has a long way to go in comparative terms. Furthermore, natural population growth is only a small component of the urbanization process. Slowing it would have little effect on the rural-urban redistribution process.

A more salient reason for population control in Latin America relates to its impact on the vital struggle for national development. From this perspective, it is a race against time rather than against space in that the high rates of population growth require high rates of economic growth in order to sustain per worker and per capita growth. A country with an annual population growth rate of three percent and economic growth rate of four percent will double in population in only 24 years while per capita income will take 140 years. These figures draw a bleak picture for countries where per capita incomes vary between $100 and $500 per year as is the case in most of Latin America. But in addition to the mathematics of population growth, its structure has implications for economic development. "A rapid increase in the quantity of people has opportunity costs in terms of the quality of people."[5] A growing population is a young, dependent population which diverts scarce capital away from direct productive investments to building hospitals and schools for the non-working proportion—in some countries approaching 50 percent—of the population under 15 years of age.

The developmental rationale for slowing Latin American population growth is not without its doubters and detractors as the selections in this book will demonstrate. It is, nevertheless, a powerful argument and one that is gaining adherents. To it, one can add a number of micro-economic and non-economic reasons. They include the financial strain on the family of too many children, the emotional costs of unwanted progeny which in turn leads to illegal abortion and child abandonment, the medical complications of high parity, and other reasons discussed by the contributors to this volume. Given the reasons for bringing down the birth rate—and recognizing that they are not unopposed in Latin America—there remains an important question. How can it be accomplished and what role can the state play? The distinguished North American demographer Kingsley Davis has written that "The rationale for population control is simple: the number of people is too important to be left to chance."[6] Not so simple is the means for achieving control.

Public Policy as a Response to the Population Explosion

With the exception of Japan, fertility declined in the developed countries in the absence of direct social intervention and government policy. The transition to low growth was accomplished virtually without notice at the time as an apparent consequence of industrialization and general modernization. There are those who predict that this is exactly how it will happen (It already has in Argentina and Uruguay.) in all Latin America. The assumption of this position is that there is very little government can do directly to bring down fertility and to think otherwise merely diverts it from assisting the modernization process.

Challenging the notion that the demographic transition will take care of itself are the proponents of organized intervention to control fertility. They point out that because death control was imposed from abroad, often in the absence of local modernization, birth control must also be instituted in advance of general development. More than just an end in itself, declining fertility is a prerequisite to completing modernization. Raulet summarizes the argument like this:

> The less developed countries are thought to be caught in a kind of low-level equilibrium trap in which high rates of population growth impede economic development and economic backwardness and traditionalism hold back the completion of the 'demographic transition.'[7]

Since, for some, population control holds the key to development as well as the resolution of other problems, they argue that government must adopt a wide variety of measures, some coercive in nature, that will force fertility down into line with mortality. Much more common is the family-planning approach to lowering the population growth rate. Berelson defines family-planning programs as "deliberate efforts, typically governmental in funding and administration, to provide birth control information and services on voluntary basis to the target population, to the end of lowered fertility . . ." [8] Family planning's great attractiveness as a governmental measure lies in its voluntarism and ambiguous objectives, although these same characteristics also raise doubts about its effectiveness in bringing about aggregate demographic changes. Consequently, contemporary antinatalist population policies in Latin America, as in the rest of the developing world, have family-planning programs as their central element.[9]

APPROACH AND SELECTIONS

One of the purposes of this book is to provide an up-to-date, empirically based description of various Latin American population policies, including the state of family-planning programs, the existence of complementary activities, and the extent to which government programs constitute a conscious, comprehensive policy aimed at controlling population growth. In effect, we are charting the recent—yet unfinished—dramatic turn away from pronatalist policies toward antinatalist policies. A second objective is to analyze the factors underlying this movement. Latin America's pronatalist roots are deep, and they have affected—but not stopped—the shift toward population control. Thirdly, through an intensive study of one particular public policy and the forces that shape it, we hope to add insight into the dynamics of Latin American policy-making in general.

To accomplish these three objectives, this book is more than another compilation of already published articles. The topic is too recent and complex for such an approach. Instead, it is a diverse collection composed of eight chapters especially commissioned to present the recent results of important field research; four chapters translating the work of Latin American authors from Spanish to English; two chapters reprinting primary source materials; and two chapters reprinting articles previously published in English. The authors represent a variety of national, professional, and in some cases, ideological perspectives. Political scientists are overrepresented in a conscious attempt to apply the theories, concepts, and methods of this discipline to the understanding of a particular policy issue. Although each chapter is written to stand on its own, they are arranged in three parts which hopefully yield a logical approach to understanding what Latin American governments are doing about population growth and why.

Part I

Part I contains four chapters which introduce the more important political dimensions of population growth in Latin America. In Chapter I, J. Mayone Stycos, a social demographer and leading United States expert on Latin American population policies, uses content analysis of Latin American newspapers and interview data to illustrate those attitudes and values—particularly nationalism and Marxism—antithetical to population control policies. In this reprint of a 1967 article he suggests such opposition be circumvented by emphasizing family planning for individual and health reasons rather than for control of national fertility. Thomas Sanders follows in Chapter 2 by challenging the widely held notion that the Catholic Church is the principal obstacle to organized family planning in Latin America. With the papal encyclical on birth control as the background, he emphasizes the complexities and contradictions in the Church as an institution and Catholicism as a body of doctrine and set of values. He also points out important national variations in the Church. Sanders concludes that ". . . the specter of a Church galvanizing millions of Latin American Catholics against family planning lacks theological or sociological reality." Next, sociologist Axel Mundigo isolates in Chapter 3 the impact of political ideology, religiosity, and modernism on the population attitudes of a sample of Honduran business, government, professional, and student elites. In general, he finds opposition quite high to antinatalist measures with political ideology the strongest explanatory variable. The last chapter in

xxiv Introduction

Part I shifts the analysis from potential opponents to perhaps the most enthusiastic supporters of Latin American population control policies. Specifically, the author and editor of this volume examines the role played by various external organizations in prodding Latin American governments to adopt antinatalist population policies. This chapter also contains a summary classification of the population policies of all 20 Latin American governments (Table 4-3).

Part II

Moving from the work of academic observers, the selections in Part II present the viewpoints of individuals and groups interested in influencing Latin American population policy-making. These selections are not meant to be inclusive nor definitive but merely representative of important positions. While containing information and analyses, they are first and foremost expressions of influential opinions on the issues of population growth and control.

In the first selection (Chapter 5), one of the leaders of the Latin American family-planning movement, Benjamín Viel, presents a long list of regional problems which are, in his view, greatly complicated, if not caused by rapid population growth. Although he is careful not to make exaggerated claims or call for family planning as the key to development, he does propose it as the logical means for restoring equilibrium between population growth and economic growth. Viel's measured appeal contrasts with Robert McNamara's more dramatic call for population control in Asia, Africa, and Latin America (Chapter 6). He warns that "The misery of the underdeveloped world is today a dynamic misery, continuously broadened and deepened by a population growth that is totally unprecedented . . ." As President of the World Bank, McNamara's urgency underlines the discrepancy between the donors of population assistance and potential recipients. Chapter 7, in reprinting the papal encyclical—*Humanae Vitae*—on birth control, presents the views of another potential source of external influence on population policy-making in Latin America, the most Catholic of the world's regions. In spite of a general prohibition against artificial contraception and a warning that solutions to the socio-economic problems of the less developed countries must not do "violence to man's essential dignity," a careful reading of the encyclical reveals room for leeway in interpretation. Furthermore, in assaying its impact in Latin America, we must keep in mind Sanders' distinction between doctrinal Catholicism and popular Catholicism.

The next two chapters present the arguments of Latin American opponents to population control. Although they start from different ends of the political spectrum—Chapter 8 from the right and Chapter 9 from the left— these selections agree on certain key points as Stycos and Mundigo argued in Part I. Both attack Malthus and the neo-Malthusian claim that rapid population growth threatens humanity, and both articulate suspicion about the motives behind the support of the developed countries, led by the United States, for population control in the developing countries. The significance of this convergence for policy-making awaits analysis in the country chapters of Part III. Meanwhile, Part II concludes in Chapter 10 with the view of a prominent Mexican demographer, Gilberto Loyo, who, after struggling with the population issue for several decades as a dedicated nationalist, shifted from pronatalism to advocacy of population control through voluntary family planning. Loyo's personal conversion previewed the change in Mexican policy which is analyzed in Chapter 16, and his conditional support for population control is increasingly typical of reform-oriented Latin American elites.

Part III
This part contains case studies of how the forces discussed in the preceding chapters, along with other factors, combine to shape the evolution of governmental policies regarding fertility and growth. The country chapters, which are based on field research, begin with introductions to national demographic characteristics and local politics; describe what the government is doing and allowing others to do to promote family planning; and analyze the political dynamics of national policy. The sample of countries includes those in which the government is acting decisively to control population growth; others with incipient antinatalist policies; and one which steadfastly clings to pronatalism.

In Chapter 11, Vivian Epstein-Orlowski compares the policies of the two countries, Chile and Costa Rica, which were the first to venture into government support for family planning in Latin America and which today have extensive national family-planning programs. She searches for relationships between their relatively advanced policies and their long traditions of democratic policy-making. Colombia, which also started relatively early, has gone furthest toward adopting an authentic population control policy. In Chapter 12, Germán Bravo, writing with the personal experience of a social scientist who has participated in the policy-making process, traces the gradual evolution of governmental commitment to population control, which culminates with the incorporation of demographic planning into general developmental planning. The next two chapters deal with countries in policy transition. The Dominican Republic (Chapter 13) has gone far in the formal adoption of an antinatalist policy—perhaps because of heavy pressure from the United States, according to author Howard Wiarda—although there is some question about the extent of policy implementation. In Chapter 14 on Venezuela, Iêda Siqueira Wiarda focuses on the roles of private organizations in providing family planning and related services and in operating within the context of "democratic development" to lobby for greater governmental involvement. The next chapter on Peru provides Richard Clinton with the opportunity to analyze the constraints on population policy in a country which has refused to abandon pronatalism. Finally, in Chapter 16, McCoy, the author and editor of this volume, offers an explanation for the Mexican government's sudden and unexpected decision in 1972 to initiate a comprehensive national family-planning program with demographic objectives.

THE DYNAMICS OF POPULATION POLICY IN LATIN AMERICA

What general conclusions can be drawn about the current evolution of Latin American population policies and their prospects for the future from the 16 selections in this book? Without going into detail and giving proper attention to national variations, several observations seem warranted.

For the reader who feels that the state must take decisive action to control fertility and bring down the national growth rate in order to achieve economic development and long range social stability, the composite picture is not overly optimistic. While Latin American governments have generally abandoned their traditional pronatalism and active opposition to organized family planning in the last decade, they have also stopped considerably short of truly antinatalist policies. What have emerged are family-planning efforts which count on varying degrees of official support, accompanied by various supplementary activities. In only a few countries—Chile, Costa Rica, Cuba, and Colombia—are these programs national in scope; and only in Colombia has the government explicitly gone beyond family planning on an individual basis to population planning as an element of national development. Therefore, the assorted activities of other governments do not in the strict sense constitute population policies since there are no *deliberate* attempts to affect *national* demographic trends.[10] The official justification of most family planning programs is not popultion control but such non-demographic rationale as eliminating illegal abortion, inculcating responsible parenthood, and lowering the number of abandoned children. Even recognizing that such efforts may have disguised or secondary demographic objectives, their low visibility and isolation in the ministry of health, far from top level national policy-making, suggests that aggregate fertility decline will be non-existent or incidental to their presence.

To say that current population/family-planning activities do not really constitute antinatalist policies is not to say that their non-demographic goals are unimportant. They are, but they are not the ends that many— particularly their external sponsors—thought these activities were serving. To understand the somewhat attenuated nature of Latin American population programs and to determine whether they will evolve into genuinely antinatalist policies, it is helpful to reflect on the forces which shape and constrain policy-making.

Following the advice of experts like Stycos (Chapter 1), the external donors of population assistance and their internal allies deliberately stressed the non-demographic aspect of family planning in order to avoid sure political controversy by raising the specter of population control. In taking the line of least resistance, they got exactly what was publicly promised: voluntary family-planning programs designed to serve the health and welfare of the individual. Thus far, these efforts have not paved the way for more inclusive attempts at fertility control and population planning, except in Colombia and, apparently, in Mexico. A major obstacle to the development of comprehensive policies seems to be the conspicuous role of external actors, especially the United States, in the family-planning movement in Latin America. As long as they are dominant, there exists considerable skepticism about the movement, and Latin American governments have little incentive to expand something which is not really theirs.

For the public policy analyst, one of the fascinating features of the Latin American population policy scene is the variation in the 20 national policies. Although they have all shifted away from pronatalism, some have gone much further than others. Why did Chile act early but then stop short of the steps taken by Colombia? Why have the Brazilian and Peruvian governments stubbornly refused to support even modest family-planning programs? Questions such as these are even more fascinating when one remembers that such variations exist despite the apparent similarity of relevant political forces in each of the 20 countries. With minor exceptions, they all have family-planning associations, doctors, and foreign organizations pushing for family planning; the Church in an ambiguous position; and groups on the political extremes attacking population control. Nor does the nature of the political regime vary systematically with policy commitment. Obviously, policy decisions and programs are the products of complex forces; nevertheless the one factor that seems to be shared by Colombia, Mexico, and to a lesser extent by Chile, Costa Rica, and Cuba is national leadership. Programs became national policies where the president and his advisers took the initiative. Without internal resolve—at the highest levels—that unrestrained population growth constitutes a threat to national development, Latin American population policies will remain of little demographic consequence. The origins of such resolve await your examination in the chapters that follow.

NOTES TO INTRODUCTION

1. Eduardo E. Arriaga, *Mortality Decline and Its Demographic Effects in Latin America,* Population Monograph Series, No. 6 (Berkeley: Institute of International Studies, University of California, 1970), p. 18.

2. *Ibid.,* p. 35.
3. Only Uruguay was under 40 per 1,000 at the beginning of this century. Andrew O. Collver, *Birth Rates in Latin America: New Estimates of Historical Trends and Fluctuations,* Research Series, No. 7 (Berkeley: Institute of International Studies, University of California, 1965), p. 30.
4. According the UN *Demographic Yearbook* for 1970 (22nd Edition), pp. 108-110, the overall population densities of the countries mentioned are as follows: Brazil, 11 persons per square kilometer; the United States, 22; El Salvador, 165; Haiti, 175; the Netherlands, 319; and Japan, 280.
5. Herman E. Daly, "The Population Question in Northeast Brazil: Its Economic and Ideological Dimensions," *Economic Development and Cultural Change* (July, 1970), p. 558.
6. Kingsley Davis, "The Nature and Purpose of Population Policy," *California's Twenty Million,* edited by Kingsley Davis and Frederick G. Styles (Berkeley: Institute of International Studies, University of California, 1971), p. 3.
7. Henry M. Raulet, "Family Planning and Population Control in Developing Countries," *Demography,* VII (May, 1970), p. 215.
8. Bernard Berelson, "The Present State of Family Planning Programs," *Studies in Family Planning,* No. 57 (September, 1970), p. 1.
9. "In general," according to Daniel Callahan, " 'antinatalist' means 'attitudes or policies directed toward a reduction of births,' and 'pronatalist' means 'attitudes and policies directed toward an increase in births.' " We shall use these terms as defined by Callahan throughout the book. Daniel Callahan, "Ethics and Population Limitation," *Science,* 175, No. 402 (February 4, 1962), p. 494.
10. "Strictly speaking, a population policy is a deliberate attempt, through governmental or quasi-governmental measures to change or maintain the rate of population growth." Davis, "The Nature and Purpose of Population Policy," p. 6.

Part I

An Overview of the Politics of Population in Latin America

Chapter One

Politics and Population Control in Latin America*

J. Mayone Stycos

The remarkable change in the United States attitude toward family planning was symbolized last October (1966) by President Johnson's acceptance of the Margaret Sanger Award for his "vigorous and farsighted leadership in bringing the United States Government to enunciate and implement an affirmative, effective population policy at home and abroad."[1] Less than a decade before, when the very mention of Margaret Sanger's name in official circles was considered risqué, President Eisenhower had made it clear that family planning was not the business of the U.S. government. Few could have predicted that in 1966 the President of the United States would say, "It is essential that all families have access to information and services that will allow freedom to choose the number and spacing of their children within the dictates of individual conscience."[2]

The change has been long in coming, is without doubt in the right direction, and is being welcomed by a number of countries. There are, nevertheless, a number of warning signals from Latin America, where North American promotional activity in the population sphere has been quite active over the past three or four years.

LATIN AMERICAN ATTENTION TO POPULATION PROBLEMS

Although most of the Latin American nations have extraordinarily high rates of population growth, the recency of this phenomenon plus the existence of vast unsettled land areas in South America have helped to suppress concern

---

*From "Politics and Population Control in Latin America," *World Politics*, XX, No. 1 (Copyright (c) 1967 by Princeton University Press), pp. 66–82.

about population problems among the region's intellectuals.[3] Because of religious taboos, moreover, public discussion of population and birth control has been muted. So effective was the blanketing of news on these themes that, as late as 1965, former Colombian President and distinguished journalist Alberto Lleras Camargo referred to population as "*el gran tabu*" of our century.

Beginning in the early 1960's, however, a combination of circumstances caused the topics of the "population explosion" and contraception to become public issues in most Latin American countries. These circumstances included publication of preliminary results from the 1960 censuses, which generally indicated higher rates of growth than had been supposed; the opening up of the topic for debate on the part of the Vatican; the technological innovations such as "the pill," which lent themselves to journalistic treatment; and the promotional activities of North American private and government agencies that had previously written off Latin America as closed to birth control programs. In 1965, the Cornell International Population Program decided to determine the extent of attention to population problems and family planning in Latin American newspapers and began to collect newspaper clippings on these topics. Through the services of the Burrelle's Press Clipping Bureau, a surprising total of six thousand clippings was obtained in 1965 and over eight thousand were gathered in 1966. Approximately three-quarters of these articles explicitly mentioned birth control or contraceptive methods.

Thus, population and birth control have become public issues in Latin America just at the time when North American official policy with respect to foreign aid on population problems is being crystallized. What have been the Latin American reactions to the emerging North American positions? Publicly, there has been an almost total absence of enthusiasm, at best, and in most cases the reactions have ranged from suspicion to hostility. The expressed opinions have contained little reference to religious questions and have been more likely to impugn North American political or economic motives. Thus, the Chilean ambassador to the United States noted that family planning "is a problem which cannot be used as a lever for the international egotism of the rich nations, in allowing them to evade their duties of assistance and solidarity with the developing nations."[4] In leading the defeat last year of a proposal that UNICEF give assistance in the family planning area, the Peruvian delegate, a former minister of health, "voicing the views of other Latin American delegates, agreed that countries like India and Pakistan have overwhelming population growth. He explained that Latin America, however, has 'empty lands and untapped resources' and if UNICEF gets itself involved in population control, rich nations might be tempted to reduce economic aid and concentrate on birth control assistance instead."[5]

In this article we shall attempt to account for such reactions, both by reference to the Latin American political ideologies and by reference to the way in which U.S. policy has been articulated. We shall rely heavily on two types of data. The first set of data is drawn from our newspaper files, particularly those of Brazilian papers of August 1966, when it was announced in Brazil that the government was planning to seek U.S. assistance in dealing with population problems. The second principle source of data is fifty-one interviews conducted with university professors in Colombia during the same month. Brazil provides us with a case example of how explosive the combination of two controversial issues—population and U.S. aid—can be among a highly nationalist people. The Colombian data provide insights into the attitudes of intellectuals just prior to public announcement of a national program of family planning.

NATIONALISM

Often fueled by anti-American sentiments, nationalism is a powerful force cutting across political identifications in Latin America. With reference to population, however, its manifestations on the Right are somewhat different from those on the Left. In large countries such as Brazil and Argentina, nationalists of the Right argue that a larger population is needed to develop the vast interior and make the nation strong. For example, during the August debate in Brazil over the possibility of U.S. aid on population problems, Dr. Fabio Fonseca, president of the Belo Horizonte Regional Council of Medicine, stated that Brazil needs a population twice its present size in order to settle the vast empty spaces of the country. He warned that "the yellow race, which is becoming more and more numerous, needs space to live and will not hesitate to seek uninhabited places like the immense Brazilian regions if this settlement is not promoted."[6]

A representative of the Brazilian Chamber of Deputies charged that population control was being "imposed on us by a country with the dimensions of Brazil but with 300 million people, giving the impression that the American people with their land already overpopulated is concerning itself with our empty spaces and intends to occupy territory."[7]

A feature article in the newspaper *O Povo* claimed that the key to Brazilian prosperity lies in her beds and hammocks. It asked for more population so that Brazil's lands will cease to figure in the schemes of Western or Eastern imperialists as reserves of natural resources or vital space. "Brazilians," the article concluded, "let us continue loving and proliferating. God did not give us all this greatness for the installation of abortion or sterilization industries. Onward! To the children!"[8]

On the issue of family planning, nationalism causes the rightists to reject American cultural and moral values while gladly accepting America's dollars. As stated by the Archbishop of Brasilia, Dom Jose Newton de Almeida Batista, "Give us dollars and we shall be powerful, provided that we also grow in number so that we can take possession of the immense territory God gave us." [9] Even more pointed was the headline in the conservative Catholic Peruvian monthly ERPA: "Latin American Needs Dollars, Not Pills." Under a photograph of President Johnson mounted on a horse, it noted, "From his Texas ranch, Johnson directs the control of births in Latin America. What about nonintervention, Mr. President?" [10] The invasion of foreign morality disturbs both religious and secular rightists, for it is a form of "psychic imperialism" that imperils spiritual and cultural values viewed as close to the heart and soul of the nation. The abortion of national growth along with the substitution of alien values is a combination especially unsavory to nationalists of the Right.

While nationalists of the Right want dollars instead of pills, nationalists of the Left feel Latin America can afford neither. Both dollars and pills are regarded as ameliorative measures to shore up a crumbling society whose demise had much better be brought about by revolution. Three Colombian university professors expressed the idea this way:

> Birth control is dangerous because it can become a distraction, or a justification for the bourgeoisie to reject change. . . . It might prevent the agrarian reform from ever taking place.
>
> With our system of production we can support about ten million. Since we have seventeen million we are overpopulated, but if our pattern of production were altered we could support fifty million or more. The reason why they want birth control is that they don't want a technical revolution. Birth control is a palliative measure which cannot lead to anything.
>
> Birth control is being proposed as a panacea, which is utopian, false, and treacherous. [11]

The following citation from the Brazilian newspaper *Correio de Manha* of August 10, 1966, illustrates the mix of nationalist and reformist sentiments:

> Neo-Malthusianism is manipulated by the big laboratories. . . and pharmaceutical houses. . . . The reactionary attitude is not that of the Catholic church but of the family planners . . . for commercial reasons, out of North American geopolitical interests (so there will not be a prevalence of underdeveloped populations, or Asiatics, or U.S. Communists), and out of fear of structural reforms. . . . Brazil, lacking in mechanical resources, depends for her economic progress on her working force. It should not be with birth control financed by the National Development Bank and the Alliance for Progress or foreign enterprises that our country will succeed in developing herself, but through drastic modification of the social and economic structures.

MARXISM

In addition to the generalized suspicion of U.S. motives which cuts across political boundaries in Latin America, there is a deep ideological basis for opposition to controls on population growth. Marxian economics and social philosophy have had a profound effect on Latin American intellectuals, whether or not they can be considered Marxists. In order to understand Latin American thought, therefore, it is necessary to understand something of the Malthusian-Marxist controversy.

Both Malthus and Marx were centrally concerned with the explanation and cure of human misery and poverty. For Marx, the cause was social and institutional, and the cure, accordingly, was the revolutionary introduction of a new institutional framework—socialism. While he saw overpopulation as possible—indeed, often encouraged—in a capitalistic society, he did not view it as a problem of any consequence in a socialist state. Malthus saw the cause of poverty as essentially biological and physical, rooted in man's instincts toward laziness and sexuality, on the one hand, and in the finite nature of food and resources on the other. His solution was accordingly individual: the curbing of the sexual drives and the stimulation of individual effort by competition—a distinctly counterrevolutionary prescription. The Malthusian approach was a damper on socialist optimism concerning man's ability to abolish misery by abolishing his social and economic systems. In Europe, Malthusian and Marxist organizations competed bitterly, with the socialists convinced that birth control was capitalism's last remaining hope for a preservation of the status quo. Pro-natalist fuel was added to the anti-Malthusian arguments as a consequence of the Soviet Union's huge losses of manpower in the world wars. Violent verbal attacks such as the following were not infrequent in the Stalinist period: "Masquerading as scientists and philanthropists, these lackeys of American monopolies openly advocate cannibalism and try to justify the demoniacal plans for the mass extermination of peoples ... Bloody wars, the atom bomb and other means of mass extermination of peoples, the devouring of nations by nations—such are the concepts of the bloodthirsty ravings of present-day Malthusians."[12]

Throughout the fifties and early sixties, the Soviet bloc in the United Nations consistently argued that the West was blaming the failures of colonialism on population increase and that birth control was a tactic to divert attention from the needs for basic reforms. Typical excerpts from discussions held by the United Nations Population Commission only four or five years ago are given below:

> The theories of Malthus and their modern variants had been used as a pretext to distract attention from the abject poverty of the

under-developed countries. The economic backwardness of those countries could not be explained away by such theories; it was the result of colonialist domination and exploitation. Malthusian and neo-Malthusian theories were unscientific, reactionary and unworthy of United Nations' support. The best way of solving demographic problems was to accelerate economic development and to promote international trade on a just and equal basis. Disarmament too could play its part. The population problem did not arise in the Ukraine for there socialist planning ensured that economic development far outstripped demographic growth.[13]

Demographic growth was therefore not the real problem and there was no justification for blaming it for the difficulties encountered by the developing countries in their economic advancement. Those difficulties were mainly due to economic backwardness, to the exploitation from which those countries had suffered at the hands of the capitalist countries and to the ineffectiveness of their policy of accelerated development. The problem could be solved only through resolute effort and radical economic and social reforms.[14]

There had been references to a population explosion presenting a threat even more serious than nuclear weapons. Some Western circles were making use of those neo-Malthusian ideas to distract world public opinion from the real causes of the poverty of the under-developed countries, by attributing economic backwardness to excessively rapid population growth, rather than to long years of exploitation in the colonial era. Efforts were being made to use the United Nations to spread propaganda on that subject and to disseminate theories which were at variance with reality.[15]

In the late 1940's, so keenly opposed was the Soviet Union to the very concept of birth control that it sought against the inclusion of "such abominable words" as "prevention of births" and "Malthusianism" in the United Nations *Demographic Dictionary*. [16]

By the 1960's, however, there were major public programs of abortion and contraception in virtually all Communist nations. Although these have been justified, probably quite sincerely, as maternal welfare and anti-illegal abortion measures rather than as population control, they have doubtless caused some strains on the ideology. For whatever reason, that lowered birth rates might not be undesirable in the developing countries has been increasingly admitted in the 1960's, but only if these occur as a result of prior changes in the economic and social structure. So intent have some writers been to demonstrate that low birth rates are an effect rather than a cause of development that they sometimes seem to believe that fertility declines magically—at the very least, without "artificial birth control":

In Europe, various artificial means of lowering the birth rate had been applied, in keeping with the pseudoscientific views of Malthus; but the actual reasons for the decline had had no connection whatsoever with Malthusian philosophy. Three main factors tended to reduce birth rates: industrialization, rising material and cultural levels of living, and increased participation by women in national economic, cultural, and political life. The operation of those factors would cause the birth rate in underdeveloped countries to decline in coming years; a decline was in fact already noticeable in some countries, including India. His country had been accused of paying no heed to the threat to the world economy posed by present rates of population growth and of taking no steps to meet it; but that criticism was unwarranted. The USSR had never ignored the facts of population growth; but it felt that the artificial ways of limiting population growth advocated by the neo-Malthusians were inhuman and that in time, through the operation of the factors he had mentioned, the birth rate would drop of its own accord.[17]

The most recent indications are that Soviet ideologists are not so far from their Western counterparts. In the illustration below, an influential Soviet writer suggests that fertility control can accelerate the developmental process:

> The basic difference between the neo-Malthusians and the Marxists is not that the former propose various measures for limiting the birth rate while the latter unconditionally reject them all. The whole point is the relative importance both attach to these measures. The neo-Malthusians impose measures to limit the birth rate in order to avoid progressive social change in society. As for the Marxists, they feel there can be no demographic solution to the vital problems facing mankind. Their solution assumes first and foremost rapid economic development and profound social change. Demographic measures are no panacea for economic difficulties and social evils. A scientific population policy which encourages both an increase in birth control in some cases and a substantial reduction in others may serve as an important secondary means for markedly accelerating social progress.[18]

MARXIST INFLUENCE ON LATIN AMERICAN THOUGHT

Whether through the writings of Marx himself or through his present-day exponents in Europe and China, Marxist ideology on population continues to have a powerful influence on Latin American intellectuals of all persuasions but the far Right. Consequently, the initial reaction of the typical intellectual to the question of population growth is that the real problems are social and economic and that any other view must be concealing ulterior motives. The need for basic social and economic reform, moreover, is obvious to virtually all persons of influence in Latin America. The Right talks about it, the Center means it, and the Left means it right now. Mass education, industrialization, agrarian reform, more equitable distribution of wealth, health, and happiness are the ingredients, which vary in priority, timing, and means of accomplishment; but nearly everyone is concerned that somehow and sometime they be realized. These needs are so crushing, so obvious, and so imminent that to talk of anything else appears to many only a diversionary tactic.

Nevertheless, there are some stark facts of population growth facing Latin America, rates of growth never experienced by Europe before or after Malthus and Marx. Increasingly, intellectuals are admitting that population growth is a problem, but for some it is just the kind of irritant needed to precipitate basic reforms in the economic and social structure. As phrased by Chile's ambassador to the U.S.: ". . . Probably the single most important factor promoting the process of modernization in the underdeveloped societies is precisely the social pressure created by population growth. . . . What would the effect be of reducing the social tensions due to population growth, in the semi-feudal and oligarchical societies of so many nations of the Third World? Could it not be that a successful birth control program carries with it the seeds of self-destruction for its principal objective of modernization?" [19] Or as phrased by a Colombian university professor: "Population growth can have a very positive role because it can break the vicious circle. If the pressures are very large, the society has to feed many people and this need can create something new. . . . Like the great intellectual advance during the population explosion in classical Athens . . . it can force new ideas and can bring about the transformation of the status quo." [20]

While few socialists admit that population growth could be a problem in a socialist state, in the light of the pattern of recent political developments in Latin America, some socialist thinkers are becoming less optimistic about the imminence of revolution. What if the socialist state is a long time in coming? Is population increase really going to accelerate its occurrence? May population control be employed to assuage the misery of the prerevolutionary period? Three other Colombian professors express their points of view:

> Given our political system and the small likelihood of change, the conservative theory that you must control fertility because the economic systems can't take care of people's needs makes more sense . . . but if we had a good revolutionary government, then we should push for another alternative, as was done by Stalin who gave prizes for mothers of large families.
>
> The revolution is not brought about by the increase in numbers but by the consciousness of the people. To try to increase population would be falling into the absurdity of trying to increase misery in order to try to solve it.

> Some say that birth control will delay the revolution. This is a simplification of Marxist theory. . . . The more poverty and misery exist, the greater the probability of revolutions. But it doesn't take into account that the masses of the poor are totally lacking in revolutionary conscience, and that things are not likely to change.[21]

The dilemma is an agonizing one for the leftist thinker, for while he basically disapproves of the birth control solution, he must consider it in some indefinite short run, if only to slow the pace of accelerating misery.

> So we have two arguments working: one of them is that we should be working toward the revolution and the more people who want to join the revolution the better. The other is that since the revolution is going to fail, then we should have birth control to avoid the vain suffering of the people.
> If all this misery is necessarily going to continue, then it is necessary to opt for birth control, at least to avoid having more people born only to end in misery and starvation. . . . While the revolution is brewing, it would be only decent to supply the population with the means they need if they want to practice birth control.
> I am lecturing to physicians about birth control and I cannot make up my mind on whether we can make policy for everybody or whether this is mainly a problem of the individual and the solution lies in the individual's mind. . . . Can we sacrifice the well-being of a generation or two in order to increase our dubious expectations of the future? We often say, "Let the population grow fast so that pressures of the status quo are increased and change comes about." But do we have the right to make such judgments on the entire population, or should we instead concentrate on curing the problems of the family as an institution itself?[22]

While politicians, social scientists, and clergy are concerned about the population question, the medical profession is doing something about it. The government of Colombia has allocated $300,000 in counterpart funds to the Association of Medical Faculties to train the nation's physicians in family-planning techniques. In Chile, the major hospitals in the major cities supply modern birth control methods, and even in Brazil a private family-planning association is gaining momentum under high-level medical leadership. Indeed, such activities in combination with a relatively permissive stance on the part of Church spokesmen have led various experts and enthusiasts to conclude that the birth control battle is more or less over in Latin America.

It is quite true that many members of the medical profession in a number of Latin American countries have accepted the principle that the public deserves contraceptive services as a means of preventing illegal abortions and that the Church has not reacted aggressively to such principles or programs. This is a remarkable story in itself and represents a revolutionary change in medical opinion. The change, however, has been much less profound among non-medical groups, who figure more prominently in policy-making circles in Latin America. It should be pointed out that while medical men in Latin America may generally be to the Left of the American Medical Association, they are generally considered to be politically conservative. Accordingly, the kinds of concerns expressed by the intellectuals quoted in this article are more rarely articulated by physicians and are almost never expressed to American birth control enthusiasts. On the other hand, in those areas where leftist physicians are a powerful force, they can become a particularly potent influence against population control. Thus the executive committee of the Guanabara Medical Association (Brazil), described by a *New York Times* writer as a group of "left-wing and anti-American physicians," announced in December, 1966, that they were preparing draft legislation to prohibit the production and sale of contraceptive pills and devices in Brazil.[23]

Further, a positive stance on the part of the Church would be a mixed blessing. Basic agreement with the Church on population problems and family planning has always been a mild embarrassment to the Left. A move by the Church to a pro-birth control policy would help to consolidate leftist opposition to birth control, since such a policy would make consistent the socialist views of the reactionary character of the Church and the reactionary character of population control. In short, the battle is not yet over.

THE UNITED STATES AND POPULATION CONTROL

Even when widespread birth control services are accepted in Latin America there will be serious questions about their role in the society and about the role that United States assistance should play. Few of the Colombians interviewed objected to U.S. aid for research or for purely technical assistance. As one respondent put it: "At the level of research it is very good . . . but the policy to be followed should not be determined by them, the foreigners. They always suggest, and that should not be, because their suggestions are often taken too seriously, and they are very often bad."[24] Or another, who had termed birth control "utopian, false, and treacherous," said with respect to aid on family planning: "We have to learn how to receive gracefully all that is knowledge or the product of culture, all that is science and technology, all that can help us."[25]

It might appear that in reality there is little danger of the United States' determining what policy Latin American nations should follow, but there is evidence that the U.S. line on population control is becoming not only clearer but harder. "There can no longer be any doubt in the administration or the country that this Congress was determined to defuse the population bomb," announced Senator Tydings last year.[26] Potentially explosive as such an activity might appear, there were signs that indelicate approaches were on the horizon. As early as mid-1965, Senator Clark told the U.S. Senate that "A.I.D. should be advocating the institution of voluntary family programs *as a necessary condition to* meeting the rising tide of unfed mouths and unfulfilled aspirations in these countries . . . and thus preventing American aid from being poured down a rat-hole. A.I.D. should move on from its attitude of limited response to initiatives made by aided governments, to an attitude of *active proselytizing of the cause of voluntary family planning,* in the many countries where that would be appropriate."[27]

Was the U.S. going to enforce birth control by holding up assistance on food, health, and economic development? What did President Johnson mean, many wondered, when he announced on January 20, 1966, that "the hungry world cannot be fed until and unless the growth in its resources and the growth in its population come into balance."[28] Was it true, as was stated in a discussion of the Food for Peace Bill, that "population control . . . by implication at least is mentioned as one of the elements to be considered in continuing U.S. aid"?[29] Was there any special significance in Secretary of Agriculture Orville Freeman's echoing the President's view of the superior value of investments in birth control?[30]

Latin American officials who had seen a withdrawal of North American support for health programs began to wonder if they were being told to stem life rather than to heal it. As the then minister of health of Peru put it, in what the journal *Caretas* termed a "sensational revelation": "The U.S. is willing to help in a campaign for the control of births but not in one to reduce the rates of death."[31] If health had been cut back, what next? Was not this concern what lurked behind UNCTAD Secretary General Raúl Prebisch's statement that lowering birth rates is not "an alternative to a broad policy of economic development"?[32]

Perhaps the burdens of the space race, hot and cold wars, and the development of nuclear facilities were causing the U.S. to look to solutions cheaper than economic development. "Heavy investments [for space research, etc.]," pointed out the Peruvian minister of health in explaining the "pessimistic" or Malthusian position of the developed nations, "are part of the struggle for world supremacy. . . . [The developed countries] are concerned about the competing demands for investments involved in this struggle."[33]

United States government economists had for some time been developing elaborate economic rationalizations for the transfer of funds from the "rat-hole" of economic aid to the haloed programs of family planning for increased per capita product. Thus, a former Deputy Assistant Secretary of Defense for Systems Analysis told the World Population Conference in 1965 that "if national economic resources were devoted to retarding population growth *rather than accelerating production growth,* these resources could be one hundred or so times more effective in raising some less developed countries' outputs per head."[34] In case such a handsome margin of profit did not seem adequate to justify the risks, the bomb-defusing experts soon produced an even more compelling argument. As stated (unofficially) by a social scientist in the Post-attack Division of the Office of Civil Defense: "Rapid population growth rates have made economic growth and political stability increasingly difficult to maintain in some parts of the world, thereby adding to the need for programs and forces *to help maintain internal order and to defend against guerilla warfare."* [35]

The culmination of the utilitarian school of thought was reached in President Johnson's San Francisco speech on the occasion of the twentieth anniversary of the United Nations, June 25, 1965. Confirming many Latins' worst fears in an admirably clear and succinct sentence, he stated: "Let us act on the fact that less than five dollars invested in population control is worth a hundred dollars invested in economic growth." Many believe that Pope Paul VI's UN message was a direct reply to this new kind of economic calculus. In a statement that, perhaps mercifully, achieved much more space in the Latin American press than did the President's, he suggested the need to increase the amount of bread rather than decrease the number of guests at the banquet of life.

The Chilean ambassador to the United States answered the argument on its own terms: "Are we looking for a cheap solution or the best solution?" he asked. " . . . It could be that the optimum return would result from our choosing the ninety dollars for economic development rather than the five for birth control."[36]

Other Latins asked themselves, if birth control programs are such a good investment, how is the Yankee capitalist, usually so astute in such matters, able to resist such an obvious bargain in the United States? That the United States has been able to point proudly only to Puerto Rico as its birth control showcase has not exactly been its strongest selling point in Latin America. However, the charge that the U.S. does not practice what it preaches was countered in mid-1965 when, in the triumphant editorial worlds of the *New York Times,* "American Indians, Eskimos and natives of the islands the U.S. holds in trust in the Pacific have just been made beneficiaries of the first Federal program offering direct help in family planning and birth control."[37] (Little noted was the unappreciative reaction of the *Navajo Times*: "We have had Washington's stock-reduction program forced on us. Now it would seem they are trying to sell us a people-reduction program.")[38]

CONCLUSIONS

In Latin America, a region deeply dedicated in spirit to freedom and liberty but often bound in fact to political tyranny and economic dependence, intellectuals are especially concerned about the freedom of choice in family matters. Indeed, even socialist opposition to population control often melts away if family planning is spoken of as increasing the scope of rational decision-making in the family. The following quotations from three Colombian professors show how birth control can be favored while population control is opposed:

> Birth control should represent an increase in the free will of the people. It should add one dimension to their possibility of choice. It should be free and available to everybody. . . . The Malthusian thesis that population growth increases misery is nothing but a comfortable way to justify the existing structures.
>
> The government should not interfere directly with family affairs. The only thing it should do is have intensive educational campaigns on family affairs . . . not to reduce the size of the family . . . but to give parents an opportunity to have the children with responsibility, to space them adequately.
>
> It is not necessary to control population in Colombia to reduce the growth rate since the people are not even in possession of their own land. Birth control can be applied only as an increase in the free will of the Colombian people.[39]

On Human Rights Day, December 10, 1966, United Nations Secretary General U Thant circulated a statement on family planning signed by the heads of twelve world states. In his covering statement U Thant noted that not only is population growth "an important factor in the rate at which nations can attain their economic goals, but . . . the size of the family is a fundamental human problem which must be based on the decisions of responsible parents concerned with the dignity and well-being of their children. . . . I feel bound to call attention to a declaration expressing concern with the quality of human life as well as with the number of human beings on earth." The national leaders, while mentioning the economic consequences of rapid population growth, also took a humanistic approach. They maintained that the "opportunity to decide the number and spacing of children is a basic human right" and that "the objective of family planning is the enrichment of human life, not its restriction; [freeing] man to attain his individual dignity and reach his full potential."[40]

Not long after, Pope Paul, in a marked change of emphasis from his earlier United Nations speech, recognized the appropriateness of government action to affect population growth, leaving it for "parents to decide on the number of their children . . . [following] the demands of their own conscience . . ."[41] More specific programmatic steps have also been taken by the World Health Organization and the United Nations in the early part of 1967, giving family planning a more apolitical world base, both ideologically and programmatically.

Our previous analysis suggests that it is precisely this kind of sponsorship combined with this kind of ideology which will create a favorable environment for the introduction of national family-planning programs in Latin America. In Brazil, the attack on Planning Minister Roberto Campos would have lost most of its steam if *international* agencies had been known to be providing assistance to Brazil on population matters. Doubtless, too, some of Lleras Restrepo's current problems with the Colombian Conservatives over the government's family-planning policies could have been avoided if international agencies had provided most of the technical and financial assistance. While the international agencies are gearing up for such aid, discreet and limited U.S. aid can be extremely useful, even more so if it comes from private organizations and foundations. With luck, within a decade much of the ideological controversy in most Latin American countries will have terminated, and the equally large problem of programmatic facilitation will have to be faced. At that time, the prediction of Marxist sociologist Jean Freville may come to pass: ". . . The people of the future . . . will be able to control the size of the population according to their potentials and needs. Far from reducing the birth rate in order to preserve the old hierarchy and to implement a reactionary imperialist policy, they will be able to control the birth rate as a factor for balance, planning and progress."[42]

NOTES TO CHAPTER 1

1. *Planned Parenthood News* (November, 1966).
2. President Johnson's Special Message to Congress on Health and Education, March 1, 1966.
3. J. Mayone Stycos, "Opinions of Latin American Intellectuals Toward Population and Birth Control," *Annals of the American Academy of Political and Social Science,* CCCLX (July, 1965), pp. 11–26.
4. *Observaciones del Exemo. Sr. R. Tomić,* Embajada de Chile (Washington, May 5, 1966).
5. Reported in *Survey of International Development,* III (June 15, 1966).
6. *Diário de Minas,* August 5, 1966. For a detailed account of the Brazilian reaction, see Cornell University International Population Program, *Latin American Newspaper Coverage of Population and Family Planning* (Ithaca, 1967).
7. *Diário de Minas,* August 17, 1966.
8. August 19, 1966.
9. *Correio Brasiliense,* August 6, 1966.
10. January, 1966.
11. As part of a 1966 summer project in Colombia of the International Population Program, Sergio Sismondo carried out an investigation of the attitudes of Colombian university professors toward economic development and population problems. Fifty-one interviews were completed, divided more or less evenly among the departments

of sociology, economics, philosophy and humanities, and psychology in a leading Colombian university. The universe was defined as the total staffs in these departments, except in the cases of economics and psychology, in which certain ranks or groupings were excluded. In only ten instances was an individual selected for the sample not interviewed. However, 198 appointments had to be made in order to obtain the 51 interviews, i.e., an average of four appointments per interview, despite the fact that most interviews were completed in one sitting. The average duration was two hours and forty minutes, with a range of from fifty minutes to six hours. Translated extracts from these interviews have been employed throughout this article.

12. A.Y. Popov (1953), cited in William Petersen, *The Politics of Population* (New York, 1964), p. 118.
13. Mr. Kochubei (Ukrainian Soviet Socialist Republic), Population Commission, A/C. 2/SR. 867, December 11, 1962.
14. Mr. Serafimov (Bulgaria), Population Commission, A/C. 2/SR. 875, December 18, 1962.
15. Mr. Solodovnikov (Union of Soviet Socialist Republics), Population Commission, E/SR. 1246, April 9, 1963.
16. Alfred Sauvy, *Fertility and Survival* (New York, 1961), p. 204.
17. Mr. Podyachikh (Union of Soviet Socialist Republics), Population Commission, E/CN. 9/SR. 170, February 11, 1963.
18. E. Arab-Ogly, in *Literaturnaya Gazeta,* cited in *Atlas* (December, 1966).
19. *Observaciones . . . R. Tomić.*
20. International Population Program interviews.
21. *Ibid.*
22. *Ibid.*
23. Juan de Onis, in the *New York Times,* December 5, 1966. In Chile, prominent leftist physicians are among the leadership of the family-planning movement. Nationalism takes a much milder form in Chile, and a more detailed comparison with Brazil might be rewarding.
24. International Population Program interviews.
25. *Ibid.*
26. Joseph D. Tydings, Speech to the U.S. Senate, October 22, 1966.
27. Joseph S. Clark, Speech to the U.S. Senate, June 14, 1965 (italics added).
28. *Population Crisis* (November, 1966).
29. *Ibid.*
30. Speech to the Organization for Economic Cooperation and Development, Development Assistance Committee, July 21, 1966.
31. "La Encuesta Hall," *Caretas* (August 28, 1964).
32. Cited in *Alliance for Progress Weekly Newsletter* (February 7, 1966).
33. Speech by Dr. Javier Arias Stella on the inauguration of the Peruvian Center of Population and Development Studies, Lima, January 14, 1965.
34. Stephen Enke, World Population Conference, September, 1965 (italics added).

35. Robert Lamson, "Needed Research for Population Policy," *American Behavioral Scientist,* IX (February, 1966), pp. 23-25 (italics added). It is stated that the article represents the views of the author and not those of the Office of Civil Defense or the Department of the Army.
36. *Observaciones...R. Tomić.*
37. "More Headway on Birth Control," *New York Times,* June 21, 1965.
38. Cited in *Indian Voices* (October, 1965), p. 5.
39. International Population Program interviews.
40. The statement was initially signed by the heads of state of Colombia, Finland, Malaysia, Morocco, Nepal, Singapore, Korea, Sweden, Tunisia, the U.A.R., Yugoslavia, and India. Several additional countries have subsequently signed.
41. *Populorum Progressio,* March 28, 1967.
42. Quoted in Arab-Ogly.

Chapter Two

The Relationship between Population Planning and Belief Systems: The Catholic Church in Latin America*

Thomas G. Sanders

It is commonly believed in the United States that the principal obstacle to family planning in Latin America is the Roman Catholic Church. In part this opinion stems from the Church's official position, which in the form of Pope Paul VI's encyclical, *Humanae Vitae,* reiterated its opposition to the most effective methods of contraception, and in part from the assumption that the Latin American branch of the Church is the world's most docile, characterized by intellectual backwardness, social conservatism, and manipulation of the populace. Observers have drawn a simple casual line between Latin America's rate of population increase, the highest of any of the world's regions, and the overwhelming adherence of its population to the Catholic faith.[1]

To those, however, really acquainted with family planning in Latin America the charge against the Church appears in practice to be grossly exaggerated. The Catholic position is certainly a cultural factor that must be taken into consideration, but any serious analysis becomes an explanation of why the Church is not as formidable an impediment as it appears on the surface. Such an enterprise is not intended for apologetic reasons, but rather to clarify what are the real problems in Latin American family planning and what are not. Catholicism as a set of values, and the Catholic Church as an institution are indispensable for understanding Latin America, but both are too complex to blame or praise facilely for a similarly complex phenomenon like the status of family planning.

One approach to this question will involve an analysis of several levels of Catholic thought and action, beginning at the top with the papal *magisterium* (teaching) and proceeding through the bishops, theologians, and priests, to the laity. It should be clear from this confrontation with the ideology

*From Thomas G. Sanders, *The Relationship Between Population Planning and Belief Systems: The Catholic Church in Latin America* [T65-5-'70], Field Staff Reports, West Coast South America Series, Vol. XVII, No. 7, 1970. Copyright © The American Universities Field Staff.

or theology of normative Catholicism that the Church, despite a certain unity of thought, allows for extensive diversity in the practices of its faithful. A second approach will focus on "popular" Catholicism. We are still at too early a stage in empirical studies to provide a complete sociological interpretation of Latin American Catholicism, but we should not assume that religious institutions, any more than other institutions, can be interpreted only by examining their ideals or ideology. We must try to understand, insofar as possible, how Latin Americans as individuals subject to a variety of cultural pressures, really think and practice their Catholicism.

The chief source of the image of the Catholic position on family planning comes from the highest teaching authority of the Church, the widely-publicized encyclical of Pope Paul VI, *Humanae Vitae*. In the controversy over its position on contraception, three aspects of the encyclical were obscured which we should examine dispassionately: (1) its authority, (2) its central themes, and (3) the background of its position on contraception.

(1) While educated people know that the Pope can speak infallibly on faith and morals, they usually do not understand the difference between infallible and ordinary teaching. If we take seriously the restricted conditions for infallibility defined by the First Vatican Council (1870), one statement only in this century, in 1950, the Assumption of the Virgin Mary, is acknowledged by theologians to be unquestionably infallible. Ordinary papal teaching like that in *Humanae Vitae* is *authoritative* for Catholics in the sense that they should seriously examine it, respect it as the voice of the Church's supreme pastor, and conform their behavior to it. Certain circumstances, nevertheless, may lead individual Catholics to demur from the official teaching when, for example, major thinkers within the Church hold a different opinion, or when they themselves, after a conscientious evaluation of their convictions and circumstances, arrive at a contrary view. While the faithful Catholic will usually find his moral outlook in harmony with the teaching of the Church, classic theology always recognized the existence of situations of genuine doubt and divergent conviction, in which case one's individual conscience is the final authority even though it contradicts the position of the Church.

(2) Although its condemnation of artificial methods of contraception received the principal attention, *Humanae Vitae* had as its central message the exposition of two themes, conjugal love and responsible parenthood. While these themes may seem obvious dimensions of an appropriate relationship between spouses and between parents and children, they represent a revolution in Catholic thought. The traditional moralists, drawing from St. Paul and St. Augustine, discussed marriage largely in legalistic and negative terms, regarding it as an instrument for procreation and a remedy for sexual sins. Its chief positive feature was as a sacramental vehicle for transmitting saving grace and motivating moral action. What the Catholic theologians now call the "humanistic" or "personalistic" side of marriage, about which statements began to appear only in the late 1920's,[2] was ignored. The best way to grasp

the shift in the Church's outlook is by contrasting Pope Pius XI's *Casti Conubii* (1930),[3] the definitive statement on sex and marriage before the Council, with the themes common today. By the time of the Council the deficiencies of the traditional outlook and the consistency of themes like conjugal love and responsible parenthood with the current Catholic theological renewal made a great impression on the assembled bishops. *Humanae Vitae* has importance in Catholic theology, then, not simply because Pope Paul VI adopted a position on contraception based on traditional modes of thought, but because he sanctioned treating marriage in interpersonal terms. The contradiction between his thinking on contraception and his affirmation of the centrality of conjugal love and responsible paternity underlie the consternation which *Humanae Vitae* provoked among many bishops, priests, and laity.

(3) The period of gestation which *Humanae Vitae* underwent gave Catholic couples time and justification for adopting modern contraceptive methods. Leading moral theologians in the early 1960's began to argue for the licitness of progesterone pills; and at the Vatican Council a number of bishops urged a decision on this matter. When the Pope himself decided to review the subject the slow process of selecting a commission, expanding it, and rejecting its recommendation in favor of a personal decision, produced a lengthy period of uncertainty during which Catholics throughout the world began using the pill. They had the willing support of priests who considered effective contraception a logical adjunct of the new matrimonial theology.

These three points apply universally to the Church and help explain the well-publicized insistence of many lay persons in Europe and North America on continued use of the pill. In Latin America also the years of delay coincided with extensive discussion of contraception in newspapers and magazines and with the initiation of private and public family-planning programs in most countries. Many urban, educated, middle- and upper-class Latin Americans, the minority of the population able to understand and care about the position of the Church, began using contraceptives on the advice of private doctors and continue to do so now. The "demonstration effect" is very strong in Latin America and extends to all articles of consumption, including the pills. Educated Latin Americans do not differ significantly in their response to such problems from educated Europeans or North Americans, even though they live in an underdeveloped part of the world. Nor, as we shall see, is their Church backward in its attitudes.

The position of bishops is important for understanding what the Church thinks in a given geographical area, but we should recognize the conformist role they play, in contrast with priests or laymen. In their dioceses they have a special responsibility to unify and defend the positions of the Church. They must bring together and meet the needs of a flock that comes from many levels of life and has sharply differing views. Obviously bishops have their own opinions and some have become spokesmen for controversial positions, but they ordinarily do not act on their own authority. They see themselves as interpreters of the Church's teaching their jurisdiction, although that teaching is sufficiently ambiguous to give them considerable leeway. The bishop, however, does not go around saying that he disagrees with the Pope—if he does disagree, he says nothing.

Before *Humanae Vitae* many Latin American bishops had an open attitude to contraceptives for several reasons. The Latin American Church was never as concerned with the use of artificial means of contraception as, for example, the North American Church. Before 1960, they apparently did not know that contraception was occurring, or if they did, it represented no great problem for them. When the issue became a reality and entered the stage of discussion, the extreme conservatives took a hard line in opposition, but the rest adopted a tolerant attitude of wait-and-see. Often they retreated by saying that the matter was under study, but many genuinely felt that effective contraception was morally significant on the personal level or that it represented an alternative to the far more serious problem of abortion. It became popular among Latin American bishops by the mid-1960's to argue that given the unsettled state of the question, the decision should be left up to the conscience of the people involved. Eighteen of twenty Chilean bishops with whom I discussed the matter shortly before *Humanae Vitae* permitted conscientious couples to use the pill or sent them to a Catholic doctor, assuming that he would probably prescribe the pill.[4] Thoughtful Latin American bishops are not insensitive to the problems of women with many children, and especially on this personal level of clear need, they discerned non-egoistic reasons for contraception.

As private and public-family planning programs appeared, many bishops expressed their fear that doctors were using psychological pressure in favor of the pill and the IUD (intrauterine device) rather than rhythm. Confronted with the obvious receptivity of "Catholic" patients to a simple and effective method, however, the bishops usually faced facts and fell back to a position of rejecting abortion and sterilization and insisting that patients not be coerced into violating their consciences. In Colombia the bishops have sporadically criticized family-planning programs—conducted with the sympathy of the nation's last three presidents—for using artificial methods, but this stems in part from the special position accorded to the Church as guardian of public morality by the Constitution. That this has not moved beyond the spoken and written level may be partly ascribed to a more dominant interest of the Church, namely, to maintain its privileges through good relations with the government.

Many Latin American bishops, while sympathizing with the desire of individuals to plan their families effectively, have opposed institutional programs because of foreign influence and financing in them. This point of view has great strength among the radical wing of the Brazilian episcopate, which is probably the most influential group of bishops in Latin America.

They believe that any program with United States government support should be resisted, because it must aim in some way at furthering North American and undermining Latin American interests. According to Msgr. Hélder Câmara, archbishop of Recife and the symbolic leader of this group, "I will never forget the words of President Lyndon Johnson—five dollars applied to birth control is a better investment than a hundred dollars used in development. I still retain that impertinence in my hearing, and I thank the Pope for taking a position although it creates problems for the underdeveloped countries.... [5] There is a certain temptation in the developed countries to regard development as a matter of birth control, and when this control is directed from abroad, it causes repugnance in me."[6] Dom Hélder and his associates, who are noted for their sensitive social conscience, have yet to resolve the anomaly of not supporting institutional means by which the lower class, which needs it most, can get effective information on contraception.

The introduction of family-planning clinics and the empirical studies accompanying them caused a profound awakening among Latin America's more thoughtful bishops to the fragility of the Church's sexual ethic in practice and led them to doubt the Church's strength in their supposedly Catholic societies. High rates of illegitimacy and abortion, as well as the readiness with which people were using contraceptive methods forbidden by the Church led them to rethink their criticisms. Did not the Church have more pressing concerns, like developing a more profound Christian consciousness in the people and promoting a more meaningful family life?

With the appearance of *Humanae Vitae,* many Latin American bishops, just like those in other parts of the world, were surprised and disappointed. I was in Chile at the time. After a hasty meeting of the bishops of the central part of the country, Cardinal Raúl Silva Henríquez of Santiago expressed their consensus in a brief television message: (1) The chief emphasis of the encyclical was on "responsible parenthood," and (2) No Catholic need ever feel alienated from the Church because he cannot fulfill all of its demands. Cardinal Silva did not mention the prohibition of artificial methods of contraception.

Cardinal Silva was typical of many prelates who now found themselves in a dilemma. Their openness to contraception on both the personal and policy level was now contradicted by the Pope. Fortunately, they could derive from the encyclical a justification for continuing in practice what they were already doing. The emphasis in *Humanae Vitae* on the extraordinary discipline, even heroism, necessary to fulfill the norms of the Church enabled bishops along with priests to take a tolerant view toward the frailties of most Christians. Pope Paul comforted persons who continued to use unacceptable contraceptives by telling them "not to be discouraged, but rather have a recourse with humble perseverance to the mercy of God, which is poured forth in the sacrament of Penance." And he called on priests to be "intransigent with evil, but merciful toward individuals.... Teach married couples the indispensable way of prayer, prepare them to have recourse often and with faith to the sacraments of the Eucharist and of Penance, without ever allowing themselves to be discouraged by their weakness." On the public level, the Pope acknowledge the existence of a problem of "rapid demographic growth" and the consequent strain on the resources of underdeveloped countries. Moreover, he admitted the right of public authorities, as he had previously in *Populorum Progressio,* to provide couples with information on acceptable methods for limiting and spacing children, consistent with the natural law.

The chief effect of *Humanae Vitae* on the bishops has been to instill a sense of obligation to give lip-service to the Pope's position, even if they personally do not agree with some aspects of it. As unifiers and transmitters the bishops have scrupulously avoided criticizing the encyclical publicly.[7] On the other hand, practical considerations and disagreements over policy in national and regional episcopal meetings have led them to emphasize the acceptable and tone down the controversial in their pastoral letters. In most cases their private comments to clergy have stressed the escapes available in individual pastoral situations.

When national hierarchies criticize family-planning programs, conservatives act from strong conviction, but in many cases the more open bishops are merely conforming to the expectations of *Humanae Vitae* and the pressure of papal nuncios. Nowhere in Latin America does a hierarchy have more than a verbal campaign against family planning, and in most countries the Church is quietly focusing on other matters. The Chilean episcopate, which initially supported contraceptive programs as an alternative to abortion, issued the following statement in August, 1969:

> We manifest ourselves to be clearly in disagreement with the anti-conception campaign which the National Health Service is developing. We reiterate our unconditioned agreement with him who fulfills the supreme *magisterium* in the Church and who in the encyclical *Humanae Vitae* reminded us of the Christian sense of marriage and the demands of the natural law, reproving the use of artificial contraceptive methods.[8]

However, the Chilean bishops, whose dominant characteristic for decades has been realism, will certainly not provoke the sophisticated middle-class and contraceptive-using lay Catholic elites in their secularized country. In Colombia, despite continued criticism of government cooperation with family-planning programs by bishops as individuals and collectively, a recent analysis of social problems in the country, the most extensive ever produced by the episcopate, emphasizes conjugal love and responsible parenthood, while referring briefly to *Humanae Vitae* "for a correct formation of the conscience of the Christian."[9] In this case, the bishops oppose the program, but lack a consensus on the proper policy to follow. The Peruvian episcopate, which denounced family planning largely on nationalistic grounds in January, 1968, (before *Humanae Vitae*), has remained silent since, in the absence of large-scale public private family-planning programs in the country. The huge and divided Brazilian hierarchy, with over 200 bishops, responded to *Humanae Vitae* with a brief pastoral,[10] but has also been quiet since. Several bishops, though, have attended as observers national seminars of the Brazilian Society of Family Welfare (Bemfam), the International Planned Parenthood Federation affiliate which operates over fifty clinics.

The nearest thing to a consensus of the Latin American bishops may be found in the document produced by the Latin American Bishops Conference (CELAM) at Medellín, Colombia, shortly after and somewhat under the pressure of *Humanae Vitae*.[11] The document treats two themes: (1) On the demographic problem in general, it acknowledges a dilemma because "our countries suffer from underpopulation and need demographic growth as a factor of development. But it is also certain that our excessively low social, economic, and cultural conditions are adverse to a pronounced demographic growth." A "unilateral" or "simplist" approach the bishops describe as "incomplete and therefore wrong," while an "antinatalist policy which tends to supplant, substitute, or lead to forgetting a policy of development" is "especially damaging." The document praises Pope Paul VI for insisting on "an integral policy focused on development" as the answer to population increase, for disowning policies of birth control as a condition for economic aid, and for defending the rights of persons, especially the poor and marginal. (2) On the personal level, the bishops describe the teaching of *Humanae Vitae* as "clear and unequivocal," but to those couples with difficulties and anxieties they offer "our support without distinction."

The relatively negative attitude of the Medellín documents toward family-planning programs does not, however, exhaust the Church's response. A more positive outlook, typified by a pastoral of the Venezuelan bishops in 1969, may also be considered part of the consensus (because at no time since the renovation of the Latin American Church began in the 1950's has anyone ever suggested that the Venezuelan bishops might be innovating or advanced). The Venezuelan bishops condemn "birth control" as a program *obliging* couples to reduce the number of children wanted, but they support "family planning" as a human right and responsibility, in the sense that parents produce only children to whom they give such decencies as food, clothing, and education. The bishops argue that the state has a role in educating and providing the means of achieving responsible paternity, as well as in combating abortion and other criminal and immoral actions against human dignity. They conclude:

> The state ought . . . to concern itself that the population receive convenient information and education about the methods approved by Christian morality for a responsible regulation of natality, especially the poorer population. Lack of economic power cannot

be a motive for discrimination in this matter. Nevertheless, in a pluralistic society with non-Catholics and non-believers, it is not forbidden to the institutions of the state to give information on other methods to those persons who may decide to use them according to their own consciences.[12]

It would be a mistake to assume that in individual dioceses the problem of contraception continues to agitate the bishop, his priests, and the laity. They determined their response to this issue before *Humanae Vitae*. The encyclical merely provided an occasion to review the practical procedures to follow, which in the end usually represented a reaffirmation of what was being done. A bishop is known for either a rigid or lenient policy toward forbidden contraceptive methods; priests have worked out their pastoral approaches; and the more sophisticated laity by-and-large have settled the matter with their consciences.

New developments could certainly lead to action by national hierarchies. For example, the initiation of publicly financed programs would undoubtedly provoke some response from the bishops of Brazil or Peru. A major factor in the nature of such a response is the consciousness of power by the episcopates. In countries like Colombia, Church leaders still believe that they exercise great influence politically and in the people's minds, but those in Brazil and Chile have no such illusions.

Descending in the Church structure we come to the intellectual expression—the theologians who interpret the *magisterium*. Few bishops are well-versed in theology and usually depend on the advice of clerical and sometimes lay experts.

Nearly all Latin American theologians studied in Europe and, consequently, their attitudes in response to *Humanae Vitae* were similar to those of their European mentors, but in most of Latin America, they have agreed not to criticize the encyclical publicly. Brazil is a notable exception. There every major Church writer on marriage and population problems, as well as the leading journals, the *Revista Ecclesiástica Brasileira* (for priests) and *Vozes* (for laymen) have openly questioned it. Both journals, which are edited by Frei Clarêncio Neotti, O.F.M., one of the priests most active in Bemfam, have a tradition since about 1962 of mediating the new marriage theology from Europe to Brazil. Articles in the *Revista Ecclesiática Brasileira* and *Vozes* since the encyclical have consistently disagreed with Pope Paul VI, chiefly over his "biological" view of human nature.[13] Against it they contend that a more diversified concept of human expression—involving reason, the capacity for relationship, responsibility, and the dedication of marriage as a whole to God's intention—entails genuinely effective contraception.

The practical justification for contraception most commonly followed in Brazil has been presented annually at the seminars of Bemfam by Dom Jerônimo de Sá Cavalcante, prior of the Benedictine monastery in Salvador,

Bahia. In this view, "responsible parenthood" as defined by the Pope requires a decision on the number and spacing of children. The only method he permitted, however, is rhythm, which has proven notably unreliable; and the Pope recognized this by calling on scientists to perfect methods acceptable to Catholic morality. Until this occurs, the Catholic couple should select one of the existent effective methods available to plan responsibly their family. According to Dom Jerônimo:

> Personally I do not make a distinction between artificial and natural methods, because what is artificial is created by man and therefore is a human method. . . . As long as medical science says that the method is not sterilizing or prejudicial to the health of the couple, and it is not imposed by any authority or power, then this method can be perfectly accepted.[14]

In Chile, the theological issue was handled by a statement of theology professors at the Catholic University of Santiago. After pointing out that the encyclical was not infallible and citing the principal themes, they confessed that on the question of contraception they were divided. The majority felt that the Pope's position was "reformable" because the matter required further study especially of the conditioning factors in human nature for making such a decision. The minority, on the other hand, believed that the force of the encyclical and its consistency with tradition made it essentially infallible. The document closes with a paragraph recognizing that Catholics might "adhere, after serious study and consultation, to one or another of the theological opinions mentioned."[15] The document thus clearly gives more emphasis than the encyclical itself to the debatable nature of its authority and provides a green light for individuals to make their own decisions.

It is not surprising, then, that all over Latin America priests in their pastoral work have agreed to encourage couples to make their own "responsible decision" and are granting absolution to those who confess use of "artificial" methods. We cannot determine what percentage this involves. Two Brazilian priests who often lead retreats and seminars on *Humanae Vitae* for clergy found about 80 percent "open" on the matter. One of them has written what being "open" means:

> Personally I found three attitudes [among couples] toward the Encyclical. One couple said to me: the Encyclical is right and we are going to return to using the charts. Another couple said: the Encyclical is nice, but we are not in a situation to observe it now. Here then would be a place for the 'law of growth.' The third attitude is of those who reflected and studied it with honesty and did not convince themselves. They disagree respectfully. In my opinion, all these attitudes are valid according to the case.[16]

Other priests are more blunt. In the wake of *Humanae Vitae*, the Carmelite fathers of the city of Belo Horizonte issued a statement complaining that the Pope did not take into consideration the opinions of the consiliar bishops and his own commission in reaffirming the traditional doctrine.

> The attitude of Pope Paul VI caused a profound sense of frustration among not a few couples wanting to maintain fidelity to the ecclesiastical authority within the demands of modern life. To ease the drama of conscience which this even brought, we should recall that each one of us will be judged by God in accordance with his own conscience. And the criterion of judgment of conscience is the Evangelical Message of the Total Liberation of man in Christ, through which we express in ourselves the image of God. To express in ourselves the image of God, everything, even the Natural Law and the Authority of the Pope, serve as instruments.[17]

In Latin America, as in other parts of the world, priests from the same religious order and diocese have met to agree on pastoral strategy. Prominent Jesuits in Colombia and Franciscans in Brazil told me that their orders had agreed in such meetings to be "open." In Latin America today the younger priests especially are in close touch with the economic problems and aspirations of the lower and middle classes. Frequently in talking with priests who work in slums, for example, I find that they do not even question the morality of contraception in a context where women struggle to support children on their husbands' minimal salaries and what they themselves can eke out from part-time work. Admitted that my contacts tend to be with the more liberal clergy, I have yet to discuss this matter with a priest in Latin America who did not in counseling leave the contraceptive method up to the individual conscience.

While we may assume that the "ideology" of the Church plays an important role in whether some Catholics use contraception or not, it is extremely doubtful that this is so for most Latin Americans. One of the curious discoveries of researchers on use of contraceptives among women in major Latin American cities was that there were no significant differences between Catholics and non-Catholics, or between Catholics of greater and lesser devotion.[18] In a recent study of slum-dwelling women in Santiago, Chile, the author concludes: "The results of the study of religious influence serves to confirm that neither the type of religious creed, nor its greater or lesser practice, are factors of real weight in the decision to use contraceptives."[19] Personnel working in family planning in many countries insist that the religious issue rarely comes up in their conversations with patients.

While facts like these have received wide publicity among students of population problems, a meaningful explanation has not. The answer seems to be that most Latin Americans adhere to various forms of culture religion which lacks a close linkage to sexual morality and accept practices contradicting normative Catholicism.

The origins of this culture religion go back to the Spanish and Portuguese conquest and to the introduction of slavery. In this clash between two sharply divergent ways-of-life, the Iberian conquerors tried to impose their culture, including religion, on the native Indians and subsequently on African slaves. The persistence of pre-Colombian religions among Andean and Central American Indians and of African religion in Brazil reveals the relative superficiality of the process of cultural imposition; but in most parts of Latin America the Iberians were more effective, at least in imparting a Catholic facade to popular religion. New symbols—Jesus, the Virgin Mary, the saints—replaced the Indian and African deities, and customary religious practice assumed a Catholic form as sacramentals, saints' feasts, and pilgrimages to shrines.

In many instances this represented a mere grafting—the Virgin Mary assumed the attributes and cult of the chief female deity, for instance, or traditional dancing became a part of the ceremony to honor a Christian saint. As one of Latin America's best-known sociologists of religion (a Chilean Jesuit) describes it:

> We live in a country in which the effort of the first centuries of civilization and evangelization produced a culture with a Catholic base. In those first centuries, the Church baptized many rites, signs, and cults, succeeding in showing in this way to people that they could encounter God through them. . . . It is true that later the rites which were Christianized came to lose their clear reference to Christianity, and on the other hand, the same Christian rites, like sacraments and sacramentals, have been distorted, becoming converted into elements more cultural and folkloric than Christian.[20]

The "conversion" of Latin America failed to communicate a strong internal perspective conforming to normative Catholicism. It is doubtful that the peasants of Spain and Portugal in the sixteenth and seventeenth century were very different, because normative Catholicism demands a sophistication that neither they nor the Latin Americans could achieve.

Sociologists working in Latin America are now moving toward a consensus on the nature of popular Catholicism. Many of the most perceptive are priests who have the advantage of close contact with the beliefs and practices of the people and who readily admit that up to 80 percent of Latin American Catholics adhere to "popular" Catholicism.

To sharpen the distinction between the two types of religion it is useful to postulate certain criteria of normative Catholicism and contrast the popular outlook with them. Normative Catholicism involves at least the following characteristics:[21]

(1) Adherence to a set of basic beliefs, such as the classical creeds and further dogmatic definitions which distinguish Roman Catholic Christianity from other forms of religion.

(2) A strong sense of identification with the institutional Church as the chief center of religious life.

(3) Participation in the sacraments administered by the Church as the basic instrument of salvation.

(4) Conformity to ethical teachings communicated by the Church and which in some instances are distinctive.

Popular Catholicism represents almost the opposite characteristics:

(1) In generalizing about Latin American popular beliefs, based on studies in a number of countries, Father Segundo Galilea, director of CELAM's Pastoral Institute, notes that although belief in God is deeply rooted in the masses, only 80 percent believe that Jesus is God, 40 percent that He is Savior, and only 55 percent believe Mary to be the Mother of God. The Trinity, the basic doctrine of Christianity, he describes as "unknown." "In any case, the most important beliefs are saints and sanctuaries, where they appear to believe in a plurality of 'virgins.' "[22] If Jesus is not the savior, what is he? According to an analysis of Brazilian Catholicism:

> Jesus is associated with Mary. Above all he is the Son of Mary, The Good Jesus, the Jesus of Sufferings, of the Cross, of Cavalry, of Passion, the Jesus whose look makes his mother suffer. He is also in the center of the religion of suffering, of piety, of resignation. Jesus is pardon, sweetness, patience. He is the rescuer in adversities and catastrophes.[23]

Essentially, popular Latin American Catholicism conforms to peasant religions in many cultures, involving a sense of kinship with a nature rich in mana and symbolized by a multiplicity of mediators who are like members of the extended family.

(2) The average Latin American has little consciousness of himself as belonging to a universal institution, and his cultic acts are centered in the community and family rather than in the church edifice. In his home are the images of the saints before which he prays. The Church building has exceptional sacred (as against profane) qualities. He crosses himself as he passes it, and often he will stop to light a candle at the altar of his favorite saint or to get some holy water for the good luck it brings. The priest is often also a respected person, because he blesses things and thus wards off evil.

(3) In Latin America, participation in the sacraments varies from country to country but is lower than most people realize. The sacraments that

serve as *rites de passage* have strong cultural, though not necessarily religious, significance. Perhaps 90 percent of the people are baptized (ranging from 95 to 98 percent in Mexico and Central America to 70 percent in Cuba), and 30 to 70 percent participate in First Communion and Marriage (though in countries like the Dominican Republic and Panama over 60 percent of the children are illegitimate). However, attendance at mass, the central cultic act of the Church, is low, with about 20 percent in the region going regularly. Variation is great among countries and even within countries. For example, Colombia as a whole registers 15 percent, but the departments of Caldas and Antiquia register 60 percent. In Mexico and Central America, mass attendance is greater in the lower classes, but in Argentina, Uruguay, and Chile, greatest among the upper-middle class. Throughout Latin America women participate disproportionately. Use of the sacraments of Penance (confession) and Eucharist is very low, usually a small minority of those attending mass taking Communion.[24]

What kind of cults makes sense to most Latin Americans? Basically a relationship with the charismatic beings of the Church (God, Jesus, the Virgin Mary, the saints) who bring blessings, good luck, benefits. Saints' days, pilgrimages, processions, candles lit at grottos—all reflect the quest of needy people for health and prosperity, and protection from evil forces. Funeral rites, visits to cemeteries, devotion to the animitas (small shrines where people have died violently) guarantee the benevolence of the dead and reflect a belief in many spirits.

(4) The average Latin American does not determine his moral behavior by the teaching of the Church. Father Galilea correctly describes the situation as follows:

> At first glance it may appear, especially to the foreign or superficial observer that the people . . . have no moral principles. This is not correct. The people have a morality, though often it is based on other norms . . . than ours. In the popular classes, for example, fornication and adultery are rather common in the men, although it is demanded that the women be faithful. The antinatural control of births and abortion has wide acceptance. . . . We should call attention . . . to the separation between morality and religious belief. It is normal to see in houses, buses, and so forth, stamps of saints next to pornography. . . . Among the moral values, friendship, affection, hospitality, are more important than efficiency and economic values. The abnegation of women in home and work is extraordinary. . . .[25]

The separation between religion and morality is central for understanding the role of Catholicism in Latin American family planning. An able interpreter of Brazilian culture who believes that the popular religion of his country differs from that of Hispanic America describes it as "a Catholicism deprived of its dogmatic and *moral* content." [26] In effect, the same Latin American woman who says, *"Soy muy católica,"* may not use contraception for a number of reasons, but religion is rarely among them. Rather, practical considerations and availability of means become decisive. It was the staggering incidence of abortion, a more serious violation of Catholic teaching than artificial contraception, in many countries of Latin America, which persuaded family planners that they could push ahead without religious or moral resistance in the popular classes.

Culture Catholicism is not limited to the lower classes, though in educated and privileged people it assumes a more complex and up-to-this-point unresearched form. Like American culture religion, participation in the Church is a matter of habit and respectability, and religion is regarded as a bulwark for preserving female virginity and the existent political and social order. The Church is honored as a pillar of the established system (although many Church leaders are desperately trying to escape this onus), but its teaching on contraception is ignored if large numbers of children stand in the way of greater material comfort and status.

The role of Catholicism in Latin America, like religion in other cultures, is ambiguous. If it sometimes stands in judgment on the values of a culture, it is also easy for individuals to find in it what they want. This is especially so with Catholicism which has spoken probably too much over many years, often with ambivalence and affirmations hedged with reservations. Moreover, the Church has changed so rapidly in the past decade that—on social thought especially—the older generation received a training almost the opposite of that which their children get today. Catholicism is more often used in the Latin American privileged classes to justify personal or class interests than the Church is able to use these same groups to further its social ethical concerns.

Despite the relatively less space devoted to the effect of culture religion on contraception practices, it far outweighs as a factor the lenient interpretations of *Humanae Vitae* within the formal structure of the Church. The dominant Irish Catholicism and the Calvinist-sectarian Protestant tradition of the United States always linked religious conviction with a strict sexual ethic. Because North Americans usually draw their impressions of Latin America from Mexico, which projects a splashy religious symbolism lacking in the secularized crescent from Brazil through Uruguay and Argentina to Chile, it is hard for them to believe that this omnipresent Catholic religiosity is not reflected in opposition to "artificial" contraception. But it is not.

Family planning does face many obstacles in Latin America. Low educational levels, subjugation of women, rural isolation, recalcitrant tradition, and lack of medical facilities will prevent many people from adopting contraception in this century. National aspirations in the region's large and relatively unpopulated countries will continue to make leaders in government and public opinion reticent. Anti-United States and anti-foreign attitudes among intellectuals and students will provide the strongest theoretical opposition. Nevertheless, the specter of a Church galvanizing millions of Latin American Catholics against family planning lacks theological or sociological reality.

Church leaders will undoubtedly want to contribute to the dialogue as family planning progresses in the future. The cooperation and mutual esteem between Brazil's Bemfam, on the one hand, and theologians and bishops, on the other, is one example. The Medical School of Colombia's Javerian University and Peru's Christian Family Movement are currently providing women with progesterone pills for two years after child-bearing, followed by the rhythm method, in experimental programs respected by family-planning leaders in both countries. Chile's Latin America Center of Population (CELAP) does research on population problems, trains leaders, and tries to clarify the Catholic position in a program with continental outreach. These efforts will probably increase, but at the same time also, leading Catholics will join other Latin Americans in pointing to anomalies in family planning, such as: (1) the desire of international and national elites for the masses to plan their families, but the unwillingness to allow them political and social participation commensurate with their numbers; (2) Americans who talk ominously of the economic consequences of demographic growth in Latin America, but spend the bulk of the national budget on a war against an underdeveloped country and in trips to the moon; (3) the unwillingness of the developed countries to devote a small percentage of their national product to development of the Third World; (4) the ignorance and indifference about Latin America in other parts of the world (for example, Uruguay and Argentina have very low and satisfactory rates of population increase).

It is regrettable that the ambivalence of the Church's position prevents it from taking a major role in the promotion of family planning in Latin America, because the Church today is producing some of the most sophisticated and socially-conscious elites in the region. However, those same elites seem likely to prevent the Church from assuming an inhumane attitude of opposition. The whole controversy over contraception has had an important role in stimulating self-criticism within the Latin American Church and has given it an excuse to turn its attention quietly to other graver problems, like doing something about the unstable and tragic family life of many people.

NOTES TO CHAPTER 2

1. The chief explanation of Latin America's high rate of population increase is its absorption of medical and sanitary advances which have reduced mortality rates while natality rates have continued high. This reflects the region's status as the most developed part of the underdeveloped world.
2. The leaders of the new marital theology are generally acknowledged to have been Dietrich von Hildebrand, H. Doms, and Bernardin Krempel.

3. *Casti Conubii,* cited in Terence P. McLaughlin, ed., *The Church and the Reconstruction of the Modern World* (Garden City: Doubleday, 1957), pp. 115-170.
4. Thomas G. Saunders, *The Chilean Episcopate* [TGS-3-'68], Fieldstaff Reports, West Coast South America Series, XV, No. 3 (1968), p. 16.
5. *Jornal do Brasil,* September 28, 1968.
6. *Diário de Notícias,* September 20, 1966.
7. One exception is Msgr. Pedro Paulo Koop, bishop of Lins (São Paulo), Brazil, co-author of "A Encíclica Humane Vitae: Análise dos Argumentos," *Vozes* (November, 1968), pp. 987-995.
8. Reported in *Noticias Aliadas* (Lima: Centro de Información Católica, 1969).
9. *La Iglesia ante el cambio* (Bogotá: Conferencia Episcopal de Colombia, 1969), p. 80.
10. "Declaração da Comissão Central da CNBB," *SEDOC,* I (February, 1969), pp. 1025-1029.
11. The Medellín document has been published in Spanish as *La Iglesia en la actual transformación de América Latina a la luz del Concilio* (Bogotá: CELAM, 1969). The sections on demography and matrimony are in Vol. II, pp. 77-88.
12. "Episcopado Venezuelano Favorável ao Planejamento Familiar," *Boletim de Bemfam* (December, 1969).
13. Typical are: Jaime Snoek, C.SS.R., "Meditando sôbre uma Encíclica," *REB,* XXIX (March, 1969), pp. 138-145; B. Beni dos Santos, "A Concepção Personalista do Matrimônio e a 'Humanae Vitae,'" *Vozes* (November, 1968), pp. 976-986. The leading Brazilian writers on the theology of matrimony are Father dos Santos (see his *O Sentido Personalista do Matrimônio* [Petrópolis: *Vozes,* 1969]); and especially Paul-Eugène Charbonneau (see his *Humanae Vitae e Liberdade da Consciência* [São Paulo: Herder, 1969]), both critical of *Humanae Vitae.* A major Brazilian Catholic demographer, Pedro Calderon Beltrão, S.J., is a professor of demography at the Gregorian University in Rome. In a country with vast unsettled regions and little public interest in population programs, Father Beltrão has written: "There is no doubt that our rate of demographic growth exceeds the optimal point and consequently, for good macro-social reasons, a policy of reduction of natality imposes itself as one of the essential elements of the national project of development and social welfare." "A transição demográfica," *Vozes,* LXIII (May, 1969), pp. 387-395.
14. Jerônimo de Sá Cavalcante, O.S.B., "Aspectos Religiosos do Planejamento Familiar," *I Seminario de Planejamento Familiar* (Rio de Janeiro: Bemfam), II, p. 49.
15. "Declaração de Professôres de Teologia da Universidade Católica de Chile," *SEDOC,* I (February, 1969), pp. 1071-1075.
16. Snoek, *"Meditando . . . ,"* p. 145.

17. "Declaração dos Padres Carmelitas de Belo Horizonte," *SEDOC*, I (February, 1969), p. 1061.
18. Carmen A. Miró, "Some Misconceptions Disproved: A Program of Fertility Studies in Latin America," *Family Planning and Population Programs* (Chicago: University of Chicago Press, 1966).
19. Josefina Lozada de Masjuan, *Comportamientos anticonceptivos en la familia marginal* (Santiago: DESAL/CELAP, 1968), p. 68.
20. Renato Poblete, S.J., "Aspectos sociológicos de la religiosidad popular, II," *Mensaje Iberoamericano*, 2a epoca, no. 52 (February, 1970), p. 14.
21. For this schema I am indebted to Thales de Azevedo, "Popular Catholicism in Brazil: Typology and Functions," cited in Raymond S. Sayers, ed., *Portugal and Brazil in Transition* (Minneapolis: University of Minnesota Press, 1968), pp. 175-178.
22. Segundo Galilea, "La práctica religiosa popular," *Mensaje Iberoamericano*, 2a epoca, no. 29 (March, 1968), p. 12.
23. Cited in Emile Pin, S.J., *Elementos para uma Sociologic do Catolicismo Latinaomericano* (Petropólis: *Vozes*, 1966), p. 70.
24. *Ibid.*, pp. 11-22, for figures on religious practice.
25. Galilea, *"La práctica religiosa . . . ,"* p. 13.
26. Thales de Azevedo, "Problemas Metodológicos da Sociologia do Catolicismo," *Cultura e Situação Social no Brasil* (Rio de Janeiro: Civilização Brasileira, 1967), p. 184.

Chapter Three

Factors Affecting the Population Attitudes of Latin American Elites*

Axel Mundigo

INTRODUCTION

The adoption and implementation of population policy, especially in developing countries experiencing high population growth, is difficult, if not impossible, where the politically and economically powerful sectors of the society are either disinterested or ignorant of population problems. Most research in the area of population attitudes in high-fertility Latin America has concentrated on lower income groups, although a few recent studies have included members of the elite.[1]

The importance of a consensus among national leaders, professionals, intellectuals, and other influential groups for the success of any innovating social policy cannot be underestimated. Population policy provides an outstanding example of the complexities underlying such policies. The majority of the Latin American nations have private family-planning programs or dispense contraceptive services through government clinics; yet their governments resist officially adopting policies committed to controlling population growth. In a few—Brazil and Peru, for example—official policy continues to call for more people. Why, it might be asked, are the leaders of a continent experiencing record demographic increase so reluctant to adopt policies designed to slow down population growth? How do negative sources of influence affect the opinions and actions of Latin American elites?

*This selection has been originally prepared for this volume by Dr. Mundigo and contains material from his dissertation: *Elites, Economic Development and Population in Honduras* (Ithaca, New York: Cornell University, Latin American Program, Dissertation Series, 1972). This research project was partly funded by Cornell University's International Population Program and partly by a Public Health fellowship (5 F03HD 36949-02) from the National Institute to Child Health and Human Development. I would like to thank Professor J. Mayone Stycos for his encouragement, suggestions, and insightful criticisms.

The elites' "privately" felt need to limit family size and their use of contraception to achieve it fails to translate itself into "public" recognition of the population problem or into wide support of family-planning programs. Several authors have pointed to two important sources of negative influence on elites: religiosity and political ideology.[2] Coupled with these roots of population opposition, most Latin American countries are overwhelmed by other developmental problems. Lack of knowledge of the extent of gains to be derived from fertility declines and lack of perception of the long-term benefits of these reductions relegate population control to an area of benign neglect.[3] Furthermore, the rise of nationalistic movements and leftist governments has thwarted the adoption of population policies in Latin America. In nations where such changes have not occurred, elites often fail to satisfy popular demands in attempting to preserve traditional values and out-moded structures. In so doing, modernism, a force that would affect the non-contraceptive status of a society, is also checked.

This chapter deals specifically with the following questions regarding the attitudes of Latin American elites as they affect population policy:

1. Is political ideology related to religiosity?
2. Is the expected influence of political ideology and religiosity with respect to birth control attitudes sustained among elite groups? How do they affect other population attitudes?
3. Is political ideology or religiosity the stronger factor in influencing attitudes towards birth control?
4. What is the predictive value of modernism in explaining population attitudes? Is modernism related to either political ideology or religiosity?
5. Who are more likely to advocate population control, established elites or upcoming elites, i.e. students?
6. How do the decision-makers in government positions differ from other elite groups in these attitudes?
7. What are the implications of answers to the above questions for the adoption of population policies?

HONDURAS: A CASE STUDY

Honduras, one of Latin America's fastest growing but least developed nations, was the locale chosen to study elite and university student attitudes on population. Although the population of the country is small—2.7 million in 1970—it is expected to reach 3.8 million by 1980 and to double in about two decades. At present there are no indications of a slowdown in population growth. The United Nations has estimated the birth rate at 47 to 50 births per thousand population, a level that has remained fairly consistent since 1945, while mortality has declined considerably in the same period, with the present rate estimated at 15 to 17 deaths per thousand population.[4]

Elites, students, and the general public at the time of the study had been exposed to the subject of population through newspaper articles, radio and television discussions, and involvement in what has been called a "demographic conflict," that is, the war that took place in mid-1969 between Honduras and neighboring El Salvador.[5] The conflict originated from the increasing numbers of Salvadorean peasants illegally entering Honduras in search of work and land. The conflict flared during a soccer match, hence its more popular name, "The Soccer War."

Interviewing began in November of 1969 and lasted through February of the next year. The study was designed so that each of the groups included would represent a majority of three positional elites: a top-level government cadre, a group of business and commercial managers, and a professional group (lawyers). Due to practical and financial reasons the elite sample was limited to a maximum of 300 persons. Quota samples were used (100 respondents for each of the above groups), which in two cases represent almost the entire universe, and in the third, 25 percent of the total. Purposely, the elite sample excludes the following: foreign nationals or members of international organizations, the military, and the non-industrial sector of the landed elite. Foreign elites are excluded because the objective was to interview "national" elites. The military is excluded unless occupying high government positions of normally civilian character. (This exclusion of the military was deemed practical since the country was still in a state of war.) The non-industrial sector of the landed elite is not very influential in a country whose agriculture is largely of plantation type requiring industrial techniques for large scale exploitation of bananas, coffee, timber, and sugar.[6]

The university student sample was "purposive" in nature, that is, neither random nor representative. The intention was to include a broad spectrum of professional interests, although about half of the students interviewed were enrolled in the school of medicine. With the permission of authorities at the Honduran Autonomous National University, a largely closed-ended, self-administered questionnaire was distributed to students during a regularly scheduled class hour. Elites were personally interviewed using a questionnaire similar in content but different in form. Their questionnaire began with open-ended questions on development, moved towards more specific questions on population topics, and ended with a closed-ended battery of scale items and personal characteristics. Many of the more specific questions had forced-choice responses but were always followed by a "Why do you think this?" or "Please explain your position" to allow for maximum flexibility and spontaneity of expression. While elite interviewing is often discarded as difficult or unattainable, the conclusion from this study is that, while difficult, it is both possible and rewarding.

ELITE ATTITUDES

Religiosity and Political Ideology. Among the factors that can be expected to affect the population attitudes of Latin American elites are religiosity and political ideology. At extremes of the political spectrum, the conservative right and the radical left oppose population control policies. Latin American Marxists see birth control as a covert policy of North American imperialism to lower the area's potential for revolution. They tend to minimize or negate the importance of demographic parameters in economic development. As a Cuban source puts it, ". . . imperialist maintenance of feudal relations in agriculture is the origin of underdevelopment, not the increase in population."[7] The political right opposes birth control both because of its effect on the supply of cheap labor and potential consumers and because of moral considerations. It is only at the center of the political spectrum, among liberals and social reformers, that birth control receives considerable support. As Stycos remarks, ". . . they [the liberals] see birth control as a social measure, as a means of reducing abortion and illegitimacy, and as a way of increasing human freedom and control over man's nature."[8] Permeating right, center and left, is a strong nationalistic feeling which favors population growth as a means to enhance national power and prestige. In Honduras, populationist sentiment was given a boost by the recent conflict with El Salvador; a low density nation of only a few millions was portrayed by nationalists as weak, defenseless, and incapable of meeting the threat of more populated neighbors.

Because of the Roman Catholic homogeneity of Latin America, religiosity should influence birth control attitudes. The Church has recently reaffirmed its anti-birth control position and demolished the expectations of many Catholics for a more liberal attitude on the use of artificial contraception. Therefore, one would expect most support for birth control from those groups least exposed to Catholic influence.

Religiosity was measured among the elites and the university students by the question, "Do you consider yourself very, somewhat, little, or not religious?" Differences are negligible: about half in each sample classify themselves as "somewhat religious," and a third as "little religious." A slightly higher proportion of the elites consider themselves "very religious" (15 percent) than do students (7 percent). Equally unsubstantial are the differences among the sub-groups in each sample (see Table 3-1).

A direct question on political affiliation was included on the first draft of the questionnaire, but after field tests, it was obvious that the question was much too controversial. The following question was substituted: "A revolution would damage the progress of Honduras and should be avoided

Table 3-1. Religiosity and Political Ideology (Percentages)

	Total Elites	Total University Students	Government Officials	Managers	Lawyers	Medical Students	Non-Medical Students
Religiosity:							
Very	15	7	14	14	16	4	8
Somewhat	49	56	45	51	52	54	58
Little	29	29	33	31	24	33	26
Not at all	7	8	8	4	8	9	8
	100%	100%	100%	100%	100%	100%	100%
Political Ideology:							
Right	23	14	20	36	13	13	15
Center	25	20	22	24	29	14	25
Moderate Left[a]	40	57	48	35	38	60	54
Radical Left	12	9	10	5	20	13	6
	100%	100%	100%	100%	100%	100%	100%
(No. of cases)	(294)	(404)	(97)	(99)	(98)	(188)	(216)

a. Group identified as favoring revolution and possibly including some liberals (see text).

at any cost. Do you agree, partly agree or disagree?" In tables showing political ideology, "right" corresponds to those in total agreement with this statement; those in partial agreement are considered "center"; and those in disagreement, are considered "moderate left." Lastly, "radical left" are respondents with a clear Marxist orientation, identified from open-ended questions in which respondents were likely to reveal their ideological positions. Following are a few examples of opinions which were considered to show a radical left orientation: "We ought to establish much closer economic ties with the Soviet block as a means to put an end to Yankee imperialism." Or, "We need an intense social and economic revolution; we must start by nationalizing all foreign enterprises and adopt a socialist model for our development." Or, "This era of capitalist domination must end by a radical revolution of the left leading to an equitable and just communist state."

Political references, plus additional comments on the question of revolution, were used to determine a radical left orientation among students. This may explain why the proportion of "radical leftists" among the elites is slightly higher than among the students—such identification was more difficult—while the opposite is more likely to be true. In all cases, the most ideologically "pure" groups are the two extremes. The "center" and "moderate left" can be considered as liberal groups. Many liberals in Honduras might advocate a revolution to overthrow a military dictatorship which has been in command for seven years but not necessarily support Castro-type revolutionary change. In contrast to religiosity, political ideological differences are marked, both

en the two principal samples and also among their sub-groups. The elites
___ ₋ higher proportion in the political "right," while two-thirds of the
students are in the two central groups, with a higher proportion in the "moderate left." Lawyers (among the elite) and medical students have the highest proportions of "radical leftists" (according to Table 3-1).

That political ideology and religiosity are not independent factors is shown in Table 3-2. The relationship is stronger among students than among elites. *As the degree of religious intensity decreases the proportion of "radical leftists" increases in both groups.* Among the "non-religious" in both samples, about a third are "radical leftists." The interrelationship between political ideology and religiosity can be expected to modify the influence of religiosity on population attitudes. It had been expected that the attitudes of the least religious groups would be the most favorable, but this might not be so in view of their higher proportion of extreme leftists, the political group most opposed to birth control.

Attitudes Towards Population Control. An underlying assumption in this study suggests that the success of a national population policy will depend largely on the support given to it by that country's elite. The support given to population policies by Honduran government officials, among whom

Table 3-2. Political Ideology by Religiosity (Percentages)

Political Ideology and Sample	Religiosity			
	Very	Somewhat	Little	Not at all
Total Elites:				
Right	23	26	20	15
Center	28	30	19	15
Moderate Left[a]	44	38	43	35
Radical Left	5	6	18	35
	100%	100%	100%	100%
(No. of cases in base)	(43)	(144)	(84)	(20)
Total University Students:				
Right	13	15	14	6
Center	33	24	14	6
Moderate Left[a]	46	55	62	58
Radical Left	8	6	10	30
	100%	100%	100%	100%
(No. of cases in base)	(24)	(227)	(117)	(31)
Correlation coefficient between Political Ideology and Religiosity:				
Total Elites	.09			
Total University Students	.15[b]			

a. Group identified as in favor of revolution and possibly including some liberals (see text).
b. Significant at 5 percent level.

Table 3-3. Attitudes Toward Birth Control and Population Policy (Percentages)

Item	Total Elite	Total University Students	Government Officials	Managers	Lawyers	Medical Students	Non-Medical Students
Birth Control[a]							
Agree	34	33	41	45	17	34	32
Partly Agree	15	47	15	20	10	44	49
Disagree	51	20	44	35	73	22	19
	100%	100%	100%	100%	100%	100%	100%
Population Policy[b]							
No government control of population	44	17	47	34	50	17	17
Policy to slow down growth rates	37	68	43	47	20	72	65
Other,[c] don't know	19	15	10	19	30	11	18
	100%	100%	100%	100%	100%	100%	100%
(No. of cases)	(300)	(404)	(100)	(100)	(100)	(190)	(214)

a. Corresponds to the following questionnaire item: "What would be your opinion about a national family-planning program to reduce the present population growth rate? Would you agree, partly agree or disagree?"

b. Corresponds to the following questionnaire item: "Would you say that the government should establish specific goals for the growth of the population of the country or that it should leave population to grow uncontrolled?"

c. Among elites includes those who wanted a policy designed to increase population growth. This distinction was not made among the students.

the implementation of such decisions rests, will be a significant indicator of the likelihood that Honduras might take serious steps to reduce the rate of her population growth in the near future. Two questions were asked of all respondents: one with regard to their support or rejection of a national birth control program, and the other about their attitude towards government involvement in setting population policy objectives (Table 3-3). While the phrase "birth control" is used throughout this chapter in Spanish, the actual question referred to "a national family-planning program to reduce present population growth rates," thus implying fertility limitation as a means to achieve a demographic objective.

A substantial proportion—14 percent—of the elites commented that there should be a population policy to *increase* population growth. Undoubtedly similar attitudes existed among students, but these were not measured in the questionnaire. In Table 3-3, the answer "no government control of population" is comparable for both elites and students. "Other," among elites only, includes those who wanted a policy designed to increase population growth. A full half of the Honduran elites is opposed to any national family-planning program. Similarly, almost half does not want government involvement in population control. This supports Stycos' assertion that ". . . the classes with the lowest fertility are generally the least favorable to the notion of a family-planning program for the nation."[9] On the other hand, the lower classes, those with the highest fertility, are overwhelmingly in favor of having contraceptive services made available to them. Of a representative sample of women in their reproductive years (15 to 45 years) from Las Crucitas, an urban lower class area of Tegucigalpa, only 15 percent opposed family planning.[10]

Student opinions on population control are not as polarized as those of the elites. While birth control opposition is weaker among students, the extent of their unqualified support for birth control is the same as among the elites. Nearly a half of the students are still making up their minds with respect to the population issue. Their indecisiveness is not affected by their age, length of study at the university, or type of academic pursuit. Only a slight increase in the negative answers is noted among the advanced medical and engineering students.

Differences among elite samples are contrary to our expectations. The more traditional and conservative managers support birth control policies more than any other group. In Honduras, where economic development is slow and characterized by low per capita income, scarcity of skilled labor, and an overwhelmingly rural population, the hypothesis that big business opposes birth control does not seem to hold. Business, it can be argued, would oppose birth control because of its deterrent effect on the continuous supply of cheap labor and on the number of potential consumers. As a leading Honduran industrialist stated it:

> While the size of our country would permit an increase in our population we must not reproduce like rabbits. We have a large unskilled labor force which only augments the problems facing industrial growth. There are jobs but we cannot fill many positions, not for lack of people, but for lack of technically qualified personnel.

Opposition to birth control was highest among the lawyers, a strongly nationalist group, and least among managers. Government officials, a key group from the viewpoint of population policy implementation were found to be roughly equally divided on the issue of birth control and nearly one-half also voiced opposition to any type of government involvement in population policy. Even more important, two-thirds of the government, legislative and political

VIP's, a group of roughly 50 leaders whose voice in national decision-making outweighs any other group, were opposed to birth control. (This included government officials with ministerial rank or its equivalent.) The extent of the opposition to birth control found among the elite strongly reinforces the belief that major obstacles exist to the implementation of a comprehensive and effective population policy in Honduras.

The Influence of Religiosity and Political Ideology on Population Attitudes. Support for birth control, in both samples, is strongest among the middle levels of religiosity. Both the "non religious" and the "very religious" are equally opposed to birth control. The greatest opposition is also found at the extremes of the political spectrum. For total elites the impact of political ideology becomes clearer when the responses are disaggregated by sub-groups. The highly nationalistic lawyers' strong opposition to birth control, regardless of their political orientation, weakens the pattern for the overall sample.

Table 3-4. Attitudes Towards Birth Control by Religiosity and Political Ideology (Percentages)

	Religiosity			
Items	Very	Somewhat	Little	Not at all
Attitude towards birth control[a] Percent who "oppose."				
Total Elites	61	50	48	60
Total Students	39	15	22	32
Government Officials	43	48	42	38[b]
Managers	50	33	33	50[b]
Lawyers	88	68	74	88[b]
Medical Students	13[b]	21	21	38
Non-Medical Students	50	12	22	27

	Political Ideology			
Items	Right	Center	Moderate Left	Radical Left
Attitude towards birth control[a] Percent who "oppose."				
Total Elites	55	55	41	68
Total Students	15	8	23	39
Government Officials	53	43	41	44[b]
Managers	49	38	11	100[b]
Lawyers	77	79	68	70
Medical Students	17	7	24	38
Non-Medical Students	13	9	22	42

a. Text of question appears in Table 3-3.
b. Based on less than ten cases.

46 An Overview of the Politics of Population in Latin America

But the strong influence of political ideology in explaining population attitudes is evident among both the government officials and the managers. It is also clear among the students.

Opposition to birth control is consistently strong among the "radical left." On the other hand, opposition from the "right" tends to vary. Among the university students it appears weak. The larger indecision and the formative nature of values and attitudes among students, in addition to a less clear position of the conservatives on matters having to do with birth control, might help to explain this apparent lack of consistency.

Of greater interest for the analysis of political influences is the peculiar behavior of the lawyers. The lawyers are a unique group in the elite sample. They are professionally the most homogeneous, and at the same time their social and personal characteristics, when compared with the managers or government officials, are the most dissimilar. They include the highest proportion of both "very religious" and of "radical left" members, and as a group, their level of political aspiration is the highest. In addition, among them religiosity and political ideology are especially correlated. Still another characteristic that sets the lawyers apart from the two other groups is their lack of cosmopolitanism. Only about a third had attended a foreign university while nearly two-thirds of the managers and half of the government officials had studied abroad. While nine out of ten of the managers spoke a foreign language, only a third of the lawyers did so.

The lawyers' background characteristics and their unusual opposition to birth control led to a check of the open-ended population questions. Among this group the influence of nationalism seems to override the influence of political ideology. Half of the respondents who believed that a birth control program would stall development were lawyers; half of those who claimed that Honduras was under-populated and needed more population to gain more prestige and power were lawyers, and three-quarters of those who believed that birth control is a United States' covert policy to slow down population in developing countries were lawyers. In short, whenever arguments implying that the country's interests were at stake were advanced against birth control, lawyers always predominated.

Lastly, an attempt has been made to separate the influence of political ideology from that of religiosity. The two extreme political groups have been left intact; the two groups in between—"centrists" and "moderate left"—have been merged. Among the religious categories, "little" and "non-religious" have been merged. The clear relationship between political ideology and religiosity once again is shown in Table 3-5. Among the "very" and "somewhat" religious groups there are no "radical leftists." The lack of conservatives among the "very religious," and, to a lesser extent, among the "somewhat religious" of the students is also striking, explaining partly the lack of consistency among the "rightists" opposition to birth control.

Table 3-5. Opposition to Birth Control by Religiosity and Political Ideology (Percentages)

Samples	Very Religious			Somewhat Religious			Little or Non Religious		
	Right	Center[a]	Radical Left	Right	Center[a]	Left	Right	Center[a]	Radical Left
Total Elite	60	58	**	54	47	**	61	44	68
(No. of cases)	(10)	(31)	**	(37)	(95)	**	(17)	(59)	(22)
Total University Students	**	37	**	3	17	31	28	20	42
(No. of cases)	**	(19)	**	(32)	(166)	(13)	(18)	(92)	(19)

a. "Centrists" and "moderate Left." (The latter group includes a considerable proportion of liberals.) were merged to leave untouched the more extreme groups.
**Based on less than ten cases, percent not shown.

The nature of the influence of these two factors can now be elucidated: (1) "rightists" tend to be strongly opposed to birth control regardless of the intensity of their religious beliefs; (2) if "centrists" are very religious, they oppose birth control; if not, they favor it highly; and (3) "radical leftists" are the most opposed to birth control; but even more so, if not religious. Table 3-5 also shows that *the strength of political ideology in predicting population attitudes is stronger than that of religiosity, and its strength increases as the intensity of religious belief decreases.* The two factors are not independent, nor should they be considered without studying their inter-connectedness. The influence of religiosity can no longer be considered to operate as a continuum.

Modernism and Population Attitudes. Demographic transition theory assumes that as societies move away from agriculture they also abandon traditional norms. The first impact of industrialization on population is in lowering mortality. Fertility decline occurs much later and its rate of change is not only slower but also difficult to predict. As industrialization progresses, pressures for better education and technical training also increase. The large family ceases to be an economic asset. Thus low fertility becomes one of the crucial variables that differentiate the traditional from the modern family.[11] Further refinements of transition theory assume that fertility declines are first achieved by the more educated (usually urban) groups in the society.[12] The Honduran elite sample is no exception; families in these groups completed their reproductive activity at levels substantially below that of a sample of Honduran urban lower-class women.[13]

Modern values can be expected to act as normative agents between socio-economic status and fertility behavior.[14] Often factors such as education or urban status seem to subsume the possible influence of modernism. Still, the relationship between modern values and population attitudes merits consideration. Modernism was measured by means of a battery of scale items which had previously been tested in Latin America by Kahl.[15] Three scales were included in the Honduran case: (1) low integration with relatives; (2) anti-big companies or the preference for smaller places of work and freer individual entrepreneurial spirit; and (3) family modernism, attitudes towards a more independent status of women within marriage. The modernism scales were then correlated with a population scale constructed using the following variables: (1) attitudes towards a national family-planning program; (2) perception of the speed of population growth in Honduras; (3) ideal family size; and (4) the effect of rapid population growth on poverty.

These variables appeared in both the elite's and the students' questionnaires. Using factor analysis, and the item with the highest loading as weight, the population scale was reduced to a single normalized score for each respondent.

Factors Affecting the Population Attitudes of Latin American Elites 49

Table 3-6. Correlations of Four Variables Used for Population Score*

Exact Questionnaire Item	Item No. 1	Item No. 2	Item No. 3	Item No. 4
1. What is your opinion about a national family-planning program to reduce the present population growth rate? Would you agree, partly agree, or disagree?				
Elites		.24	.44	.22
University Students		.07	.25	.25
2. What has been the most important tendency in the population of Honduras during the last 30 years? Has it grown: (1) very fast, (2) fast, (3) slowly or (4) has been stable.				
Elites			.23	.06
University Students			.01	.05
3. In your opinion, which is the convenient (or ideal) number of children a family should have?				
Elites				.14
University Students				.15
4. Rapid population increase is an important factor contributing to the increase of the poverty of the masses. Do you agree, partly agree or disagree?				
Elites				
University Students				

*Correlation is significant at the 5 percent level if above .12 for the Elites and above .10 for the University Students.

The generally low order of the correlation coefficients shown in Table 3-6 suggests that the influences that affect "population control" attitudes (questions 1 and 3) might not have much effect upon attitudes towards the possible consequences of population programs (questions 2 and 4). Knowledge, as measured in question 2, might depend on other factors, such as type of education or the attention given by the respondent to the overall issue of population.

Modern orientations seem to have little or no predictive value with respect to population (Table 3-7). The three modernism scales—on integration with relatives on attitudes toward work and large corporations, and on family life—are not significantly correlated with the population score. Only among university students does "family modernism" associate with the population score. The factor analysis reveals the independence of the modernism scales from the population score. On the other hand, the correlation is significant between "foreign education" and the population score, and there is a tendency to associate in the factor rotation.

These findings seem to agree with the hypothesis advanced by Clifford where "value orientations [are seen] as dependent on status, so that people in upper levels of socio-economic status tend to be modern . . . and

Table 3-7. Population Score and Modernism Scales: Rotated Factors*

	Elites			University Students	
	First	Second	Third	First	Second
Modernism I.	.74	—	—	.53	—
Modernism II.	.64	—	—	.56	—
Modernism III.	.55	−.45	—	—	.75
Population Score[a]	—	—	.68	—	.68
Foreign Education	—	—	.77	.	.
Religiosity	—	.83	—	.54	—
Political Ideology	.41	.39	—	.63	—

*Loadings below .35 not shown. Third factor did not rotate for students. Modernism I. refers to scale on "Low Integration with Relatives." Modernism II. refers to scale on attitudes toward "Big Companies." Modernism III. refers to scale on "Modern Family Attitudes." Includes also normalized scores for "foreign education," "religiosity" and "political ideology."

a. Composite, including four population variables and obtained from factor rotation using highest loading as weight.

which sees specific attitudes and behavior, such as family size and birth control effectiveness, as reflections of value orientations."[16] It might then be added that, as socio-economic status decreases, there might be an increasing tendency to link birth control attitudes as part of a set of modern values. Among the elites, as in this case, other influences would take over and modern values would have only a tangential or supportive role in influencing or predicting population attitudes.

Foreign Education. Foreign education's influence on birth control attitudes appears well defined only when those who attended United States schools are compared with those who went to other countries or did not study abroad. Rejection of birth control is consistently lower among the United States educated, regardless of whether they are lawyers, government or industrial leaders (Table 3-8). The attitudes of those who have not had foreign education tend to be similar to those who went to countries *other* than the United States. This group went, for the most part, to countries of a similar culture as that of Honduras, specifically to Latin America or Spain. The argument can be advanced that exposure to these countries would not have as strong an impact on attitudes as going to a different culture such as is the case of the United States.

As a counter-argument, it would be possible to hypothesize that those who have gone to the United States for their education are a special group responding to some selectivity process. By most characteristics it would appear that no differences exist between the United States educated and others in the elite sample. The former are only slightly younger, tend to be "single,"

Table 3-8. Elite Rejection of Birth Control by Type of Education (Percentages)

	Foreign Education:[a]		
Sample	At a United States University	At a University or Training Institute in other countries	No Foreign Studies
Total Elite:	31	60	55
(No. of cases)	(70)	(121)	(95)
Government Officials:	31	55	38
(No. of cases)	(29)	(52)	(16)
Managers:	23	43	37
(No. of cases)	(31)	(35)	(27)
Lawyers:	60	82	70
(No. of cases)	(10)	(34)	(52)

a. Excludes 14 persons who had high school education abroad but attended university in Honduras. No. of cases refers to all cases in the base for that particular category.

and tend, for the most part, to be engineers, architects, economists and business administrators. For some of those who chose these careers it might have been essential to go abroad, especially for the architects who could not pursue their academic interests at home since there is no school of architecture in Honduras. This suggests still another link in the chain of interrelationships that appear to exist among the factors that affect population attitudes, as foreign education and political ideology are not totally independent from each other. There are practically no "radical leftists" among the U.S. educated, and, from the viewpoint of the political spectrum, the proportion with "no foreign education" rises in a continuum from right to left. It is also doubtful that a "radical leftist" might want to go to the United States even if he were admitted. A selectivity process, then, does appear to be at work with political ideology influencing the nature of the pattern of response to population attitudes by foreign education.

The Extent of Influences on Population Attitudes. Does the predictive value of religiosity and of political ideology in explaining birth control attitudes extend to knowledge about population and/or perceptions about population size and growth? The lack of correlation between "knowledge" and "population control" items (Table 3-6) suggests that perhaps the predictive value of political ideology and of religiosity might not be as great when applied to issues not clearly or immediately related to population control. Thus the following hypothesis is suggested: the pattern of response by religiosity and political ideology will be more sharply defined the closer the issue is to population control.

Table 3-9. Selected Population Knowledge and Attitude Items by Religiosity of Elites (Percentages)

	Religiosity			
Population Item	Very Religious	Somewhat Religious	Little Religious	Not at all Religious

Knowledge:

1. Percent who recognize that the rate of population growth in Honduras is high

   80   74   80   80

2. Percent who know the correct order of population size of the Central American countries

   48   49   51   55

3. Percent who know it takes about 20 to 25 years to double Honduras population

   52   51   50   45

Population Control:

4. Percent who advocate government action in the control of population growth

   30   40   38   25

5. Percent who give total support to a national family-planning program to lower birth rates

   14   36   37   30

6. Percent who give full support to family planning whether it be to lower birth rates or to help solve illegal abortion problem

   47   51   47   35

7. Percent among those opposed to birth control who would favor it as a preventive measure to help solve illegal abortion problem

   47   37   27   12

8. Percent who are opposed to the World Bank's position on population

   57   37   49   55

Size and Growth:

9. Percent who do *not* believe that Honduras faces a population growth problem

   80   75   75   90

10. Percent who believe that the population size of Honduras is adequate as is

    12   28   35   23

11. Percent who oppose the idea that population growth increases the poverty of the masses

    47   29   27   42

Saliency:

12. Percent declaring to have paid *no* attention to population or related issues during past year

    12   39   29   7

Average number of cases in base   (44)   (143)   (83)   (20)

The above correspond to the following questionnaire items:

1. "What has been the most important tendency in the population of Honduras during the past 30 years?: Stability, Slow growth, or Fast growth."
2. "Would you please rank the Central American countries according to their population size; which is the largest in population, the second, etc."

3. "How long does it take Honduras to double its population size under present rates of growth?: 10 years, 15 years, etc."
4. "Should the government establish specific goals for the growth of the country's population or should it let the population grow without any controls?"
5. "What is your opinion of a national family planning program which would be directed at lowering the rate of population growth of Honduras?: Do you agree, partly agree or disagree?"
6. "Those against a national family planning program were asked: Would you agree to a family planning program designed to help solve the high incidence of illegal abortions recorded presently in Honduran hospitals? Would you agree, partly agree or disagree?"
7. From same question as No. 6.
8. "Recently the newspaper *El Dia* published the following declaration made by the World Bank: The major obstacle to economic and social progress in the developing countries is rapid population growth? Do you agree, partly agree or disagree with this statement?"
9. "Does Honduras face a population problem?"
10. "Is the present population size of Honduras adequate?"
11. "A rapid increase in population is an important factor contributing to the increase of poverty among the masses. Do you agree, partly agree or disagree with this statement?"
12. "During the past year did you have a chance to pay attention to population problems?"

The pattern by religiosity of 12 population items is shown in Table 3-9. "Knowledge" of population trends (items 1 to 3) does not respond to the influence of religiosity. But the expected pattern by religiosity—with the most opposed at each end of the religious spectrum—is maintained in all population control items where it applies. (The exception is item 7 which is based on those "opposed" to birth control only.) In all cases the most support for birth control comes from the middle levels of religiosity. Among the three items on "size and growth" (items 9 to 11), the pattern is maintained in two cases: the middle levels of religiosity give more support to the idea that Honduras does face a population problem and believe that rapid population growth increases the poverty of the masses. Lastly, the extremes of religiosity paid the most attention (item 12) to population issues. It is not inconsistent that the two groups most opposed to birth control be the most concerned with population problems, the root of their hostility.

The pattern of response to the same twelve population-related items by political ideology is shown in Table 3-10. in addition to the responses of the total elite sample, a second set of data (shown in parenthesis), consisting of government officials and managers only, is included in the table. Lawyers, a group that is somewhat atypical in personal characteristics as well as attitudes (especially extreme negativism towards birth control), were removed to eliminate possible distortions and to verify the extent of the influence of political ideology when they were excluded.

The influence of political ideology is clear in each of the population control variables with opposition being highest at both extremes of the spectrum. One exception is the item on the World Bank's position on population where the "right" shows the least opposition and the "radical left"

Table 3-10. Selected Population Knowledge and Attitude Items by Political Ideology of Elites* (Percentages)

		Political Ideology		
Population Item	Right	Center	Moderate Left	Radical Left

Knowledge:

1. Percent who recognize that the rate of population growth in Honduras is high

	80	71	82	71
	(78)	(78)	(85)	(79)

2. Percent who know the correct order of population size of the Central American countries

	53	49	47	49
	(55)	(51)	(48)	(50)

3. Percent who know it takes about 20-25 years to double Honduras' population

	57	42	51	58
	(61)	(53)	(58)	(79)

Population Control:

4. Percent who advocate government action in the control of population growth

	34	33	43	24
	(39)	(42)	(52)	(29)

5. Percent who give total support to a national family planning program to lower birth rates

	31	32	40	18
	(35)	(40)	(52)	(21)

6. Percent who give full support to family planning whether it be to lower birth rates or to help solve illegal abortion problem

	45	49	52	21
	(50)	(56)	(63)	(21)

7. Percent among those opposed to birth control who would favor it as a preventive measure to help solve illegal abortion problem

	35	39	39	13
	(45)	(56)	(61)	(12)

8. Percent opposing the World Bank's position on population

	31	41	48	68
	(28)	(31)	(42)	(57)

Size and Growth:

9. Percent who do *not* believe that Honduras faces a population growth problem

	75	71	78	92
	(70)	(67)	(71)	(86)

10. Percent who believe that the population size of Honduras is adequate as is

	26	27	27	34
	(27)	(34)	(35)	(36)

11. Percent who oppose the idea that population growth increases the poverty of the masses

	30	36	28	42
	(24)	(25)	(21)	(50)

Saliency:
12. Percent declaring to have paid *no* attention to population or related issues during past year

	54	55	54	43
	(48)	(47)	(47)	(36)
Average number of cases in base:				
Total Elite	(67)	(74)	(119)	(34)
Elite excluding lawyers	(54)	(45)	(81)	(14)

*The figures shown in parentheses are for the elite sample excluding the 100 lawyers whose strong anti-birth control position dampens the influence of political ideology and is presumably caused by a strong nationalistic feeling. For wording of items see Table 3-9.

the most. This is not inconsistent since the more conservative leaders of government and industry would not react negatively against a measure which might otherwise imperil international credit and affect adversely an already faltering economy. For every case where the influence of political ideology is shown to exist, the pattern of response becomes more sharply defined when the lawyers are excluded (figures in parenthesis).

As with religiosity, political ideology shows only slight influence on population "knowledge" items. The relation to political ideology is clearer among "size and growth" variables, with the "radical left" taking in every case a consistent position: being the most in disagreement with the idea that Honduras faces a population problem or being the least to agree with the proposition that population growth might increase poverty. The "radical left" was also the only group to differ in the amount of attention paid to population matters, being the group most concerned with the issue.

CONCLUSIONS

At the beginning of this chapter seven questions were asked dealing with the nature and influence of the factors that affect population attitudes. Now they can be answered:

1. The pattern of the relationship between political ideology and religiosity is characterized by an increase in the proportions of "extreme leftists" as religious intensity decreases. Thus these two factors, political ideology and religiosity, are not independent.
2. The "expected" pattern of response by religiosity (a continuum with most opposition to birth control among the "most religious" and least among the "non-religious") does not materialize. Most support for birth control is found among the "middle levels" of religiosity, and opposition, as in the case of political ideology, at both extremes of the spectrum.

3. The disaggregation of religiosity and political ideology reveals that: (a) rightists tend to be strongly opposed to birth control regardless of their intensity of religious belief; (b) when centrists are very religious they oppose birth control but when not, they favor it highly; and (c) radical leftists are the most opposed to brith control, even more so if not religious. The strength of political ideology in predicting birth control attitudes is stronger than that of religiosity and its strength tends to increase as the intensity of religious belief decreases.
4. The extent of the influence of political ideology and religiosity in predicting population attitudes is greater the closer the issue is related to population control (as opposed to other population issues). The influence of these factors is weak on some attitudes relating to problems of population growth or pressure and none on variables dealing with population knowledge.
5. Modern value orientations seem to have little or no predictive value with respect to population. This is especially true among the elites where the influence of political ideology and religiosity have greater definition than among students. It can be hypothesized (in line with other studies in this area) that modernism is contingent on social status, having its smallest influence among the elites. At a lower socio-economic status there might be an increasing tendency to associate birth control with modern values. Partial support for this was found among the students.
6. A full half of the elite sample is opposed to birth control, but the incipient elites (or students) are more favorably disposed with only one in five taking a negative position. Because of the greater polarization of attitudes among elites and the high proportion of undecided among the students (47 percent), full support for birth control among both the elite and the students is the same, roughly one-third.
7. Nearly half the government officials, a key group from the viewpoint of policy implementation, oppose any type of government involvement in birth control. Within the elite, a special sample made up of ministers, legislative and political leaders, and other notables, showed even less enthusiasm, with two-thirds of this group opposed to birth control.

If the hypothesis that the support of the elites is vital for the adoption of a comprehensive birth control policy (meaning a fully and widely backed government effort) is accepted, it can be concluded that Honduras, as most Latin American countries, appears to be a long way from attaining that objective. Honduras is a rapidly growing nation whose population is mostly rural. Family-planning services are offered mostly in urban clinics whose targets are the city poor. In short, the demographic impact of such token programs cannot be expected to be too great. If the purpose of birth control programs was to decelerate population growth to the point where economic indicators might be noticeably affected, it must be concluded that to succeed, such efforts should enlist the support of the elites, especially of those in powerful government positions. In Latin America the interaction of important influences, especially political ideology and religiosity, are a block to such support.

NOTES TO CHAPTER 3

1. J. Mayone Stycos, ed., *Ideology, Faith and Family Planning in Latin America* (New York: McGraw Hill, 1971), pp. 37-45.
2. See, for example, David Chaplin, ed., *Population Policies and Growth in Latin America* (Lexington, Mass.: D.C. Heath & Co., 1971), pp. 1-22; and Barent Landstreet, Jr. and Axel Mundigo "University Students," in Stycos, *Ideology, Faith . . .*, pp. 191-211.
3. Simon Kuznets, "Economic Aspects of Fertility Trends in Less Developed Countries," cited in S.J. Behrman, Leslie Corsa and Ronald Freedman, eds., *Fertility and Family Planning: A World View* (Ann Arbor: The University of Michigan Press, 1969), pp. 157-179; and Dudley Kirk, "Natality in the Developing Countries," *ibid.*, pp. 75-98.
4. United Nations, *Demographic Yearbook 1970* (New York, 1971); and "Total Population Estimates for World, Regions and Countries," ESA/P/WP.34, 1970.
5. *The New York Times* of August 4, 1969, ran an editorial on the war referring to it as the demographic clash.
6. Axel Mundigo, *Elites, Economic Development and Population in Honduras* (Ithaca, Cornell University: Latin American Program Dissertation Series, 1972). See especially Chapters II, III, and V.
7. Barent Landstreet, Jr., "Marxists," quoted in Stycos, *Ideology, Faith . . .*, pp. 89-144.
8. Stycos, *Ideology, Faith . . .*, p. 11.
9. J. Mayone Stycos, "Public and Private Opinions on Population and Family Planning," *Studies in Family Planning,* 51 (March, 1970), p. 15.
10. Axel Mundigo, "Scarcity and Family Planning in Honduras," *Cornell Journal of Social Relations,* 5, No. 2 (Fall, 1970), pp. 102-116.
11. Rupert B. Vance, "The Development and Status of American Demography," cited in Philip M. Hauser and O.D. Duncan, eds., *The Study of Population* (Chicago: University of Chicago Press, 1959), pp. 286-316.
12. John C. Caldwell, *Population Growth and Family Change in Africa* Canberra: Australian National University Press, 1968).
13. Axel Mundigo, *Elites, Economic Development . . .*, pp. 151-159.
14. Joseph A. Kahl, *The Measure of Modernism* (Austin: The University of Texas Press, 1968); and Kingsley Davis and Judith Blake, "Social Structure and Fertility: An Analytic Framework," *Economic Development and Cultural Change,* 4 (1956), pp. 211-235.
15. Kahl, *The Measure of Modernism.*
16. William B. Clifford, "Modern and Traditional Value Orientations and Fertility Behavior," *Demography,* 8, No. 1 (1971), pp. 37-48.

Chapter Four

Linkage Politics and Latin American Population Policies*

Terry L. McCoy

INTRODUCTION

One of the most striking features of Latin American population policies is the extent to which they have attracted the interest of a variety of external actors. Beginning in the mid-1960's, a major campaign was mounted by certain of the developed countries to induce action on behalf of governments in the developing countries to slow their rates of population growth. This effort spilled over into international and regional agencies with the developing nations remaining the main "beneficiaries" or targets. Symptomatic of the great urgency given to population control by representatives of developed nations and international agencies was a 1969 declaration by Robert McNamara, recently named President of the World Bank, that, "... the greatest single obstacle to the economic and social advancement of the majority of the peoples in the underdeveloped world is rampant population growth."[1] Latin America, with the highest regional rate of demographic increase in the world and a strongly pronatalist tradition, was a prime target of the various efforts to induce government action aimed at slowing growth.

---

*This selection was prepared originally for this volume, and research for it was supported by the Mershon Center of the Ohio State University. The author would particularly like to thank Professor Mary Ellen Caldwell, Director of the Mershon Caribbean Seminar, and the Brookings Institution where he was a visiting scholar during the summer of 1970. Earlier versions of this paper were presented as "The Taxonomy of External Assistance Organizations" in *The World Population Crisis: Policy Implications and the Role of Law* (Charlottesville, Virginia: The John Bassett Moore Society of International Law, 1971), pp. 56–63 and "External Inputs and Population Policy in Latin America" (paper presented at the 1971 Annual Meeting of the American Political Science Association, Chicago, September, 1971). Aage Clausen, Robert Kaufman, William Liddle, and Giacomo Sani all made useful suggestions for the final draft.

At the outset, there was opposition and apathy in the developing world, Latin America included, to the campaign. Writing in 1970 Bernard Berelson observed that:

> At present . . . there is a discontinuity of will between the donor and recipient agencies: they do not fully share the common objective of population control. The irony is that, with a few exceptions on each side, the donors are more committed than the recipients, yet it is the latter who must do the job.[2]

However, it was not long until a distinct trend developed in the direction of adopting what appear to be population control policies. In Latin America, where every national policy was either officially or in fact pronatalist as late as 1960, only four countries—Argentina, Brazil, Peru, and Uruguay—retained such policies in 1973. Despite initial opposition then, national policies have changed in the direction desired by the sponsors of the international population control campaign. The primary purpose of this chapter is to isolate the role of external forces in the evolution of "legislative measures, administrative programs, and other government actions" designed to control population size and rate of growth in Latin America.[3] An auxilliary purpose served by the study is that of advancing our general understanding of external participation in Latin American policy-making. It is in this general context that the present study is set; a brief exposition of this setting follows.

Latin America's strong ties to the outside world have been widely acknowledged since the colonial period. Yet until recently scholars have not explored the full implications of the contemporary situation. From the perspective of political science this omission is in part due to the rather artificial distinction between comparative politics and international relations as disciplinary subfields. Both Kling and Anderson in their pioneering attempts to abstract the Latin American political system recognize the importance of external forces, but neither deals with the extra-national origins and structures of these "foreign power contenders," to use Anderson's terminology.[4] Students of international relations, in contrast, dwell upon United States dominance of the Western Hemisphere without analyzing its domestic implications for Latin America.[5]

Economists working with the United Nations Economic Commission for Latin America (ECLA) began to bridge the gap by advancing the "center-periphery" thesis in the early 1950's. Led by the Argentine economist Raúl Prebisch, they argued that Latin American underdevelopment stemmed from the region's status on the periphery of the international economic system as an exporter of primary products and importer of manufactured goods from the industrial countries at the center of the system. Until they industrialized, the Latin nations were condemned to this inferior position in an economic interchange conducted at increasingly disadvantageous terms of trade.[6] Combining ECLA's center-periphery thesis with Marxist-Leninist theory, a group of Latin American social scientists have developed a more inclusive "dependency" model in which the region is "... part of an international system dominated by the now developed nations, and Latin American underdevelopment is the outcome of a particular series of relationships to that international system."[7] Capitalism is the essence of contemporary dependency but its effects are more than economic. "Politically ... Latin American development has been limited by the fact that policy decisions ... are conditioned, and options limited, by the interests of the developed societies."[8]

Dependency theory focuses attention on an aspect of Latin American reality too long ignored. Thus far, however, its political dimensions remain in the form of amorphous deductive assertions rather than precise empirically demonstrated relationships.[9] Economic dependence is relatively easy to demonstrate with the analysis of trade, investment, balance of payments, and foreign aid flows, but assessing its political consequences and actual political transactions across national boundaries is more difficult. The international campaign for population control carried out in Latin America provides an excellent opportunity to study the flow of external influence at the policy level. To structure our endeavor and provide it with conceptual precision, we shall rely upon the framework of "linkage politics," developed by James N. Rosenau and applied to Latin America by Douglas A. Chalmers.[10]

Rosenau defines a linkage as "any recurrent sequence of behavior that originates in one system and is reacted to in another."[11] Typically the framework has been used to study foreign policy, specifically how domestic factors affect foreign policy and how the foreign policy and behavior of one country affect those of another.[12] It is also well suited for breaking down and analyzing the impact of external factors on domestic policy. In discussing Latin American linkage patterns, Chalmers directs our attention to four variables, which by extension can be hypothesized to affect policy-making: the character of the international system, external linkage groups, internal linkage groups, and the character of the local polity.[13] In addition to using these variable clusters to determine the role of external factors in Latin American population policy-making along with an added category of input type, we shall look for confirmation of those of Chalmer's hypotheses relevant to policy-making, some of which agree with and others which challenge dependency theory.

EXTERNAL LINKAGE GROUPS

With the international system constant for all of Latin America at any one time, its "impact on a polity will vary according to the particular nations, structures and groups to which the polity is linked and the nature of that link."[14] These nations, structures, and groups are called "external linkage groups." This section presents an inventory of the external linkage groups seeking to influence Latin American population policies and the techniques utilized by them. (As used here, "Latin America" specifically refers to the 20 traditionally Latin American countries of Middle and South America.) Taken as a whole they exhibit two important characteristics. First, the number of organizations active in the population control campaign along with the amount and variety of their inputs has increased dramatically in recent years. Discovery of the "population explosion" detonated a secondary explosion of external linkage groups dedicated to slowing population growth. Prior to 1960 international population-related foreign aid was the purview of several private foundations primarily supporting biomedical research. Now the range of assistance encompasses major public bilateral and multilateral programs as well as expanded private efforts, both of which support a wide variety of population-related activities with special emphasis on family planning and population control. According to one estimate, the total value of world population assistance, the vast majority going to developing nations, grew from $5 million in 1962 to $95 million in 1968.[15] By 1971 it reached the $225 to $250 million level.[16] The second significant characteristic of external linkage groups in the population control campaign is the overwhelming presence of the United States government, principally through its Agency for International Development (USAID). Roughly one-half of all world population assistance comes from official United States sources.[17]

Latin America does not significantly deviate from either of the above patterns. The number of donors and amount of population assistance increased exponentially until recently, and as Chalmers points out, "One of the most enduring features of Latin American linkages has been the predominance of one other nation . . ."[18 In the twentieth century that nation has been the United States. Consequently, one would expect the United States to loom large in Latin American population policies, even larger than in other developing regions. But Chalmers also hypothesizes that various sorts of international agencies are emerging to compete as external linkage groups with the United States in Latin America.[19] We must be very careful, therefore, to determine the genesis and flow of influence in the population policy case.

The Network of Donor Organizations:
Governmental

In contrast to its outspoken leadership of population control efforts today, the United States government resisted early efforts to enlist its participation. Its conversion into the dominant external linkage group resulted not from requests for population assistance from developing nations but from the work of a small band of notables with important allies in Congress. They succeeded in making United States assistance for population-related activities the largest bilateral effort in the world with considerable impact on other forms of population aid quite independently of what the projected recipients, especially those in Latin America, wanted.

The first public suggestion that the United States government include support for population control in its foreign aid program came in 1959 in the so-called Draper report on foreign economic and military assistance.[20] When President Eisenhower replied that the federal government should stay out of such matters,[21] the advocates of government intervention launched a campaign to educate the public and force government action to curb population growth at home and abroad. They worked through private organizations, such as the Planned Parenthood Federation of America and Population Crisis Committee, and in Congress, especially through the Senate Subcommittee on Foreign Aid Expenditures, chaired by Democrat Ernest Gruening of Alaska, a physician and former governor of Puerto Rico. From 1965 through 1968, the Gruening subcommittee held a series of hearings on the "Population Crisis" that provided a forum for the proponents of government action to air their views. In addition to building a public case for action with an impressive parade of supportive witnesses, the subcommittee badgered government officials about their opposition to population assistance. Under congressional pressure, the executive branch took a first significant—yet reluctant—step in 1965 by agreeing to authorize $6 million under the Foreign Aid Act for research on population growth.[22] It was about this time that President Johnson became convinced of the necessity of population control. But with a few exceptions, the foreign aid bureaucracy, especially USAID officials in Latin America, was slow to act. They feared the political repercussions of moving into such a sensitive area. In order to circumvent this resistance, Congress earmarked foreign aid funds for population assistance in 1968. Even this did not satisfy some Congressmen and their supporters, as the following exchange between Senator Gruening and William Gaud, the Director of USAID indicates:

> *Gruening:* How, in view of the fact that the appropriations for AID have been reduced in Congress, and this population problem is pressing, can you not adopt a policy of pointing out to those nations that do something that they will get more help proportionately in relation to what they do to solve their population dilemma? . . .
>
> *Gaud:* Yes sir. If I understand you, I do not think that I agree with you. I agree 100 percent that we should do everything we can by way of education, persuasion, action, and so forth and so on, and assistance to induce the developing countries to adopt and carry out effective programs. But I do not buy the proposition that we should make such a program a condition of aid.[23]

Thus, the small antinatalist lobby and its allies in Congress forged a crucial initial link in the population assistance network. They pressured the executive branch into incorporating support of population control activities as a prominent part of the foreign aid program. During a period of declining congressional funds for foreign aid, USAID appropriations for population assistance grew from nothing in 1964 to $100 million in 1971. In 1971, USAID was providing direct help to population and family-planning programs in 33 countries representing more than half of the population of the developing world.[24]

The Latin American Bureau of USAID had established a Regional Population Reference Unit and urged country missions to appoint a local officer to oversee the development of population and family-planning programs, a suggestion which was rather coolly received in the field where the subject was perceived as much too controversial for official involvement.[25] In 1967, central USAID created the Office of Hunger, which included the Population Service, and called for the designation of Population Officers in both regional bureaus and country misssions.[26] In 1973, the Office of Population prospered as part of the Bureau of Technical Services while local population officers remained in most embassies despite a general dismantling of central USAID and its country missions.[27]

Other government agencies joined the drive to control population growth in the developing world. For instance, the Peace Corps trains volunteers for family-planning programs, and, since 1966, the State Department has had a Special Assistant to the Secretary for Population Matters who lobbies for the cause of population control with other governments and international bodies.

Why this large United States commitment to population control, resulting in efforts to influence public policy in Latin America and other areas? Clearly world population growth is today widely perceived as a problem in the United States. Hence, it is legitimized for foreign policy discussion. Furthermore, beyond the altruistic impulse to help others solve this new problem, it is probably fair to surmise that in the minds of many policy-makers rapid population growth posed a threat to the strategic interests of the United States in the form of growing unrest in Asia, Africa, and Latin America.[28] For others close to foreign aid, population assistance represented an alternative to the frustrating and unrewarding venture of developmental assistance. A majority in Congress eventually came to see rapid population growth as the principal obstacle to development and to feel that foreign aid was wasted unless it helped to slow population growth. President Johnson identified himself with this school when he issued his frequently cited statement that $5 spent on population control is worth $100 invested in economic growth.[29] In his 1969 report to President Nixon on Latin America, Governor Rockefeller declared that the region's rapid population increase "cancels out so much of the economic growth achieved to make improvement of living standards difficult, if not impossible."[30] From this perspective, population assistance was both necessary and a bargain.

As a consensus favorable to population assistance grew at the top levels of the foreign aid bureaucracy, opposition at the lower levels faded. The pressure to fall into line was particularly intense due to the general reduction and reorganization of USAID's activities. Officials interested in staying with the Agency climbed aboard the population band wagon. This is not to say that those with doubts about population assistance simply caved in. They did not, and there are instances, such as the embassies in Brazil and Mexico, of successful resistance to Washington's call that population control be pushed on the host country. Nevertheless, they were under constant pressure. For instance, in 1970, USAID/Washington dispatched a special committee to Latin America to evaluate the activities of country missions. In its report (the "Haroldson Report," named after the chairman), the committee criticized the local missions and urged a more vigorous approach to population assistance.

In summary, a mixture of considerations underlie United States population assistance: a genuine desire to help others coupled with definite ideas about the most effective and inexpensive way of providing this help; preoccupation with preserving world stability in order to protect United States strategic interests; and concerns internal to the bureaucracy. Let me emphasize once again that it did not emerge and is not sustained primarily in response to requests from the developing world for help in controlling population growth. The impetus comes from within the United States.

The existence of other nations and organizations giving population assistance would appear to support Chalmer's hypothesis on the increasingly competitive nature of external linkage groups in Latin America and a decline in United States influence. Closer examination reveals that this competitiveness may be more apparent than real. The United States has encouraged other developed nations to offer population assistance, since, even though their contribution does not amount to much monetarily—especially in Latin America— it does give the appearance of a multi-national effort. Guiding the developmental aid of major Western nations is the Organization for Economic Cooperation and Development (OECD), which, under the leadership of Sweden and the United States, established a population unit in 1968 to encourage and coordinate member assistance.[31] Beyond merely coordinating bilateral assistance, there has been a distinct trend toward multilateralism. The United States fully supports this shift, not only because it corresponds with the general foreign aid policy of President Nixon, but also because, as Richard Gardner points out, "In a sensitive area like family planning, the case for multilateral aid is particularly compelling."[32] The loss in direct control is more than offset by the "cleansing" of assistance to make it more acceptable to countries which fear North American domination, or at least the charge of succumbing to it. The shift became possible only as resistance to population assistance from the members and bureaucracies of intergovernmental organizations (IGO's) declined in the late 1960's.

Change in organizational policy came easily to the World Bank Group, while it was considerably more complicated in the United Nations system. Two factors explain the position of the World Bank: the predominant role of the United States in its affairs and the personal convictions of its president. As the largest single contributor, the United States government has an important voice in Bank policy. More important was Robert McNamara's assumption of the presidency, a post traditionally held by a North American, in 1968. In his first public address as president McNamara told the Bank's Board of Governors that, population control

> ... is a thorny subject which it would be very much more convenient to leave alone. But I cannot because the World Bank is concerned above all with economic development, and the rapid growth of population is one of the greatest barriers to the economic growth and social well-being of our member states.[33]

With this he announced a Bank program of population assistance and launched his own outspoken, controversial advocacy of population control for developing nations. Almost immediately Latin America got McNamara's special attention. Speaking to a meeting of the Inter-American Press Association in Buenos Aires, he told the delegates and their audiences in Latin America that the Bank expected a "realistic appraisal" of rapid population growth and an "earnest effort" to cope with it.[34] McNamara's public lecturing on the necessity of population control created a storm of protest in Latin America. In fact the World Bank's most significant role, under McNamara's leadership, has been to raise the issue and force its discussion throughout the developing world. In contrast to its public statements, the Bank has actually allocated little money to national population control programs with none going to Latin America.[35]

Opposition to UN population assistance came from Catholic and Communist countries and the internal inertia of the UN bureaucracy and the network of specialized agencies. The fight for action was led first by a group of Scandinavian and Asian nations which was later joined by the United States with its considerable resources. The antinatalist forces ultimately resorted to the established tactic of creating a new agency to deal with population, the Fund for Population Activities (UNFPA).[36]

Into the 1960's UN population activities were limited to the demographic projects of a minor division in the Secretariat. Then in 1962 the General Assembly agreed to debate a resolution jointly sponsored by Sweden and Denmark, on "Population Growth and Economic Development." The United States in a reversal of previous policy supported the Scandinavian initiative since it offered an opening to deal with the population explosion on a multilateral basis.[37] The 1962 resolution, as passed, instructed the Secretary General and Population Commission to conduct an inquiry into population problems and assist member governments.[38] It was followed by other General Assembly resolutions, and the entire UN family of agencies began debating the desirability of population-related activities.[39] But policy outputs lagged behind policy pronouncements. In an effort to invigorate the UN effort, certain of the antinatalist countries sponsored the creation of the semi-autonomous UNFPA in 1967. Its resources grew rapidly under the commitment of the United States to stimulate donations from other countries. In 1970, against a matching United States grant of $7.5 million, the Fund received an additional $7.7 million from 24 other governments.[40]

UNFPA, not an operating agency, uses voluntary contributions from member states to induce other UN bodies, private organizations, and even national governments to undertake population programs.[41] For example, a 1968 grant from the Fund to the Population Division led to the appointment of UN population officers throughout the world for the purpose of creating interest in and coordinating requests for population assistance from the UN. By 1969, two such officers were stationed in Latin America in preparation for a general expansion of UN population activities in that area.[42] Symbolic of the headway made in Latin America is the fact that a Latin American will act as Secretary General of the UN-sponsored 1974 World Population Conference.

The UN population linkage has grown tremendously thanks in large part to the establishment of a mechanism that allows bilateral funds to be channeled into the network of specialized agencies. UNFPA provides a multilateral outlet for the growing pool of population assistance without directly challenging either pronatalist countries in the General Assembly or the vested interests of the specialized agencies. Despite its formally multilateral character, the United States, through the Fund's dependence on voluntary subscriptions, plays a very important role.[43] While this may not include dictating specific policies, it undoubtedly involves setting the general orientation of UN population assistance.

Three regional UN affiliates—the Economic Commission for Latin America (ECLA), Latin American Demographic Center (CELADE), and the Pan American Health Organization (PAHO)—have been particularly important in the movement toward population control in Latin America because of their perceived independence from the United States. Throughout the postwar period ECLA has been the fount of economic wisdom for Latin America. Its economists, led by former director Raúl Prebisch, and their pronouncements are influential with national policy-makers. Consequently, both the advocates and opponents of birth control saw ECLA's prestige as crucial to their respective causes. For its part ECLA seemed reluctant to be drawn into the controversy. Its executive secretary declared that ECLA should not have "any point of view about population growth" but merely supply essential demographic data.[44] However, in 1967, it agreed to undertake a three-year study of the relationship between population dynamics and economic development. By the early 1970's ECLA's position had evolved from "hands-off" to support for demographic policies as integral components of national development planning.[45]

Founded in 1957 with its headquarters in Santiago, Chile, the Latin American Demographic Center initiated demographic analysis in the region through its research and training program. It produced both the personnel and data essential to the current debate over population trends. Its reputation for dispassionate, objective analysis is such that when CELADE speaks, Latin American governments and scholars listen. Therefore, even though the Center avoids policy recommendations, only recently moving into research that is directly policy relevant, it receives financial support from a variety of international donors (see Figure 4-1) who perceive it influential in the struggle against rapid population growth.

PAHO, the Western Hemispheric affiliate of the World Health Organization, entered the population field only after overcoming considerable opposition from its Latin members. In order to mute a resurgence of this opposition, PAHO's population assistance is justified as a logical extension of its health focus.[46]

The prestige and influence of ECLA, CELADE, and PAHO stem in part from their statuses as Latin organizations. Nevertheless, there is evidence of strong United States involvement in their population work. Part of the first United States contribution to UNFPA was earmarked to finance a population adviser for ECLA.[47] Both CELADE and PAHO receive significant financial support from USAID. PAHO has even "fronted" for a USAID financed program in Colombia and the first director of its Department of Health and Population Dynamics was an employee of the United States Public Health Service. Therefore, the legitimacy conferred by these organizations to population control in Latin America was not internally generated.

Two other hemispheric organizations are only marginally involved in population activities because the United States plays too direct a role for them to ever be above suspicion and credible with the Latin Americans. The Inter-American Development Bank (IADB), which receives the bulk of its funding through annual appropriations from the United States Congress, theoretically offers population assistance, but in fact no Latin member has ever requested such aid.[48] The population activities of the Organization of American States (OAS) are more impressive on paper—within the Secretariat there is a formal "Population Program" in the Department of Social Affairs with its own staff and responsibilities—but in practice its effort has been modest, directed primarily at sponsoring regional meetings and coordinating inter-agency activities.[49]

The Network of Donor Organizations: Non-Governmental

Accompanying the explosion of governmental population assistance has been a similar expansion in non-governmental aid. In part this growth reflects a reorientation of the resources of private organizations, especially large North American foundations like Ford and Rockefeller, whose support for population-related research abroad antedates that of all IGO's. In the 1960's, it expanded dramatically in both amount and scope. Since 1952, the Ford Foundation has committed over $147 million to population work with increasing amounts going to developing countries either through direct grants or through other organizations such as the Population Council.[50] Ford has placed emphasis in Latin America on working with private groups and universities to build an institutional infrastructure for subsequent policy development.[51] Rockefeller's funds for population assistance have likewise grown recently with important support going to the Population Council. Pressure for the shift in foundation spending came from the same people lobbying for action by the United States government since they also influence the affairs of major philanthropic institutions.[52]

The expansion of private population assistance is only partially accounted for by the redeployment of private resources. The rest comes from channeling increased public aid through non-governmental organizations (NGO's). The Director of USAID testifying before a congressional audience in 1968 expressed his agency's philosophy on the use of private organizations:

> ... one of my fundamental tenets is this: If we can do a job, whether it is in the family-planning field or any other field, through existing private institutions rather than bringing people on a Government payroll, I would prefer to do it that way.[53]

In addition to the efficiency argument, NGO's are attractive conduits of government aid because they are more flexible and less controversial. They can do things in foreign countries that agencies of the United States government could not do.

IPPF and the Population Council are the two most important private organizations granting population assistance. IPPF is directly concerned with policy questions as an international lobby for family planning while the Population Council is more research oriented, although it does not avoid policy questions. Both came into existence in 1952, and, therefore, both were present to benefit from the explosion of public and foundation support for population activities. From the standpoint of primary donors, IPPF and the Population Council were convenient, reliable, and credible linkages to the population policies of developing countries. The infusion of this new funding

Table 4-1. USAID Grants to IPPF ($1,000's)

	FY1968	FY1969	FY1970	FY1971
Worldwide Grants	3,500	4,000	5,500	3,000
Western Hemisphere Grants	500	1,964	1,750	2,000

Source: USAID, *Population Program Assistance* (1971), p. 220 and p. 227.

dramatically increased the budgets and activities of both organizations. IPPF's total budget went from $325,000 in 1962 to $23.8 million in 1973 with, as Table 4-1 demonstrates, an important share of the increments coming from USAID.[54] The situation of the Population Council was similar.[55] In their total budgets Latin America came to occupy increasingly larger shares. For instance, by 1973 over one-third of all IPPF expenditures were targeted for the Western Hemisphere.

Other specialized non-governmental organizations benefited from the growth in the availability of public and foundation support. Several are creatures of it. The Pathfinder Fund, for example, is a small Boston-based charitable foundation devoted to supporting family planning which received a new lease on life with massive infusions of USAID funds in the late 1960's.[56] It became an appendage of USAID, working where the latter could not. Through foundation grants the Population Reference Bureau (PRB) of Washington, D.C., was able to establish an office in Bogotá, Colombia, in order to extend its informational and educational activities into Latin America.[57] Various Protestant religious organizations, because of their missionary work in Latin America and support of birth control, became conduits of population assistance. Even regional Catholic organizations have moved into the population field with outside support. The Latin American Center for Studies of Population and Family, which was founded in 1965 as part of a liberal Catholic social science research center in Chile (it later moved to Colombia), has received significant amounts of external financing. Another regional recipient of external aid is the Pan American Federation of Medical School Faculties (FEPAFEM) which has sponsored workshops on the integration of demography into medical education. Finally, the International Union for the Scientific Study of Population (IUSSP), a prestigious professional organization, channels outside money into population activities through its sponsorship of Latin American regional meetings.

Figure 4-1 summarizes the network of external linkage groups. The central position of the United States government in this network is very evident in the figure. Not only does USAID support other countries directly, but it provides financial or commodity assistance to almost all of the other linkage groups, some of which would not even be offering population assistance were it not for agency financing. Furthermore, the second leading primary donor of

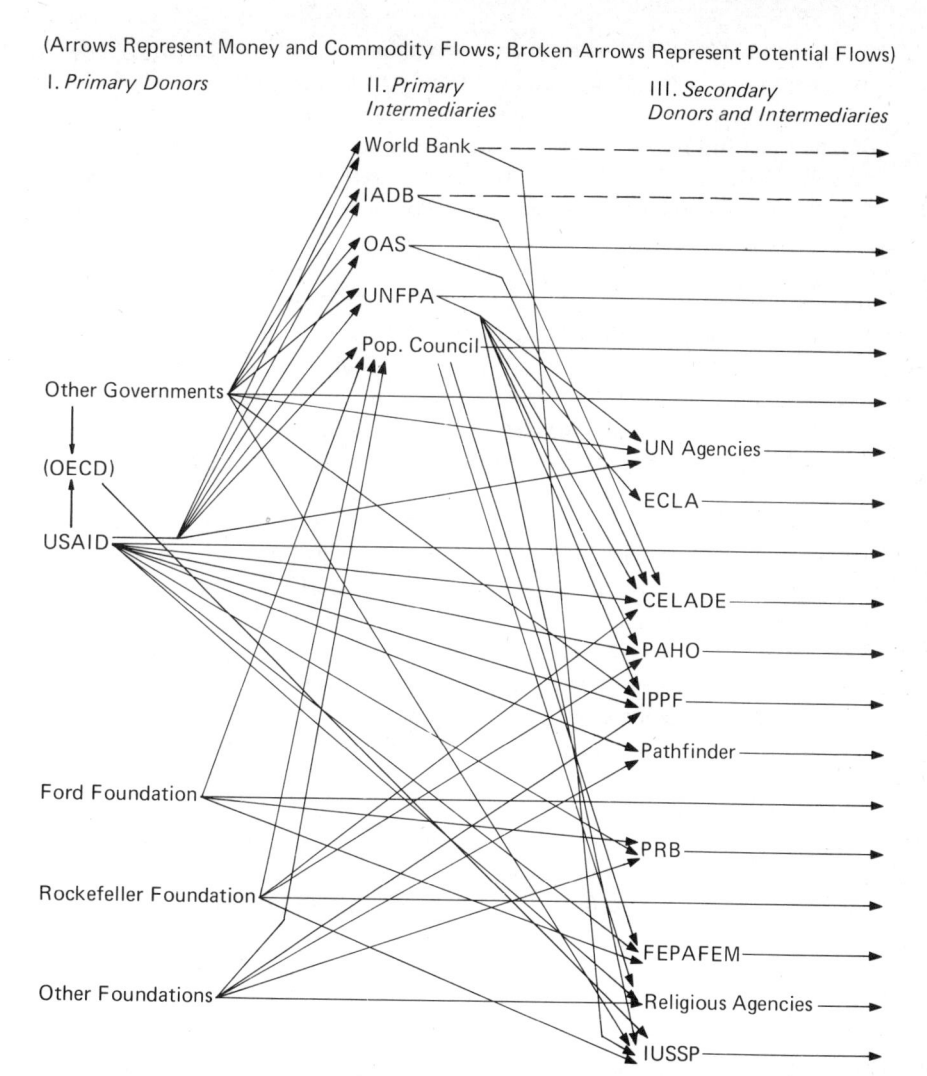

Linkage Politics and Latin American Population Policies 71

(Arrows Represent Money and Commodity Flows; Broken Arrows Represent Potential Flows)

I. *Primary Donors* II. *Primary Intermediaries* III. *Secondary Donors and Intermediaries*

- World Bank
- IADB
- OAS
- UNFPA
- Pop. Council

Other Governments
(OECD)
USAID

- UN Agencies
- ECLA
- CELADE
- PAHO
- IPPF
- Pathfinder

Ford Foundation

- PRB

Rockefeller Foundation

- FEPAFEM
- Religious Agencies

Other Foundations

- IUSSP

Sources: USAID, *Population Program Assistance* (1969, 1970, 1971); OECD, *Population: International Assistance and Research* (1969); PAHO, *Population Dynamics* (1967); UNDP, Fund for Population Activities, *1970 Allocations and Projects for 1971-74* (1971); Population Council, *Annual Reports* (1962-1971); various reports of OAS Advisory Committee on Population and Development; IPPF, *News*; the Pathfinder Fund, *Annual Report* (1971); and personal correspondence and interviews.

Figure 4-1. External Linkage Group Network for Latin American Population Assistance

population assistance are North American foundations, followed finally by other governments; and as has been pointed out, policy leadership of these foundations and the government overlap. Robert McNamara and McGeorge Bundy moved from the executive branch of the United States government to the presidencies of the World Bank and Ford Foundation respectively. John D. Rockefeller III is Chairman of the Board of Trustees of the Population Council and was Chairman of President Nixon's Commission on Population Growth and the American Future. William Draper, who helped initiate the debate on population assistance, served as Chairman of the Population Crisis Committee and as an official United States delegate to the UN Population Commission.

Did these men design assistance for population control in Latin America, and the developing world in general, to advance the strategic and corporate interests of the United States?[58] Such considerations probably crossed their minds, although their motives are not easily unraveled. Regardless of whose interests are served, we know that the United States initiated and sustains the world campaign to control population. Its dominance is particularly pronounced in Latin America. This situation contradicts Chalmer's hypotheses regarding the proliferation of competing external linkage groups in Latin America. In the realm of assistance for population control, although there is a formal diversity of groups, they are hardly competing. At best they act to disguise and dilute the role of the dominant external linkage group, but basically they are there because it wants them to be, not because they are reacting to their own perceptions of the situation or to Latin American demands. Nor has the United States and its collaborators been effectively challenged by external linkage groups of a pronatalist bent. True, the Catholic Church occasionally speaks out against programs based on artificial contraceptives. It does not, however, have the material resources to reward desired policy actions (or non-actions). In the same vein, certain Latin American countries, such as Brazil and Peru, inveigh against population control in regional bodies and meetings, but they too lack the resources to influence program decisions. Brazil cannot pay Bolivia, for instance, not to initiate family planning. The Soviet Union, which is nominally pronatalist and which does have the potential resources, neither feels strong enough on the issue nor well enough established in the Western Hemisphere to enter the debate.

Consequently, the United States dominates external efforts to influence Latin American population policy. Although in part based on its position of overall hegemony in the region, the principal source of its influence is financial. Money still speaks authoritatively in any international effort depending on voluntary contributions. This is only one type of external policy linkage. Others may produce different patterns. But, when it is a case of initiating new government programs of a distributive nature, the United States has the resources, not only to finance such programs bilaterally, but also to bring multilateral agencies into the picture. Now let us look at specifically how outside money is used to influence population policy and demographic trends within Latin America.

The Mix of External Inputs

There is little disagreement among external linkage groups that the key to population control in Latin America and the rest of the developing world is the adoption of antinatalist population policies by national governments. In justifying special emphasis on the Western Hemisphere, IPPF declared in 1972 that, "The programme of work is aimed first and foremost at convincing Latin American governments that they have a duty to provide family-planning services for all their people."[59] The OAS specified that the "principal objective" of its population program is "the adoption by countries of population policies in the context of their general development plans and programs."[60] In seeking the adoption of such policies, external agencies make inputs that vary from support of existing programs to assistance for activities designed to pressure national decision-makers.

Table 4-2 contains a summary of the inputs of each external linkage group dealing directly with at least one Latin American country. Those in

Table 4-2. External Population Policy Inputs in Latin America

External Linkage Groups	Program Support	Information and Promotion	Institution Building
I. Governmental			
A. *Bilateral*			
Government of the U.S.	X	X	X
Other Governments	X	X	X
B. *Multilateral*			
UN Family		X	X
World Bank		X	
ECLA		X	
CELADE		X	X
PAHO	X	X	X
IADB		X	
OAS		X	
II. *Non-Governmental*			
Ford Foundation		X	X
Rockefeller		X	X
Population Council	X	X	X
IPPF	X	X	X
Pathfinder	X	X	
PRB		X	
FEPAFEM			X
Religious Agencies		X	X
IUSSP		X	

Sources: Same as those for Figure 4-1.

the columns labeled "Program Support" include money and commodity transfers and other direct support of established government programs, especially family-planning programs in the Ministry of Health which are currently the policy actions most relevant to population control. In other words, to assist government family-planning efforts, outside agencies provide financial support to pay specialized personnel or purchase equipment, grants of contraceptives or other supplies, and technical advice and training. As an example, let us look at Costa Rica where, beginning in 1967, USAID gave the Ministry of Health equipment, training, and commodity support; the Ford Foundation provided consultants for the Ministry; UNFPA sponsored an inter-agency evaluation mission; and PAHO supported postpartum programs in both the Ministry and Social Security Institute.[61] Throughout Latin America, USAID supplies the bulk of program support, though it is often funneled through intermediary groups since direct government-to-government assistance would be unacceptable on the receiving end.

External support can act as an incentive to initiate a government program or expand an existing one. But the process is usually more complicated than that in Latin America where the primary obstacle to national family-planning programs has been a lack of will rather than a shortage of materials and personnel. Instead of waiting for governments to develop the resolve, external linkage groups generate inputs designed to mobilize the public and officialdom in support of population control.

Informational and promotional inputs are externally supported activities usually aimed at making the Latin American people and their governments aware of rapid population growth as a problem and educating them on how to cope with it. They are based on a widely held rationalist assumption that inaction is a function of ignorance.

> The basic belief of the [Population Reference] Bureau is that people will take corrective action to control births when they understand that too rapid growth dilutes living levels.[62]
>
> The Population Crisis Committee is a private nonprofit organization established to promote public understanding and action in the face of the world population crisis.[63]
>
> The field of population is not birth control alone. It relates to letting people know the dimensions of their problem, involving their biologists, sociologists, and economists because they are the people that give the political backstopping to the leaders of the society. (President of Population Council).[64]
>
> AID must help awaken other governments to a full realization of the nature of the population problem, and respond quickly and imaginatively to requests for assistance....[65]

Such sentiments resulted in a rather massive flow of resources into information and promotion. An organization such as PRB is devoted exclusively to such pursuits. Others like IADB and OAS seem to grab at them as opportunities for demonstrating their concern to the United States without directly challenging their Latin American constituents. Virtually all external linkage groups in Latin American population matters pursue informational and promotional activities.

The eventual targets of these inputs are national policy-makers, although most approaches are indirect through national elites and public opinion. One tactic for reaching elites is the sponsorship of regional conferences and meetings dealing with population. In Latin America, where the regional environment is perhaps more salient than in other developing areas, there was a concerted attempt, beginning in the mid-1960's to recast the population issue in antinatalist terms through a series of conferences.[66] National elites from the public and private sectors came together to discuss population-related topics in regional meetings largely financed with external funds. For example, the 1970 Latin American Regional Population Conference in Mexico City drew its budget of $95,000 from the UNFPA ($25,000), the Mexican Government, IADB, World Bank, USAID, Rockefeller Foundation, Swedish International Development Agency ($10,000 each), Population Council ($5,000), OECD ($3,000), and Social Science Research Council ($2,500).[67] Without dictating the agendas of the regional meetings, their financial sponsors were able to suggest the inclusion of certain topics which served to redefine uncontrolled population growth as a problem. Latin American elites are also reached through smaller, more specialized conferences. PRB tackles the growth question directly in its "Population Dialogues" for government officials, political figures, and business and labor leaders, while the OAS sponsored a series of seminars for national planners on "Development Planning and Population."[68] In addition to working elites, external agencies support activities designed to mobilize public opinion. Central to IPPF strategy is the tactic of providing private family-planning services in order to build demand for expanded public services. Accompanying the establishment of private clinics are mass media campaigns to educate the public about family planning. In order to demonstrate systematically a widespread desire for family planning—to convert private needs into public demands—external groups finance KAP (Knowledge, Attitudes, Practices) surveys.[69] Finally, some external agencies approach national policy-makers directly in order to promote their action on population control. The UN, USAID, and Ford Foundation all have population officers in residence whose purpose is to lobby with local officials for policy changes which then can be supported with external funds.[70]

The line between informing governments of alleged demographic problems and threatening to retaliate should they not act is very fine. The World Bank and USAID, for instance, as major donors of foreign aid may only have to stress the harmful consequences of rapid population growth in order to suggest that unless it is dealt with requests for subsequent development assistance will not be favorably received. According to an official publication, the World Bank does not condition its loans on population planning but does "remind" its borrowers that "unduly rapid population growth" poses a threat to their economic progress.[71] USAID also denies attaching any population control conditions to its other assistance, but once again recipients are undoubtedly made aware of how the Agency and the United States Congress feel about the futility of assisting development without controlling population growth.

In their informational and promotional activities, external linkage groups seek to move population control onto the national agenda and convert it to official policy. The linkage politics framework does not adequately account for these types of inputs. They most closely fall between being "penetrative" and "reactive" in Rosenau's terms.[72] That is, external linkage groups stop short of actual participation in policy-making, yet they go beyond simply awaiting a desired reaction to structure one. The "structuring" of policy decisions is also characteristic of our final category of external inputs, institution-building. Here we are concerned with support for the construction of national population control infrastructures. From one perspective, the institutions in this infrastructure serve as alternatives to government action; however, their mere existence also puts added pressure on the government and supplies it with the instruments for action. The basis of this latter proposition becomes dear as we explore the nature of institutional inputs.

Research is an institutional input that performs the dual function of providing knowledge for action and of building local awareness and commitment under the guise of intellectual discovery. Significant biomedical and social science research does take place in the more advanced Latin American countries like Argentina, Mexico, and Chile with external assistance, including support from multinational pharmaceutical corporations. But to quote an USAID document, "Perhaps more important than the research itself is the fact that it is performed within the country and probably has more acceptance and relevance than the same finding based on work done in other countries."[73] Consequently, the emphasis of external funders is on local policy oriented research as a means of legitimating already established knowledge rather than on original scientific discovery. A leading Mexican economist complains that this narrow focus even excludes basic demographic research.

> There is a certain impatience on the part of organizations in the United States, foundations, for example. If you say you are going to do some work on family planning you get an immediate grant from an American foundation. If you say you are going to do some demographic research ... then the answer is less enthusiastic.[74]

In the social science realm, virtually every country has had an externally-financed KAP study carried out by the local university or family-planning association that inevitably "demonstrates" significant popular support for family planning.

Externally supported research not only provides locally generated rationales for population control activities but it also serves to get a first foot in the door in situations where such activities would be too threatening. The best example of this tactic is the Population Council's International Postpartum Family Planning Program, which is described as a "demonstration-research."[75] Furthermore, those participating in population research, either as researchers or subjects, form a natural lobby for subsequent population activities. Given its relatively non-controversial nature and multiple functionality, it is not surprising that population research commands widespread external support.

Externally supported personnel training is another input that serves more than one purpose from the donors' perspective. First, it helps provide the human resource base needed for operating population programs. Second, it contributes to local advocacy of government action by further sensitizing the recipients to demographic trends and creating in them vested interests in family planning and related activities. An official of USAID reiterates the familiar theme that:

> ... advocacy and prescriptions for change are more acceptable and effective when made by informed local citizens. Foreign technical assistance, therefore, ought to be used to strengthen the capacity of strategic local leaders, public or private, to analyze and act on population problems.[76]

Personnel training ranges from short courses to graduate training abroad. It is aimed at medical, para-medical, and social science personnel with a heavy, but not exclusive, family-planning emphasis. CELADE plays an important role in the training process. Beyond training and research, foreign agencies provide short-term technical assistance for everything from setting up a local family-planning clinic to conducting a national census.

In the mid-1960's external linkage groups, led by the United States, quickly abandoned any hope that Latin American governments would have the "good sense" to undertake population control programs on their own. Instead they began attempting to actively stimulate the desired policy changes. External inputs in this regard range from the offers to subsidize antinatalist activities in the hopes of eliciting favorable Latin American reactions to more direct efforts at structuring the local policy process in favor of population control. Before evaluating the results of these inputs, we must complete the policy linkage by examining the internal channels through which they are funneled.

INTERNAL LINKAGE GROUPS

Since external groups are not linked directly to authoritative decision-makers in the early phases of the drive to produce policy changes, they are dependent upon local intermediaries—internal linkage groups—to make their antinatalist inputs. Chalmers suggests that the internal linkage group network be analyzed in terms of its dependence on foreign sources of support, its proximity to authoritative decision-making, the range of issues in which it is involved, and its coherence.[77] As our analysis will demonstrate, the network concerned with population control is, in most Latin American countries, coherent with a narrow focus on the population issue, yet heavily dependent on foreign support and fairly far removed from top-level decision-making. This would indicate that the network's influence on national policy has definite limits.

Family Planning Associations

In most Latin American countries the national family-planning association (FPA) is the most important link between external groups and domestic policy-making. Although bearing a variety euphemistic names, the 18 Latin American associations—only Bolivia and Cuba have none—are quite similar in their organization and functions, due to the fact that they are organized and supported by IPPF. Beginning in Chile in 1962, IPPF representatives galvanized local elites, especially physicians, into the establishment of national associations, the first objective of which is to "assist in the creation of a climate of opinion which will enable or impell Governments to accept their proper responsibility . . ."[78] To create the proper "climate of opinion," local FPA's promote the cause of family palnning among the public and targeted elites, train the personnel necessary for national programs, conduct policy-oriented research, and operate local clinics that serve both to meet interim needs and to demonstrate the demand for family planning. As the climate changes they turn many of their services over to the government and retire into an auxiliary role.[79]

There are other private organizations offering family-planning services, but the national IPPF affiliate is the primary beneficiary of external support for family-planning-related activities. The outside money comes from IPPF, from other donors through IPPF, or directly from other donors.[80] Without this assistance, all Latin American FPA's would experience drastic reductions in their activities, thus impairing their performance as lobbies for government programs, since little of their revenue is locally generated.[81]

Academic and Research Organizations

An important share of external population assistance goes to Latin American research organizations. There are three reasons for this. First, the rationalist perspective stresses research and dissemination of knowledge at the local level as the key to resolution of the "problem." Second, those Latin Americans commissioned to do the research are influential in national policy-making. Their opposition, acquiescence, or support can make or break a policy regardless of its objective merits. Third, strong linkages between international agencies and local research organizations already existed when population became perceived as a problem. It was therefore natural for this aid pipeline to continue to be used with only a shift in the research content.

Two important recipients of research and training inputs are the medical profession and social scientists. The former is covered through its participation in local family-planning associations, since physicians form the core membership of most FPA's. Academic medicine gets special attention because of its research in reproductive biology and because of its influence of future doctors. In Colombia, the Association of Medical Schools literally launched the national family-planning effort, now the strongest in Latin America. With heavy outside assistance, it trained the medical and para-medical personnel who later formed the nucleus of the government program, coordinated university research, operated a postpartum program, and in general, acted as a pressure group for government action.[82] Throughout the region, there has been a concerted effort, supported by external funds, to integrate demographic and family-planning materials into medical school curricula.[83] Although there are some pockets of resistance within the medical profession to the expansion of population control activities, it has generally been supportive. However, serious opposition from Latin American social scientists, especially those in academic settings, presents external linkage groups with a dilemma. On the one hand, outsiders see a need for supporting demographic research in Latin America and with it possibly winning converts in the local social science community. On the other hand, the Marxist, anti-American predispositions of many Latin American social scientists act as a deterrent. In 1971, Stycos warned of growing opposition to family planning among Latin American social scientists that was spilling over into the medical schools.[84] Rather than provoking confrontation with leftist intellectuals in the social science departments of the national universities, much external support for social science research is channeled into private or semi-autonomous universities, such as Los Andes in Colombia, El Colegio de México, and even various Catholic Universities. Sizeable research grants also go to non-academic organizations, the Mexican Institute for Social Studies for example, or directly to individuals.[85]

Government Agencies

Population assistance goes to government agencies in many Latin American countries as another form of pressure for policy change in which government agencies are the internal linkage groups. Thus, in countries which may be officially pronatalist, external inputs of an antinatalist nature often flow into public agencies because of bureaucratic slippage and the variety of ways in which population assistance can be packaged. Support for improved census-taking or a pilot abortion control clinic appears innocuous enough, but external linkage groups use them as wedges for awakening interest in population growth among specialized low level bureaucrats in the hope that they will push it up and out into the rest of government. In actual practice, however,

80 An Overview of the Politics of Population in Latin America

the spread has been limited with the exception of Colombia. Externally supported population activities remain isolated in intragovernmental linkage groups of secondary influence, usually in the Division of Maternal and Child Health of the Ministry of Health. And there is a distinct reluctance to admit that even these programs are of relevance to population control.[86]

While approaching the population problem through the medical establishment—defining it as a health question—tends to minimize domestic opposition, it also relegates the resultant programs to low governmental priority and public awareness. One of the failures of the population control campaign thus far has been its inability to link up with more powerful, broader gauged internal groups, especially those with developmental interests and responsibilities. This failure indicates the attenuated evolution of Latin American population policies.

CONCLUSIONS

We have now described the population policy linkage network in Latin America. Figure 4-2 abstracts the network. To recapitulate, its main features are first, an explosion of external programs directed at convincing Latin American governments to adopt antinatalist policies and implement family-planning programs. Second, despite the proliferation of organizations offering population assistance, the United States government is the dominant external linkage group. Third,

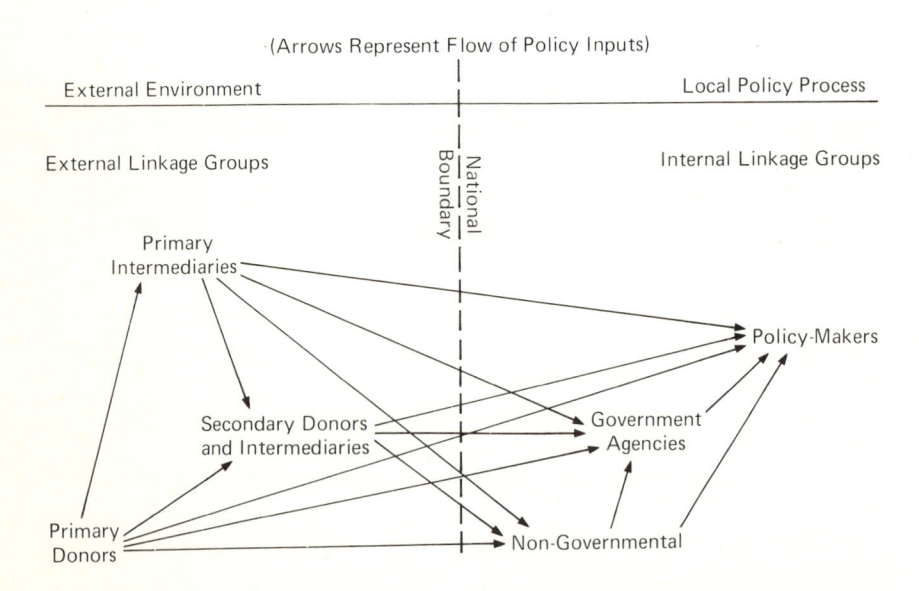

Figure 4-2. Linkage Network for Latin American Population Policies

external attempts to influence national population policies have resulted in an ingenious combination of direct and indirect policy inputs. And, fourth, these inputs are funneled through various internal linkage groups. What have been the policy results of this network?

Impact

For our purposes "population policy" refers to the spectrum of *governmental* decisions and actions that are intended to affect national fertility and with it the population growth rate. They can vary from fully articulated, codified, and programmed commitments to increase fertility (and lower mortality) to equally explicit and comprehensive efforts to decrease fertility (but not to increase mortality). In practice, pronatalist policies tend to be reflected in attitudes and statements rather than programs, while antinatalist policies rely on family planning as the means for slowing growth. Changing policy in the Latin American case would thus consist of movement away from traditional pronatalism toward organized family-planning programs, accompanied by supplementary—yet voluntary measures—with demographic objectives.

Although limited by severe data constraints, the policy ranking presented in Table 4-3 goes beyond existing nominal classifications to capture more of the complexities and variations in Latin American policies.[87] Each nation's score represents a composite evaluation of the essential policy components, with the range varying from minus one for pronatalist to plus three for explicitly antinatalist. Because organized family planning remains the key to contemporary control policies, each score on this component is doubled for a maximum of six points. "Other Programs" are the research, training, and public educational activities that complement family planning while the next column refers to the existence and age of a governmental agency in charge of population/family-planning programs. The first policy component column rates the statements of top-level leaders, and the last indicates the extent to which population planning is integrated into national developmental planning. (In order to check the interrelatedness of the policy components as shown in Table 4-3, Goodman and Kruskal's gammas were calculated. With the exception of the Agency scores, the gammas ranged from .47 to .92, being highest for Family Planning and other Programs. For the Agency they ranged from -.06 to .46. The Agency component was kept in the policy score despite its relatively low interrelatedness with the other dimensions, since it is the only one that directly taps the length of time that the policy has been in existence.)

The policy data in Table 4-3 documents a pronounced shift in Latin American population policies since the early 1960's. Every government has at the minimum allowed private organizations to initiate family planning and related programs. Colombia has gone the farthest with not only national family planning and the full range of supporting activities but also the integration of demographic analysis and population planning into developmental

Table 4-3. Latin American Population Policies and External Inputs

Country	Statements	Family Planning	Other Programs	Agency	Pop. Planning	Policy Score	Per Capita External Assistance ($US)	Fertility (births/1000)
Colombia	3	6	3	2	3	17 (1)	.2182 (8)	45 (14.5)
Chile	0	6	3	3	0	12 (2.5)	.4322 (4)	33 (4)
Costa Rica	1	6	3	2	0	12 (2.5)	.6940 (1)	45 (14.5)
Dom. Rep.	3	4	2	2	0	11 (4.5)	.2145 (9)	49 (19.5)
El Salvador	0	6	2	2	1	11 (4.5)	.3868 (5)	47 (18)
Mexico	3	4	2	1	0	10 (6.5)	.0843 (14)	43 (9.5)
Panama	0	4	1	2	3	10 (6.5)	.5928 (2)	40 (6)
Cuba	−1	6	1	3	0	9 (8.5)	.0000 (20)	27 (3)
Ecuador	1	4	1	2	1	9 (8.5)	.0842 (15)	45 (14.5)
Honduras	0	4	1	3	0	8 (10)	.3816 (6)	49 (19.5)
Guatemala	0	4	1	2	0	7 (11.5)	.2716 (7)	43 (9.5)
Nicaragua	0	4	1	2	0	7 (11.5)	.4943 (3)	46 (17)
Venezuela	0	2	1	3	0	6 (13)	.0845 (13)	41 (7)
Peru	−1	2	1	3	0	5 (14)	.1082 (11)	42 (8)
Bolivia	0	0	1	2	0	3 (16)	.1053 (12)	44 (11.5)
Paraguay	0	2	0	1	0	3 (16)	.1900 (10)	45 (14.5)
Uruguay	0	2	1	0	0	3 (16)	.0452 (17)	21 (1)
Argentina	−1	2	1	0	0	2 (19)	.0529 (16)	23 (2)
Brazil	−1	2	1	0	0	2 (19)	.0295 (18)	38 (5)
Haiti	0	0	1	1	0	2 (19)	.0202 (19)	44 (11.5)

Sources:

1) "Policy Components": Numerical scores vary from −1 to 3 (except for Family Planning where scores are doubled) and translate as follows: −1 equals overtly pronatalist; 0 equals none, neutral, ambiguous; 1 equals mildly antinatalist usually through recognition of value of family planning although not necessarily to control growth, existence of private programs; 2 equals more explicitly antinatalist, public-private mix in programming; 3 equals unmistakenly antinatalist; comprehensive public programs:

a) "Statements" refer to public pronouncements of top leadership about what their policy is and its objectives; gleaned from wide variety of sources including Dorothy Nortman, "Population and Family Planning Programs: A Factbook," *Reports on Population/Family Planning,* No. 2 (Fourth Edition, September, 1972);

b) "Family Planning" is the actual state of organized family planning within the country in which 2 equals limited private programs, sometimes in public facilities, 4 equals significant programs of public-private mix, and 6 equals family planning as an integral part of public health care; variety of sources;

c) "Other Programs" refer to research, training, and public educational efforts with the score increasing as their extent and relevance to national family-planning increase; variety of sources;

d) "Agency" refers to the existence of a public agency specifically and solely charged with population/family-planning matters and the scoring is based on the agency age with 1 equals 1–2 years, 2 equals 3–5 years and 3 equals 5 plus years, derived from wide variety of sources (no reference to a Cuban agency was found but it is assumed that, because of the overall age and comprehensive nature of Cuban family planning, there is a coordinating agency);

e) "Pop. Planning" is the extent to which population growth and control are integrated into national developmental planning; 1 equals mention of these considerations in plan while 3 equals inclusion of specific reduction targets in plan; from B. Maxwell Stamper, "Population Policy in Development Planning: A Study of Seventy Less Developed Countries," *Reports on Population/Family Planning,* No. 13 (May 1973), pp. 8–9;

2) "Policy Score": Calculated by policy components;

3) "Per Capita External Assistance": calculated using 1970 population and total population assistance from the Ford Foundation, 1963–1970 (official foundation records); Pathfinder Fund *(Annual Report, FY 1970–1971)*; Population Council, 1962–1969 *(Annual Reports)*; OECD *(Population: International Assistance and Research,* p. 113); UNFPA, 1970 *(Allocations Issued by the UNFPA in 1970)*; USAID, 1963-mid 1970 (Statistics and Reports Division, *Operation Report,* June 30, 1970); and the Rockefeller Foundation, 1964–1971 (letter from Foundation to author). The major missing donor is IPPF for which figures were not available;

4) "Fertility Rate, 1970": Organización de Estados Americanos, Departamento de Asuntos Sociales, *Datos básicos de población en América Latina, 1970* (Washington, D.C.: OAS, 1971).

planning. Most of the other governments are developing family planning and related programs although they do not yet justify them in demographic terms nor tie them into developmental policy-making. A few, most importantly Brazil and Peru because of their large populations and high fertility rates, officially cling to pronatalism and only grudgingly permit scattered private activities.

At the very least, we know that a regional change in population policies closely followed the upsurge in external assistance. But beyond this gross correlation, there are indications that external inputs played, and continue to play, significant causal roles in domestic policy-making. In the first place, they pushed the issue into the policy arena, redefining population growth as a *problem* demanding *government* action, thus confirming Chalmer's point that "... one of the ways linkages affect Latin American politics is through making certain types of issues prominent within the system and influencing the ways in which others are faced."[88] As population control goes on the national agenda, external linkage groups back up their demands for local action with offers for assistance to a variety of activities. In the initial stages of Latin American family-planning programs, external resources play an inordinately important role. Support for personnel training, for example, is almost exclusively international in character.[89] Without the relatively massive combination of external inputs described in this paper, Latin American population policies would not have changed as rapidly and as extensively as they have. An exploration of national differences further substantiates this conclusion. Thus, we find a relatively strong positive correlation (.46), using a measure of rank order correlation (Kendall's tau), between the policy scores and per capita external assistance (Columns 6 and 7 of Table 4-3). The major deviant case is Cuba, which has a moderately strong policy but receives very little, if any external assistance. (In fact even Cuba had received some population assistance and participated in some international programs although its family-planning program can hardly be explained in terms of external inputs which are still very limited. There is no evidence of assistance from the Socialist countries for Cuba's impressive family-planning program.) Dropping it out of the rank order correlation, on the justification that its external linkages in general are radically different from the other Latin American countries, raises the value of tau to .53.

Policy Linkages and Dependency

In addition to establishing the importance—perhaps dominance—of external linkages in Latin American population policies, the data analyzed here seem to indicate general policy dependency. External organizations did manipulate public policy away from pronatalism toward antinatalism. In concluding, we shall examine some qualifications to the policy results of population linkages before speculating about the findings of this case for Latin American policy-making.

Some countries, like Chile, Colombia, Mexico and especially Cuba, were influenced by factors other than external assistance to adopt population family-planning measures. Others like the Middle American countries (minus Costa Rica) seem to absorb high levels of external inputs without converting them to effective policy. This latter pattern suggests the hypothesis that population assistance tends to flow into countries already heavily dependent on external aid. Ranking the 20 according to total per capita public assistance of all kinds from the United States in the period 1946-1969 and correlating this with per capita population assistance produced a Kendall's tau of .54.[90] Thus the small client states of the United States in Middle America receive more external aid regardless of its content and of their performance in using it. A second qualification regarding the impact of external linkages concerns the lack of desired policy outcomes. That is, they have not produced lower fertility and growth rates. The rank order correlation between per capita population assistance and crude fertility (last column in Table 4-3) is -.33. It is important, however, to emphasize that the assistance has probably not been effective long enough to have trickled down through government policies into fertility rates, but this observation brings us to a third qualification. Even discounting the time factor, most Latin American governments seem to be stopping considerably short of full-fledged population control policies. (The correlation for policy score and fertility is -.23 for all 20 countries. Dropping Argentina and Uruguay, which had low fertility before the population control campaign began, virtually washes out any correlation [tau = -.08]. There is scattered evidence linking fertility declines to organized family planning in Cuba, Chile, and Costa Rica. Elsewhere there is no evidence of demographic impact.) Only Colombia, and perhaps Mexico, are current exceptions to the rule of keeping population/family-planning activities at a low profile and in a health context. In some of the remaining 20 countries, such activities hardly constitute antinatalist policies since they are of so little consequence and since they are not deliberately used to control national growth rates.

The very prominence of external linkages in policy-making limits their impact, producing unintended consequences counterproductive to the achievement of effective antinatalist policies. In the worlds of an ECLA study:

> ... recent insistence on the overriding importance of curbs to population growth, under prevailing conditions of political *dissensus,* has brought forth suspicions and accusations of concealed motivations. The high-income countries are suspected of wishing to limit the population growth of their poor neighbors, whether to reduce future claims for aid or to guard against shifts in relative power.... Such suspicious [sic] constitute a factor that cannot be ignored in considering the probable viability of population policies concentrated on fertility control, and complicate every effort at objective analysis of the problem.[91]

The active leadership of the United States in the population control campaign redoubles Latin American wariness of the entire effort and makes an easy target for ideological opponents of the "Colossus of the North." As Gregory and Martine point out ". . . it is evident that a large number of persons on this continent stopped believing a long time ago in the altruism of their benefactors."[92] Consequently, in order to satisfy powerful external linkage groups and take advantage of population assistance without at the same time creating domestic political controversy, governments quietly channel external assistance into unobtrusive family-planning and research programs in the Ministry of Health or private agencies. Such responses are unlikely to generate significant demographic results.

The long run prospects for the modest family-planning programs, begun with foreign assistance and encouragement, becomes even more problematic when we add a feedback loop to the linkage network. What happens when the United States Congress begins to question, as it inevitably will—especially in an era of domestic budgetary cuts—what it is getting for the $125 million per year it appropriates for population control? At best, USAID officials, who now have an enormous stake in the program, can present some impressive data on programs initiated with foreign assistance, but when it comes to results, the findings are not so impressive. Only in a few Latin American countries is there even circumstantial evidence that these programs have affected the growth rate. There is no evidence of a broader impact, i.e., that population assistance leads to family-planning and related measures which lead to declining fertility which results in accelerated economic development and finally greater social stability. As a matter of fact the most visible cases *could* be interpreted to demonstrate the opposite. Brazil with no population assistance and little family planning is experiencing a highly publicized economic boom and relative (if enforced) stability while Chile with a fairly well-developed population policy is experiencing economic stagnation, social unrest, and political radicalism. Obviously, causality in these and other instances is difficult to establish, but congressional appropriations are made in the short run with imperfect information. It is not hard, therefore, to imagine growing congressional disillusionment with population assistance resulting in its abandonment and a renewed search for alternative varieties of developmental aid. Under present conditions, such a shift would effectively destroy many Latin American population programs as well as the work of intermediate external and internal groups.

Using the linkage politics framework of Rosenau and Chalmers, this study has explored the role of external forces in the making of Latin American population policies. The findings do point to significant dependency at the policy level. (See Part III of this volume for intensive analyses of the role of external and other factors in the population policy-making of individual countries.) The initial flow of influence and pressure was essentially one way, with the Latin American polities reacting to a configuration of outside groups dominated by the United States government. One cannot, however, conclude that Latin American policy dependency is total. To begin with, this case concerned linkages to only one particular category of policy, a relatively low priority, non-antagonistic policy compared with, say, national defense, foreign investment, or internal security. The influence of the United States in this case grew out of its willingness and ability to commit considerable resources to slow population growth in Latin America and the rest of the developing world rather than directly out of the United States' alleged economic and strategic dominance. Furthermore, even when external actors decide to mobilize their resources and ingenuity to provoke policy changes, the population case would indicate that their influence has limits in Latin America. Foreign governments, international agencies, and private organizations can reward, cajole, and pressure, but they cannot dictate policy and guarantee its results. They can raise issues for consideration, but often their participation obstructs effective domestic action on the proposed policy. And, with the failure of foreign aid to produce the desired commitments, demonstrable results, and recipient gratitude, there is a decline in external support, regardless of the state of the problem which provoked the original concern. This decline in external support has yet to occur with population control assistance; however, there is no reason to believe that it will not. When it does the chronic instability of externally linked Latin American policies will again be painfully confirmed.[93]

NOTES TO CHAPTER 4

1. "Address to the University of Notre Dame" (May 1, 1969, World Bank Reprint), p. 3.
2. Bernard Berelson, "The Present State of Family Planning Programs," *Studies in Family Planning,* No. 57 (September, 1930), p. 11.
3. Policy components from Hope Eldridge, "Population: Population Policies," *Encyclopedia of the Social Sciences,* XII, pp. 381-382.
4. For two classic macro-level theories of Latin American politics see Merele Kling, "Toward a Theory of Power and Political Instability in Latin America,"*Western Political Quarterly,* IX, No. 7 (March, 1956), pp. 21-35; and Charles W. Anderson, *Politics and Economic Change in Latin America: The Governing of Restless Nations* (New York: D. Van Nostrand Company, Inc., 1967), especially Part I.
5. ". . . we badly need empirical studies of the actual and potential impact of U.S. foreign-policy instruments on the economics, social systems, and especially politics of these countries [of the Third World]. Not only the academics but also the government research and evaluation organs have practically ignored these questions." Robert Packenham, "Political Development Doctrines in the American

Foreign Aid Program," *World Politics,* XVIII, No. 2 (January, 1966), p. 230.
6. Raúl Prebisch, *Toward a Dynamic Development Policy for Latin America* (New York: United Nations, 1963).
7. Susanne Bodenheimer, "Dependency and Imperialism: The Roots of Latin American Underdevelopment," *Politics and Society,* I, No. 3 (May, 1971), p. 330.
8. *Ibid.,* p. 334.
9. For a recent attempt to test some of the major dependency hypotheses see Robert R. Kaufman, Harry I. Chernotsky, and Daniel S. Geller, "A Preliminary Test of the Theory of Dependency" (unpublished paper, Rutgers University, 1973).
10. For a general discussion of linkage politics see James N. Rosenau, ed., *Linkage Politics: Essays on the Convergence of National and International Systems* (New York: The Free Press, 1969). Chalmer's chapter is "Developing on the Periphery: External Factors in Latin American Politics," pp. 67–93.
11. *Ibid.,* p. 45.
12. For two case studies of linkage politics in Latin America, see Rod Bunker, "Linkages and the Foreign Policy of Peru, 1958–1966," *Western Political Quarterly,* 22 (June, 1969), pp. 280–297; and Robert J. Clark, Jr., "Economic Integration and the Political Process: Linkage Politics in Venezuela" in *Contemporary Inter-American Relations,* edited by Yale H. Ferguson (Englewood Cliffs, New Jersey: Prentice-Hall, Inc., 1972), pp. 522–543.
13. Chalmers, "Developing on the Periphery," p. 68.
14. *Ibid.,* p. 69.
15. Theodore K. Ruprecht and Carl W. Wahren, *Population Programmes and Economic and Social Development* (Paris: Development Centre of the Organization for Economic Cooperation and Development, 1970), pp. 47–49.
16. USAID, Bureau of Technical Assistance, Office of Population, *Population Program Assistance* (Washington, D.C.: Agency for International Development, 1971), p. 2.
17. USAID alone had a population budget of $100 million in FY1971. *Ibid.*
18. Chalmers, "Developing on the Periphery," p. 71.
19. *Ibid.*
20. The chairman of the committee issuing the report, General (ret.) William Draper, later claimed that his attention was focused on the population issue by a wire from Hugh Moore charging that the committee would be derelict in its duty if it did not deal with the population explosion. Draper, Moore, and others with close government ties later formed the Population Crisis Committee to lobby for government action. The Victor-Bostrom Fund for the International Planned Parenthood Federation, *Report,* No. 16 (Winter, 1972–73).

For more on the Draper Committee see Phyllis Tilson Piotrow, *World Population Crisis: The United States Response* (New York: Praeger Publishers, 1973), pp. 36–42.
21. Cited in David A. Baldwin, *Foreign Aid and American Foreign Policy: A Documentary Analysis* (New York: Frederick A. Praeger, Publishers, 1966), pp. 218–219.
22. U.S., Congress, Senate Committee on Government Operations, *Population Crisis: Hearings before the Subcommittee on Foreign Aid Expenditures of the Committee on Government Operations, Senate on S. 16776*, 89th Congress, 1st Session, 1965, p. 67.
23. *Ibid.*, 90th Congress, 2nd Session, 1968, p. 626.
24. USAID, *Population Program Assistance* (1971), p. 22.
25. U.S., Congress, *Population Crisis*, 89th Congress, 2nd Session, 1966, pp. 884–886. Piotrow examines in detail the positions and organization of USAID over time. See also Frances Lavinia Edwards Winslow "American Aid to Population Programs in Latin America: A Case Study in Penetration Politics" (unpublished MA thesis, Drew University, 1971).
26. USAID, *Population Program Assistance* (1969), pp. 11–14.
27. According to one source, the total number of U.S. personnel serving in Latin America decreased from 2,129 in FY1967 to 869 by the end of FY1972. Figures from a House hearing cited in Yale H. Ferguson, "An End to the 'Special Relationship': The United States and Latin America," *Revista InterAmericana,* II, No. 3 (Fall, 1972), p. 370.
28. "The *sine qua non* goal and justification of aid is that it be an instrument of foreign policy and justified in terms of the national interest. If other goals and justifications can be added, all the better; if they cannot, the decision to go ahead is forthcoming anyway. In no case, however, does the doctrine justify using aid for humanitarian purposes when the justification in national interest terms is lacking." Robert Packenham, "Foreign Aid and the National Interest," *Midwest Journal of Political Science,* X No. 2 (May, 1966), pp. 218–219. Packenham's article and the above quotation is based upon a survey of USAID officials.
29. Cited in Piotrow, *World Population Crisis*, p. 90.
30. Nelson A. Rockefeller, *Quality of Life in the Americas: Report of a U.S. Presidential Mission for the Western Hemisphere* (Washington, D.C.: Agency for International Development, 1969), p. 13.
31. The population unit is part of the Development Assistance Committee, the permanent chairman of which always comes from the United States. Goran Ohlin, "The Organization for Economic Cooperation and Development," *The Global Partnership: International Agencies and Economic Development,* edited by Richard N. Gardner and Max F. Millikan (New York: Praeger, 1968), p. 235. Sweden and the United

States made the initial grants to establish the population unit. Together OECD members account for 90 percent of all developmental assistance.
32. Richard N. Gardner, "Toward a World Population Program" in *The Global Partnership*, p. 342.
33. Robert S. McNamara, "Address to the Board of Governors" (September 30, 1968, World Bank Reprint), p. 11.
34. Robert S. McNamara, "Address to the Inter-American Press Association," (October 18, 1968, World Bank Reprint), p. 8.
35. *The New York Times*, July 8, 1973, Section 3, p. 1. McNamara explains the apparent discrepancy between public commitments and actual Bank practices in terms of not knowing *how* to reduce population growth on p. 9 of this article.
36. For more detailed examinations of UN population activities see Piotrow, pp. 66-69 and 199-219, and John Corwin Burt, "Decision Networks and the World Population Explosion: The UN and Institutional Innovation for Social Crises," *A Sage Professional Paper in International Studies Series*, I (1972).
37. Piotrow, *World Population Crisis*, pp. 66-69.
38. Burt, "Decision Networks . . . ," pp. 19-20.
39. Charles F. Gallagher, *The United Nations System and Population Problems*, American Universities Field Staff Reports, West Europe Series, V, No. 5 (General, April, 1970), p. 5.
40. *Population Crisis*, VII, 2 (March-April, 1971). For 1972 the United States offered matching funds of $24 million. *International Letter*, No. 86 (July 25, 1972), p. 6.
41. Interview with UNFPA official, May 18, 1971. In 1970 the Fund allocated $6.7 million to seven UN agencies plus $0.5 million to IPPF and $2.3 million directly to national projects. *Population Crisis*, VII, 2 (March-April 1971). Only six percent of the $6.7 million went to Latin America. UNDP Fund for Population Activities, *1970 Allocations and Projects for 1971-74* (UNFPA/1ACC/2/Rev. 2), (UNFPA/AB/III/4), January 31, 1971.
42. UN, *Population Newsletter*, No. 5 (May, 1969), p. 18. Plans for 1971-1974 called for an increase in the percentage of UNFPA aid going to Latin America. *1970 Allocations and Projections for 1971-74*, pp. 4-5. In fact there has been a steady expansion of UN work in Latin American population matters.
43. In 1969, UNFPA was transferred from the Secretary General's office to the UN Development Programme where, Cox and Jacobson argue, the United States, because of its generous contributions, "seems to have retained a de facto right to appoint the administrator of that program and an undoubtedly great—albeit indirect—influence over its management." Robert W. Cox and Harold K. Jacobson, *Anatomy of Influence: Decision Making in International Organization* (New Haven: Yale University Press, 1973), p. 433.

44. Interview with Dr. Carlos Quintana in Stanley Johnson, *Life Without Birth* (Boston: Little Brown and Company, 1970), p. 53.
45. *Población*, (Spanish language newsletter of the Population Reference Bureau), II, No. 9 (1971).
46. PAHO, "Population Dynamics Policy of the Organization" (Mimeo, 1970).
47. Winslow, "American Aid to Population Programs in Latin America," p. 60.
48. Personal interview with IADB official, August 12, 1970, and subsequent review of IADB loans.
49. OEA, Depto. de Asuntos Sociales, *Boletín de Población*, No. 9.
50. USAID, *Population Program Assistance* (1971), p. 54.
51. "Summary of Ford Foundation Strategy in Latin America and the Caribbean" (Xerox, n.d.), and review of Ford Foundation population grants to Latin America.
52. See Piotrow, *World Population Crisis*, pp. 15-19.
53. U.S., Congress, *Population Crisis*, 90th Congress, 2nd Session, 1968, p. 624.
54. 1973 projected budget from *IPPF News*, No. 223 (November, 1973).
55. In 1963 the Council received a total of $3,030,853 in gifts and grants with the biggest contribution being from the Ford Foundation. *Annual Report, 1962 and 1963*, p. 78. In 1971 the total had risen to $15,980,857 with $6,515,588 from the United States government and $4,926,230 from Ford. *Annual Report*, 1971, p. 92.
56. In unrestricted USAID grants the Fund received $700,000 in 1968, $2,500,000 in 1969 and $2,266,000 in 1971. For Latin America it received $300,000 in 1969 and $800,000 in 1971. USAID, *Population Program Assistance* (1971), p. 220 and p. 228. During FY1971 the Fund had 22 active projects in nine Latin American countries. *Annual Report, Fiscal Year Ending June 30, 1971*, p. 1 of Appendix III.
57. In 1971 the Kellogg Foundation awarded PRB a four-year grant of $325,000 to support the Bogotá office. *IPPF News*, No. 206 (May, 1971).
58. For interpretations of population assistance stressing these motives see Bonnie Mass, *The Political Economy of Population Control in Latin America* (Montreal: Editions Latin America, 1972); and William Barclay, Joseph Enright, and Reid T. Reynolds, "Population Control in the Third World," *NACLA. Newsletter*, IV, No. 8 (December, 1970), pp. 1-18.
59. *IPPF News*, No. 223 (November, 1972).
60. OEA, *Boletín* (Población), No. 9.
61. USAID, *Population Program Assistance (1971)*, p. 150 and USAID, Regional Office for Central America, *Report on Population Activities in the Central America and Panama Region for Calendar Year 1969* (Washington, D.C.: Agency for International Development, 1970).
62. U.S., Congress, *Population Crisis*, 89th Congress, 1st Session, 1965, p. 917.
63. USAID, *Population Program Assistance* (1971), p. 56.

64. U.S., Congress, *Population Crisis*, 89th Congress 1st Session, 1965, p. 849.
65. *Ibid.*, 90th Congress, 2nd Session, 1968, p. 516.
66. Rosenau posits the regional environment as one possible source of external influence on national polities in *Linkage Politics,* pp. 61-62.
67. Unión Internacional para el Estudio Científico de la Población, *Conferencia regional latinoamericana de población, Actas I* (Mexico, D.F.; Colegio de México, 1972) p. xix.
68. OEA, *Boletín* (Población), No. 12.
69. "The most important function of such surveys is similar to any market research project: to demonstrate the existence of a demand for goods or services, in this case birth control." J. Mayone Stycos, *Human Fertility in Latin America: Sociological Perspectives* (Ithaca: Cornell University Press, 1968), p. 83.
70. "The PPO's [Population Programme Officers] represent an innovation in the UN family of organizations; never before has a secretariat group been granted a mandate so explicitly promotional of UN services to member governments." Burt, "Decision Networks . . .," p. 24.
71. *World Bank: 100 Questions and Answers* (Washington, D.C.: The World Bank, 1970), p. 38. Both the Bank and USAID have multiple opportunities to issue reminders to their borrowers about the dangers of uncontrolled population growth.
72. Rosenau, *Linkage Politics,* p. 46. Rosenau here is not classifying external inputs per se but the processes linking outputs and inputs across systems.
73. USAID, *Spring Review Population Programs, May 11-13, 1970: Getting A.I.D. Population Programs Started* (Washington, D.C.: Agency for International Development, 1970), p. 9.
74. Victor Urquidi in Philip B. Taylor, Jr. and Sam Shulman, *Population and Urbanization Problems in Latin America* (Houston: Latin American Studies Committee, Office of International Affairs, University of Houston, 1971), p. 31.
75. Population Council, *Annual Report,* 1969, p. 53.
76. Rutherford M. Poats, *Technology for Developing Nations: New Directions for U.S. Technical Assistance* (Washington, D.C.: The Brookings Institution, 1972), p. 147.
77. Chalmers, "Developing on the Periphery," p. 72.
78. OECD, *Population . . . ,* p. 131 Latin American was selected as an area of special attention in the 1972 IPPF work plan. IPPF News, No. 214 (January, 1972).
79. USAID, ROCAP, *Report on Population Activities in the Central America and Panama Region for Calendar Year 1969,* p. 37. In several Latin American countries FPA clinics have been turned over to the government. Chile and Costa Rica are leading examples.
80. As USAID is the biggest source of IPPF funds, a 1971 Agency decision to allow its support to come in the form of general program assistance without prior earmarking for specific countries, as had previously

been the case, represented a major breakthrough for IPPF and its affiliates. It not only gave the Federation greater control, but it also permitted USAID funds to be commingled and channeled into countries where they had previously been forbidden by USAID policy. *IPPF News,* No. 208 (July, 1971). As an example of the diversity of funding, the Costa Rican Demographic Association has received direct assistance from IPPF, USAID Sweden, the Ford Foundation, and Population Council.

81. Despite recent attempts to increase local financial support for IPPF affiliates, they are still overwhelmingly dependent on outside sources. The 1972 IPPF budget called for expenditures in the Western Hemisphere totaling $10,684,200 of which more than $7.7 million was to come from IPPF headquarters. Much of the remainder was accounted for by direct grants from other external sources to local FPA's, *IPPF News,* No. 214 (January, 1972). In July, 1971 representatives from various Latin American Associations set the goal of raising $1.4 million from local sources by June, 1972. *IPPF News,* No. 208 (July, 1971).

82. Information from former Colombian Minister of Health in Taylor and Shulman, *Population and Urbanization Problems of Latin America,* p. 55.

83. The Pan American Federation of Medical Schools (FEPAFEM) devotes special attention to the teaching of demography in Latin American medical schools. *DIME Dialogue,* 4, No. 1 (January-February-March, 1971), p. 3.

84. J. Mayone Stycos, "Latin America: Programs, Politics, and the Universities", *Concerned Demography,* 2, No. 4, (March, 1971), p. 17.

85. In 1972 the Ford Foundation announced a $365,000 two-year grant, to be foundation administered, for fellowships and research awards in Brazil to develop a community of scholars in demography and related fields. *Ford Foundation Letter,* 3, No. 6 (September 1, 1972), p. 7.

86. In 1972 the Chilean government announced the signing of an agreement with the UNFPA for $3,198,000 over four years. The announcement made no direct mention of family planning though this was presumably an important aspect of the grant. Republic of Chile, *The Chilean Report,* No. 5 (June 15, 1972), p. 8.

87. The most important attempt to classify world population policies is done yearly by Dorothy Nortman, "Population and Family Planning Programs: A Factbook," *Reports on Population/Family Planning,* No. 2. There were four editions as of September, 1972.

88. Chalmers, "Developing on the Periphery," pp. 80–81.

89. María Luisa García, "Programas de planificación familiar en America Latin (1969)" in *Conferencia regional latinoamericana de población, Actas 2,* p. 396.

90. Total foreign aid per country is from USAID, Office of Statistics and Reports, Bureau for Program and Policy Coordination, *U.S. Overseas*

Loans and Grants and Assistance from International Organizations, Obligations and Loan Authorizations, July 1, 1945-June 30, 1969. (Washington, D.C.: Agency for International Development, 1970), pp. 31-62. Each country's total was divided by its 1970 population. The per capita total ranged from $174.25 for Chile to $6.24 for Cuba. Kendall's tau was used instead of Pearson's *r* because the data intervals of the policy score column are the product of the author's evaluation while the per capita assistance figures are hard data. A Pearson's *r* would undoubtedly produce a higher coefficient.

91. UN, ECLA, *Social Change and Social Development Policy in Latin America* (E/CN.121826/Rev. 1) (May, 1970), p. 288.
92. Alfonso F. Gregory and George Martine, "Interrelaciones de los aspectos micro y macrosociológicos en las políticas de población," *Conferencia regional latinoamericana de población, Actas 2*, p. 434.
93. Chalmers in "Developing on the Periphery," p. 84, delineates policy instability as one of the results of Latin American linkages.

Part II

Perspectives on Population Control

Chapter Five

The Population Explosion*

Benjamín Viel

Current Status of the Demographic Problem *(pp. 241-242 and p. 245)*

At the beginning of this century the population of Latin America was calculated to be about 60 million habitants. In 1920 it approached 90 million; in 1960, 212 million; and in 1969, the best estimate was about 272 million. In the period of 69 years this region of the American continent has seen its population multiply 4.5 times.

In 1900 the percentage of annual growth was only 1.5; in 1969 it was calculated at 2.9 percent. The human mind is not accustomed to comprehending the true magnitude of the problem in percentages as 2.9 percent growth does not seem, at first glance, to be an excessive figure to those unfamiliar with this type of information. For them, the problem would be clearer if they realized that in 1969 a new country of 7,900,000 inhabitants joined the continent, or practically one more Guatemala plus one more El Salvador—not in production terms as these countries are today but two additional infant countries requiring 18 years of investment.

In 1970 the population of the Latin American continent will reach 280 million, and then a new country of 8,100,000 infants, the present size of Cuba, will join our population. Since the percentage of annual growth is by nature cumulative, by projecting the 2.9 percent growth rate, the year 1993 will see a population of 544 million and then the country of "newborns" that will join us will be about 15,800,000—a little more than the present population

---

*Translated excerpts from Tercera Parte, "El problema demográfico de la América Latina," of *La explosión demográfica; ¿Cuántos son demasiados?* (México, D.F.: Editorial Pax-México, Libería Carlos Césarman, S.A., 1970) by Benjamín Viel. Reprinted by permission of the publisher and translated by Pat Tolliver and the editor. Notes have been retained and renumbered.

of Peru. Such growth, that could well qualify as monstrous, without historical precedent, is the consequence of a dramatic and spectacular decline in the number of deaths without a decline in the number of births. . . .

The analysis of demographic data allows us to conclude that we inhabit a continent, with annual growth, which is condemned to double its population in the brief period of 24 years. Those who want to sleep tranquilly contrast these figures with the low density of inhabitants per square kilometer, a density much lower than that of Europe. But they present averages, and the averages are figures that do not always show reality.

Population Projections *(pp. 255-257 and 259-260)*

Carmen Miró, Director of the Latin American Demographic Center, estimates 592 million as the probable number of Latin American inhabitants that will exist in the year 2000.[1] The same author, in her paper, "The Population of Latin America in the Twentieth Century," presented at the first Panamerican Assembly of Population celebrated in Cali in 1965, estimated the population for 1980 as 364,398,000 and established an annual growth rate of 2.7 percent between 1980 and 1990 and one of 2.5 percent between 1990 and 2000.[2] Using this base to calculate the population for the year 2000, one would arrive at 608,194,000, practically 16 million more than Miró's first publication, and even the latter assumes that the annual growth rate has to diminish beginning in 1980. The Population Reference Bureau . . . with data from 1969 predicts a population of 376 million for the year 1980, 12 million more than that which Carmen Miró predicted in 1965. If the prediction of the Population Reference Bureau, based on a sustained annual growth of 2.9 percent, is carried to the year 2000, Latin America will have a population of 756 million or 148 million more than Miró's 1965 estimate which based on the declining growth rate beginning in 1980. The Population Reference Bureau estimate illustrates what occurs when the annual growth does not decline. . . .

When the press informs us of a distant catastrophe, such as the death of 5,000 people in China from flood or the famine of prolonged drought, the news does not have the emotional impact of only 100 deaths in an air accident in one's own country. That which is distant is little understood, attracting only superficial attention. For this reason, perhaps, to say that the total population of the world will reach eight billion in a short time is similar to lack of emotion with which one reads notice of Oriental catastrophe. . . . Thinking of Brazil in the short span of 40 more years as having a population of 240 million inhabitants, more than the current population of the U.S.A.— the richest country in the world—constitutes a catastrophe difficult to imagine for those who have seen close up the present misery of Northeast Brazil or the "Favelas" of Rio de Janeiro, both which exist with a present population of only 71 million inhabitants.

Food Production *(pp. 262-263 and 270-271)*

The desolate panorama of widespread, chronic malnutrition among the inhabitants of Latin America, as Dr. Sen, Director of FAO, pointed out in 1965, could be irradicated by increasing agricultural productivity.[3] Dr. Sen says textually: "It is certain that the countries with excessive foodstuffs could export food to low calorie countries, but it is also certain that as yet no one has studied nor resolved all of the problems that accompany great transfers. The final solution of the problem must be found in increasing of the agricultural productivity of developing countries."

Latin America understands the problem and desperately seeks to increase its agricultural production. One cannot say that there has been culpable neglect. According to CEPAL, in the decade between 1956 and 1965, the production of foodstuffs increased 32 percent, a 3.2 percent annual rate that cannot be considered slight and that compares favorably with experimental increases in other areas of the world.[4] But such an increase is reduced to nothing when it is related to population. The same CEPAL publication establishes that, using 100 as an index for the production of food per inhabitant in the period 1952-1955, in 1958 there was a rise to 104; in 1960 a decline to 98; and in 1965 a return to 100. In 10 years the production of food increases 32 percent; yet hunger persists.

Faced with a production of foodstuffs insufficient to solve the problem, it is not strange that the importation of food increases in spite of the drain of capital it represents. The same CEPAL publication reports that, with an index equal to 100 for the period of 1951-53, the importation of cereals in the period 1961-63 was 153 and that of livestock products was about 152. Resorting to the importation of food from developed areas is without doubt harmful; it diverts funds from imports that could have been used for industrial development, that is, from the expansion of the infrastructure necessary for agriculture's own development. To spend continuously for more time than an emergency justifies impedes progress and necessitates a policy of growing external spending. . . .

In summary, population growth appears compatible with what could be called the reserve food production capacity of Argentina and Uruguay. However, in semi-urbanized America, demographic growth is superior to the known resources, and while potential resources certainly exist, their exploitation will demand a capital investment that this zone can only make with great difficulty without sacrificing the standard of living to its population even more. (*Viel divides the countries of Latin America into "Urbanized" [Argentina and Uruguay], "Semi-Urbanized," and "Rural or Agricultural" in analyzing population growth and its impact.*) In this zone, demographic growth accompanies misery. In the agricultural zone, owing to its poor present conditions and limited potential in regards to economic development, such growth condemns the zone to misery.

The alarming nutritional situation facing Latin America is not new; it was visible, as it is logical that it would have been, many years ago, and it served to goad countries into seeking to increase agricultural production by all possible means. One cannot blame laziness or slowness; the 3.2 percent increase in agricultural production is solid proof that effort was expended. That such effort was not translated into substantial improvement in the nutritional state of the poorly fed is the consequence of a demographic increase that has consumed the gains and of insufficient capital investment.

Sources of Labor in Latin America
(pp. 271-273 and p. 275)

If someone would check the correlation between the number of beggars and the indexes of production, it is evident that he would find a strong negative relationship. Logically, a lower index of production means a smaller number of workers. Many upon seeing the out-stretched hand of a young man who lives—or better said, vegetates—by begging will be tempted to ask him: "You are young, you are strong, why aren't you working?" Few think "and at what?"

From the invention of machines until the present, humanity has suffered the progressive substitution of human muscle, which has invaded all types of productive activity—today, including intellectual activity with the invasion of the electric computer. In primitive agricultural life, an illiterate with a plowshare and a farm animal was a worker; many were necessary to sow a small plot—just as the arms of the women and children were necessary to harvest the product. Into the midst of this came the tractor and the mechanical harvester. Production increased enormously when the land could be plowed more extensively and when the harvest could be done more rapidly, but with these enormous advantages came the fact that one man could replace ten. And that one man had to be specialized, a costly process since training was necessary before he could work.

At the beginning of the industrial revolution a machine could do the work of ten men. Now a machine is capable of replacing 100 or 1,000, and industrial countries are obligated to diminish hours in the work week to avoid dismissals caused by the greater efficiency of factory equipment. Automation, which increases yields and permits price reductions, brings the serious inconvenience of decreasing the openings in the labor market.

Building a factory requires a capital investment of $10,000, according to a 1963 estimate for the United States, for each worker the factory employs. To achieve efficiency from such capital means installing machinery requiring the least operating cost and consequently a minimum of manual labor. The capital necessary to put a man to work in agricultural activity was always less, but automation has also invaded agricultural production, and surprisingly in 1963, the capital investment that a new man would mean in the agriculture in the United States reached the same $10,000 figure as required in industry.

In Latin America the problem is to produce more. To achieve this it is necessary to introduce a certain degree of automation into production, be it agricultural or industrial. Such automation means an investment of scarce capital, and also it means denying job opportunity to the growing mass that joins the labor pool daily. Latin America's problem is not, then, easy to resolve. It must protect itself from unemployment by keeping factories of lower yield and higher cost than if they were automated in operation, and it has to increase its agricultural production avoiding useful mechanization that unfortunately reduces manual labor. Such facts create a situation of compromise which renders increases in either agricultural or industrial production even more difficult. . . .

Unemployment, a genuine specter hanging over the underdeveloped or developing areas of our continent, has to be a fundamental cause of a political instability. In as much as young people in search of non-existent remunerative work can only blame their situation on existing economic structures and on the present systems of government, they necessarily must look for the solution to their tragic condition in social revolution.

Generating employment, raising the level of our primary education as well as the number of those benefiting, raising and diversifying the quality of our higher education to achieve higher technology are aspirations that require money to be converted into reality. Unfortunately obtaining that capital is not easy.

Developmental Capital *(pp. 277-278)*

Without pretending to argue that slowing the velocity of population growth would by itself be a panacea to cure all evils, from the data one can obviously deduce that an increase in the gross national product diminishes substantially upon being divided among a larger number of heads thus making the building of working capital difficult. [Our data] . . . clearly shows that there are more possibilities of investment and, therefore, of progress in the zones of low population increase. If for circumstantial reasons economic difficulties appear in the urbanized zone, as an international economist has noted in a bitter, witty manner, they are serious but with hope, whereas the tragic crises of the rest of the continent are not serious but of little hope.

There are those who deny that a decrease in the growth rate could affect the accumulation of a country's working capital, and they argue that such capital ought to come from outside, be it through credit or limits on the earnings of companies with foreign capital. Traditional sectors advocate a credit policy; for the rest, it is already widely used. Those influenced by Marxism advocate nationalization of those sources of production using foreign capital. This attitude frightens away the money that might come from outside, thus aggravating the problem in addition to accentuating the nationalistic feeling of our republics with the consequent endangering of the concept of a common market and economic integration. Neither of the two groups publicly recognizes the obstacle that an excessive population growth rate represents for economic development.

Since it is very improbable that the political instability of our continent, derived in good part from the misery that excessive population growth encourages, will facilitate foreign investment, it is not possible to be very optimistic about the future. We urgently need greater production of food, better education, and more sources of employment. All these require capital, and since internal investment is very low and the hope for external capital is low, we come to the conclusion that our governments ought to have, along with their economic policies, clear and well-defined demographic policies.

The Necessity for Demographic Policy in Latin America *(pp. 278-281)*

The preceding analysis was intended to show that, with the exception of Argentina and Uruguay, Latin American population is increasing out of proportion to the increase in the means of production and that such growth in the purely agricultural countries is approaching saturation. The analysis also permits the conclusion that only with great difficulty can education absorb the exaggerated growth which threatens more unemployment upon not fitting into the labor market. If the reader thinks that the solution to such serious problems lies in stopping the growth of the population—stabilizing it at its present level—my proposal will undoubtedly be seen as traitorous. Stopping demographic growth is biologically impossible. As Harold Thomas has demonstrated, a population that reduces its birth rate by one half will still see its population doubled only in a longer time.[5] Chile with its present annual growth rate will have its population double in 26 years; if it reduces its annual growth to one half of what it is today, it would see its population double in the course of the next 60 years. That which we have tried to show leads only to realizing the necessity of reducing the growth rate to the point where it is parallel with the increase in the means of production as well as with satisfaction of the educational and nutritional necessities of the newborn.

A demographic policy designed to facilitate equilibrium between the increase in men and that in the means of production in the Latin American environment demands that the governments of the respective countries dedicate themselves to providing the family with the necessary means to reduce births according to its economic resources as well as the physical, mental, and emotional state of the couple. Such a policy involves an indispensable educational campaign, so that the people can make use of the means offered them. But this absolutely does not imply a mandatory atmosphere destined to limit the number of births to less than that which couples really desire. It is well known that such a restrictive policy would never succeed since legislation cannot regulate the intimate life of human beings.

The policy required of governments is nothing other than giving impetus to education in the fundamentals of reproductive physiology, in the knowledge of the contraceptive methods, and in the moral fundamentals of the concept of responsible paternity. It also implies they will not continue placing restrictions on importation of contraceptive products not manufactured domestically. And finally, the policy should stimulate doctors, educators, and sociologists to study the acceptability of such practices in the population, especially in the rural population which in a good part of Latin America constitutes more than 50 percent of the total.

If such a policy is imposed and achieves an equilibrium between economic and demographic growth, we would have to add to the advances obtained in the fight against misery advances in the field of health where there could be a decline in the harmful effects of illegal abortion as well as in infant mortality which thrives due to multiparity.

The document known as the Declaration of the Heads of State magnificently summarizes that which, in my opinion, constitutes a demographic policy that ought to be adopted by the nations of Latin America.[6] The document concludes by declaring that: "As heads of governments actively concerned with the population problem, we share the following convictions:

WE BELIEVE that the population problem must be recognized as a principal element in long range national planning if governments are to achieve their economic goals and fulfill the aspirations of their people.

WE BELIEVE that the great majority of parents desire to have the knowledge and the means to plan their families; that the opportunity to decide the number and the spacing of children is a basic human right.

WE BELIEVE that lasting and meaningful peace will depend to a considerable measure upon how the challenge of population growth is met.

WE BELIEVE the objective of planning families is the enrichment of human life, not its restriction; that family planning, by assuring greater opportunities to each person, frees man to attain his individual dignity and reach his full potential.

Recognizing that family planning is a vital interest of both the nation and the family, we, the undersigned earnestly hope that leaders around the world will share our views and join with us in this great challenge for the well-being and happiness of people everywhere."

This declaration, signed by more than 40 Heads of State, upon appearing publicly included only the signatures of the Presidents of Colombia and the Dominican Republic as beautiful and unique exceptions of this continent.

Despite the fact that their governments have not signed the declaration, some countries tolerate the existence of programs created by doctors with the primary objective of combating the effects of illegally induced abortion. Among such countries, which did not sign, Chile has incorporated education and distribution of contraceptives into the action program of the Maternal-Infant Service of its National Health Service. Other countries allow action by private associations, which because of budget limitations has slight repercussion on the birth rate. Others have created Centers of Demographic Studies without permitting them to do anything other than draw graphs showing birth rates. Others prohibit all mention of the problem, declaring that use of contraceptives "limits the creative and expansionist potential of the race and the country."

It is difficult to understand such an attitude in the face of a Latin America suffering from the effects of demographic growth before obtaining the benefits of the industrial revolution. Delaying population policy means favoring a vicious circle in which the increase engenders misery and pain and drags along a catastrophe that could destroy many values which man ought to try to conserve. Such slowness of action cannot be easily understood and requires analyzing some of the factors that are blinding those who have responsibility of acting before it is too late.

Potential Effects of Family Planning on the Latin American Population Explosion
(pp. 288-290)

The answer [concerning the impact of family planning] depends entirely upon what is intended to be the ultimate proposition of a family-planning program receiving governmental aid. If what is desired is that the human family of this region of the world produces only those babies who are desired, which without a doubt would mean a considerable decline of our present birth rates, I believe that it can be achieved in a short time. If one defines the solution to the demographic explosion as a halt in the growth of the human species, as though the present number of people represents maximum saturation, the answer would be negative.

Writing in *Science* in 1967 Kingsley Davis says that, ". . . the present programs in the countries that have adopted them as government policy are not more than successful attempts at reducing births. That if South Korea with an annual population growth of 2.9 percent in 1960 could reduce it to 1.2 percent in 1980, it would mean that a country, already densely populated, would duplicate its population in 60 years."[7] His analysis can be extended to Latin

America. If in the short run our present growth of 2.9 percent annually, which means doubling our population in 24 years, could be reduced to 1.5 percent per year, the doubling time would be extended to 47 years. That would not resolve Latin America's population explosion but would give us time to think of more effective solutions in addition to reducing a good proportion of the human pain of which we are victims.

If a doctor treating a gravely ill patient uses a therapy designed to prolong his life, allowing time for new drugs to appear that would definitely cure him, the doctor is fulfilling his obligations. In Latin America the problem of the population growth must be approached using a similar criterion. The ultimate goal must be to reduce the velocity of population growth to the point that it is less than the rate of economic growth, thus giving time to improve the standard of living. This does not mean that in the long run the shadow of the threat of saturation does not exist, but as no one today can say how much time will delay such a possibility, especially given continuous technological progress, I believe that now is not the time to discuss how to stop growth. Rather we should concentrate on slowing it down.

Reduction in growth rate has been accomplished in other regions. In 1920 Japan had 154 births for each 1000 women of fertile age while in 1966 the figure was little more than 60. In Taiwan in 1951, 211 children were born per 1000 women of fertile age, but in 1966 it was only 149, reducing the birth rate from 50 per thousand to 32.7 per thousand. Logically no one could argue that this considerable reduction is the exclusive consequence of family-planning programs which were more successful in Japan where legalized abortion joined the use of contraceptives. It is well known that changes in living style and growing urbanization brought on by economic development contributed to the reduction, but one can ask "Would this rapid economic development have been possible, without a parallel reduction in population growth?"

If other regions have realized success, could Latin America achieve it? I think so. Chile is a good example of what can be attained with a permissive policy. The family planning carried out in the western area of Santiago has already been mentioned. That—achieved between May, 1964, and December, 1968—is for me sufficient proof that the growth rate can be reduced in Latin American populations and that such success is proportional to the intensity of effort devoted to it.

NOTES TO CHAPTER 5

1. C. Miró, "Demografía y salud," *Cuadernos Médico Sociales,* V, Nos. 2 y 3 (1964).
2. C. Miró, "La población de la América Latina en el Siglo XX" (paper presented to the Primera Asamblea Panamericana de Población, Cali, Colombia, August, 1965).

3. B.R. Sen, *Alimentos, población, progreso* (Rome: FAO, 1915).
4. CEPAL, "El desarrollo agrícola de América Latina" (document prepared jointly with FAO for 1969).
5. H. Thomas, "Orientation and Goal of the Harvard Center for Population Studies," *Harvard Alumni Bulletin,* 22, No.1 (1965).
6. "Declaration on Population: The World Leaders Statement," *Studies in Family Planning,* No. 26 (1968).
7. K. Davis, "Population Policy: Will Current Programs Succeed?" *Science,* 158, No. 3802.

Chapter Six

The World Bank Perspective on Population Growth*

Robert S. McNamara

I

I want to discuss with you this afternoon a problem that arose out of that recent past; that already plagues man in the present; and that will diminish, if not destroy, much of his future—should he fail to face up to it, and solve it.

It is, by half a dozen criteria, the most delicate and difficult issue of our era—perhaps of any era in history. It is overlaid with emotion. It is controversial. It is subtle. Above all, it is immeasurably complex.

It is the tangled problem of excessive population growth.

It is not merely a problem, it is a paradox.

It is at one and the same time an issue that is intimately private—and yet inescapably public.

It is an issue characterized by reticence and circumspection—and yet in desperate need of realism and candor.

It is an issue intolerant of government pressure—and yet endangered by government procrastination.

It is an issue, finally, that is so hypersensitive—giving rise to such diverse opinion—that there is an understandable tendency simply to avoid argument, turn one's attention to less complicated matters, and hope that the problem will somehow disappear.

What may disappear is the opportunity to find a solution that is rational and humane.

If we wait too long, that option will be overtaken by events.

*This chapter is from "Address to the University of Notre Dame," May 1, 1969, by Robert S. McNamara, President of the World Bank Group, and is reprinted in its entirety, with the exception of the first two paragraphs, by permission of the International Bank for Reconstruction and Development.

We cannot afford that. For if there is anything certain about the population explosion, it is that if it is not dealt with reasonably, it will in fact explode: explode in suffering, explode in violence, explode in inhumanity.

All of us are, of course, concerned about this.

You, here at Notre Dame, have been giving constructive attention to this concern for several years. And yet it may seem strange that I should speak at a center of Catholic thought on this awkward issue which might so conveniently be ignored, or left to demographers to argue.

I have chosen to discuss the problem because my responsibilities as President of the World Bank compel me to be candid about the blunt facts affecting the prospects for global development.

The bluntest fact of all is that the need for development is desperate.

One-third of mankind today lives in an environment of relative abundance.

But two-thirds of mankind—more than two billion individuals—remain entrapped in a cruel web of circumstances that severely limits their right to the necessities of life. They have not yet been able to achieve the transition to self-sustaining economic growth. They are caught in the grip of hunger and malnutrition; high illiteracy; inadequate education; shrinking opportunity; and corrosive poverty.

The gap between the rich and poor nations is no longer merely a gap. It is a chasm. On one side are nations of the West that enjoy per capita incomes in the $3,000 range. On the other are nations in Asia and Africa that struggle to survive on per capita incomes of less than $100.

What is important to understand is that this is not a static situation. The misery of the underdeveloped world is today a dynamic misery, continuously broadened and deepened by a population growth that is totally unprecedented in history.

This is why the problem of population is an inseparable part of the larger, overall problem of development.

There are some who speak as if simply having fewer people in the world is some sort of intrinsic value in and of itself. Clearly, it is not.

But when human life is degraded by the plague of poverty, and that poverty is transmitted to future generations by too rapid a growth in population, then one with responsibilities in the field of development has no alternative but to deal with that issue.

To put it simply: the greatest single obstacle to the economic and social advancement of the majority of the peoples in the underdeveloped world is rampant population growth.

Having said that, let me make one point unmistakably clear: the solution of the population problem is in no way a substitute for the more traditional forms of developmental assistance: aid for economic infrastructure; aid for agriculture; aid for industrialization; aid for education; aid for technological advance.

The underdeveloped world needs investment capital for a whole gamut of productive projects. But nothing would be more unwise than to allow these projects to fail because they are finally overwhelmed by a tidal wave of population.

Surely, then, it is appropriate that we should attempt to unravel the complexities that so confuse this critical issue.

II

One can begin with the stark demographic dimensions. The dynamics are deceivingly simple. Population increase is simply the excess of births over deaths. For most of man's history the two have been in relative equilibrium. Only in the last century have they become seriously unbalanced.

Though the figures are well known, they are worth repeating—if for no other reason than to forestall the familiarity with unpleasant facts from cloaking itself with complacency. It required sixteen hundred years to double the world population of 250 million, as it stood in the first century A.D. Today, the more than three billion on earth will double in 35 years time, and the world's population will then be increasing at the rate of an additional billion every eight years.

To project the totals beyond the year 2000 becomes so demanding on the imagination as to make the statistics almost incomprehensible.

A child born today, living on into his seventies, would know a world of 15 billion. His grandson would share the planet with 60 billion.

In six and a half centuries from now—the same insignificant period of time separating us from the poet Dante—there would be one human being standing on every square foot of land on earth: a fantasy of horror that even the *Inferno* could not match.

Such projections are, of course, unreal. They will not come to pass because events will not permit them to come to pass.

Of that we can be certain.

What is not so certain is precisely what those events will be. They can only be: mass starvation; political chaos; or population planning.

Whatever may happen after the year 2000, what is occurring right now is enough to jolt one into action.

India, for example, is adding a million people a month to its population—and this in spite of the oldest family-planning program in Southern Asia.

The Philippines currently has a population of 37 million. There is no authorized government family-planning program. At the present rate of growth, these limited islands—in a brief 35 years—would have to support over one hundred million human beings.

The average population growth of the world at large is 2 percent. Many underdeveloped countries are burdened with a rate of 3.5 percent or more. A population growing at 1 percent doubles itself in 70 years; at 2 percent it doubles in 35 years; at 3.5 percent, it doubles in only 20 years.

Now, if we are to reject mass starvation and political chaos as solutions to this explosive situation, then there are clearly only three conceivable ways in which a nation can deliberately plan to diminish its rate of population growth: to increase the death rate; to step up the migration rate; or to reduce the birth rate.

No one is in favor of the first choice. On the contrary, under the impact of public health programs, death rates are falling throughout the underdeveloped areas. Even simple medical improvements—better sanitation, malaria suppression, widespread vaccination—bring on a rapid and welcome decline in mortality. The low-level death rates which Europe required a century and a half to achieve are now being accomplished in the emerging areas in a fifth of that time.

The second choice is wholly inadequate. Increased migration, on any scale significant enough to be decisive, is simply not practical. Countries concerned about their own future crowding are understandably disinclined to add to it by accepting more than a limited number of foreigners. But the more important point is that the continually expanding increment, on a global basis, is already so massive that migration as a solution to population pressure is manifestly unrealistic. We can put a man on the moon. But we cannot migrate by the millions off our own planet.

That leaves the third choice: a humane and rational reduction of the birth rate.

Is it feasible? It is.
Is it simple? It is not.
Is it necessary? Without question.

It is necessary because the consequences of continuing the present population growth rates are unacceptable.

III

Let us examine those consequences.

One cannot sense the inner significance of the cold, remote, impersonal demographic data by merely tracing a line upward on a graph, or by scanning the print-out from a computer.

The consequences of rapid population growth—piled on top of an already oppressive poverty—must be grasped in all their concrete, painful reality.

The first consequence can be seen in the gaunt faces of hungry men.

One half of humanity is hungering at this very moment. There is less food per person on the planet today than there was 30 years ago in the midst of a worldwide depression.

Thousands of human beings will die today—as they die every day—of that hunger. They will either simply starve to death, or they will die because their diet is so inadequate that it cannot protect them from some easily preventable disease.

Most of those thousands of individuals—individuals whose intrinsic right to a decent life is as great as yours or mine—are children. They are not mere statistics. They are human beings. And they are dying; now; at this very moment; while we are speaking.

They are not your children. Or my children. But they are someone's children. And they are dying needlessly.

And yet thousands who die are perhaps the more fortunate ones. For millions of other children, suffering the same malnutrition, do not die. They live languidly on—stunted in their bodies, and crippled in their minds.

The human brain reaches 90 percent of its normal structural development in the first four years of life. We now know that during that critical period of growth, the brain is highly vulnerable to nutritional deficiencies: deficiencies that can cause as much as 25 percent impairment of normal mental ability. Even a deterioration of 10 percent is sufficient to cause a serious handicap to productive life.

This is irreversible brain damage.

What is particularly tragic in all of this is that when such mentally deprived children reach adulthood, they are likely to repeat the whole depressing sequence in their own families. They perpetuate mental deficiency, not through genetic inheritance; but simply because as parents they are ill-equipped mentally to understand, and hence to avoid the very nutritional deprivations in their own children that they themselves suffered.

Thus hunger and malnutrition forge a chain of conditions that only spiral the total human performance dismally downward. Alertness, vitality, energy, the ability to learn, the desire to succeed, the will to exert an effort—all these inestimable human qualities drain away.

How many children today are caught up in this crisis? How many of them subsist at levels of hunger and malnutrition that risk their being irreversibly mentally retarded for the rest of their lives? Some three hundred million.

But the population explosion's corrosive effects on the quality of life do not end with hunger. They range through the whole spectrum of human deprivation. With entire national populations, already caught up in the dilemmas of development, now doubling in as short a time as 20 years, there is a chronic insufficiency of virtually every necessity.

Current birth rates throughout the emerging world are seriously crippling developmental efforts. It is imperative to understand why. The intractable reason is that these governments must divert an inordinately high proportion of their limited national savings away from productive investment simply in order to maintain the current low level of existence.

Each additional child brought into the world must not only be fed, but clothed, housed, medically cared for, and supported by at least minimal educational services. All of this requires new capital—new capital that cannot be invested in other desperately needed sectors of the economy. For approximately the first 15 years of their lives, children cannot contribute economically to the nation: simply because they are young they are consumers rather than producers.

If the number of children in the total population—as a result of high birth rates—is very large, a nation is under the compelling necessity to expend ever greater resources simply to keep its people from slipping beneath minimum subsistence levels. A treadmill economy tends to emerge in which the total national effort will exhaust itself in running faster and faster merely to stand still.

More and more classrooms must be built; more and more teachers must be provided; more and more vocational training facilities must be established. But despite all this effort both the quantity and quality of education will inevitably decline. It simply cannot keep pace with the mounting waves of children. Thus, one of the prime movers of all human development—education—is sacrificed.

Further, as ill-educated, perhaps wholly illiterate, children reach the age when they ought to become producers in the economy, they are engulfed by the hopelessness of underemployment. In many of the world's shanty towns 50 to 60 percent of the adolescents are out of work.

Not only are these youngsters unequipped for the jobs that might have been available, but the total number of meaningful jobs itself tends to decline in proportion to the population simply because the government has been unable to invest adequately in job-producing enterprises. The capital that ought to have been invested was simply not available. It was dissipated by the ever rising tide of additional children.

This, then, is the cruel and self-perpetuating dilemma that governments face in underdeveloped countries overburdened for long periods with high birth rates.

Their plans for progress evaporate into massive efforts merely to maintain the status quo.

But what is true at the national level is repeated with even greater poignancy on the personal family level. Millions of individual families wish to avoid unwanted pregnancies.

And when these families cannot find legal and compassionate assistance in this matter, they often turn to desperate and illegal measures.

Statistics suggest that abortion is one of the world's commonly chosen methods to limit fertility—despite the fact that in most societies it is ethically offensive, illegal, expensive, and medically hazardous.

In five countries of western Europe, it is estimated that there are as many illegal abortions as live births.

In India, the estimate is that each month a quarter of a million women undergo illegal abortion.

In Latin America, illegal abortion rates are among the highest in the world. In one country, they are said to total three times the live birth rate; in another, to be the cause of two out of every five deaths of pregnant women. Further, there are indications that the illegal abortion rate in Latin America is increasing, and that multiple illegal abortions among mothers are becoming common.

The tragic truth is that illegal abortion is endemic in many parts of the world. And it is particularly prevalent in those areas where there is no adequate, organized family-planning assistance.

The conclusion is clear: where the public authorities will not assist parents to avoid unwanted births, the parents will often take matters into their own hands—at whatever cost to conscience or health.

IV

Now I have noted that this entire question of population planning is incredibly complex. There are, of course, certain precise and painful moral dilemmas. But quite apart from these, there is a vague and murky mythology that befogs the issue. Not only does this collection of myths obscure the essentials of the problem, but worse still, it builds barriers to constructive action.

I should like to turn now to that mythology, and examine some of its irrational premises.

There is, to begin with, the generalized assumption that somehow "more people means more wealth." As with all fallacies, there is a deceptive substratum of plausibility to the thesis. With the earlier rise of nationalism in the West—and the more recent emergence of newly independent countries in Asia and Africa—rapid population growth has often been regarded as a symbol of national vigor. It provided, so it was believed, the foundations of a more powerful military establishment; an economically advantageous internal market; a pool of cheap labor; and, in general, a prestigious political place in the sun.

But in the underdeveloped world, nearly every one of these assumptions is false. Because rapid population growth tends seriously to retard growth in per capita income, the developing nation soon discovers that its economic vigor is diminished rather than enhanced by the phenomenon of high fertility. The hoped-for internal market becomes a mere mass of discontented indigents, without purchasing power but with all the frustrations of potential consumers whose expectations cannot be met.

"Cheap labor" in such countries turns out not to be cheap at all. For sound economic growth requires technological improvements, and these in turn demand higher levels of training than the strained government resources can supply. Though individual workers may be paid lower salaries than their counterparts abroad, their efficiency and productiveness are so low that the nation's goods are often priced out of the competitive export market. The "cheap" labor turns out to be excessively expensive labor.

Even the argument of expanding the population in order to provide a powerful military force is suspect—not merely because the expansion of one nation's forces will, in time, lead to a reactive expansion of its neighbors' forces, but also because modern defense forces require an increasing ratio of educated recruits rather than mere masses of illiterate troops.

As for political prestige, nations caught in the catastrophe of an uncontrolled population growth do not enhance their position in the family of nations. On the contrary, they find it slipping away as their once optimistic plans for progress turn inevitably to the politics of confrontation and extremism.

Akin to the myth that "more people means more wealth" is the notion that countries with large tracts of uninhabited open land have no need to worry about birth rates, since there is ample room for expansion.

The argument is as shallow as it is misleading. For the patent fact is that mere open land does not, in and of itself, support a high rate of population growth. Such open land—if it is to become the home of large numbers of people—must be provided with a whole panoply of heavy government investments: investments in roads, housing, sanitation, agricultural and industrial development.

The sound economic argument is quite the other way round. What such raw space requires first is not surplus people, but surplus funds for investment. And it is precisely surplus people in a developing economy that make the accumulation of surplus funds so incredibly difficult.

What is equally overlooked is that a rational restraint on fertility rates in an emerging country never implies an absolute reduction of the total population. It simply hopes for a more reasonable balance between birth and death rates. And since death rates in the future are certain to drop with continued advances in medicine—and in highly underdeveloped countries the drop in the death rate is characteristically precipitous—there are no grounds whatever for fearing that a nation's population, under the influence of family planning, will dangerously ebb away. The danger is quite the opposite: that even with family planning—should it be inadequately utilized—the population will proliferate in the future to self-defeating levels.

A still more prevalent myth is the misapprehension that official programs of family planning in a developing country are wholly unnecessary since the very process of development itself automatically leads to lowered birth rates. The experience of Europe is cited as persuasive proof of this theory.

But the proof is no proof at all, for the theory is hopelessly irrelevant to today's conditions in the underdeveloped world. There are no comparable circumstances between what happened in Europe's early period of modernization, and what is happening in the emerging world today.

Aside from a lapse of logic which fails to grasp that the current population growth in these areas inhibits the very economic development which is supposed to curb that growth, the historical fact is that conditions in Europe during its initial developmental period were far more favorable to lower rates of population growth. The birth rates were much lower than they are in the underdeveloped world today, the death rates had not yet drastically fallen, and by the time public health measures had accomplished that, the infrastructure of industrialization was already in place.

Further, in nineteenth century Europe, unlike in the developing countries today, marriages were entered into later, and the level of literacy—always an important factor affecting population growth—was considerably higher.

Even in spite of all these advantages, it required some 70 years for Europe to reduce its birth rates to present levels. Today the average birth rate for developing countries is 40 to 45 per 1000 of population. To get this rate down to the 17 to 20 per 1000 that is common in contemporary Europe would require a reduction in the developing world of some 50 million births a year. To suppose that economic advancement by itself—without the assistance of well organized family planning—could accomplish this in any feasible timeframe of the future is wholly naive.

Indeed, even with family planning, no such promising results are feasible in less than two or three decades. What is feasible—indeed what is imperative—is the establishment of family planning on a scale that will stave off total economic and political disintegration in those countries where social progress is being seriously limited by the glut of unwanted births.

No government can, of course, ultimately succeed in convincing its own population to undertake family planning, if parents themselves do not really want it.

But the almost universal fact is that parents do want it. They often want it far more than their own political leaders comprehend.

People—particularly poor, ill-educated people—may not understand the techniques of family planning. Most of them have only the most tenuous understanding of human biology. Often their limited comprehension is tragically confused by gross misinformation.

But the notion that family-planning programs are sinister, coercive plots to force poor people into something they really do not want, is absurd.

The pervasive prevalence of voluntary illegal abortion should be enough to dispel that fiction.

The poor do not always know how to limit their families in less drastic and dangerous ways, but there is overwhelming evidence that they would like to know how.

Another serious misunderstanding is the fear that family planning in the developing world would inevitably lead to a breakdown of familial moral fiber—and that it would encourage parents to limit the number of their children for essentially frivolous and selfish reasons: that it would trade the responsibility of having a large number of children for the opportunity of acquiring the needless gadgetry of an advancing consumer economy.

But one stroll through the slums of any major city in the developing world is enough to dispel that concept. If anything is threatening the fiber of family life, it is the degrading conditions of subsistence survival that one finds in these sprawling camps of packing crates and scrap metal. Children on the streets instead of in non-existent classrooms. Broken men—their pride shattered—without work. Despondent mothers—often unmarried—unable to cope with exhaustion because of annual pregnancies. And all of this in a frustrating environment of misery and hunger and hopelessness. These are not the conditions that promote an ethically fibered family life.

Family planning is not designed to destroy families. On the contrary, it is designed to save them.

All of us accept the principle that in a free society, the parents themselves must ultimately decide the size of their own family. We would regard it as an intolerable invasion of the family's rights for the State to use coercive measures to implement population policy. We can preserve that right best by assisting families to understand how they can make that decision for themselves.

The fact is that millions of children are born without their parents desiring that it happen. Hence, a free, rational choice for an additional child is not made in these cases. If we are to keep the right of decision in the hands of the family—where it clearly belongs—then we must give the family the knowledge and assistance it requires to exercise that right.

Nor need anyone be deterred from appropriate action by the pernicious, if pervasive, myth that the white Western world's assistance in family-planning efforts among the non-white nations of the developing areas is a surreptitious plot to keep the whites in a racial ascendancy. The myth is absurd on purely demographic grounds, as well as on many others. Non-white peoples on the planet massively outnumber whites. They always have and always will. No conceivable degree of family planning could possibly alter that mathematical fact.

But a more relevant answer is that if the white world actually did desire to plot against the non-white nations, one of the most effective ways possible to do so would be for the whites to deny these nations any assistance whatever in family planning. For the progressive future of the non-white world is directly related to their indigenous economic development—and that, in turn, as we have seen, is dependent upon their being able to bring birth rates down to a level that will allow a significant increase in per capita income.

V

There is one more myth that obstructs the road to action. It is the belief that the time for decisive action is past, and that sweeping famine is inevitable.

The distinguished British scientist and novelist, C.P. Snow, has recently noted that it is the view of men of sober judgment that "many millions of people in the poor countries are going to starve to death before our eyes."

"We shall see them doing so," he adds, "upon our television sets."

He stresses that when the collision between food and population takes place "at best, this will mean local famines to begin with. At worst, the local famines will spread into a sea of hunger. The usual date predicted for the beginning of the local famines is 1975-80."

In summing up his own view, he suggests that "The major catastrophe will happen before the end of the century. We shall, in the rich countries, be surrounded by a sea of famine, involving hundreds of millions of human beings."

"The increase of population," he predicts, "all over the rich world may get a little less. In the poor world it won't, except in one or two pockets. Despite local successes, as in India, the food-population collision will duly occur. The attempts to prevent it, or meliorate it, will be too feeble. Famine will take charge in many countries. It may become, by the end of the period, endemic famine. There will be suffering and desperation on a scale as yet unknown."

Now, though Lord Snow is a brilliant and perceptive man of good will, I simply do not believe that one need feel quite so near despair—even in the face of a situation as ominous as this one.

Wholesale famine is not inevitable. I am convinced that there is time to reverse the situation, if we will but use it. Only barely sufficient time. But time nevertheless.

It is the time which has been given us by those who have created the revolution in agricultural technology: a revolution based on new seeds, hybrid strains, fertilizers, and the intensified use of natural resources.

It is a revolution which already has increased the yields of food grains by more than 100 percent in parts of Southeast Asia, and which promises to boost yields by one-half ton per acre throughout Asia. It is a revolution which has expanded the number of acres sown with the new seeds from 200 in 1965 to 20,000,000 in 1968—and an estimated 34,000,000 in 1969—but which has yet to touch more than a small percentage of the rice and wheat-producing acreage of the world.

If we will but speed the spread of this agricultural revolution—by adequate and properly administered technical and financial assistance to the developing countries—we can expect that for the next two decades the world's food supply will grow at a faster rate than its population.

The predicted spectre of famine can be averted.

It will take immense energy and organizing skill, and significant infusions of new capital investment—but it is possible to stave off disaster.

What is required to accomplish this is not so much a psychologically comforting optimism, as an energetic, creative realism.

I believe enough of that realism exists among men of good will—both in the developed and in the emerging world—to do the job.

This is the fundamental reason I do not share Lord Snow's degree of discouragement.

There is no point whatever in being naively over-optimistic about a situation as full of peril as the population problem.

But I am confident that application of the new technology will dramatically expand the rate of agricultural growth and will buy two decades of time—admittedly the barest minimum of time—required to cope with the population explosion, and reduce it manageable proportions.

VI

How can this best be done?

To begin with, the developed nations must give every measure of support they possibly can to those countries which have already established family-planning programs. Many have. The governments of India, Pakistan, Korea, Taiwan, Hong Kong, and Singapore have established both policies and specific targets for reducing population growth rates and have shown some measurable progress.

Ceylon, Malaysia, Turkey, Tunisia, the United Arab Republic, Morocco, Kenya, Mauritius, Chile, Honduras, Barbados, and Jamaica are giving government support to family-planning programs, but need substantial technical or financial assistance before any significant reduction in birth rates can occur.

Some 20 other governments are considering family-planning programs.

In other countries, where governments are only dimly aware of the dangers of the population problem—but would like, nevertheless, to ponder the matter—the developed nations can quietly assist by helping with the demographic and social studies that will reveal the facts and thus point up the urgency of the issue, and the disadvantages of delay.

It is essential, of course, to recognize the right of a given country to handle its population problem in its own way. But handle it, it must.

The developed nations can point out the demographic facts; can explain the economic realities; can warn of the consequences of procrastination. They can—and should—inform. They should not—and cannot—pressure.

Technologically advanced countries can make one of their greatest contributions by initiating a new order of intensity in research into reproductive biology. They have starved their research facilities of funds in this field. The result is that we are still only on the threshold of understanding the complexities of conception, and therefore only at the outer edge of the necessary knowledge to help make family planning in the developing countries beneficial on a meaningful scale.

Annual worldwide expenditures for research in reproductive biology now total roughly 50 million dollars. The hardheaded estimate is that the sum should treble to 150 million dollars annually—for the next ten years—if we are to develop the knowledge necessary for the most effective and acceptable kinds of family planning.

Our parsimony in this matter in the United States is illustrated by the discouraging fact that out of a total budget of nearly one billion dollars, the National Institutes of Health this year are spending less than ten million dollars for research in population-related phenomena. Hundreds of millions of dollars for death control. Scarcely 1 percent of that amount for fertility control.

And research efforts should range far beyond biology.

Demography, as a fully developed science, remains in its infancy. It is likely that fewer than half the world's births are even registered. And while the crude estimates of birth rates almost inevitably turn out to be too low, it is essential that more precise data be developed in those areas where the population problem is the most acute.

Similarly, there is a pressing need for far more research in the sociocultural aspects of family planning. There is manifestly a great deal more to population planning than merely birth control. Attitudes, motivation, preferences differ from country to country, and this essential research can clearly best be conducted locally. The developed nations should be generous in their financial support for such studies and surveys.

Above all else, there is a need to develop a realistic sense of urgency in all countries over the population problem.

Programs are beginning to show progress in limited areas. But no reduction in birth rates has yet been achieved anywhere in the underdeveloped areas which can significantly affect overall world population totals.

This means that family planning is going to have to be undertaken on a humane but massive scale. Other massive efforts in our century—for example, in the field of public health—have been mounted and have been successful. And granted all the difficulties, there is no insuperable reason this one cannot be.

The threat of unmanageable population pressures is very much like the threat of nuclear war.

Both threats are undervalued. Both threats are misunderstood.

Both threats can—and will—have catastrophic consequences unless they are dealt with rapidly and rationally.

The threat of violence is interwined with the threat of undue population growth. It is clear that population pressures in the underdeveloped societies can lead to economic tensions, and political turbulence: stresses in the body politic which in the end can bring on conflicts among nations.

Such violence must not be allowed to happen.

You and I—and all of us—share the responsibility of taking those actions necessary to assure that it will not happen.

There is no point in despair.

There is every point simply in getting busy with the job. That is surely what God gave us our reason and our will for: to get on with the tasks which must be done.

I do not have to convince you of that here at Notre Dame.

You, and the Roman Catholic Church at large, are completely dedicated to the goal of development. One has only to read the Second Vatican Council's *Pastoral Constitution on the Church in the Modern World,* and Pope Paul's *Populorum Progressio* to understand that. Both these impressive documents call for a solution to the population problem as it relates to development. Such controversy as remains in this matter is merely about the means, not at all about the end.

I am confident that you in this university, and those in the Catholic community that reaches out around the globe, and the fatherly and compassionate Pontiff who stands at your helm—as well as men everywhere of whatever religious allegiance—I am confident that all of us are dedicated to that end however much we may disagree on the specifics of the means.

The end desired by the Church—and by all men of good will—is the enhancement of human dignity. That, after all, is what development is all about.

And human dignity is severely threatened by the population explosion—more severely, more completely, more threatened than it has been by any catastrophe the world has yet endured.

There is time—just barely time—to escape that threat.

We can, and we must, act.

What we must comprehend is this: the population problem will be solved one way or the other. Our only fundamental option is whether it is to be solved rationally and humanely—or irrationally and inhumanely. Are we to solve it by famine? Are we to solve it by riot, by insurrection, by the violence that desperately starving men can be driven to? Are we to solve it by wars of expansion and aggression? Or are we to solve it rationally, humanely—in accord with man's dignity?

There is so little time left to make the decision. To make no decision would be to make the worst decision of all. For to ignore this problem is only to make certain that nature will take catastrophic revenge on our indecisiveness.

Providence has placed you and me—and all of us—at the fulcrum-point in history where a rational, responsible, moral solution to the population problem must be found.

You and I—and all of us—share the responsibility, to find and apply that solution.

If we shirk that responsibility, we will have committed the crime.

But it will be those who come after us who will pay the undeserved . . . and the unspeakable . . . penalties.

Chapter Seven

On the Regulation of Birth: Humane Vitae*

Pope Paul VI

1. The most serious duty of transmitting human life, for which married persons are the free and responsible collaborators of God the Creator, has always been a source of great joys to them, even if sometimes accompanied by not a few difficulties and by distress.

At all times the fulfillment of this duty has posed grave problems to the conscience of married persons, but, with the recent evolution of society, changes have taken place that give rise to new questions which the Church could not ignore, having to do with a matter which so closely touches upon the life and happiness of men.

I. NEW ASPECTS OF THE PROBLEM AND COMPETENCY OF THE MAGISTERIUM

2. The changes which have taken place are in fact noteworthy and of varied kinds. In the first place, there is the rapid demographic development. Fear is shown by many that world population is growing more rapidly than the available resources, with growing distress to many families and developing countries, so that the temptation for authorities to counter this danger with radical measures is great. Moreover, working and lodging conditions, as well as increased exigencies both in the economic field and in that of education, often make the proper education of a larger number of children difficult today. A change is also seen both in the manner of considering the person of woman and her place in society, and in the value to be attributed to conjugal love in marriage,

*This chapter presents the English translation of the Encyclical Letter, *Humanae Vitae,* issued by Pope Paul VI on July 25, 1968. It is reprinted with the permission of the United States Catholic Conference which issued this translation. Footnotes in the original have been eliminated along with minor sub-headings.

and also in the appreciation to be made of the meaning of conjugal acts in relation to that love.

Finally and above all, man has made stupendous progress in the domination and rational organization of the forces of nature, such that he tends to extend this domination to his own total being: to the body, to physical life, to social life and even to the laws which regulate the transmission of life.

3. This new state of things gives rise to new questions. Granted the conditions of life today, and granted the meaning which conjugal relations have with respect to the harmony between husband and wife and to their mutual fidelity, would not a revision of the ethical norms, in force up to now, seem to be advisable, especially when it is considered that they cannot be observed without sacrifices, sometimes heroic sacrifices?

And again: by extending to this field the application of the so-called "principle of totality," could it not be admitted that the intention of a less abundant but more rationalized fecundity might transform a materially sterilizing intervention into a licit and wise control of birth? Could it not be admitted, that is, that the finality of procreation pertains to the ensemble of conjugal life, rather than to its single acts? It is also asked whether, in view of the increased sense of responsibility of modern man, the moment has not come for him to entrust to his reason and his will, rather than to the biological rhythms of his organism, the task of regulating birth.

4. Such questions required from the teaching authority of the Church a new and deeper reflection upon the principles of the moral teaching on marriage: a teaching founded on the natural law, illuminated and enriched by divine revelation.

No believer will wish to deny that the teaching authority of the Church is competent to interpret even the natural moral law. It is, in fact, indisputable, as our predecessors have many times declared, that Jesus Christ, when communicating to Peter and to the Apostles His divine authority and sending them to teach all nations His commandments, constituted them as guardians and authentic interpreters of all the moral law, which is also an expression of the will of God, the faithful fulfillment of which is equally necessary for salvation.

Conformably to this mission of hers, the Church has always provided—and even more amply in recent times—a coherent teaching concerning both the nature of marriage and the correct use of conjugal rights and the duties of husband and wife.

5. The consciousness of that same mission induced us to confirm and enlarge the study commission which our predecessor Pope John XXIII of happy memory had instituted in March, 1963. That commission which included, besides several experts in the various pertinent disciplines, also married couples, had as its scope the gathering of opinions on the new questions regarding

conjugal life, and in particular on the regulation of births, and of furnishing opportune elements of information so that the magisterium could give an adequate reply to the expectation not only of the faithful, but also of world opinion.

The work of these experts, as well as the successive judgments and counsels spontaneously forwarded by or expressly requested from a good number of our brothers in the episcopate, have permitted us to measure more exactly all the aspects of this complex matter. Hence with all our heart we express to each of them our lively gratitude.

6. The conclusions at which the commission arrived could not, nevertheless, be considered by us as definitive, nor dispense us from a personal examination of this serious question; and this also because, within the commission itself, no full concordance of judgments concerning the moral norms to be proposed had been reached, and above all because certain criteria of solutions had emerged which departed from the moral teaching on marriage proposed with constant firmness by the teaching authority of the Church.

Therefore, having attentively sifted the documentation laid before us, after mature reflection and assiduous prayers, we now intend, by virtue of the mandate entrusted to us by Christ, to give our reply to these grave questions.

II. DOCTRINAL PRINCIPLES

7. The problem of birth, like every other problem regarding human life, is to be considered, beyond partial perspectives—whether of the biological or psychological, demographic or sociological orders—in the light of an integral vision of man and of his vocation, not only his natural and earthly, but also his supernatural and eternal vocation. And since, in the attempt to justify artificial methods of birth control, many have appealed to the demands both of conjugal love and of "responsible parenthood," it is good to state very precisely the true concept of these two great realities of married life, referring principally to what was recently set forth in this regard, and in a highly authoritative form, by the Second Vatican Council in its pastoral constitution *Gaudium et Spes*.

8. Conjugal love reveals its true nature and nobility when it is considered in its supreme origin, God, who is love, "the Father, from whom every family in heaven and on earth is named."

Marriage is not, then, the effect of chance or the product of evolution of unconscious natural forces; it is the wise institution of the Creator to realize in mankind His design of love. By means of the reciprocal personal gift of self, proper and exclusive to them, husband and wife tend towards the communion of their beings in view of mutual personal perfection, to collaborate with God in the generation and education of new lives.

For baptized persons, moreover, marriage invests the dignity of a sacramental sign of grace, inasmuch as it represents the union of Christ and of the Church.

9. Under this light, there clearly appear the characteristic marks and demands of conjugal love, and it is of supreme importance to have an exact idea of these.

This love is first of all fully *human,* that is to say, of the senses and of the spirit at the same time. It is not, then, a simple transport of instinct and sentiment, but also, and principally, an act of the free will, intended to endure and to grow by means of the joys and sorrows of daily life, in such a way that husband and wife become one only heart and one only soul, and together attain their human perfection.

Then, this love is *total*, that is to say, it is a very special form of personal friendship, in which husband and wife generously share everything, without undue reservations or selfish calculations. Whoever truly loves his marriage partner loves not only for what he receives, but for the partner's self, rejoicing that he can enrich his partner with the gift of himself.

Again, this love is *faithful* and *exclusive* until death. Thus in fact do bride and groom conceive it to be on the day when they freely and in full awareness assume the duty of the marriage bond. A fidelity, this, which can sometimes be difficult, but is always possible, always noble and meritorious, as no one can deny. The example of so many married persons down through the centuries shows, not only that fidelity is according to the nature of marriage, but also that it is a source of profound and lasting happiness.

And finally this love is *fecund* for it is not exhausted by the communion between husband and wife, but is destined to continue, raising up new lives. "Marriage and conjugal love are by their nature ordained toward the begetting and educating of children. Children are really the supreme gift of marriage and contribute very substantially to the welfare of their parents."

10. Hence conjugal love requires in husband and wife an awareness of their mission of "responsible parenthood," which today is rightly much insisted upon, and which also must be exactly understood. Consequently it is to be considered under different aspects which are legitimate and connected with one another.

In relation to the biological processes, responsible parenthood means the knowledge and respect of their functions; human intellect discovers in the power of giving life biological laws which are part of the human person.

In relation to the tendencies of instinct or passion, responsible parenthood means that necessary dominion which reason and will must exercise over them.

In relation to physical, economic, psychological and social conditions, responsible parenthood is exercised, either by the deliberate and generous decision to raise a numerous family, or by the decision, made for grave motives and with due respect for the moral law, to avoid for the time being, or even for an indeterminate period, a new birth.

Responsible parenthood also and above all implies a more profound relationship to the objective moral order established by God, of which a right conscience is the faithful interpreter. The responsible exercise of parenthood implies, therefore, that husband and wife recognize fully their own duties towards God, towards themselves, towards the family and towards society, in a correct hierarchy of values.

In the task of transmitting life, therefore, they are not free to proceed completely at will, as if they could determine in a wholly autonomous way the honest path to follow; but they must conform their activity to the creative intention of God, expressed in the very nature of marriage and of its acts, and manifested by the constant teaching of the Church.

11. These acts, by which husband and wife are united in chaste intimacy, and by means of which human life is transmitted, are, as the Council recalled, "noble and worthy," and they do not cease to be lawful if, for causes independent of the will of husband and wife, they are foreseen to be infecund, since they always remain ordained towards expressing and consolidating their union. In fact, as experience bears witness, not every conjugal act is followed by a new life. God has wisely disposed natural laws and rhythms of fecundity which, of themselves, cause a separation in the succession of births. Nonetheless the Church, calling men back to the observance of the norms of the natural law, as interpreted by their constant doctrine, teaches that each and every marriage act (*quilibet matrimonii usus*) must remain open to the transmission of life.

12. That teaching, often set forth by the magisterium, is founded upon the inseparable connection, willed by God and unable to be broken by man on his own initiative, between the two meanings of the conjugal act: the unitive meaning and the procreative meaning. Indeed, by its intimate structure, the conjugal act, while most closely uniting husband and wife, capacitates them for the generation of new lives, according to laws inscribed in the very being of man and of woman. By safeguarding both these essential aspects, the unitive and the procreative, the conjugal act preserves in its fullness the sense of true mutual love and its ordination towards man's most high calling to parenthood. We believe that the men of our day are particularly capable of seizing the deeply reasonable and human character of this fundamental principle.

13. It is in fact justly observed that a conjugal act imposed upon one's partner without regard for his or her condition and lawful desires is not a true act of love, and therefore denies an exigency of right moral order in the relationships between husband and wife. Likewise, if they consider the matter, they must admit that an act of mutual love, which is detrimental to the faculty of propagating life, which God the Creator of all, has implanted in it according to special laws, is in contradiction to both the divine plan, according

to whose norm matrimony has been instituted, and the will of the Author of human life. To use this divine gift destroying, even if only partially, its meaning and its purpose is to contradict the nature both of man and of woman and of their most intimate relationship, and therefore it is to contradict also the plan of God and His will. On the other hand, to make use of the gift of conjugal love while respecting the laws of the generative process means to acknowledge oneself not to be the arbiter of the sources of human life, but rather the minister of the design established by the Creator. In fact, just as man does not have unlimited dominion over his body in general, so also, with particular reason, he has no such dominion over his generative faculties as such, because of their intrinsic ordination towards raising up life, of which God is the principle. "Human life is sacred," Pope John XXIII recalled; "from its very inception it reveals the creating hand of God."

14. In conformity with these landmarks in the human and Christian vision of marriage, we must once again declare that the direct interruption of the generative process already begun, and, above all, directly willed and procured abortion, even if for therapeutic reasons, are to be absolutely excluded as licit means of regulating birth.

Equally to be excluded, as the teaching authority of the Church has frequently declared, is direct sterilization, whether perpetual or temporary, whether of the man or of the woman. Similarly excluded is every action which, either in anticipation of the conjugal act, or in its accomplishment, or in the development of its natural consequences, proposes, whether as an end or as a means, to render procreation impossible.

To justify conjugal acts made intentionally infecund, one cannot invoke as valid reasons the lesser evil, or the fact that such acts would constitute a whole together with the fecund acts already performed or to follow later, and hence would share in one and the same moral goodness. In truth, if it is sometimes licit to tolerate a lesser evil in order to avoid a greater evil or to promote a greater good, it is not licit, even for the gravest reasons, to do evil so that good may follow therefrom; that is, to make into the object of a positive act of the will something which is intrinsically disorder, and hence unworthy of the human person, even when the intention is to safeguard or promote individual, family or social well-being. Consequently it is an error to think that a conjugal act which is deliberately made infecund and so is intrinsically dishonest could be made honest and right by the ensemble of a fecund conjugal life.

15. The Church, on the contrary, does not at all consider illicit the use of those therapeutic means truly necessary to cure diseases of the organism, even if an impediment to procreation, which may be foreseen, should result therefrom, provided such impediment is not, for whatever motive, directly willed.

16. To this teaching of the Church on conjugal morals, the objec-

tion is made today, as we observed earlier (no. 3), that it is the prerogative of the human intellect to dominate the energies offered by irrational nature and to orientate them towards an end comfortable to the good of man. Now, some may ask: in the present case, is it not reasonable in many circumstances to have recourse to artificial birth control if, thereby, we secure the harmony and peace of the family, and better conditions for the education of the children already born? To this question it is necessary to reply with clarity: the Church is the first to praise and recommend the intervention of intelligence in a function which so closely associates the rational creature with his Creator; but she affirms that this must be done with respect for the order established by God.

If, then, there are serious motives to space out births, which derive from the physical or psychological conditions of husband and wife, or from external conditions, the Church teaches that it is then licit to take into account the natural rhythms immanent in the generative functions, for the use of marriage in the infecund periods only, and in this way to regulate birth without offending the moral principles which have been recalled earlier.

The Church is coherent with herself when she considers recourse to the infecund periods to be licit, while at the same time condemning, as being always illicit, the use of means directly contrary to fecundation, even if such use is inspired by reasons which may appear honest and serious. In reality, there are essential differences between the two cases; in the former, the married couple make legitimate use of a natural disposition; in the latter, they impede the development of natural processes. It is true that, in the one and the other case, the married couple are concordant in the positive will of avoiding children for plausible reasons, seeking the certainty that offspring will not arrive; but it is also true that only in the former case are they able to renounce the use of marriage in the fecund periods when, for just motives, procreation is not desirable, while making use of it during infecund periods to manifest their affection and to safeguard their mutual fidelity. By so doing, they give proof of a truly and integrally honest love.

17. Upright men can even better convince themselves of the solid grounds on which the teaching of the Church in this field is based, if they care to reflect upon the consequences of methods of artificial birth control. Let them consider, first of all, how wide and easy a road would thus be opened up towards conjugal infidelity and the general lowering of morality. Not much experience is needed in order to know human weakness, and to understand that men—especially the young, who are so vulnerable on this point—have need of encouragement to be faithful to the moral law, so that they must not be offered some easy means of eluding its observance. It is also to be feared that the man, growing used to the employment of anti-conceptive practices, may finally lose respect for the woman and, no longer caring for her physical and psychological equilibrium, may come to the point of considering her as a mere

instrument of selfish enjoyment, and no longer as his respected and beloved companion.

Let it be considered also that a dangerous weapon would thus be placed in the hands of those public authorities who take no heed of moral exigencies. Who could blame a government for applying to the solution of the problems of the community those means acknowledged to be licit for married couples in the solution of a family problem? Who will stop rulers from favoring, from even imposing upon their peoples, if they were to consider it necessary, the method of contraception which they judge to be most efficacious? In such a way men, wishing to avoid individual, family, or social difficulties encountered in the observance of the divine law, would reach the point of placing at the mercy of the intervention of public authorities the most personal and most reserved sector of conjugal intimacy.

Consequently, if the mission of generating life is not to be exposed to the arbitrary will of men, one must necessarily recognize insurmountable limits to the possibility of man's domination over his own body and its functions; limits which no man, whether a private individual or one invested with authority, may licitly surpass. And such limits cannot be determined otherwise than by the respect due to the integrity of the human organism and its functions, according to the principles recalled earlier, and also according to the correct understanding of the "principle of totality" illustrated by our predecessor Pope Pius XII.

18. It can be foreseen that this teaching will perhaps not be easily received by all: Too numerous are those voices—amplified by the modern means of propaganda—which are contrary to the voice of the Church. To tell the truth, the Church is not surprised to be made, like her divine Founder, a "sign of contradiction", yet she does not because of this cease to proclaim with humble firmness the entire moral law, both natural and evangelical. Of such laws the Church was not the author, nor consequently can she be their arbiter; she is only their depositary and their interpreter, without ever being able to declare to be licit that which is not so by reason of its intimate and unchangeable opposition to the true good of man.

In defending conjugal morals in their integral wholeness, the Church knows that she contributes towards the establishment of a truly human civilization; she engages man not to abdicate from his own responsibility in order to rely on technical means; by that very fact she defends the dignity of man and wife. Faithful to both the teaching and the example of the Saviour, she shows herself to be the sincere and disinterested friend of men, whom she wishes to help, even during their earthly sojourn, "to share as sons in the life of the living God, the Father of all men."

III. PASTORAL DIRECTIVES

19. Our words would not be an adequate expression of the thought and solicitude of the Church, Mother and Teacher of all peoples, if, after having re-

called men to the observance and respect of the divine law regarding matrimony, we did not strenghten them in the path of honest regulation of birth, even amid the difficult conditions which today afflict families and peoples. The Church, in fact, cannot have a different conduct towards men than that of the Redeemer: She knows their weaknesses, has compassion on the crowd, receives sinners; but she cannot renounce the teaching of the law which is, in reality, that law proper to a human life restored to its original truth and conducted by the spirit of God.

20. The teaching of the Church on the regulation of birth, which promulgates the divine law, will easily appear to many to be difficult or even impossible of actuation. And indeed, like all great beneficent realities, it demands serious engagement and much effort, individual, family and social effort. More than that, it would not be practicable without the help of God, who upholds and strengthens the good will of men. Yet to anyone who reflects well, it cannot but be clear that such efforts ennoble man and are beneficial to the human community.

21. The honest practice of regulation of birth demands first of all that husband and wife acquire and possess solid convictions concerning the true values of life and of the family, and that they tend towards securing perfect self-mastery. To dominate instinct by means of one's reason and free will undoubtedly requires ascetical practices, so that the affective manifestations of conjugal life may observe the correct order, in particular with regard to the observance of periodic continence. Yet this discipline which is proper to the purity of married couples, far from harming conjugal love, rather confers on it a higher human value. It demands continual effort yet, thanks to its beneficent influence, husband and wife fully develop their personalities, being enriched with spiritual values. Such discipline bestows upon family life fruits of serenity and peace, and facilitates the solution of other problems; it favors attention for one's partner, helps both parties to drive out selfishness, the enemy of true love; and deepens their sense of responsibility. By its means, parents acquire the capacity of having a deeper and more efficacious influence in the education of their offspring; little children and youths grow up with a just appraisal of human values, and in the serene and harmonious development of their spiritual and sensitive faculties.

22. On this occasion, we wish to draw the attention of educators, and of all who perform duties of responsibility in regard to the common good of human society, to the need of creating an atmosphere favorable to education in chastity, that is, to the triumph of healthy liberty over license by means of respect for the moral order.

Everything in the modern media of social communications which leads to sense excitation and unbridled customs, as well as every form of pornography and licentious performances, must arouse the frank and unanimous reaction of all those who are solicitous for the progress of civilization and the defense of the common good of the human spirit. Vainly would one seek to justify such depravation with the pretext of artistic or scientific exigencies, or to deduce an argument from the freedom allowed in this sector by the public authorities.

23. To Rulers, who are those principally responsible for the common good, and who can do so much to safeguard moral customs, we say: Do not allow the morality of your peoples to be degraded; do not permit that by legal means practices contrary to the natural and divine law be introduced into that fundamental cell, the family. Quite other is the way in which public authorities can and must contribute to the solution of the demographic problem: namely, the way of a provident policy for the family, of a wise education of peoples in respect of moral law and the liberty of citizens.

We are well aware of the serious difficulties experienced by public authorities in this regard, especially in the developing countries. To their legitimate preoccupations we devoted our encyclical letter *Populorum Progressio*. But with our predecessor Pope John XXIII, we repeat: no solution to these difficulties is acceptable "which does violence to man's essential dignity" and is based only on an utterly materialistic conception of man himself and of his life. The only possible solution to this question is one which envisages the social and economic progress both of individuals and of the whole of human society, and which respects and promotes true human values. Neither can one, without grave injustice, consider divine providence to be responsible for what depends, instead, on a lack of wisdom in government, on an insufficient sense of social justice, on selfish monopolization, or again on blameworthy indolence in confronting the efforts and the sacrifices necessary to ensure the raising of living standards of a people and of all its sons.

May all responsible public authorities—as some are already doing so laudably—generously revive their efforts. And may mutual aid between all the members of the great human family never cease to grow: This is an almost limitless field which thus opens up to the activity of the great international organizations.

24. We wish now to express our encouragement to men of science, who "can considerably advance the welfare of marriage and the family, along with peace of conscience, if by pooling their efforts they labor to explain more thoroughly the various conditions favoring a proper regulation of births." It is particularly desirable that, according to the wish already expressed by Pope Pius XII, medical science succeed in providing a sufficiently secure basis for a regulation of birth, founded on the observance of natural rhythms. In this way, scientists and especially Catholic scientists will contribute to demonstrate in actual fact that, as the Church teaches, "a true contradiction cannot exist between the divine laws pertaining to the transmission of life and those pertaining to the fostering of authentic conjugal love."

25. And now our words more directly address our own children, particularly those whom God calls to serve Him in marriage. The Church, while

teaching imprescriptible demands of the divine law, announces the tidings of salvation, and by means of the sacraments opens up the paths of grace, which makes man a new creature, capable of corresponding with love and true freedom to the design of his Creator and Saviour, and of finding the yoke of Christ to be sweet.

Christian married couples, then, docile to her voice, must remember that their Christian vocation, which began at baptism, is further specified and reinforced by the sacrament of matrimony. By it husband and wife are strengthened and as it were consecrated for the faithful accomplishment of their proper duties, for the carrying out of their proper vocation even to perfection, and the Christian witness which is proper to them before the whole world. To them the Lord entrusts the task of making visible to men the holiness and sweetness of the law which unites the mutual love of husband and wife with their cooperation with the love of God the author of human life.

We do not at all intend to hide the sometimes serious difficulties inherent in the life of Christian married persons; for them as for everyone else, "the gate is narrow and the way is hard, that leads to life." But the hope of that life must illuminate their way, as with courage they strive to live with wisdom, justice and piety in this present time, knowing that the figure of this world passes away.

Let married couples, then, face up to the efforts needed, supported by the faith and hope which "do not disappoint . . . because God's love has been poured into our hearts through the Holy Spirit, who has been given to us"; let them implore divine assistance by persevering prayer; above all, let them draw from the source of grace and charity in the Eucharist. And if sin should still keep its hold over them, let them not be discouraged, but rather have recourse with humble perseverance to the mercy of God, which is poured forth in the sacrament of Penance. In this way they will be enabled to achieve the fullness of conjugal life described by the Apostle: "husbands, love your wives, as Christ loved the Church . . . husbands should love their wives as their own bodies. He who loves his wife loves himself. For no man ever hates his own flesh, but nourishes and cherishes it, as Christ does the Church . . . this is a great mystery, and I mean in reference to Christ and the Church. However, let each one of you love his wife as himself, and let the wife see that she respects her husband."

26. Among the fruits which ripen forth from a generous effort of fidelity to the divine law, one of the most precious is that married couples themselves not infrequently feel the desire to communicate their experience to others. Thus there comes to be included in the vast pattern of the vocation of the laity a new and most noteworthy form of the apostolate of like to like; it is married couples themselves who become apostles and guides to other married couples. This is assuredly, among so many forms of apostolate, one of those which seem most opportune today.

27. We hold those physicians and medical personnel in the highest esteem who, in the exercise of their profession, value above every human interest the superior demands of their Christian vocation. Let them persevere, therefore, in promoting on every occasion the discovery of solutions inspired by faith and right reason, let them strive to arouse this conviction and this respect in their associates. Let them also consider as their proper professional duty the task of acquiring all the knowledge needed in this delicate sector, so as to be able to give to those married persons who consult them wise counsel and healthy direction, such as they have a right to expect.

28. Beloved priest sons, by vocation you are the counselors and spiritual guides of individual persons and of families. We now turn to you with confidence. Your first task—especially in the case of those who teach moral theology—is to expound the Church's teaching on marriage without ambiguity. Be the first to give, in the exercise of your ministry, the example of loyal internal and external obedience to the teaching authority of the Church. That obedience, as you know well, obliges not only because of the reasons adduced, but rather because of the light of the Holy Spirit, which is given in a particular way to the pastors of the Church in order that they may illustrate the truth. You know, too, that it is of the utmost importance, for peace of consciences and for the unity of the Christian people, that in the field of morals as well as in that of dogma, all should attend to the magisterium of the Church, and all should speak the same language. Hence, with all our heart we renew to you the heartfelt plea of the great Apostle Paul: "I appeal to you, brethren, by the name of Our Lord Jesus Christ, that all of you agree and that there be no dissensions among you, but that you be united in the same mind and the same judgment."

29. To diminish in no way the saving teaching of Christ constitutes an eminent form of charity for souls. But this must ever be accompanied by patience and goodness, such as the Lord himself gave example of in dealing with men. Having come not to condemn but to save, he was indeed intransigent with evil, but merciful towards individuals.

In their difficulties, may married couples always find, in the words and in the heart of a priest, the echo of the voice and the love of the Redeemer.

And then speak with confidence, beloved sons, fully convinced that the spirit of God, while He assists the magisterium in proposing doctrine, illumines internally the hearts of the faithful inviting them to give their assent. Teach married couples the indispensable way of prayer; prepare them to have recourse often and with faith to the sacraments of the Eucharist and of Penance, without ever allowing themselves to be discouraged by their own weakness.

30. Beloved and venerable brothers in the episcopate, with whom we most intimately share the solicitude of the spiritual good of the People of God, at the conclusion of this encyclical our reverent and affectionate thoughts turn to you. To all of you we extend an urgent invitation. At the head of the

priests, your collaborators, and of your faithful, work ardently and incessantly for the safeguarding and the holiness of marriage, so that it may always be lived in its entire human and Christian fullness. Consider this mission as one of your most urgent responsibilities at the present time. As you know, it implies concerted pastoral action in all the fields of human activity, economic, cultural and social; for, in fact, only a simultaneous improvement in these various sectors will make it possible to render the life of parents and of children within their families not only tolerable, but easier and more joyous, to render the living together in human society more fraternal and peaceful, in faithfulness to God's design for the world.

31. Venerable brothers, most beloved sons, and all men of good will, great indeed is the work of education, of progress and of love to which we call you, upon the foundation of the Church's teaching, of which the successor of Peter is, together with his brothers in the episcopate, the depositary and interpreter. Truly a great work, as we are deeply convinced, both for the world and for the Church, since man cannot find true happiness—towards which he aspires with all his being—other than in respect of the laws written by God in his very nature, laws which he must observe with intelligence and love. Upon his work, and upon all of you, and especially upon married couples, we invoke the abundant graces of the God of holiness and mercy, and in pledge thereof we impart to you all our apostolic blessing.

Given at Rome, from St. Peter's, this 25th day of July, feast of St. James the Apostle, in the year 1968, the sixth of our pontificate.

Chapter Eight

The Population Explosion Myth*

Jorge Iván Hubner Gallo

THE INOPPORTUNE RETURN OF MALTHUS

The Historical Evolution of Birth Control
(p. 13)

The problem of birth control is as old as man himself. Since time immemorial, humans have used their inventiveness to exercise influence over their offspring, creating or avoiding them by conscious and voluntary means. In many communities, sterility has been considered a shameful misfortune. This in turn stimulated marriage and the procreation of large families. On the other hand, religious and moral beliefs have always been a guiding force for natural order and value of life. The Bible mentions the case of Onan, the Hebrew, who practiced contraception. God put him to death as a punishment befitting such a detestable act![1]

Repudiation of procedures meant to impede procreation must have been common among ancient peoples, except during periods of corruption and decadence such as the Roman Empire. "During much of the Middle Ages and most of the Modern Age, they were reserved for prostitution, illicit love affairs, especially adultery."[2] Only towards the middle of the eighteenth century were these practices extended to marriage, beginning with the upper classes but spreading during the nineteenth and twentieth centuries into other social strata.[3]

---

*This chapter contains excerpts from Jorge Iván Hubner Gallo, *El mito de la explosión demográfica: La autorregulación natural de las poblaciones.* (Buenos Aires: Joaquín Almendros Editor, 1968). It has been translated by Philip Choate, Barry Nobel, and the editor and reprinted by permission of the publisher. Notes have been retained but renumbered.

The actions of an individual nature, which logically occur first, become governmental measures in a more advanced period of civilization with the tendency to reduce or increase population for economic, social or military reasons. In an even more advanced phase of cultural maturation this process leads to the formulation of diverse demographic theories.

Demographic Theories: The Doctrine of Malthus *(pp. 15 and 16)*

Thomas Robert Malthus (1766-1834), Protestant pastor and professor of history and economics, published his celebrated *Essay on the Principle of Population* in 1788. This work constitutes the foundation, not only for contemporary demographic theories of an economic nature, but also for the neo-Malthusian school of birth control and for contemporary campaigns in favor of so-called "family planning" (although, as will be seen, Malthus condemned all artificial procedures limiting natality).

In this work, Malthus formulated his simple and attractive Law of Population. According to it population grows in geometrical progression, doubling every 25 years (if there are no obstacles impeding it), while food resources increase by only an arithmetic progression.[4]

The disequilibrium between population growth and food production, on a worldwide scale, must therefore get larger and larger, until it ends in war, hunger, and misery. In order to avoid this ultimate disaster, the author, who professed solid moral and religious convictions, proposed that fertility be limited by means of moral constraints, celibacy, and voluntarily delaying the age of marriage. Malthus explicitly affirmed that use of any other means to impede births would vilify human nature and deny man's dignity.

The Facts Disprove Malthus
(pp. 16-20)

The so-called law of population was very quickly demonstrated to be false in its two basic principles. In the first place, while it is certain that in theory the population could double every 25 years, in practice this has not occurred nor does it ever occur, save in rare exceptions. Many complex natural factors, which cannot be reduced to the obstacles described by Malthus in his book, impede it. It is therefore a flagrant error to confuse the potential human fertility with actual birth rates, which have experienced appreciable variation at various times and places due to factors many of which are merely biological. The true demographic growth curve is not progressive and continuous, but an irregular line with many ups and downs. The periods of over-population and under-population have alternated through history like rising and receding tides, as Wagemann and Roscher note.[5] Thus, for example, during the first centuries of our era and the larger part of the Middle Ages, the population of Europe remained more or less stationary.[6]

From the tenth to the thirteenth centuries, an appreciable population increase occurred; in the fourteenth century, the "black plague" caused a reduction; in the fifteenth century, population remained stable; in the sixteenth century there was a considerable increase in Central Europe; in the seventeenth century European population levels once again stagnated and diminished; in the eighteenth and nineteenth centuries there was an irregular increase; and in recent decades of the twentieth century a new upward push is observed.[7] According to the estimates of Professor Wilcox, the number of inhabitants in Africa and Oceania remained constant between 1650 and 1850.[8] Also, in each historical period great differences in the indices of natality and mortality for the different regions of the world were observed.

It is fitting to remember, moreover, that Malthus himself observed that among Negroes of the West Indies, and in one or two similar cases, population did not even rise to the level permitted by subsistence.[9] It is a fact, on the other hand, that there are human groups that have been shrinking in numbers little by little towards extinction, such as the Alacalufs and the Onas of extreme southern Chile.[10] There is no reason to suppose that these primitive tribes use contraceptive methods.

In conclusion, as the Brazilian scientist and writer Josué de Castro notes, "Malthus' first error was to consider population increase as an independent variable."[11] This phenomenon in fact depends upon many complex political, social, economic and especially natural and biological factors. History "completely discredited his rigid and simplistic formula."[12]

> The increase of world population during the first years following the publication of his theories seemed to confirm Malthus' predictions, but before the end of the century the initial rhythm of this increase had slowed down considerably. The birth rate diminished in several countries, and the danger switched from overpopulation to underpopulation. While today countries such as India, China, Egypt and Central America continue with high indices of population increase, others—in Western Europe, North and South America, and Africa—are entering a stage of transitory equilibrium. The United States, Australia, and New Zealand have reached a point which Notestein calls incipient population decrease. This is how the principal doctrine of Malthus was completely contradicted by natural evolution, according to a statement by the famous demographer Imre Ferenczi.[13]

It is interesting to note, finally, that according to Malthus' own data at the time of the publication of his book, the earth had one billion inhabitants.[14] If his theoretical progression had overcome the many impediments to growth, by 1973—or in five years—the world wide population would reach 128 billion people. Since the present figure scarcely exceeds three billion, a number not capable of great variations during the indicated time lapse, it is easy to see that the theory's predictions diverge astronomically from the facts. This is because of the numerous complex and unforeseen factors that come into play in this area.

In the second place it is not true that food resources increase slower than the population. The truth is that one cannot establish any fixed rules in this respect, except that, as a general rule, food production has always more or less kept pace with the necessities of consumption. Furthermore, in recent times the increase in production of foodstuffs has amply exceeded the most optimistic of predictions. Between 1895 and 1912, "world population increased by 12½ percent. At the same time, wheat production increased by 45 percent, corn by 43 percent, oats by 53 percent, rice by 40 percent, etc."[15] Within the last few decades, the increase in food production in many areas of the planet has achieved spectacular dimensions. In the United States, for example, where population has increased at a very rapid rate, food production levels have increased so much that during some years gigantic surpluses have to be stored because internal consumption of them would be impossible. The country then has to export food, in large part through aid programs to underdeveloped countries.

According to well-founded studies, at least 75 percent of the cultivatable land on the planet is not even exploited.[16] More recent authoritative appraisals put the figure at 90 percent.[17] In 1952, the experts gathered at the 17th International Congress of Geography in Washington estimated that, given the technical means of that time, the world capacity for food production was sufficient to satisfy the needs of 13 billion people.[18] In 1954, the sociologists of Malinas drew up a declaration on the same problem in which they affirmed that "use of better techniques which can be put into practice immediately on land already under cultivation, plus the addition of one-tenth of the world's reserve of uncultivated but cultivable land, would be enough to insure satisfactory nutrition to all the world's people, even allowing for its probable expansion for the next few generations."[19] In 1960, Josue de Castro, who in addition to his other honors was World President of the Food and Agricultural Organization until recently ago, wrote with justified optimism:

> In spite of the tendency of our civilization not to produce enough to prevent malnutrition among the people of the world by applying newly acquired techniques of science in order to use soils to the maximum benefit, food production has come to surpass population increase in the last decade. While the latter increases at an annual rate of 1.5 percent, the former exceeds 2 percent. This means the total destruction of neo-Malthusianism.[20]

It is fitting at this point to add that since 1960 science and technology have continued to advance the frontiers of agriculture.

In addition to the ever more productive exploitation of the land, we can mention the unlimited possibilities of food from the ocean and the fabulous new food synthesis promised by recent progress in chemistry. A group of English scientists from the University of Cambridge, to cite only one recent example, has just succeeded in transforming methane into an edible protein. This has been tested by animals and humans and can be manufactured on a large scale.[21] Along with other contemporary North American authors, Arthur Salter says that we will have the material resources and the technical capability to raise the standards of living of all humanity to levels much higher than what we know today, even if world population grows to several times its present size.[22] Doctor Athebstar Spilhaus, member of the Executive Council of UNESCO and Dean of the Minnesota Institute of Technology, has written:

> Atomic and solar energy will be exploited to satisfy many needs of growing humanity such as: low cost distillation of sea water, utilization of frozen fresh water from the poles, hydropanics, transformation of vegetable organisms into edible food, exploitation of the oceans, technical knowledge about fish, sea nurseries, the use of the nutritive value of algae, weather control . . .[23]

Furthermore, Colin Clark, in his recent book *Population Growth and Land Use,* estimates that with present technical resources the world can feed a population of 47 billion persons at a level similar to that of the United States, or 150 billion at a level typical of Asia.[24]

The somber pessimism of William Vogt has been refuted in his own lifetime as having no bearing on reality. Two decades ago he maintained that there was no road for survival other than to limit population by reducing medical and hygienic assistance to underdeveloped peoples who multiplied too quickly. The alarmist warning of Fairfield Osborn has even less foundation. He asserts that the large nations have ransacked the planet by exhausting the land. This, together with erosion, will destroy the fertility of the land. Science has authentically demonstrated that present agricultural possibilities and the development of food from more varied sources permits us to look into the future with complete tranquility. The necessity of limiting births has not been demonstrated. Instead, it is necessary to concentrate international cooperation and the internal powers of each nation in order to apply new scientific and technological discoveries to the mass production of consumer goods.

The Untimely Return of Malthus
(pp. 22 and 23)

During the first decades of the twentieth century, Malthus' theory became only one chapter in the history of economic doctrine. It was an ingenious but superficial thesis which no longer exercised major influence in scientific and academic circles. In the nonacademic realm, however, neo-Malthusian activist groups arose in a number of countries. While ignoring the strict moral principles of Malthusianism and invoking principally reasons of convenience, they engaged in public campaigns and established organizations in favor of birth control. In the beginning there were small groups active, and frequently accompanied by scandal, in England, France, and the United States and later, in Germany, Sweden, Holland, and other countries. But with the advance of the twentieth century, this trend intensified and extended into all parts of the world in different forms.

In the last 15 years, the movement has been preoccupied with strengthening its fundamental theory and doctrine, revitalizing the old and feeble conceptions of Malthus, and acquiring a veritable worldwide span. Its expansion is based on a new and powerful argument, which has gained the official support of several governments: the contemporary population explosion. Its diffusion is being realized under a new name which disguises its discredited origins and is better adapted to contemporary mentality: "family planning" (or "planned parenthood").

Why has Malthus returned from the grave, after giving the impression of being quite dead, to knock on the world's door? The explanation does not really lie in the strong increase which population growth has recently experienced, since resources have increased fantastically, but with powerful political and economic forces. Frequently these are hidden behind other appearances, to which we will refer later.

FAMILY PLANNING

The Specter of Over-Population (p. 25)

In recent years, a torrent of publications in all languages has inundated the world with alarming statistics about population increase and related catastrophic predictions. It is not necessary to read them one after the other because in general they all say the same thing. The figures, the arguments, and the conclusions are repeated with wearisome uniformity, as if obeying a single commanding voice. Most of these works are based on data provided by international organizations and are written by North American, English, or Latin American sociological and demographic experts. Expressly or tacitly, almost all affirm that the solution to the problem consists in providing birth control programs, especially in the underdeveloped countries where the indices of population growth are particularly high.

Neo-Malthusianism in Action
(pp. 27-29)

The same voices are raised everywhere, inspired by invisible but powerful forces. In one form or another, the problem is under discussion in the International Food and Agriculture Organization (FAO), the World Health

Organization, the Commission on Population, the General Assembly of the United Nations, and the Organization of American States. In some parts of the world, the campaign to stop life at its source relies on the assistance of international organizations and is directed and financed by governments or by other public entities. Among these, the government of the United States is the leader. In Japan, India, Ceylon, Malaysia, Turkey, and the United Arab Republic, among other countries, there are official birth control programs.

In the private sector, various important foundations, especially the American Ford and Rockefeller Foundations, plus other associations in places like England and Scandinavia, are pledged to this same idea. Among these, several should be explicitly mentioned: "The Population Council," founded in 1952, and the "International Planned Parenthood Federation" (IPPF), which was created in the same year to group together national associations throughout the world. IPPF presently has its world headquarters in London and its Western Hemisphere headquarters in New York. This vast organization operates by means of centers situated in five large geographic zones: Europe, Middle East and Africa, Indian Ocean, Southeast Asia, and the Western Pacific.

At the population symposium held at the Washington office of the Panamerican Union (the General Secretariat of the Organization of American States) in September, 1964, Dr. Alan G. Guttmacher, President of "Family Planning/World Population," explained that the "Committee of Finances and Budgets" of the IPPF "distributes funds for each region according to their need." "In the last four years, the sum distributed has grown from $150,000 to $500,000." In the speaker's judgment, this "is undoubtedly a miniscule quantity if one considers the vast global work that is being attempted."[25] One can assume that these figures have continued to increase since 1964.

The "International Planned Parenthood Federation" has held eight world conventions to date in order to exchange information and spread contraceptive plans and methods. The last of these Congresses, with large amounts of foreign financing and ample publicity, was held in Santiago, Chile, between April 9 and 15, 1967. More than a thousand delegates from numerous countries attended.

Direct action by the United States government and official entities in favor of birth control plans in various parts of the world (which will be discussed later) has strongly reinforced the contemporary neo-Malthusian offensive is based on arguments related, in part, to what some have claimed to be the needs of a developing economy, and in part to the supposed necessity of combating abortion by spreading contraceptive methods.

Overpopulation and Economic Development *(p. 29, pp. 31-33 and 34-35)*

The trite old Malthusian argument, repeatedly refuted by fact and theory, that population growth is more rapid than the increase in food resources, has currently been remolded into a new pretentious facade. English-speaking statesmen, experts from international organizations, and "family planning" propagandists disseminate its latest watchword to the world: The "population explosion" holds back "economic development" to such an extent that not even outside help can overcome it.

This thesis is "demonstrated" with impressive statistical evidence, which no one has bothered to analyze sufficiently, showing high indices of fertility and slow growth of per capita income in "Third World" regions. As corollary to these studies, it is concluded expressly or tacitly that slowing population growth . . . is indispensable.

However, if we analyze the question both in theory and in the light of historical experience, we will have to conclude that the assertion that accelerated population growth slows economic development lacks a solid basis.

In theory, the thesis is based on Malthus' archaic principles of population supported by modern statistical and mathematical methods. However, it has been exhaustively demonstrated that population does not increase indefinitely at the same rate and that food resources do not increase at a rate which is slower than necessary.

Limiting ourselves to this latter aspect . . . we would like to point out that all the works published by international organizations and many of those by demographers and economists concerning production, national income, and "per capita income" are based on the false assumption that the rate of economic development are rigid and invariable. This supposition, accepted as proven with no further inquiry, does not take into account that any increase in population and, therefore, in the work force can by itself provide a much larger increase in income. This takes place because demographic pressure generates increased exploitation of natural resources, greater development and diversification of industry, and a lessening of costs due to the increase in the size of the market. Neither can this hypothesis account for the unlimited prospects for technological progress, which in modern times has surpassed even the most optimistic forecasts about its applications to agricultural, mineral, and industrial production. The spectacular perspectives of atomic energy, cybernetics, simple automation, and the breakthroughs in chemistry have led us to discard all previous calculations on the rise in living standards of humanity.

The eminent contemporary economist W.W. Rostow, whose theory constitutes one of the major hopes for developing communities, has demonstrated that economic growth historically follows a process characterized by five grand stages or links. These begin with the most primitive and backward phases of society and end with the period in which high standards of living and mass distribution of goods and services are attained.[26] Rostow has shown clearly that population and economic growth continue at more or less parallel rates, until they reach the point where the necessary conditions for the ascending impulse or economic "take off" are met. From that instant, economic development accelerates in geometrical progression, as if investments and "per capita" income were drawing compound interest, and the problem of eventual overpopulation becomes meaningless. The "take off," with its consequent profound transformations in systems and means of production, completely supercedes the written calculations of those experts who base their projections on dead and stagnant figures. Argentina and Mexico between 1930 and 1940, and India and China towards 1956, have begun the "take off." Other nations of the "Third World," with greater or lesser speed, will be reaching the conditions necessary to begin the great leap from underdevelopment to maturity and material abundance, using both international assistance and their own internal efforts. Therefore, the authentic solution to the socio-economic problems of these nations does not include limiting population size, whose total energy is necessary to take the decisive step. The real solution is to dedicate ourselves to creating the conditions necessary for further expansion, following the same route that the underdeveloped nations of long ago travelled in order to become the great powers of this age.

In fact many countries which have experienced an explosive population increase in recent times did not suffer an economic setback, but rather a considerable improvement in their cultural, educational, and socio-economic situation. The most eloquent example of this is the United States. From less than 4 million inhabitants in 1790, it has grown to 188,643,000 in 1963, or an increase of 4,700 percent in 173 years.[27] With no fear of any "population explosion," the United States has attained the highest levels of civilization and affluence known to man. The same phenomenon, although without such a monumental increase in population, has occurred in the great industrial powers of the Western World. Together with a high population growth, they have raised their "per capita" incomes to much higher levels. Why deny the underdeveloped nations of today the possibility of following the same developmental stages (as some Spanish American countries are doing) by increasing industry rather than limiting population? . . .

The hour has arrived when we must treat the statistical speculations of certain "experts" with the skepticism which they deserve, and not allow ourselves to be convinced that a reasonable and normal population increase in a country will harm its cultural, social and economic development. However, it must be pointed out that our optimism on material questions presupposes the existence of a hard-working population actively disposed to assimilate scientific progress and apply technological advances to the processes of production. Neither communities nor individuals can progress without sacrifices and hard work. This simple principle can explain the stagnation of certain Asian nations, a condition caused not by an excess of population (as has been falsely alleged by some authors) but by the inability of their inhabitants to adapt to the new conditions of discipline, industry, and technological advance which civilized life demands.

Neo-Malthusianism and Abortion
(pp. 35-37)

Birth control policy also is justified today as a means of preventing abortion. Thus, teaching a human couple contraceptive techniques will enable them to avoid unwanted pregnancy and its subsequent violent interruption. It is emphasized that, especially where resources are scarce and fertility high, education on this matter constitutes the most effective means of combating the serious social and moral illness of abortion, which some countries have come to consider as extremely serious.

In our opinion, looking at the matter from a doctrinal point of view, the solution to this undeniable problem is not found in the dehumanizing and simplistic suppression of conception, but in the determination and substantiation of the causes that prompt abortion. These are principally of cultural, moral, social and economic character. . . . we will refer to the general basics of a truly positive demographic policy, which, instead of reducing and undermining the family, will assist and fortify it as the most important pillar of civilized society.

Disregarding the moral judgments and negative policy that birth control entails as a supposed means of preventing abortion, let us review expert analysis of concrete results which have been obtained in countries where such methods have already been tried.

In the first place, we must point out that the indices which are usually used to demonstrate the effectiveness of these plans must be viewed with much caution. As J. Sutter of the French National Institute of Demographic Studies observes, "the figures which are given on the number of abortions are fundamentally meaningless. On what basis can they be established? All real specialists who have forced themselves to determine scientifically the number of induced abortions in any country, even approximately, have completely renounced [them] . . . Any conclusion or hypothesis which gives only a decline in abortions after general diffusion of contraceptive methods can have no foundation whatever."[28] In another work, Dr. Sutter adds, "We completely lack the data that could demonstrate the extent to which the diffusion of contraceptive methods reduces abortions. The principal argument of the neo-Malthusians cannot receive even the slightest numerical confirmation."[29]

One fact, however, has been completely established: in nations where the use of contraceptive methods has been officially promoted, such as the United States, criminal abortion is far from disappearing. The same observation also holds with respect to Sweden, a country which is famous for its extremely liberal and audacious practices in these matters. Dr. Axel Westman, a Swedish delegate to the 5th International Congress of Family Planning held in Tokyo in 1959, publicly acknowledged that in his country the legalization of contraceptive practices on June 17, 1938, did not produce the anticipated reduction in criminal abortions. He also noted that since that time, criminal abortions have been growing more frequent, since the possibility of terminating pregnancy was publicized and became a popular topic of conversation.[30]

In other countries, for example certain regions of Japan where an intense "family-planning" campaign took place, the absolute number of abortions went down as did the birth rate; however, the percentage of abortions increased. This phenomenon is not surprising, since according to the results of a survey done in 1952 of 3,500 Japanese homes by the Demographic Investigation Commission of Mainichi, "couples using contraceptives obtained abortions up to six times more frequently than those who rejected birth control." The Royal Population Commission of Britain had already come to this conclusion in 1949. "The proportion of abortions was 8.7 times higher among British married people who were accustomed to contraception than among the others."[31]

The solution to this apparent paradox is simple enough: convinced of the necessity to avoid procreation at all costs, or having lost respect for life, whichever takes greater importance, the couple ends the pregnancy by means of abortion. Furthermore, legalization of contraception very quickly leads to legalization of abortion and sterilization as social and eugenic devices. This constitutes the next step on the road to contempt for life and human dignity.[32]

New Contraceptive Methods
(pp. 37-38 and p. 41)

In spite of the pervasive weakness of its theoretical and practical foundations, the "family-planning" campaign has acquired increased publicity and popularity in the last few years throughout the entire world. Aside from other very significant factors which we will analyze later on, it is undeniable that this expansion has been aided by the notable scientific progress over the last few decades in the study of the processes of human reproduction. Special progress has been made in perfection of old contraceptive procedures and in the creation of new ones which are easier and more economical to use.

Among these systems, which we will not detail at this point, "intra-uterine devices" and "anti-ovulation" drugs are the most widely known. . . .

The anti-ovulants have acquired wide diffusion due to their simple use and the continual publicity given them by communications media. We can now speak of the "pill civilization." Large commercial enterprises, which have found the curtailment of life to be a most profitable business, have produced great quantities of these products in order to create the habit of using them.[33] North American foundations are disseminating them with the mistaken impression that they are beneficial.[34] A recent press release announced that the United States government will begin in the next few months to send "oral contraceptives" through its "aid" program to those underdeveloped countries that need them to contain the "population explosion."[35] We have thus, come to the point in which the "pill" is distributed on a massive worldwide scale as carelessly as if it were nothing but an innocent stick of chewing gum. But the "pill" will not only compromise the moral life of the "aided" community, but will soon create a new problem which is much more serious than the one they are trying to solve: the progressive depopulation of nations.

Birth Control from Religious and Moral Perspectives *(pp. 41-43)*

A matter like birth control, closely affecting the very foundations of life and intimate human conduct, falls directly into the sphere of religion and morality.

Since ancient times, the use of contraceptive procedures has been known and generally censured by religious beliefs. The primitive Vedic texts of India reject contraception.[36] (In our century, Mahatma Ghandi, following the ancient spiritual Hindu laws, also catagorically condemned it.)[37] In reference to the people of Israel, we have already mentioned the case of Onan referred to in the Bible.

Traditionally, Christian morality also rejected birth control. However, this standard suffered an important change in the Protestant branches of Christianity with the Declaration of the Conference of Lambeth of 1930. In it, the Anglican Church admitted that in those cases in which there is clear "moral obligation" [?] to limit or prevent birth, it is legitimate to employ means to obtain this result, each married couple determining for itself the respective methods according to Christian principles. The Council of the Church of England and the Council of Churches of America have made similar pronouncements. In support of this position, outstanding Protestant theologians like Leslie Weatherhead, Otto Piper, Emil Brunner, Reinhold Niebuhr, and Sherwin Bailey have maintained that conjugal sexuality has a considerable positive value in and of itself with procreation not being the principal aim of matrimony.[38] In a certain sense, the Protestants are promulgating the illegal ethic of individual responsibility and liberty before faith.

The doctrine of the Catholic Church has invariably condemned all artificial means of birth control. Opposing official teaching, based on the interpretation and exposition of natural law by Church doctrine, some divergent theological opinions have appeared in recent years. We will refer to these later.

The theological-moral foundation on which the traditional Catholic doctrine is based is very clear. Reproductive function is ordained by nature itself (and therefore by God) for procreation; consequently, it is contrary to natural order and intrinsically immoral to employ any means to violate artificially the proper effects of this function.

No matter what the motive or desired end used to justify such procedures, the amoral character of the deed does not change, since the end does not justify the means. A just cause can never be advanced by illegitimate means. On the other hand, this thesis does not in any way imply that all sexual acts ought to be fecund, or that conjugal partners should live in absolute abstinance if for physiological reasons they cannot have children. It only contends that one ought to respect the natural order. The sexual act is destined by its very nature to produce children: this in no way changed if, because of other natural causes, it does not produce these effects. For these reasons, the Church has legitimatized the judicious use of the system of periodic abstinence or the Ogino-Knaus cyclic method, which is founded on the knowledge of the woman's sterile periods. By this method, the prevention of conception is not the result of artificial methods but of physiological mechanisms of natural laws discovered by science.

However, we must also affirm the sublime value and transcendental significance of the sex act, through which God calls upon humanity to collaborate in His creative work. It is plainly stupid to defraud natural order in the only area in which we have been permitted to cooperate as instruments of the Supreme Maker—the marvelous plan of creation.

Finally, one must keep in mind that "the life of mankind and the mission of transmitting it is not limited to this world, nor can it be measured and fully appreciated only at this level. It is always aimed at the eternal destiny of man." [39]

Current Trends in the Catholic Church
(p. 50 and pp. 57-58)

In spite of repeatedly strong pronouncements by the Apostolic See, an intense offensive by the so-called "progressive" sector has begun in recent years, especially during Vatican II. These forces have drawn world attention to their defense of moral licenciousness regarding contraceptive methods and to their demand that the Church modify its intransigent attitude. The action of these theologians has been assisted by a number of press reports, petitions directed to the Apostolic See, and by street demonstrations, an unusual tactic for this type of controversy. We must add that the problem under discussion is one of extreme gravity, transcending its own specific importance. It affects the authority of the Roman Pontiff and Ecclesiastic Majesty, the philosophical bases of the moral order, the concepts of nature and natural law the doctrine of marriage, etc. . . .

We will therefore leave our review of this great theological and moral controversy which is presently raging within Catholicism. Undoubtedly, the doctrinal problem arouses passionate interest, since its clarification concerns fundamental aspects of doctrine and morality. Nevertheless, we cannot help but think that the attitude of those who predict a change in the Church's unvarying position on this subject involves a tacit but basic lack of faith in the action of Providence (especially when they use demographic and socio-economic arguments) and an unconfessed desire to make religion more mundane by making it easier and more convenient to observe. Although some theologians of this new tendency believe that, by overcoming the rigidity of certain moral norms and by exalting the role of love and individual responsibility, a greater perfection of married couples would be achieved, it seems evident to us that in practice often no motives are lacking for justifying egotistical behavior, a lamentable abandonment of ascetic spirit, the negation of self, and the feeling of eternity which characterizes the evangelical message.

The theological controversy has not ended. But for the present Catholics can accept only the norms already established by the Magistrate of Rome as guidance and try to form a virtuous and solid conscience with regard to new materials which must be questioned because they have not yet been neatly defined. Above all, Catholics must patiently wait for the definitive pronouncement of the Roman Pontiff, the repository of the dogmatic and moral truth of the Church.

The Political, Commercial and Economic Origins of the Contraception Campaign
(pp. 58-59 and 64-65)

In spite of its lack of sufficient scientific, social, and economic evidence and the moral and religious objections to it, the campaign in favor of a worldwide birth control policy has intensified noticeably in the last ten years. The underdeveloped countries are the favorite targets of a gigantic propaganda offensive, which, using all available publicity techniques, is attempting to convince them of the necessity and urgency of slowing their demographic growth.

Nobody would deny that there are many idealists in this movement—politicians, sociologists, economists, demographers, doctors—who are sincerely convinced that birth control is necessary to advance the welfare and progress of the "Third World" and, for some, to avoid an imminent and grave crisis of misery, starvation, and civil strife.

There is no doubt that the collective efforts of a well-intentioned group of people from many different countries, no matter how great, are not sufficient to explain the dimensions that the pro-birth control activities have acquired. In reality, powerful political, economic, and commercial forces are at work underneath all the ideas and theories. It is necessary to clearly identify these forces, which have succeeded in enslaving and controlling this worldwide campaign.

Within the last few years, the ruling circles of the United States have become convinced that the rapid population increase in Latin America, Asia, and Africa constitutes, not only a supposed obstacle for economic development, but also a source of revolutionary disruption and problems of civil disorder which can seriously compromise the well-being and security of a nation. This conviction seems to have developed into a truly psychotic panic, compelling United States leaders to use every conceivable means to limit the population increase of the "Third World." . . .

Continually pushing this policy, the United States has been appropriating vast sums of money, directly and indirectly subordinating other aid programs to the condition that birth control is accepted, promoting the massive distribution of contraceptive methods, and spreading propaganda on a large scale in "Third World" countries. The United States is thereby assuming an historical responsibility of incalculable proportions whose ramifications have certainly not been fully considered.

This attitude is especially deplorable for a nation that in the last few decades has defended democracy and liberty throughout the world and given constant and generous aid to the underdeveloped peoples. Until a short time ago, this aid was not subordinated to the foregoing conditions.

With sweeping action of North American political and financial power in favor of the convenient new birth control products, the cultural and spiritual integrity, family life, and the moral customs of an entire people can be rapidly undermined.

From another point of view, the diffusion and massive use of these procedures constitutes bloodless and refined genocide, in a metaphorical sense of the word, in those nations where the population lacks the cultural development and moral responsibility necessary to resist this influence and to ascertain its possible consequences. Contemporary native populations are not massacred; that would contradict the sentiments of the great civilized neo-Malthusian society. But it does not hesitate to prevent the proliferation of future generations in the unfortunate, underdeveloped countries. Without exaggerating we can affirm (as we have already demonstrated in another part of this book) that the prosecution of this policy, undertaken under the pretext of avoiding the disastrous effects of the "population explosion," is destined to cause even more catastrophic results: moral corruption, the aging of the population, and, finally, the massive annihilation of a community where there is no new blood to compensate for the natural loss of people through death. In currently vigorous regions of the "Third World" depopulation and death are threatening to conclude the international offensive destined to smother the sacred seed of life at its roots. One recalls this episode from the history of ancient Egypt: confronted with the rapid population increase of the people of Israel, the Pharoah ordered the Egyptian midwives to kill all Hebrew male infants. Since this measure did not have the intended affect, the king ordered "that all male children born to the Hebrews be thrown into the river, saving only the female children." (*Bible*, Exodus 1.) Nowadays, in a more refined civilization in which similar ideas have intruded, there are governments that propose the bloodless but efficient elimination of children, yet to be born to underdeveloped peoples, by massive diffusion of contraceptive methods. Is

THE NATURAL SELF-REGULATION OF POPULATIONS

The Basic Error of Neo-Malthusianism
(pp. 67-68)

After having indicated the fallacies of neo-Malthusianism in its various aspects, we have come to the most important part of this work: the formulation of the theory of natural self-regulation of the species.

As a final synthesis of the basic error of the current dire predictions whose lack of consistency has stimulated the search for a more objective explanation of the facts, we reiterate that these ideas come from a hypothesis which is, not only undemonstrated, but proven false, that is, if nature is left to itself, population continually increases without limit in accordance with more or less invariable indices of progression.

In other words, using this criterion it is supposedly possible to predict precisely how much world population will grow, on the abstract level, by means of certain mathematical progressions. But proceeding in this way, it is necessary to assume that the rates of population increase are constant, uniform, and permanent. In reality, they neither have nor have ever possessed these attributes. On the contrary, the huge expansion of humanity of the last decades with its higher growth indices does not constitute the general rule. In fact, it represents a demonstrably rare exception which has a profound *raison d'être,* as we shall see later on. It would be incorrect to presume that it will continue indefinitely at this inflated rate.

History and current demographic facts show that rates of population increase are very relative and variable, since they are influenced by numerous unknown and complex factors. The total population of any human group is extremely fluid and variable, depending on the era, the place, and the circumstances. It is therefore scientifically impossible to make any sure predictions concerning future developments. It is a well-known fact that any one particular human group, can increase, decrease, or remain stationary, regardless of its previous tendencies, due to factors still insufficiently known, but whose mechanisms can be partially explained. This fact alone leads us to suspect that biological laws exist by which the human population regulates itself in the same manner as other species, according to physical and social conditions, never exceeding a maximum limit or saturation point. This is more than a merely speculative hypothesis, since there is a considerable collection of systematically ordered factual material which permits us to establish definitely that the true "law of populations" is not one of indefinite growth by geometric progression but self-regulation by natural mechanisms.

Ecological Equilibrium among Animals
(pp. 68-69)

Ecology, or the study of reciprocal relationships among living entities and the environment in which they evolve, has pointed out the marvelous ability of life to adapt to its surroundings. It is an established fact that the animals as well as the plants of any given region are tied together and to the surrounding environment, living in harmony and interdependence. This harmony is especially evident in the regulation of the population sizes of the various species so that a state of equilibrium is maintained with respect to both themselves and to the other species in the environment.

Potentially all species have the possibility of unlimited multiplication. This possibility is especially impressive among micro-organisms and insects. Bacteria, for example, reproduce themselves by dividing at a fantastic velocity. Some subdivide every twenty minutes, representing a geometrical increase of population over short time spans. As Claude A. Villee, professor of biology at Harvard University, notes, "At this velocity, if one bacterium has sufficient food and no interference, it can create about 500,000 bacteria in six hours. After 24 hours, the resulting mass of bacteria would weigh more than 4,000,000 pounds, and in less than a week this one bacterium could create a mass the size of the earth."[40] Two fruit flies freely reproducing could produce $3,368 \times 10^{52}$ (10 raised to the 52nd power) offspring in just one year.[41] Fish lay eggs by the thousands, so that only one progenitor could populate all the oceans in a short time. The high fertility of rabbits is legendary. If they could multiply without impediment, they would quickly saturate vast regions.

There is no doubt that, if fruit flies, for example, were an intelligent species, they would have by now produced some expert who would warn about the dangers of the "population explosion," an imminent catastrophe worse than a cloud of DDT. Actually, neither bacteria, flies, fish, rabbits, nor any other species can overrun the earth by multiplication. It is evident that thanks to inexorable natural laws, not the intervention of contraceptives, a certain equilibrium is maintained between the number of individuals of each of the thousands of extant species and the surrounding environments. The total population of a species never rises to a dangerous level. Since man is also a species of the tree of life, he is subject to the same laws as other living beings, with a few modifications due to his uniqueness. In this respect, we must note that with man, the concept of "environment" to which one must adapt has a much richer, more varied, and complex structure than a simple physio-chemical and biological one. This environment also consists of a conjunction of artificial conditions such as culture, society, and technology, which have considerable influence on the mechanisms of fertility and morality. Later, we will refer in greater detail to this important phenomenon.

Aside from the scientific foundations of our statements, as believers we must add that if the Supreme Creator ordered the world in such a way that there exists a balanced proportion of all species, it would be absurd to think that He would have excluded man, the apex of visible creation, from His providential laws. Man would thus be put into the terrible dilemma, implied by an absence of connection between natural order and the reproductive process, making him suffer the consequences of disastrous overpopulation. To appreciate the harmony of the universe, life, and the actions of Divine Providence would suffice to make one understand that the human species would not have been excluded from the natural laws, placed in a disadvantaged state compared with other living species.

The Demographic Development of the Human Species *(pp. 86-89)*

In our opinion, we are now witnessing a third demographic revolution, which is even more important than the previous ones, and of which the demographers still have not taken complete notice. The period of liberal-individualist political and socio-economic organization found in oligarchical capitalist democracies having ended, the evolution of ideas and the giddy progress of science and technology have completely transformed our world. In some regions of the planet, totalitarian socialist life-styles have emerged; in others, state-regulated popular capitalism has completely changed the conditions of social existence. Everywhere, especially in Western countries, the levels of human existence have been elevated, or are now being elevated to extraordinary heights. The peaceful use of atomic energy, the electronic automation of the means of production, and the imminent practical applications of cybernetics are heralding a new unprecedented world of abundance and prosperity. In addition, integration of large groups of nations, greater ease in crossing international frontiers, and accelerated progress in transportation and communication have considerably enlarged the spatial environment in which the average person grows. All of these factors have profoundly modified the human habitat, giving rise to a new demographic revolution whose effects are only just beginning to be realized. We will add that voluntary limitation has also contributed to lower birth rates. However, with the exception of some countries where birth control has been widely diffused, this factor has generally not been truly significant in comparison to the natural mechanisms of self-regulation which we will consider in greater detail below.

From this discussion we can extract some important conclusions about the demographic development of the human species:

1. Man, like all other living beings, has a great expansive potential. He tends to multiply and to extend his population throughout the environment in which he finds himself.
2. This biological potential, although theoretically unlimited in an infinite environment, must adapt itself to the forever limited possibilities of the real environment.

3. In the human species, as in all other species, population increase proceeds according to the inflexible biological laws which determine natural self-regulation of population in relation to environment. The concept of "logistic curve," stripped of its mathematical rigor, or the less ambitious idea of "demographic cycle," augmented by the several known characteristic stages of the cycle (take off, accelerated increase, decrease in rate of increase, final equilibrium, and sometimes extinction), accurately describe the process of human population.
4. The environment or habitat of the human species, which must be taken into account when considering the application of these biological laws, has very little in common with the physical environment which influences the life of other animals. Civilized man, in contrast to animals which are enslaved by their environments, artificially creates his own habitat consisting of a conjunction of cultural and social conditions such as religion, art, science, education, politics, socio-economic organization, urban life, housing, nutrition, heating and refrigeration systems, transportation and communication, manufacturing industry, technological progress, psychological tensions, etc.
5. All positive and important changes in the conditions of the habitat create a new base for population growth and give rise to new growth curves which are subject to the demographic cycle. Eventually, a new state of equilibrium is reached, unless the environment undergoes another significant transformation. The present-day demographic revolution originated in a huge, world-wide enlargement of the geographical environment and of the various resources which technology has put at the disposal of humanity. This permits a vast increase in population expansion. Pearl's bottle has become a hundred times larger. The population increase curve has once again begun to rise from a new horizon in a situation which has changed fundamentally from previous periods of history.

The Natural Regulating Mechanisms of Human Populations *(pp. 90-91)*

Now that we have established the fact that human populations do not increase progressively and indefinitely but pass through a cycle of development related to the conditions of their respective environments until reaching a certain stationary limit, it is necessary to consider the natural mechanisms which regulate this development. Science has not yet attained a completely clear view of the nature and causes of this phenomenon, just as it has not been able to determine precisely how individual organisms develop from fertilization to birth or from birth to maturity. It is probable that the study of cybernetics with its mechanisms of retroaction and self regulation will shed light on some issues, giving us a better understanding of life processes which are much more complex than man could contrive. We believe that current biological investigations on fertility and sterility in humans will help to clarify the problem of demographic development.

In spite of the lack of complete and systematic knowledge of this phenomenon, various independent authors have succeeded in discovering some of the factors which regulate human population increase. It would seem beyond doubt that the importance of some factors has been overestimated in relation to many other complicated mechanisms which deserve further coordinated study but have been subordinated or even eliminated. All factors which potentially affect the regulation of populations should be systematically studied together. Furthermore, it is very probable that such mechanisms do not always operate in the same way and the same proportion, since the relative importance of each variable depends on the particular situation and the characteristics of each population group and its respective environment.

By the same method we followed when we considered population regulation among animal species, we will attempt to first consider the factors which control fertility. Later, we will briefly mention the control exercised by mortality.

We can classify the natural mechanisms which regulate fertility into two groups: endogenous (directly influencing internal generation of sex cells via physio-chemical and biological processes), and exogenous (acting externally to cause indirectly an increase or reduction of fertility). This classification is not rigid since in some cases we must consider mixed factors which act from the outside to produce internal biological effects.

The New Conditions of Today's World
(pp. 108-109 and 110-111)

Using the scientific fundamentals developed on the preceding pages, it has been demonstrated that natural mechanisms exist which regulate human population increases, assuring that no population can exceed a certain limit or "ceiling" based upon the characteristic possibilities of the environment. The threatening spectre of the "population explosion" raised nowadays by many politicians, writers, journalists, and the bureaucrats of modern international agencies is therefore nothing more than one of the great myths of our time. We will consider their deepest motivations later.

But before we begin to consider this point, we must stop in order to refute the main argument which the neo-Malthusians use to bring the law of natural self-regulation of populations into question.

No serious author with any knowledge of the fundamental notions of biological sciences can deny the existence of a universal equilibrium among all species including man, and their environments. This constitutes a general principle of nature. But the exponents of the "population explosion" and the birth control campaign tell us that due to medical progress, the reduction of death from many diseases, and a longer life span, man has broken this equilibrium and an alarming increase in the population must therefore occur, especially in the underdeveloped regions of Asia, Africa, and Latin America. . . .

The idea that science has broken the ecological equilibrium—as someone would break a dike holding back water—thus provoking an uncontainable and disastrous human flood neither reflects the true situation nor lessens the validity of those arguments claiming the existence of a natural law of population self-regulation.

In order to understand present reality, it is necessary to remember that by virtue of a universal mechanism of nature each group of living beings regulates its own volume, not abstractly, but in relation to its environment, and that with man the medium is not only constituted by the physical and biological framework in which he develops but also by a complex of civilized and cultural conditions.

Neo-Malthusian spokesmen highly value the demographic changes artificially obtained through the advance of medicine, but they forget that that which is artificial in the transformation of the environment becomes natural in man's habitat. In effect the biological laws which govern the species do not operate on a naked and inert being, like other living organisms, but on a being who, from the beginning, has used his intelligence and will to overcome his environment. If science and technology have made great progress in the present in the transformation of nature, for example, in disease control, this fact does not substantially alter the peculiar conditions of human existence. Among its other fundamental features, life is characterized by an extraordinary capacity to adapt to the environment; even more, it is a question of beings, who by their very nature, live by transforming their very environment. Just as biological laws have had to adapt to the fact that man creates his own climate, travels at supersonic speeds, eats synthetic elements, and is surrounded by a series of other artificial conditions, in the same way these laws will operate to adjust birth rates to the new possibilities of each age in order not to produce disequilibria, either due to an excess or shortage in population.

It is then unquestionable that the great demographic leap of the last 30 years, which worries many authors, coincides with a great step forward in scientific, technical, and socio-economic progress. The latter manifests itself in, among other ways, significant advances not only in medicine but also in food production, the construction and clothing industries, and the production of manufactured goods. Population has grown considerably, but at the same time today's standard of living, even in regions of the so-called "Third World," is much higher than 30 years ago.

The environment has changed in terms of increasing resources of all kinds in terms that justify and perfectly explain the great increase in world population, which is simply growing to adjust to the new conditions of its environment. In no way does this fact imply that the current growth will be indefinite but only that the new limit or "plafond" will permit our species higher development than previously for the same reason that population is scarce in the polar regions and dense in temperate and fertile zones. There is no doubt that once this new margin is achieved—the limits of which no one can predict—the upward curve of demographic growth will tend once again to stabilize....

Factors Favoring the Spread of Neo-Malthusianism *(pp. 113-115)*

As a conclusion... let us summarize those factors already mentioned or hinted at in this book which are aiding and abetting the world wide contraception campaigns.

Certainly many politicians, economists, demographers, writers and journalists sincerely believe that a cataclysm caused by overpopulation is imminent. They also think that the only way to stop this catastrophe is to start immediately on projects designed to provoke vigorous mass action in favor of birth control. In this way they believe that they are lending a great service to mankind. Because of the law of degradation of ideas, this thesis has reached the masses in its most deceptive and simplistic form, disseminated over a wide area by a huge publicity campaign directed mostly from the United States.

It is undeniable that this campaign has been a great success. Not only has neo-Malthusianism succeeded in convincing the great masses of people, who lack the education necessary to analyze this type of problem more deeply and therefore accept everything they read in print as truth, but it has also influenced the mentality of many people at higher cultural levels. The leaders of various non-Catholic religious groups have already accepted the supposed innocence and legitimacy of contraceptive methods, as we pointed out in a previous chapter. Even within the Catholic Church, that bulwark of revealed truth and moral discipline, there has been a tendency, known as progressivism, to call for a relaxation of the traditional norms that have always defined the ethics of married life.

What is the reason for this success? Beyond the obvious visible personal motivations of birth control partisans, what are the political and economic forces behind the prent day worldwide neo-Malthusian campaign?

In our opinion, the deep penetration of these essentially materialistic and disruptive ideas has succeeded thanks to a "deChristianization" of the Western World and a weakening of the non-Christian religions in other parts of the world. This progressive lessening of the moral strength of religious faith over large sectors of humanity is paralleled by the insidious growth of materialism and paganism in everyday life. Human ideals have thus come to center exclusively upon immediate gain and pleasure. The enormous progress of technological civilization, the elevation of living standards, and the shortening of the work week and concomitant increase in leisure time have not generally been accompanied by any increase in religion or spiritual and moral values. The indispensable "supplement of the soul," which, according to Bergson, must accompany the material advance of mankind, has been lacking. Eternal morals have been replaced in millions of disoriented minds by concern for only the moment in which they live. The supreme objectives of human destiny have been taken over by the immediate concrete considerations of physical existence. Knowledge of humility has been displaced by a constant search for pleasure.

Famous writers and philosophers are contributing to this spiritual degradation of mankind. Even the most evil of sins are presented as natural and respectable, or at least dignified by ample justifications and excuses. Some superficial, unconcerned authors are praising free instinctual licentiousness in the name of science, thereby corrupting the true meaning of some important modern ideas. Materialism and eroticism are spread night and day by the cinema, television, and the press, infecting minds like a soft, penetrating rain of mud. There are even religious leaders of certain sects who consciously or unconsciously believe that they can preserve the fundamental values of faith by yielding to the general decadence. They are trying to offer a religion which is easier and more comfortable to their congregations by making certain moral norms more flexible, softening the disagreeable notion of "sin," and rejecting the disturbing threat of hell.

Evidently a world undermined by materialism and ruled by the pleasure principle is excellent ground for the cultivation of neo-Malthusian ideas. In this contaminated environment, modern man could ask for nothing better than the distribution of economical and efficient contraceptives so that he could seek after pleasure without responsibility. At the same time, an apparently scientific doctrine is being offered to justify his conduct and to assuage his conscience, in case it is still bothering him.

Furthermore, gigantic political and economic forces are taking advantage of this moral atmosphere, managing and financing the worldwide contraceptive campaigns. The United States government and various important North American foundations, seconded principally by certain English and Swedish organizations, are carrying out a broad action aimed at disseminating neo-Malthusian dogma and promoting the massive use of contraceptives among the underdeveloped countries. Thus, in a manner which in a certain sense can be viewed as mass "genocide," they think they are contributing to the solution of man's problems. At the same time, large and powerful commercial producers of contraceptives are aiding these campaigns by inundating the world with their products. They are earning millions of dollars from this sad work of blinding life and facilitating the death of national customs.

The principle objects of this political and economic strategic operation are the nations of Africa, Asia, and Latin America. To stop the feared population growth in the underdeveloped countries, thus avoiding certain pressures and dangers, and to create fantastic commercial profits are the two political and economic motives which together form the most powerful force on

Earth. They are two huge engines whose action is not always clearly manifested in their international declarations and treaties on the matter. They constitute the main forces behind the world birth control campaign.

We will let the reader judge these events for himself, especially if he is one of those unwanted inhabitants of the "Third World."

NOTES TO CHAPTER 8

1. *Bible,* Genesis 38:6-10.
2. André Armengaud, *La explosión demográfica* (Madrid: Ediciones Aid, S.A., 1967), p. 55.
3. *Ibid.*
4. Thomas Robert Malthus, *Essai sur le Principe de Population,* 2a. ed. (Paris: Ed. Guillaumin et Cie., Libraires, 1852), pp. 5-11.
5. Ernesto Wagermann, *La población en el destino de los pueblos* (Santiago: Editorial Universitario, S.A., 1949), p. 37.
6. Dr. Raoul dé Gutcheneer, *La limitación de la natalidad: Birth Control* (Madrid: Editorial Razon y Fe, S.S., 1942), p. 20.
7. Wagermann, *La población . . . ,* p. 77.
8. W.F. Wilcox cited in Amos H. Hawley, *Human Ecology: A Theory of Community Structure* (New York: The Ronald Press Company, 1950).
9. Malthus, *Essai . . . ,* p. 11.
10. A century ago there were around 4,000 Alaeulufs; today there are only about 20.
11. Josué De Castro, *El libro negro del hambre,* 2a. ed. (Buenos Aires: Editorial Universitaria EUDEBA, 1965), p. 29.
12. *Ibid.*
13. *Ibid.*
14. Malthus, *Essai . . . ,* p. 11.
15. Gutcheneer, *La limitación . . . ,* p. 25.
16. *Ibid.,* p. 24.
17. De Castro, *El libro negro . . . ,* p. 30-31.
18. *Ibid.,* p. 30.
19. *Ecclesia,* XV, No. 711 (26 de febrero de 1955), pp. 11-12.
20. De Castro, *El libro negro . . . ,* p. 31.
21. *Boletín de las Universidad de Chile,* No. 73 (April, 1967), p. 47.
22. In Arturo Aldunate Phillips, *Al encuentro del hombre* (Buenos Aires: Editorial Guillermo Graft Ltda, 1953), pp. 178-179.
23. In S.J. Martín Brugarola, *Sociología y teología de la natalidad* (Madrid: Editorial Stxdium, 1967), p. 264.
24. Colin Clark, *Population Growth and Land Use* (London: Macmillan & Co., 1967), p. 153.
25. Dr. Alan G. Guttmacher, "¿Qué se está haciendo?" *Población: Simposio realizado en la Unión Panamericana* (México; D.F.: Secretario General de la Organización de los Estados Americanos, n.d.), p. 32.

26. W.W. Rostow, *Las etapas del crecimiento económico: Un manifesto no comunista,* 2a. ed. en español (Mexico: Editorial Fondo de Cultura Económica, 1963), and *El desarrollo económico.*
27. Rupert B. Vance, "El credimiento de la población norteamericana," cited in Ronald Freedman, *La revolución demográfica mundial* (Mexico: Editorial U.T.H.E.A., 1966), p. 178.
28. Dr. J. Sutter cited by S.J. Stanislas de Lestapis, *La limitation des naissances* (Bourges: Institut Catolique de Paris-Institut d'Estudes Sociales, Editorial SPES, 1959), p. 61.
29. *Ibid.*
30. *Ibid.,* pp. 60-61.
31. *Ibid.,* pp. 62-63.
32. *Ibid.,* pp. 65-70.
33. Benjamin Viel, *La explosión demográfica* (Santiago: Ediciones de la Universidad de Chile, 1966), p. 163.
34. *Ibid.*
35. *El Mercurio* (Santiago, Chile), July 16, 1967, p. 9.
36. Lestapis, *La limitación* . . . , p. 47.
37. *Ibid.,* pp. 49-50.
38. *Ibid.,* pp. 28-36.
39. *Concilio Vaticano II, Constituciones, Decretos, Declaraciones, Legislación Posconcilar,* Tercera Edición (Madrid: Biblioteca de Autores Cristianos, Editorial Católica, S.A., 1967), p. 339.
40. Claude A. Villée, *Biología,* p. 145.
41. *Ibid.,* p. 657.

Chapter Nine

Birth Control as a Weapon of Imperialism*

José Consuegra

THE RATIONALE OF THE ANTINATALIST THESIS

The "Population Explosion" as a Diversionary Fallacy *(pp. 19-31)*

Perhaps it would not be exaggerating to say that the thesis of the so-called population explosion in the underdeveloped countries, advanced by the neo-imperialists, is not worth pausing to analyze and refute. But the even more disturbing proposals emanating from such propaganda obligates economists (who are bound to inquire into the real causes of underdevelopment through the examination of history and analytical observation of the economic problems of our peoples) to speak out on this phenomenon, to denounce the malicious interpretations which are hidden behind false positions, and to test, under the light of growth theory, the positive goals of a demographic policy directed at adequately exploiting human resources which are both the foundation and objective of productive activity.

The thesis that the population explosion is an obstacle to development of the Indo-American countries began to be sketched out at the very moment when the post-war liberation efforts were renewed in dominated and colonial regions. And at the same time economists and researchers in these regions conscientiously began to examine reasons behind their unfavorable situation.

---

*This chapter contains excerpts from *El control de la natalidad como arma del imperialismo* (Buenos Aires: (c) Editorial Galerna, 1969). It has been translated by the editor with the assistance of Barry Nobel and reprinted by permission of the publisher. Notes have been retained but renumbered.

When the serious study of development replaces previous speculations, an avalanche of interpretations and judgments from outside the field as to the possible causes of underdevelopment also appears. On the one hand, a number of serious and honest researchers from the developed nations are taking charge of making an inventory of the historical bases which produced the economic inequalities of developing countries. (These contributions are recognized by economists of the Indo-American countries, who at the present time are engaged in adjusting the theoretical foundation that must serve as the strategy and guide for future developmental policy.) On the other hand, the majority of the professors and economists from the developed countries, acting as spokesmen for their own dominant economic systems, are assuming the task of interpreting the problems in their own way by presenting a series of arguments. These vary from the most superficial and slanderous (for example, those arguments which stress racial make-up, emotional characteristics, or eating habits such as consumption of spicy food) to those based on demographic and climatic factors, to the very tendentious and fallacious arguments of the so-called vicious circles, social dualism, etc. Precisely in the first group we find the notions associated with the population explosion thesis, which has been converted in our time into a favorite theme, not only in the area of speculation, but also in the work of a well-organized campaign by foreign governments and private organizations.

In this way, in our view, the population explosion thesis can be seen as a new diversionary tactic directed at impairing the work of those who denounce the contradictions and structural inequities of our underdeveloped economic systems as the only sources of misery, exploitation, and dependency of their peoples.

Furthermore, the truth is that once the economic invalidity of neo-Malthusianism is demonstrated, it has to be interpreted as an exclusively political thesis which responds to the interests of the economically powerful countries. These interests wish to preserve the status quo and blame those people who are suffering for their own problems.

The Arguments of the Population Explosion

The commentaries regarding the major changes in the size of world population in recent decades serves as the first justifications for the apologists of pessimism when they point out how serious it would be if current trends continue. While ignoring the study of differences in production and population growth indices in the developed areas or capitalist or socialist worlds, they maliciously use the same standards for the underdeveloped countries. Thus by observing the high rate of population growth and low rates of growth of production in underdeveloped countries, they deduce that only by lowering population growth can substantially better incomes be gained for the citizens of those countries.

Through this deformed conceptualization of demographic phenomenon and of the relations of population growth to increases of global and per capita income, it appears that the population explosion is the cause of underdevelopment, and not a simple and natural consequence of certain economic structures. (It would be stupid and reckless to speak of a demographic explosion in Latin America with a density of 12 inhabitants per square kilometer, while in Europe the density is 90 and in Asia 63. In Colombia in 1964 the population was 17,482,420 in a territory of 1,138,338 square kilometers for a density of 15. In the jungle areas, rich in wood and criss-crossed by abundant rivers which represent about half of the national territory, density is less than one inhabitant per square kilometer.)

To contradict this point of view it is sufficient only to remember some facts about changes that have occurred in those economies classified as developed. In the past, they maintained very high birth rates, but, as these declined, the rates of economic growth diminished to the point of worrying the theoreticians. An examination of the increases in generated wealth, which in the long run have led to surprising average income, produces an even more elequent argument.

Nevertheless, it is indispensible to indicate that in spite of previous global comparison between developed and underdeveloped economies, population growth, whatever its intensity and whatever the characteristics of the country, constitutes a real problem only in the context of a particular economic system. Even though the neo-Malthusian presumption is essentially political, in reality, capitalist private ownership of the means of production, the preponderant role played by the market, and profit as the only incentive of productive activity determine disfigurations in the social composition. In the long run, new births in a part of the population, added to those without permanent work, become a problem that reflects the contradictions and the crisis in the decomposition of the capitalist system.

Rather, it can be considered that the relatively large population, or the "population explosion" in neo-Malthusian terms, can only be explained as a phenomenon determined by structures existing in developed capitalist countries, given the dynamics of capital. In underdeveloped countries it will be explained by an array of phenomena which will be constantly referred to in this study. In the United States, for example, recent reports by sociologists show that along side of the "affluent society," there are some 50 million persons whose living standard is equal or inferior to the average of the Latin American countries. [1] The growth rate of this sector alarms certain groups. In spite of periodic expansions and relative stability, due primarily to the arms industry, unemployment is growing progressively worse to the point that the English economist, Joan Robinson, concludes that since this is one of the most protuberant characteristics of underdeveloped countries, the United States can soon be classified as underdeveloped. According to the observations of this famous English economist, in recent United States history each economic recovery has left a larger residue of unemployed. Even the North American Academy of Sciences recognized that "millions of North American citizens do not have work and the problem of unemployment is complicated . . . by the growing number of young people entering the working class. Postwar population increases aggravate urban problems such as slums, delinquency, etc."[2] And former President Kennedy, in one of his speeches, spoke of 17 million Americans who go to bed every night without dinner.

But for neo-Malthusians the population problem is limited to underdeveloped economies, and their presentation borders on terrorism. One of their spokesmen, for example, said, "Since the Second World War ended, certain events have brought the problem of population growth into the category of World Problem Two, occupying second place only to the problem of avoiding nuclear war."[3]

There is neither an economist nor politician in developed world who has not spoken in one way or another about the population explosion. But without a doubt, those most interested in spreading the new doctrine are found in international credit organizations or in those social science research centers which are sponsored by the great financial corporations with operations in underdeveloped countries.

But along side foreign expositions also appear some within the underdeveloped countries which utilize instruments provided by foreign capital to spread their doctrine. More than once, for example, we have read in the magazine *Visión* the disquisitions of former Colombian President Lleras Camargo on such matters, and the so-called economic studies centers of some Colombian universities, financed and directed by foreign foundations, have reduced almost all of their activity to measuring the intensity of population growth and subverting development.

In general, the assumptions of population "explosivism" posit that reduction in rate of population increase is the only way to achieve development. Given that miracle drugs of recent times have begun to exercise a certain "control over death," it seems to be logical that the high birth rate must be controlled. All means are valid for achieving this objective, even though they may violate the most elementary principles of humanity. Only a few months ago President Johnson, in one of the most disconcerting and sadly celebrated declarations known to history, said: "He who is not born costs us five dollars but he who is born costs us ninety." This was fearfully interpreted by many as a prelude to a new wave of genocide. One university professor commented on the seriousness of these words with a little irony but also with much uncertainty for the destiny of our peoples when he recalled Chesterton's description of the conduct of the Malthusians in the following anecdote.[4] Once some recent converts of Malthus invited some peasants over to indoctrinate them, using sombreros as bait. Ten peasants came to the meeting, but there were only eight sombreros. In the face of this predicament, it occurred to one of the intruders that two more sombreros should be made. This proposition was flatly rejected by the Malthusians as being too complicated and inoperable, since the obvious solution was to cut off the two extra heads.

In their purely economic argument, the neo-Malthusians use mathematics to arrive at accommodating, reactionary conclusions. Without considering underlying causes, they use objective statistics to "measure" the efforts that an underdeveloped economy would have to make (greater external debt, limitation of consumption to obtain savings, etc.) in order to achieve given levels of economic growth and in per capita income. For example, if the 5 percent minimum growth rate set by the United Nations were achieved in a country whose annual population increase was two percent, and whose personal income was one hundred dollars, after a decade the new per capita income would be only one hundred and twenty-three dollars, *ceteris paribus.* If population growth in this country was three percent, a more reasonable figure for Latin America, then in the same period per capita income would increase to only one hundred and eleven dollars, *ceteris paribus.* These assumptions, responding to *ceteris paribus,* blithely ignore the social essence of the problem and its connection to economic structure.

In order to criticize the statistical point of view, it is necessary to express the variable of economic growth concretely. Also, vigorous research into resource potentiality is needed in order to calculate the possible magnitude of investments which can be channelled into profitable activities.

Other more sophisticated authors add new details to the analysis in order to create equations that yield similar conclusions. For example, Dobb expounds on how the rate of income growth equals the investment rate divided by the capital-product ratio.[5] This gives primary importance to the rate of population growth in the analysis of economic growth. As will be remembered, the rate of investment is the percentage of resources which is spent on new capital equipment. The capital-product ratio expresses the ratio between the value of capital utilized in the private production sector and the value of the product obtained during a specified period. This ratio can be high or low depending on how much capital equipment is used. For example, in economies with demonstrable market imperfections such as in Columbia where supply is dominated by monopolies and cartels, and many enterprises barely work one shift, the value of the ratio is high. On the other hand, in economies planned for more complete exploitation of resources, the value of the ratio is low. Let us suppose, as in the previous example, that income is equal to 100 pesos, that the rate of investment is six percent of income, and that the capital-product ratio is high, for example four. Then the annual investment of six percent would permit only a 1.5 percent (6/4 = 1.5) increase in income to 150 pesos. With a lower capital-product ratio, for example two, the rate of income growth would be doubled. Let us relate these figures to an annual population growth of 3 percent (in Colombia it is 3.3 percent). When it is 2, per capita income stays even. This means that in order to achieve an economic growth rate of 5 percent (in Colombia it is 4.2 percent) and at the same time an increase in per capita income of 2 percent, an investment rate of 20 would be needed, given the capital-product ratio of four (20/4 = 5 - 4 = 2). [sic] As is easy to conclude, an investment rate of 20 percent under existing conditions would demand such a great effort from the majority lower income population that it would be necessary to consider a drastic reduction in population growth rate plus foreign financing of development schemes. It is worth noting that with the fatalism of the mathematical formula, one arrives at accomodating conclusions. These lead, in turn, to proposals which are in the economic interests of those who indulge in such reasoning.

The previous arguments can be refuted by citing many of the characteristics of dependent and underdeveloped economies. But it is enough to bring to mind the well-known phenomena of the unequal income distribution and the associated waste of savings. As we have seen, it is customary to speak of per capita income, which is a false arithmetic average. Without vigorous analysis of arithmetic averages, the grave problems caused by concentration of private property and poor utilization of resources remain obscure. The privileged classes squander resources when they consume ostentatiously, invest their capital abroad, and support large bureaucracies and military establishments. But even more important than the preceding problems are those concerning foreign relations. These include repatriation of profits and interest to other countries, draining of general service payments, and the constant deterioration of prices in commercial relations. All of these things keep the rate of investment from being much greater, sometimes because resources are poorly utilized or partially exploited due to structural obstacles, and sometimes because a good part of the income which could be used for investment is wasted on conspicuous consumption or used in other ways such as repatriations of profits.

The apparently simple reasoning based on the deceptive logic of mathematics makes the mistake of taking certain situations as given without trying to explain them. In reality, this system of analysis forms part of a chain of static models which try to avoid the study of structural problems. In the long run, they lead to the thesis that only internal finance of "development" with foreign resources can solve the economic problems of underdeveloped countries.

Given the contemporary situation, the aforementioned mental exercises only provoke people to consider seriously the desirability of effecting those revolutionary changes which would permit full exploitation of resources.

The aim of these changes would be a rate of growth approximating those of postwar socialist economies, about 10 percent, or those of capitalist countries like Japan, with 9 percent, or Germany, with 6 percent. The contrary is only valid for clarifying, as Aguilar does, that "the so-called population explosion is only the explosion of a social system incapable of rationally utilizing the productive potential that humanity has at its disposition to satisfy its necessities."[6]

Malthusian Reasoning
(pp. 40–41)

The discussion developed by the antipopulationists contains nothing new: it has all been presented in those historical periods when the social relations of production led to profound contradictions. When the dominant and exploiting social classes of the Malthus' period felt pressured by the demands of the exploited classes, they tried to divert attention by presenting problems for which they blamed the victims themselves. The same tactic is used by modern imperialist powers when pressured by underdeveloped countries. It is an exceedingly well-known tactic which imputes the blame for death on interference with the bullet's path.

In reality, Malthus was not original. Before him many authors spoke of the problem during similar periods of fear, contradictions, or the beginnings of social upheavals. As Farriera said, Malthus' importance and his great success in his position of spokesman for his country's governing class was in putting the blame for crisis not on the regime, but on precisely that part of the population which suffered.[7] Thus he avoided revolutionary answers. The conduct of Malthus is paradoxical: he spoke of a population explosion and future misery during one of the most auspicious moments in the history of English economic growth. The fact that he wrote during the great industrial revolution only serves to increase doubts about the scientific validity of the presumed "law" of the increase of population and production. As Sauvy noted, Malthus, as a self proclaimed enemy of the French Revolution and its conquests, saw the proliferation of the poor as a threat to property. He made the fears of the conservatives of the period his own.

Neo-Malthusian Reasoning
(pp. 48–55)

Neo-imperialism, or the attitude which capitalist economic powers, especially the United States, have adopted in the postwar period toward the dependent countries, now uses the same tactics to justify the exploitation of some peoples by others. The neo-imperialists try to fix responsibility for their condition upon the very people who are forced by all conceivable means (including armed invasion, as occurred recently in Santo Domingo) to remain in that condition.

Neo-imperialism takes four major forms:

1. giant corporations not only exploit mineral resources but also install primary manufacturing and assembly industries. In this way, or by direct purchase of all or part of pre-existing industry, they gain the power to syphon off ample profits, which are sent back to headquarters ;
2. the so-called aid and loan program, direct or through international credit organizations, deplete currency reserves with their high interest;
3. trade agreements are fixed so that income from the export of products is kept low;
4. finally, penetration and economic domination leads to complete domination of the political and social life of the country.

To cover up this reality, dominating foreign powers have revived the thesis that population growth is dangerous. Moreover, in the face of growing skepticism among people who no longer wish to accept responsibility for crimes that they do not commit and rejection of such futile and deceptive arguments by researchers and economists, the conduct of imperialist monopolies and official agencies has become so rash that they are trying to impose acceptance of their thesis by force, threatening to curtail all kinds of "aid" or finance of development programs.[8] They simply want to force the Latin American countries to accept the population problem as the principal cause of their economic lag.

The insistence of the United States is very understandable. Within it the real obstacles to progress are covered up, or at least a smoke screen of distraction is draped over the research that is taking place in responsible universities and organizations such as the United Nations Economic Commission for Latin America (ECLA).

How convenient it would be for the imperialist forces to have the underdeveloped peoples believe that their backwardness, poverty, and frustration are due exclusively to irresponsible procreativity. As the more audacious authors say when they speculate merrily about development, these countries do not change because they are opposed to change. They are underdeveloped because *they are underdeveloped.*

To think in this way so favored by neo-imperialists would be to ignore the course of our history (the conquest, the colonial period, republican free trade and imperialist periods) and some contemporary practices of imperialism: foreign exploitation of resources, imposition of specialization in primary products for the benefit of powerful countries, importation of capital as a means of immediately repatriating not only more capital but also the work of the oppressed nations. These practices prevent these nations from taking off economically.

What is really frightening the imperialist theoreticians and agents is that we economists of the backward countries are trying to formulate a body of theory that can serve as the basis for a policy and strategy of development for our peoples. In these times of uncertainty and liberated hopes, we are enumerating in rigorous order of priority the authentic causes of the present situation. Leaving aside past events for reasons of presentation, it can be said that the principal factors obstructing Latin American development are:

(1) *The misuse of available human and natural resources.* The people of Latin America, many kept in the darkness of illiteracy, removed from technical culture and those tools which are for achieving different productive goals, hardly even figure as a valuable resource for the future. Likewise, the natural riches of uncultivated lands, rivers which are potential sources of electrical energy, minerals and hydrocarbons, forests, seas, and, finally, the labor of her inhabitants, are hardly even partially exploited. Where they are exploited it is mostly for the benefit of foreign interest.

(2) *The growing waste of potential capital.* This is represented by the large proportion of foreign currency, earned from the export of primary goods, which escapes through the purchase of foreign goods and services which could be produced locally. Although Latin America pays more than 60 percent of its general export earnings in service costs, it receives barely one-sixth of export earnings for its services. This marked imbalance in the service portion of Latin American balance of payments has to be considered as the principal obstacle to economic and social development. In these services the principal shares are represented by the repatriation of capital, transportation payments, tourism, etc. To such measurable losses must be added the clandestine flight of capital, which for Colombia alone was calculated in 1965 at more than one billion dollars.

The remainder of exports, once services are deducted, consists mostly of non-durable goods, primary materials found at particular locations (petroleum, iron, copper, aluminum, etc., exploited by foreign capital) and agricultural products, among them cereals, which could easily be produced in uncultivated lands.

Finally, because of her structural dependence, Latin America must resort to the importation of capital by direct investments or loans in order to acquire capital goods.[9]

(3) *Capital imports.* They increase the drain on foreign currency and potential capital and enlarge the vicious circle of financial dependence. This leads to greater political, technical, and cultural dependence, for instance on universities which must repay various "aids," gifts, and loans.

Importation of capital, independently considered, constitutes the third fundamental obstacle to the development of our peoples. More than 28 percent of the income received by Latin America from exports of goods and services goes into the repatriation of profits and payment of interest and amortization of the external debt. This percentage grows daily (in 1956 it represented 15.6 percent, in 1963 it reached 28.5 percent) taking the characteristics of a boomerang effect. Capital is imported to cover balance deficits or the lack of capital, but at the same time, the balance becomes more deficient because these resources are used to pay interest, profits, and repatriation of original capital. A careful examination of how foreign capital operates proves that Latin America is not really an importer but an exporter of capital. Instead of financing her own development with external resources, in many cases Latin America finances the development of the industrialized countries by sacrificing to the point of exhaustion of natural and mineral resources, by exploiting labor, and by distorting development.

(4) *Deterioration of prices of export items.* In recent times, this appears to have worsened, according to the clear expositions of ECLA. For example, in 1964 the unitary value of Latin American exports was 35.8 (base 100 in 1950) and that of imports was 116.4. This shows a trade relationship of 82.3.[10]

To stress the economic importance of this phenomenon, let us cite the commentaries of CEPAL and Prebisch. They say that the amount of money which Latin America loses through price relationships in her commerce with the economic powers could offset general capital imports. In other words, by overcoming the injustice of present trade relationships in which imported manufactured goods become more expensive and primary products become cheaper, our countries could cover present investment expenses without having to resort to foreign capital and without increasing the external debt.

In Colombia, as a result of the coffee crisis provoked by the developed consumer countries, the terms of trade have become even worse: in 1964, the ratio was 72.3. The aggravation of this problem even forced the President of the Republic to respond, publicly denouncing the manuevers of the industrialized countries which were designed to divide the coffee producing countries, thereby achieving new lows in the price of this primary export so important to many Latin American economies.

To the previously discussed problems are added those of internal origin, such as land tenure, monopolistic concentration of private capital, and its associated uneven income distribution. Taken all together, these problems serve as a complete superstructure for dependent policy and culture, a deformed state organization, and for a defective administrative and fiscal organization. And according to our understanding (in spite of the preachings of *pill* advocates) these are the true, authentic obstacles which today keep underdeveloped people off the road to economic recovery, social development, and human and political dignity.

ECONOMIC THOUGHT AND POPULATION GROWTH *(pp. 59-60)*

A rapid review of the history of economic thought shows that the most eminent researchers have always learned to appreciate the positive role that population plays in economic development, and how its growth has forced the most revolutionary innovations in development. In the field of inventing, for example, new instruments of production have appeared, due to demographic pressure. Population increase encounters obstacles, but it can overcome them. Man's inventive power has appeared as the social solution of production. In this universal historical analysis, Silva Herzog says that as the demand for goods increases, be it through population growth or through increased purchasing power, or both, national and international markets rapidly expand. The urge to satisfy the new demands stimulates man's ingenuity to produce inventions.

Economists have proven the unquestionable reality of the creative and energizing power of population, which is especially evident during the most successful periods of economic systems. One could even say that in the dialogues between populationists and antipopulationists, the former embrace the optimistic thinking of the growth theorists, whose ideas reflect revolutionary times, that is, the first stages of a new system. But the antipopulationists, led by Malthus, embrace the conservative thinking of false pessimism. This only hides their fears of change, the breakdown of the status quo, and the replacement of those structures from which their own privileges and advantages emanate.

Socialist Thinking *(pp. 71-76)*

Socialist doctrine is clear and emphatic in rejecting Malthusianism. No one was more unrelenting than Marx in unmasking the reactionary and unscientific position of Malthus. Marx was not only irritated with Malthus' theoretical superficiality, but he fiercely fought his plagiarist style and his incorrect position in the face of Ricardo's scientific maturity. While Ricardo personified the dynamic elements of bourgeois society in the sense that it signified the unlimited and inexorable development of the productive forces of society, Malthus, especially in his value theory, glorified the vestiges of feudal society with its landlords, its fiefdoms, its tithes, its tax collectors, its speculators, its executioners. He glorified everything that Ricardo fought as useless and dangerous vestiges of pre-bourgeois production.[11] "We have already seen ... how childish, feeble, vacuous and trivial Malthus' position is ... but also a graver accusation weighs on him: his incapacity to renounce his innate vice of plagiarism...." *Principles of Political Economy* is a simple translation, slightly rearranged, of Sismondi's *Nouveaux Principes de L'économie Politique.*

Marx commented that Malthus advocated development of capitalist society, but thought that this mode of production should be adjusted at the same time to meet the needs of everything in the Church, and which reflected the hereditary interests of feudalism and absolute monarchy . . . "Malthus always favors bourgeois production when it is not revolutionary, i.e. when it does not represent a new historical element and is limited to establishing a wider and more comfortable material base for the sustenance of the old society."[12] With regard to the concrete case of the *Essay on the Principle of Population,* Marx said: "In reality, this work of Malthus' on population was a pamphlet directed against the French Revolution and the reformist aspirations manifested in England. It was an apology for the misery of the working class. In writing it he simply plagiarized Townsend."[13]

It would be easy to believe that as the father of scientific socialism and critic of capitalism, Marx used this same kind of language when referring to the capitalist theoreticians. Such was not the case. He repeatedly recognized the merits of the great economists who preceded him, whom he labeled the "classical." He not only calls Petty the founder of modern economics, but he speaks of his "genius and originality."[14] He recognizes the valuable scientific contribution of Smith, Ricardo, and almost all of the liberals. Perhaps nothing is more appropriate to demonstrate his spirit of vigorous scientific criticism than his comparison of Ricardo's and Malthus' concepts of the worker:

> It is not dishonest for Ricardo to compare the proletariat to machinery, to beasts of burden or to goods. This is stoic, objective, scientific. Whenever he could do it without violating his science, Ricardo spoke out as the philanthropist which he really was in practical life. On the other hand, 'pastor' Malthus, without relegating the worker to the role of beast of burden, condemned him to death and celibacy. And whenever the demands of production cut into the landlords' rent, the churches tithes, or the tax collectors' take, whenever sacrifices had to be made in the interests of production, 'pastor' Malthus always put the private interests of the dominant classes above the needs of production. Malthus never hesitated to falsify his pseudoscientific conclusions in favor of the aristocracy, or the conservative, or reactionary bourgeoisie when it came into conflict with the progressive bourgeoisie. Apart from his professional plagiarism, his scientific dishonesty and sin of perverted science are found here. The scientific consequences reached by Malthus are full of considerations favoring the most reactionary elements of the dominant classes in particular, which means that he falsifies science to serve these interests. In contrast, they are without scruples when it is a question of the subjected classes. Not only are scruples lacking, but they even boast of it, they cynically take pleasure in it, and they even exceed in their favor against those who live in misery that from their own point of view would be scientifically justified.[15]

Besides, Marx repeatedly made explicit reference to the relative excess of population which formed in the process of capital accumulation. See for example Chapter 23 of the first book (on the *Organic Law of Capital Accumulation*) and Chapter 14 of the third book (on *Contrary Causes* . . .). This is typical of the dialectic contradictions of the system. The process of reproduction modifies the organic composition of capital, as the goods of production and other elements essential to production increase in relation to the variable of labor. The same thing occurs in underdeveloped as well as industrial countries when foreign capital moves in with great technology and automation; a noticeable modification develops in the relationship between constant capital and variable capital. In short, the greater the use of machines, the lesser the relative use of workers. "With the growth of the total capital, its variable constituent or the labor incorporated in it, also does increase, but in a constantly diminishing proportion."[16] This relative decrease of the variable portion of capital is the reason for the great number of unemployed in the working classes of the underdeveloped countries. As accumulation of capital increases, so does the volume of "excess population or population superfluous to the average needs of capital valuation."[17] And this relative population surplus, notes Marx, shows up much more in a country where capitalist production is more developed.[18] In citing J. Robinson's motions, we pointed out what has been happening in the United States. The army of the unemployed has been growing markedly, even during cyclical phases of expansion, and it can only be reduced by conducting war or by building a gigantic army. Marx affirms: "This is a law of population peculiar to the capitalist mode of production; and in fact every special historic mode of production has its own special laws of population historically valid within its limits alone."

Latin American Thinking
(pp. 91-92 and 119-122)

Latin American economic thinkers almost unanimously reject neo-Malthusian superficiality. Exceptions include some young professional graduates of United States universities who were influenced by their tendentious teachings, members of University Centers financed by great foreign monopolies through the Ford and Rockefeller Foundations, professionals who are either uninformed or who are well remunerated in foreign cash (doctors, demographers, professors, etc.), and disoriented or complacent politicians with foreign commitments. In general, the social scientists of the continent know how to interpret the population problem and evaluate the importance of human resources in development.

From past times to the present, responsible investigation has weighed the importance of population density as the foremost factor in the achievement of development.

We have already mentioned, among others, Alberdi of Argentina and Narváez of Colombia as clear exponents of past populationism. In our times the most brilliant thinkers have consistently rejected neo-Malthusian fallacies:

Oreste Popescu in Argentina, Jesús Silva Herzog, Alonso Aguilar, Fernando Carmona, H. Flórez de la Peña, André G. Frank in Mexico; Humberto Espinoza, Carlos Capuñay Mimbela in Peru; Marcio Mejía Ricart, Bolívar Batista in the Dominican Republic; Josué de Castro, Celso Furtado in Brazil; Manuel Pernaut, Armando Alarcón, Armando Córdoba, Gastón Parra in Venezuela; Antonio García, Eduardo Arias, Carlos Calderón, E. Ahumada, H. Vergara in Colombia. The books and essays of these authors are well-known as representing the ideological expressions of our peoples. They have elucidated and clearly explained the fact that the problems of misery, unemployment, and other frustration, although apparently related to some mythical "population explosion," originate and feed on the faults of an archaic structure filled with vicious institutions that respond to neither the necessities of the modern world nor to the social structures achieved by other countries.

It is thus demonstrated that economic theorists have been and continue to be aware of the dynamic and stimulating role of population, not only in achieving economic growth under adequate conditions for normal development of productive activity, but also in overcoming the obstacles that obstruct development of the economy and new forms of social organization.

This intrusive force, generated by population density, is what prevailing forces fear, because they are incapable of resolving the profound disequilibriums that accumulate as collective necessities increase. For this reason, their neo-Malthusian proposals really ought to be considered as expressions of a special political doctrine which is interested in avoiding revolutionary pressures from new generations of unemployed and starving people.

We saw in the first chapter how an analysis which is limited to the infantile objectivity of population and production variables is simplistic and unscientific. On the contrary, investigation of the phenomena characteristic of population dynamics yield twice as much in the fields of production and consumption. Furthermore, because of the huge costs of installing the large mass production factories needed these days for manufacturing heavy machinery, industrial plants, tractors, and automobiles, existing national markets seem too small. Countries have therefore seen the necessity of commercial integration, of regional common markets. Necessarily, when we are explaining the rationale and importance of the Latin American Free Trade Association, Andean Zone, and Central American Common Market, we speak of the impossibility of achieving industrialization in countries with markets of a few million inhabitants in contrast to that which would presumably occur with the bigger markets resulting from the projected integration schemes. This means that the complexity of modern production and commercial competition demands not less, but more population in order to guarantee development. Greater demand can be created through combining populations and markets previously separate. Naturally, we do not assume that this broadening of demand through integration would alone yield change. In the last analysis, a common market is not an end, but a means or tactic whose results and benefits are relative. But at least we have clarified the importance which general integration places on a large population as prerequisite for markets capable of justifying the costs of certain industrial installations. It is worth saying that, in general, the theory of common markets and integration of independent geographic units validates the idea that more extensive demographic groupings and higher population volumes are needed.

Spokesmen for special interests, who are responsible for the misery of the masses in undeveloped countries, unfurl the phantom of the population explosion, lift the banners of birth control, and use sophisms in order to misrepresent and obscure the correct interpretation of the origins of the given situation. They exhibit extreme cynicism when they try to shift the responsibility for misfortune to the victims themselves. In the long run however, they end up allowing the truth of their political proposals be known. This leads them to the realization that the hungry, the dispossessed, those with no future, those with neither land nor work, will tomorrow, as the torrent feeds on and grows bigger with drops of persistent rain, break the gates that they encounter and follow the route which historical destiny and the laws of social evolution have reserved for them.

And if the reactionary forces, represented by prevailing structures and institutions, are fully aware of it, then those who desire a different society also ought to know how to appreciate the importance of demographic expansion. That which represents fear and guilt for some is a sign of great things to come for others. To paraphrase an old saying we could well say, "It is necessary to have hope in those who today are born without hope."

NATURAL RESOURCES AND POPULATION
(pp. 125-128)

The ideas of Malthus, like those of his predecessors and present disciples, maintain mistaken assumptions about the rhythm growth between variables supposedly independent of each other, that is, the exaggerated increase of population and slow development of productive activity. Furthermore, these pessimistic disciples even believe that there is a natural barrier impeding man from obtaining the amount of food necessary to cope with population growth.

In Malthus' time, statements about declining yields were in their apogee. In spite of the beginning of the extraordinary innovations which would later be known as "Industrial Revolution," structural obstacles, which in England were manifest in land tenure, led to pessimistic conclusions and even served to support the differential theory of income.

In our time, history has fully disproven the hypothesis of the past. Through the analysis of production statistics, it is now possible to appreciate how those countries where man's creativity and labor have not encountered obstacles have attained a productivity growth which has surpassed all previous calculations. Thus European and North American capitalism has reached its well-known affluence and mass consumption, while socialist economies have attained their lightening growth.

Referring to past beliefs, Eric Roll has said: "The law of 'diminishing returns' was clearly refuted as a dynamic principal; its place in contemporary economies is that of a law which only holds under the ideal situation of a stationary equilibrium."[19]

This is a correct estimation, because only in conditions of hypothetical stagnation can one imagine a decline in the production of some product when the use of those factors involved in its production is increased. In underdeveloped economies, because of characteristics typical to these economies which we will study later (the exploitation and uncontrolled destruction of vegetation, mineral, forest, and fishing resources; the permanent depilating cultivation of small plots; the growing infecundity of large estates which are wasted with erosion and devegetation, etc.), one can partially appreciate the kinds of problems which demand immediate action. For example, foreign capital freely exploits our natural resources so that only exhausted holes are left where the oil trust acted, and only stony ground remains where the mining excavators passed. These are real facts that cannot be denied but must be explained as the unavoidable consequences of economic and political dependence. These phenomena are all expressions of particular prevailing structures and institutions which will have to be either corrected or superceded by different forms of production and social organization.

In the same manner it could be asserted that by dominating supply, concentrated or monopolistic property rigidifies production, conditioning it exclusively to the interests of capital. Thus industry becomes insensitive to changes in demand resulting from natural population growth.

As we have already mentioned, the statistics on capitalism in its early stages give eloquent proof that economic growth in every sector exceeded the highest population growth rates. This is presently happening in some socialist economies, where production levels are surpassing the highest rates of the past, exceeding by five or six times the rates of population growth.

But naturally it is almost impossible to evade the reality of a system where production does not satisfy human necessities, but where certain men earn profits; where wealth is not enjoyed by the natives, but by strangers who acquire it by their own efforts or from productive relationships which they themselves have imposed; where technical progress represented by the machine does not serve society but benefits only a few.

The truth is that, given recent scientific advances along with unlimited natural resources, the earth could support a population 50 times its present size.

Latin American Resources
(pp. 152-154 and 172-174)

Now in the particular case of our continent, the resource inventory is prodigious. The richness of its land is so complete in contrast to the misery of its inhabitants. In comparing the data described by resource experts with statistics on the hunger and deprivation of Indians in Peru, Bolivia, and Ecudar, or peasants in Brazil, Colombia, or Nicuragua, one is reminded of a well-known phrase by Engels which refers to a contradiction inherent in the capitalist system during a crisis of relative overproduction. A moment arrives, said the great dialectic thinker, in which "the working masses lack the means of life because they produce too much of the means of life." The abundance of mineral resources in Latin America was in the past the cause of the destruction of aboriginal culture, developmental distortion, and the annihilation of peoples; and in the present it is the prevailing economic system which causes her economic, political, and cultural submission.

In his studies, Josué de Castro emotionally recalls the significance of Latin America's wealth and the role that its exploitation has played in the development of those countries which have conquered it. He comments:

> From her immense natural resources, she derives only wretchedness. She is in agony in the presence of innumerable resources. Latin America supplies the needs of the world, but there is not enough for her. It is the booty and power base of others. According to Davidson, it possesses more arable tropical land per capita than Asia, and the greatest forest reserves in the world. Under this land lie incalculable reserves of petroleum, iron, copper, tin, gold, silver, zinc, and lead. The list is endless, including practically every ordinary and precious metal, and every industrial chemical element known by man. With her petroleum and hydroelectric energy, she has one of the greatest energy reserves in the world. But through the centuries the gold and silver have been stripped for the benefit of Europe. She has handed over her raw materials for a very low price. In contributing to the fortunes of the Spanish, Portuguese, English, French, and now the Americans, her own misery has increased.[20]

Now we can go back and think a bit about the bad faith of the propogandists of antinatalist terrorism, and about the insensitivity of students who unquestioningly accept irresponsible proposals. The abundance of nature and man's creativity present eloquent testimony against their clamor. It is true that current conditions cause anguish. But in the future, changes implied by social laws will permit us to overcome the obstacles which today cause inequality among men.

We have already mentioned the inventory of world resources, particularly that of our continent. Latin America's problems can only be explained as resulting from a historical linkage to an economic system, because huge mineral reserves and fertile soils are just waiting for the changes leading to a new social order which will harness them to serve the people.

It is not important, one could say, that spokesmen for the fallacious

180 Perspectives on Population Control

thesis are echoed by certain groups who share the booty which foreign organizations and enterprises extract from the dependent countries. In the last analysis, the future belongs to those who would crush individual selfishness.

But before concluding these remarks, it would be interesting to mention that some researchers complement the theoretical criticisms that they outline against antinatalism by observing the very suggestive attitude adopted by the United States' laboratories which produce birth control pills. To many observers, the close relationship between the "aid" programs of the U.S. government and the sale and manufacture of its pills is conclusive. At a seminar in Chile sponsored by foreign organizations to study problems of population growth, a high percentage of the delegates represented American manufacturers of contraceptives.

Because truthfully, this antinatalist uproar hides a gamut of chilling intentions related to business calculations and dealings. Referring to an aspect which we commented on in the first chapter, the weekly *El Catolicismo,* organ of the Curia Romana of Bogotá, said in an edition of October, 1968: "It is a question of numbers—a pill or intrauterine coil costs less than a napalm bomb— and of principles. It is better to kill potential subversion at its roots, without suffering, than to let it be born and grow only to exterminate it 20 years later having put up with its nuisance. After killing Asians, MacNamara [sic] solemnly declared that even the World Bank would dedicate to preventing the births of underdeveloped barbarians."[21]

NOTES TO CHAPTER 9

1. M. Harrington, *La cultura de la pobreza en los Estados Unidos,* cited by Carlos Calderón Mosquera, *La nación norteamericana y sus minorías* (Bogotá, 1967).
2. Cited by Ernest Havemann, *El control de la natalidad* (n.p.: Life, Informe Internacional, 1967).
3. Joseph Marion Jones, *Sobreproducción significa pobreza?* (Washington, 1962). Edited by the Center for International Development, with Prologue by Eugene R. Black, President of the International Bank of Reconstruction and Development.
4. Gregorio García, at a conference held at the University of Cartagena, 1967.
5. Maurice Dobb, *Capitalismo, crecimiento económico y subdesarollo* (Barcelona, 1964).
6. Alonso Aguilar, *Teoría del desarrollo en América Latina* (México, 1967).
7. Farreira, *Ensayos sobre el principio do la población* (Buenos Aires: Editorial Intermundo, 1945), Prologue.
8. On October 2, 1967, the A.P. news agency, in an article published in *El Tiempo,* said that the United States made it known before the Inter-American Committee of the Alliance for Progress meeting in Rio de Janeiro that it would condition the aid of the Alliance to family planning in Latin America. This threat has since been repeated to

the point of causing a general reaction. For example, *El Tiempo* published a caricature by Chapete (representing Northern imperialism) trying to deceive a little girl (Latin America) with a carmel (projected loans) so that she would accept his antipopulation thesis.
9. Statistics from ECLA, André Frank, ¿*Servicios extranjeros o desarrollo nacional?* (México: Revista Comercio Exterior, n.d.); José Consuegra, *Los economistas ante el desarrollo nacional* (Bogotá, 1967).
10. ECLA, *Estudio económico de América Latina* (1964).
11. Carlos Marx, *Historia critica de la plusvalía,* III (n.p.: Fondo de Cultura Económica, n.d.), p. 44.
12. *Ibid.,* p. 45.
13. *Ibid.,* p. 53. In volume II of the cited edition he adds, "Malthus was a professional plagiarist. It is enough to compare the first edition of his work, with its niceties of geometric and arithmetic progressions, with the work of Reverend Townsend to be convinced that he did not work with his own creations, but simply copied and paraphrased like a common plagiarist . . ." p. 245.
14. *Ibid.,* I, p. 3.
15. *Ibid.,* II, pp. 250, 251.
16. Carlos Marx, *El capital,* II (México: Fondo de Cultura Económica, n.d.), p. 126 (from the English edition).
17. *Ibid.*
18. *Ibid.,* IV, p. 236.
19. Eric Roll, *Historia de las doctrinas económicas* (México: Fondo de Cultura Económica, n.d.), p. 181.
20. Josué de Castro, "El oro y la América Latina," *Desarrollo Indo-americano,* no. 5 (Colombia), 1967.
21. *El Catolicismo* (Bogotá), October, 1968.

Chapter Ten

The Demographic Problems of Mexico and Latin America*

Gilberto Loyo

The following facts of importance characterize today's world:

1. great scientific and technological progress;
2. popular revolutions against the colonial powers, against what has been called neo-colonialism, and naturally against imperialism which in this epoch has assumed new forms and a new nature, even though it still retains some of the aspects acquired in the beginning of the century;
3. the unprecedented accelerated growth of the world population which is especially high in the underdeveloped countries;
4. at the same time that the nationalistic ideas and attitudes are becoming stronger in the backward but developing countries, aspirations of improving the standard of living and of participating in the governmental decisions are also growing among the masses, that is to say, people no longer wish to remain on the fringe of the political life of their nations;
5. the tendency of the small and middle-size countries toward political and economic integration as a reaction to the three continental nations (United States, USSR, and China).

The great scientific and technological progress has lead scientists, politicians and humanitarians (capitalists as well as socialists) to believe that with the existing scientific and technological state we can feed, clothe, house, and educate the world population even if it should double or triple in the future. These observers point out that the difficulty of eliminating hunger in

*This chapter contains a translation of "Algunos problemas demográficos de México y América Latina" *Cuadernos Americanos,* CL, No. 2 (enero-febrero de 1967), pp. 41-64. It is reprinted by permission of the publisher and translated by Jennie Lincoln and the editor.

the world is of a social, political and economic character, that the prevailing social, political and economic system impedes proper use of the world's production capacity to attend to the needs of the population even if it were doubled or tripled.

Other men, however, are of the opinion that scientific and technological progress is not enough, even where it might be possible to obtain favorable results through the social, political and economic reforms, because underdeveloped societies present obstacles to the adoption and application of new techniques of production, and it is difficult to change the social attitudes which impede scientific and technological progress. Likewise, these men believe that, while nationalism creates a favorable force in the evolution of countries, it also generates resistance to international solutions of problems based on a rational distribution of the population on the planet as well as a distribution of food and other articles of primary necessity. Others believe that institutional and social factors are not properly valued in relation to the technological and economic factors of development.

In the first quarter of the nineteenth century most of the Latin American countries gained their independence just as many of the African and Asian countries did after World War II. The process of decolonization came about because of the political, economic and moral decline of some of the mother-countries, the new correlations of economic , political and military forces resulting from World War II, and the demographic and economic evolution of the people who had been colonial subjects. At the same time that these factors were in operation, in the latter part of the 1940's, notable progress was made in the fields of medicine and hygiene which decreased infant mortality as well as general mortality thereby increasing the population. Thus the demographic pressures of the 1960's, which continue to grow and may do so for decades to come, were generated. Associated with these demographic pressures were other causes that awaken the desires of people to improve their lives and accelerate their economic development at the same time that political and social pressures mentioned earlier combined with the rapid growth of the cities of the underdeveloped countries from the increase in population and the growing emigration from the rural areas to the cities.

In 1700 the life expectancy of the white population of North America and of Western Europe was 33 years. Now many countries involved in the development process have a life expectancy of more than 60 years. In the United States in 1950, it was 69 years. In the countries of North America and Western Europe there had been an equilibrium between fertility and mortality for many centuries. Then, when the growth rate began to increase, birth control methods were adopted to control fertility in those countries of primarily white population. In 1930 the birth rate had diminished in these countries with some demographers fearing the decline of the white populations of North America and Western Europe and projecting their probable decrease.

The low growth rate which these countries reached resulted from low mortality rates and only moderate fertility rates that were due to voluntary birth control. This is what was called the demographic revolution which was the transition from an age of high fertility and declining mortality rates to the equilibrium mentioned earlier. At the beginning of the 1930's the Mexican population grew only slightly because, even though the fertility rate was high, both the infant and overall mortality rates were very high. In 1929, I stressed the necessity of increasing the population growth rate that was at the time slow as a way to defend ourselves from the expansive foreign powers which threatened to take or "to buy" some of our northern states.

At that time some Malthusians argued that Mexico was a country of deserts that could not support a population of more than 20 million inhabitants. In 1966, Mexico had a population of 44 million people and the living standards of important parts of the people were much improved as compared to the 1920's or 1930's.

It has been estimated that by 1975 the population of the world will be four billion and that it will reach 32 billion a century later. (Continuing this reasoning, the year 2200 will see 500 billion people). Professor Harold F. Dorn says that these statistics are frightful and that:

> we are not able to conceive of a population so numerous. It seems that man must establish some conscientious manner of controlling his reproductive capacity in order to balance fertility with mortality rates before another century passes. . . . The world does not constitute one single unit from the point of view of its necessities nor in the availability of resources, ability, and knowledge to attend to these, nor with respect to population growth. As a result of the existing political barriers, population growth will become a serious problem in some countries much before it becomes a world problem with no existing boundaries for the redistribution of the population. Except in a very general sense, there does not exist a world population problem, but there are many different problems in the different nations of the world. There is no solution that might be equally applied to all the countries.

The cause of the high rates of population growth is said to consist of a combination of medieval fertility rates and twentieth century mortality rates. There are no indications that these high fertility rates will begin to decline in years to come. The age structure of the population in most of the underdeveloped countries is the factor which explains why even in fifteen or twenty years these countries would not be able to register any significant decreases in the population growth, even if they were to initiate family planning and responsible parenthood programs of sufficient magnitude immediately. Almost all of the demographers of Europe and the United States agree that rapid population growth in Asia, Africa and Latin America hinders economic development since a large part of resources goes to feed, clothe and educate the infant and adolescent portions of the population which are constantly growing.

I believe that Mexico's population growth has until now not hindered its economic development, but that it could diminish the rhythm of economic development in the coming years if it continues at the growth rate of the early 1960's. Furthermore, I believe that the accelerated growth of the population of Mexico is a fundamental fact which must be taken in account in the planning and execution of economic and social policies.

Proliferation in the means of communication, the fight against illiteracy, the use of computers, the political and social literature, and the growing contrasts between affluence and misery in the underdeveloped countries coincide with the formation and amplication of individual attitudes of malaise, of desires for a better standard of living as well as better incomes and social security. These increasing aspirations for material and cultural betterment are getting stronger because of the accelerated population growth and because of the density of the urban and suburban areas. The process, therefore, generates political and social tensions and factors favorable toward changes in the political and economic structures of the underdeveloped countries. It also strengthens resistance to imperialistic penetration and neo-colonialism.

The most important demographic problems of Mexico may be divided into two classes: those that are derived from the accelerated population growth and those that result from historic, economic, social and political factors which have determined the evolution and the characteristics of the Mexican nation. Most demographic problems in the second category are related to characteristics of the social and economic structure such as illiteracy, indigenous languages, land tenure practices and other economic activities, housing, family organization and distribution of income and population.

The national population has an annual growth rate of 3.5 to 3.6 percent and is one of the highest in the world. The figure of 44 million people in 1966 is not in itself high in relation to the natural resources and the levels of available technology; however, in some zones the growing population threatens the already low levels of agricultural and, in some sectors, industrial production. In the country as a whole it reinforces insufficient capital formation. It is a demographic statistic which—because of natural resources and available technology as well as the advanced unity of the country expressed in its traditions, history, national language, and national conscience formed through the War of the Independence, the War of the Reform and the Mexican Revolution—is compatible with the first stage of modern development of a peaceful, middle-size nation that for well-known reasons does not spend a great part of its gross national product on the military. Instead, it dedicates the greatest proportion of the federal budget to education and an important part to building infrastructure and investments which are directly or indirectly productive.

Neither does the general density of the population (22 persons per sq. kilometer) constitute a demographic problem, even though disproportionate growth of the Federal District (Mexico City) generates grave economic and social problems, such as obstructing the industrial development of other regions of the country. Such obstacles tend to be overcome by stimulating development in areas such as Guadalajara, Monterrey, el Bajio, Puebla, part of Veracruz, and some regions of the North and of the Southeast.

Agrarian reform, in the areas where it has had medium or good results, has settled the rural population. Where the results have not been good due to the poor quality of the land or other causes, it has stimulated the migration of rural workers to the United States and to other rural areas in Mexico as well as to the large cities. In addition to the internal movement of agricultural workers, a new agricultural system has developed in Mexico. Above all there is cotton which moves from area to area because of the high costs of re-cultivation resulting in less yearly production and higher costs of controlling pests, etc. Indigenous groups are not very geographically mobile, but the efforts made to modernize their material and cultural conditions have had good results. These efforts were counteracted in part by the rapid increase in the indigenous population due to decreasing mortality, a rate still sometimes higher than the national average.

The accelerated growth of the Mexican population is due to the accentuated decline in general and infant mortality rates while the birth rate remains high. The latter constitutes a demographic problem of primary importance and results from the underdeveloped economy, low cultural levels, the low income of the masses, paternal irresponsibility, maternal irresponsibility, and ignorance of family planning, which contrasts with the growing abortion rate and use of ineffective contraceptive devices. It can be said that to some degree in the rural areas and to a greater degree in lower class urban areas women—oppressed by the number of children they have, by their poverty, and by the irresponsibility of their husbands—attempt to control birth by inducing abortion, (many times with regrettable consequences) or by ineffective contraceptive methods. There is, then, a clear tendency for lower class urban women to hold down the number of children, after having had four or five surviving children, in spite of the poverty, because of the factors which have produced a decline in infant mortality. Religious factors play less of a significant part than is usually attributed to them in Mexico, in both the urban and rural areas.

The primary demographic problem is the age composition of the national population. High proportions of children and adolescents burden the active population of 15 to 64 years of age. A large part of the theoretically active population is underemployed and another part unemployed. The composition by ages of the population with its high proportions of young adults of both sexes, on the one hand, produces a high fertility rate and, on the other, pressures the labor market and raises the investments needed to provide employment for this growing young population.

A significant proportion of the young population in the cities express desires for an improved life-style with such things as electrical appliances, motorcycles, cars, as well as sports and other entertainment, imitating the customs and attitudes of the young people of the upper-middle and upper classes. Poverty greatly reduces access to high school and university educations for many young people. The aspirations and ambitions of the young women pressure the labor market, aggravate the low purchasing power of fathers, husbands and brothers and sharpen discontentment, ultimately stirring family tensions whose characteristics and intensity vary in the different urban and rural strata.

The accelerated growth of the infant population intensifies the race between the growing number of school age children and the construction of primary schools and preparation of teachers and doctors. The necessity of eliminating illiteracy and raising the levels of education in a developing country is clear and urgent; and the obstacles to obtaining it grow in proportion to the accelerated growth of the infant and adolescent population. The imperatives of economic development and the growth in the number of young people increase the need for secondary schools, technical and professional schools as well as extra-curricular activities such as sports and other youth organizations. It also accentuates the urgency for reforms in both the universities and at the primary and middle levels of the national educational system.

The high proportion of youths produces changes in the customs, in the structure of the family, in the distribution of income, in social consciousness, and in the characteristics of the juvenile delinquency. The accelerated growth of the young generates political and social pressures and tends to create a political and social network acting in defiance of the older generation, thus stimulating improvision and substitution.

The composition of the national population by sex is normal. Only in the rural zones where there has been great emigration of workers or in the small cities which are university or industrial centers is there a moderate disproportion in the composition of the young population by sex.

The doors of our northern neighbor remain closed to the seasonal emigration of Mexican farm workers called "braceros." Because of this, rural unemployment has grown and income declined in several zones. In some— especially rural—areas and some urban strata the tendency to emigrate to the United States has increased. It is known that the emigrants generally have qualities of energy and initiative superior to that of the average population from where they came. In the last few years there has been noted an increase of young emigrants to the United States, especially qualified and professional workers. This fact is not important because of its magnitude, but because of the insufficient number of these qualified workers left in the country—doctors and engineers, for example.

Most of the national population is concentrated in an axis that goes from the Gulf of Mexico to the Pacific Ocean, crossing the country as a wide band that climbs moderately toward the North as it gets farther away from the Gulf of Mexico. Its direction corresponds to the volcanic axis. However, in analyzing the changes in population during the last 30 years, we see that the uneven distribution of the population has decreased because of increased population in various regions of the North and other border zones. Problems of this uneven distribution of population persist in areas characterized by small *ejidal* parcels and poor quality soils. Irrigation and transportation policies have contributed to a better distribution of the population to some areas which before were almost depopulated. Regional agriculture crises of pests and drought or low prices in the international markets have generated internal migration when changes in agricultural cultivation were not opportune and sufficient to retain the population in that area. It is convenient to remember that the official intentions of colonizing the interior have been limited in scope, of little importance, and therefore have not had satisfactory results.

In 1960, the economically inactive population of ages 0 to 14 years numbered 16.4 million people, who were dependent for food, clothing, entertainment, medical services, and education upon an economically active population of 11 million people. These 11 million people represented 31.7 percent of the national population. In 1965, the inactive population was estimated to be 20 million people out of total population of 43 million people. In 1970, the national population will be 51 million people with 24 million people in the ages 0 to 14. In 1970, Mexico will have to produce material and cultural necessities satisfactorily for 24 million children. In 1975, the 0 to 14 population will reach approximately 28 million people of a national population of 61 million people. In 1980, with a national population of 72 million people, the 0 to 14 segment will have reached 33 million. It should be noted that the problems related to the accelerated growth of inactive population tend to grow and become more complicated in that a larger proportion of the gross national product will have to be dedicated to education and other public services for the larger number of young children and adolescents. Social investments will have to increase at least proportionally, and for that reason, it will be difficult to increase direct productive investments more than proportionally.

The growth of Mexico's gross national product is small when compared to the economies of some socialist and capitalistic countries. In 1965, according to published data, the increase in gross national product was 6.1 percent and the increase in population 3.5 percent yielding an increase in per capita gross national product of 2.6 percent, which is small even though larger than many other Latin American countries. Although our economic development has been sustained for the past two decades, it is still small. We have not achieved an economic and political organization which assures rapid and effective advances in economic and social planning for the most efficient use of our human, technological, financial, economical, institutional, and natural resources. We have not lived in a social climate of austerity, collective discipline, and an abundance of work. In the near future we cannot expect a substantial elevation of our economic growth, but with great efforts and a firm will applied to the popular ideals we could develop at a 6.5 to 7 percent annual increase in gross national product.

It is estimated that the rural population, which was 17.7 million in 1960, will reach 20.9 million in 1970 and 23.7 million in 1980. It will, however, have diminished from 49.2 percent of the total population in 1960 to 32.8 percent in 1980. New areas of cultivation and technological advances in agriculture, as well as effective progress in land tenure, land utilization, and the reorganization of small holdings and *ejidos* to improve their productivity will generate work for a large number of the people in economically productive ages who form a part of the rural population of 23.7 million people. And so the accelerated growth of the rural population (naturally less than that of the urban population) aggravates the problems of land tenure, use of the land, agricultural technique, rising yields, production, and industrial organization as well as the problems of medical services, education, electricity and roads for the rural population. As for the urban population, the problem will be sharper as it grows from 18.3 million in 1960 to probably 30 million in 1970 and 48.6 million in 1980 not only because of the natural increase of the population but also because of current emigration from the rural areas to the urban areas, especially to the large cities.

Strong investments in the social and economic infrastructure, in factories, plants and mines as well as in transportation will be required to employ the people of active age in this urban population of 48.6 million people. The effort that this country ought to make in 1960 to 1970 to maintain its growth of the gross national product must be vigorous and well-directed in order to overcome many obstacles; but the effort that will have to be made in 1970 to 1980 will have to be even greater because of the extremely rapid growth of the urban population. It will be a crucial decade for the Mexican economy which will test economic and social planning, or put differently, the experience and the techniques which are supposed to bring about progress. Our political and social stability will also be tested because the accelerated increase in the urban population could intensify social and political tensions.

The birth rate in 1965 is estimated to be 45.5 or 46 per 1000 inhabitants; if the death rate is 10.5 per 1000, then the natural increase is 3.5 percent. In 1970, the primary sector of the economically active population will still be important, since it could represent 50.2 percent of the total active population. Of this proportion 48.9 percent could be in agriculture, cattle raising, forestry, hunting and fishing and 1.3 percent in extractive industries. The secondary sector will account for 21.6 percent of the active population of which 16.3 percent will work in manufacturing, 5 percent in construction, and 0.4 percent in electricity and gas industries. In the tertiary sector (commerce, transportation and services), which tends to increase greatly in the developing countries with almost pathologic growth which hides behind the euphemism of "services," 28.2 percent of the active population will work. More people will work in this sector than in industry. Of this 28.2 percent, 10.8 percent will be in commerce, in which there now exists a high proportion of underemployed people who work in tiny businesses on the streets, in the markets, or in the traditional *"tianguis"* of small and medium towns. Possible 3.9 percent of the active population in the tertiary sector in 1970 will work in transportation and 13.5 percent in a wide variety of "services" distinct from commerce and transportation.

So the proportion of the active population in the primary sector will have scarcely diminished from 55.8 percent in 1960 to 50.2 percent in 1970. It is a small advancement for a decade in an age as dynamic as this. The population dependent on agriculture will diminish from 54.6 percent of the total active population in 1960 to 49 percent in 1970. The end of the decade will still see a very high proportion of the population dedicated to agriculture. Therefore we will begin the decade of the 1970's with such a high proportion occupied in agriculture that an important part of the excess population will push to emigrate abroad and to the large Mexican cities. The proportion of the population in extractive industries will increase slightly. The rate of economic development in the country will probably allow an increase of active population in the secondary sector from 17.8 percent in 1960 to 21.6 percent in 1970. The active population in the tertiary sector will increase from 26.3 percent to 28 percent in 1970, according to the present trends, if factors which are conducive to a major increase in population in this service sector that is almost marginal and which has a tendency to increase in developing countries, are not aggravated. These small anticipated changes for 1970 well-illustrate the seriousness of our demographic situation.

According to the 10 year plan (1961 to 1971) for the provision of water in urban and rural Latin America, it is estimated that in Mexico the population without water services in 1961 was 8.3 million people and that it will increase to 18 million in 1971 in spite of investments and extraordinary efforts to provide potable water. According to this plan, Mexico needs to supply at least 963,000 more urban inhabitants each year and at least one million more rural inhabitants annually.

According to the Economic Commission for Latin America (ECLA) Mexico has an estimated deficit of 1,600,000 housing units of which 1,000,000 are in urban areas and 600,000 in rural. In order to attend to the housing needs of an increasing population, Mexico needs to build at least 194,000 housing units each year in urban zones and 85,000 in rural. These 280,000 housing units per year are required to cover the population increase and replace useless housing. In the face of this theoretical housing need, ECLA estimated that Mexico was building approximately 57,000 housing units per year so that the deficit or the number of additional necessary units is very large—222,000 units per year—which gives a clear idea of the seriousness of the housing problem in the next decades due primarily to rapid population growth.

In the United States, the number of doctors per 10,000 inhabitants is 14.8, in Argentina 14.9 and in Canada 11.3. Meanwhile the number in Mexico in 1961 was scarcely 5.7. Without a doubt this proportion has improved slightly in the last years. In Mexico in 1960, the number of doctors per 10,000 inhabitants was 11.9 in the provincial capitals and important cities but only 4.2 in the rest of the country. The extension of social security services to some agricultural areas has tended to improve this deplorable situation. Thus, interdependence between the rapid increase of population, low standards of living, insufficient housing condition, unemployment, underemployment, and new social and political tensions is coming to our attention.

Ideological differences within a country generate political tensions, but great inequality in the income distribution and therefore in the standards of living of the backward and developing countries, places even greater difficulty in the way of accelerating economic and social development and consolidating political institutions. The increase in the population in countries of limited development tends to augment internal demand if it is accompanied by good economic policy and social security, but it can decrease savings and the capacity to increase productive investments. Finding an adequate equilibrium in the underdeveloped countries with accelerated population growth between increases in levels of consumption and the capacity to strengthen and diversify productive investments only can be the result of sane, well-planned, and precisely executed policies in the diverse economic and social areas.

I consider equally simplistic the following positions: the position of those who affirm that the accelerated population growth devours the increase in the gross national product and prevents the attainment of higher levels of income per capita and the position of those who maintain that accelerated population growth forces intensive and rational development of natural resources of underdeveloped countries, thus permitting accelerated economic development. This second position is misleading as generally our countries have very deficient and incomplete knowledge of their natural resources and, in many instances, do not arrange financial and technological resources to provide intensive and rational exploitation. Even achieving intensive and rational exploitation of those resources, prices of primary materials and basic products with their well-known tendency to decline on international markets are factors contrary to development.

One may not contemplate the future economic development of Mexico without considering the demographic variable not only in terms of the high growth rates and global statistics by decade but also in terms of the age structure of the population, urban and rural proportions, and the possible composition of the active population by economic activity.

When the Mexican population in the 1920's was increasing at a modest rate and when Mexican independence and sovereignty were threatened by foreign forces, it was desirable to accelerate national population growth through decreases in general and infant mortality rates. During this period, a demographic policy aimed at increasing population and distributing it appropriately was called for, and when population growth greatly increased due to progress in medicine and hygiene after the World War II, we have seen how the absolute figures reached in themselves did not arouse serious concern in relation to our economic and social development. But now the facts that our birth rates remain high in the face of declining mortality; that our growth rates in the next decades are going to be very high, decreasing only slightly; and that the age structure of the national population makes it difficult to obtain sensible reductions in birth growth rates during the period 1960 to 1980 must be examined in the light our hope to maintain the same or even reach higher rates of development. If the tendencies of the last two decades of the twentieth century continue, accelerated demographic growth may raise new obstacles, and aggravate existing ones, to economic and social development. The very high proportions of young in the population will necessitate increases in social investments—in order to creat jobs for the burgeoning population from 15 to 64 years of age—that may reach enormous figures. Therefore, we should be aware that it is necessary to proceed without delay and with social consciousness to do something about these acute problems. This awareness should not come from fear when facing rapid population growth but from objective, well-founded knowledge in order to propose education policies and technical assistance of a medical and social nature that would bring about responsible family planning.

It is not possible for a country with a high rate of population growth to sustain indefinitely the birth rate of a backward country, the mortality rate of a developed country, and at the same time to aspire to accelerate the growth rate of its per capita gross national product. These are simple facts. We have not raised doctrines but facts and demographic tendencies.

The appreciable increase in abortions in Mexico is, on the one hand, a sad, undesirable aspect of a responsible and insufficient means of birth control; that is, it is not a real control but an attempt to control. On the other hand, abortion is a crime and a poor method of controlling the birth rate; it is unacceptable in its legal, moral and human aspects. Modern contraceptives, scientifically chosen and applied, could, with social consciousness, begin to decrease Mexico's high birth rate. They would not only have positive democ affects in decreasing the population growth rate after some decades, ey would also strengthen the moral and social structure of urban and rural families. They would allow extension to a large stratum of the national population notions of responsible parenthood which are contrary to Don-Juanism, *machismo,* and the other antisocial and anachronistic forms of relations between men and women characteristic of some sectors of our population.

Family planning, through strengthening the effective and moral bonds of the family, would reduce the action of cultural and economic factors that are conducive to the exploitation of children, school desertion, begging, and other social phenomena just as deplorable. Family planning can stimulate better distribution of the income of the head of the family, thereby strengthening general consumer demand. It also allows better utilization of medical services, social security, and mass education as well as occupational orientation services for young people. It can, moreover, improve the family environment, diminish the penalties of being Mexican mothers in the poorest strata, increase the capacity of these women to educate their children and to diminish their wants and their anguish.

The United States and Canada with a population of a little more than 6 percent of the world total have a production of more than 39 percent of the world's production. Euroepe, including the USSR, has a population which is 22 percent of the world's total and produces more than 37 percent of the world's production. To sum up, the so-called highly developed countries with less than 30 percent of the world's population account for more than 80 percent of the world's production. The Third World, or the underdeveloped countries, with 70 percent of the world's population now can hardly produce 20 percent of the world's production.

The simple statistics above are eloquent. On the other hand, the distance between the developed and underdeveloped countries is getting dangerously greater since the growth in per capita income of the developed countries is more than fifteen times bigger than that of the so-called underdeveloped countries. This is one of the fundamental problems of the contemporary economy which for its part hides serious weaknesses of the economic, political and social structures, of monetary exchange rates, of the qualitative and the quantitative structure of production in the underdeveloped countries, and of the causes which tend to lower the prices of primary goods and basic products while raising the prices of the manufactured goods that the developed countries produce with their great technology. These countries raise the already high standard of living of their population to an annual rate of 5 percent, while some of the developing countries which have progressed greatly in the last decades scarcely reach 1.5 to 2 percent annual increase in their per capita income.

It is clear that, on one hand, economic, social and political structures and, on the other, trade relations between the countries that produce primary good and those which are highly industrialized are two of the primary causes of the dramatic poverty and slow development that afflict two-thirds of the population of this planet. Accelerated population growth is only one factor down the hierarchical level that combines with other fundamental factors to aggravate the unfavorable aspects of relatively slow development. Therefore, even when the accelerated population growth demands more extensive study in each country and even when it is appropriate for underdeveloped countries to become consciously aware of the causes and consequences of rapid population increase and to initiate the sociological, biological, and medical studies which form the base for family planning, it is necessary to point out that a good policy of family planning is not, and cannot be, a panacea nor a remedy for the fundamental causes of the economic backwardness and low development rates of the underdeveloped countries.

It is important to remember that a policy of lowering the birth rate cannot by itself accelerate economic development if the economic and social policies are not correct and if the means of implementing them in each country are not adequate. Mexico, fortunately, in the last decades has been developing and clarifying a national consciousness of the necessity of good economic and social planning. Some steps have been taken timidly, while others have been taken firmly. There have been improvements in the training of professionals for economic and social planning, recognition of policies and experiences of other countries with different political systems, and the majority of the private sector has seen the advantages of proper economic planning. Also there is a tendency toward coordination of public investments and the activities of ministries, decentralized organisms, and federal enterprises.

The President of the Mexican Republic in his Second State of the Union Address to Congress on the first of September of 1966 said: "We have a special pledge to the planning of economic and social development of the country and to programming the public sector." He said that the Intersecretarial Commission charged with elaborating the feature project for socio-economic development in 1966 to 1970 issued the following orientations and national objectives:

1. to achieve at least a 6 percent annual economic increase;
2. to give priority to the agricultural-livestock sector to accelerate its development and to strengthen the domestic market;
3. to give impetus to industrialization and improve the productive efficiency of industry;
4. to diminish and correct disequilibria in development, regional as well as different economic sectors;

5. to distribute better national income;
6. to improve education, housing, sanitary conditions, social security and, in general, social welfare;
7. to promote domestic savings;
8. to maintain the stability of the exchange rate and combat inflationary pressures.

And the President added: "It is anticipated that Mexico will face a greater increase in population (in the next few years) compared to the past."

Afterwards the President said that, in order to raise the rate of increase in the standard of living to 6.5 percent per year in the 1966 to 1970 period, Mexico would require investments of 275 billion pesos, 95 billion from the public sector and 180 billion from the private sector. He added that the 95 billion from the public sector will be distributed in the following way: 39.5 percent to industry; 22.6 percent to communications and transportation; 14.2 percent to agriculture and fishing; 22.1 percent to social projects; and the remaining 1.6 percent to administration and defense. Likewise, he announced that from 1966 to 1970 the amount of irrigated land would be expanded by 850,000 hectares. Thus, it is clear that the Federal Government of Mexico is aware of the seriousness of the rapid population increase, of the pressing necessity of economic and social planning. It has ideas and objectives regarding the policies that ought to be formulated and carried out in order to achieve an annual increase of 6.5 percent from 1966 to 1970, considering that the Mexican population grows at 5.6 percent per year. Moreover, the President pointed out, regional planning has begun.

It is important to warn the national public that some may attribute the character of a panacea to birth control. National attention devoted to problems derived from rapid population growth should not distract our people, as I pointed out at the First Panamerican Population Assembly in Colombia in 1965, from the basic social and economic reforms that the Latin America countries must implement if they want to take care of the aspirations and necessities of their people. My warning was unanimously endorsed by the Latin Americans at the Assembly.

The Latin American population of 207 to 212 million inhabitants in 1960 is expected to reach between 275 and 282 million inhabitants in 1970 and 365 to 374 million in 1980. The average annual growth rate in Latin America from 1950 to 1960 was 2.7 percent; from 1960 to 1970 it is expected to grow at 2.9 percent annually and 2.8 percent from 1970 to 1980. Given the age structure of the American population, if well-organized national programs of family planning are not initiated, it is likely that in 1990 the growth rate will have been 2.7 percent in the preceding decade with only a slight drop to 2.5 percent in the next decade. It seems, therefore, that a slight decrease in the growth rate may be anticipated in the next decades. This decrease may be accentuated only if family-planning programs are initiated soon and carried out efficiently with proper adjustment to the conditions of each country and each social sector.

The proportion of inactive population by age (less than 15 years old) will remain stable from 1960 to 1980 (41.7 percent of the total population in 1960 and 41.6 percent in 1980). Because of this, the demographic evolution of Latin America until 1980 could constitute a grave situation complicating economic and social problems. It is estimated that in the year 2,000 the proportion of minors less than 15 years old in the Latin Americas will have decreased to 37.8 percent. The active population (from 15 to 64 years old) represented 55 percent in 1960.

The years between 1966 and 1980 constitute an interesting, critical period in the economic, social, and political evolution of Latin America. In order to successfully emerge from it, the following are required:

1. clear, honest planning and the effective realization of economic and social basic reforms;
2. acceleration of economic integration in Latin America;
3. the elevation and maintenance of per capita gross national product growth rates;
4. the execution on an appropriate scale of family-planning programs in which the sense of maternal and paternal responsibilities may be strengthened and medical assistance can be given to the families that freely seek it.

These are four fundamental tasks facing the Latin American countries from 1966 to 1980; that is to say, that they are primary objectives which peoples and their governments should make a great effort to achieve in each country.

In almost all Latin American countries characteristics of the struggle between the social groups which are surreptitiously opposed to basic reforms and progressive groups that are motivated by the conviction that it is indispensable to bring about these reforms as soon as possible are becoming clearer. These groups differ with regard to the nature, breadth, intensity, and implementation of reforms.

The slow increase in the growth of gross national product and the greater knowledge about the major obstacles to their increase and maintenance, which generates hope in some people and desperation in others, are facts that form the social situation in most Latin American countries. Growth of the desire for the economic integration of Latin America is a result of a process that was initiated with the economic disillusionment that these countries suffered in the first years following World War II. In addition, the accelerated increase of the population in a major part of the Latin American countries intensifies the pressure for the structural reforms clearly demanded by the people.

Planning and the application of family-planning measures, based on a couple's right to determine the dimensions of its family—according to their moral, religious and social ideas—using adequate means voluntarily chosen, would permit in the 1980's most of the Latin American countries with high birth rates to register significant decreases. Thus, in the last two decades of the Twentieth Century, the Latin American countries would be able to extend and improve training of their labor forces in various ways.

The figure of 366 million inhabitants which could be reached by 1980 indicates the importance that the Latin American countries could have if they make substantial progress toward economic integration. To the extent that basic economic and social reforms are achieved, it will be less difficult to overcome obstacles to economic integration and growth and distribution of growth national product. If these reforms are realized and national income increases with improved distribution, the factors favorable to family planning and those which raise the productive and social value of human resources will be strengthened.

There will be a demographic transition of approximately 15 to 20 years in the progress of Latin America, which is only a part of the countries of low industrial development and very low standards of living. Historical, cultural, geographic, and economic factors have shaped Latin America as a ruptured union of peoples who need economic integration in a relatively short time if they want to maintain their historical and cultural originality and if they want to achieve development rather than growing poverty and economic and political weakness in a world of intense rapid changes, dominated by the four great powers: Western Europe, the United States, the Soviet Union, and the Republic of China.

A stage of great and rapid scientific and technological advancement and of important social, economic, and political changes in the more developed parts of the world is at the same time for the underdeveloped countries a time of low economic development and of accelerated population increase with popular unrest and anxiety for improvement of standards of living.

Their pre-Colombian history, colonial past, the similarities of the two romance languages, their republican tradition, their frustrated experiences with democracy, their decided inclination toward Western culture, the battles waged during the nineteenth and twentieth centuries to maintain their liberty in the face of imperialistic aggressors, and geographic conditions are all factors favorable to the economic integration in Latin America. The Latin American countries also have unfavorable characteristics derived from the structures, interests, and intentions of the oligarchies and of the privileged classes.

The principal economic, social and political problems of Latin America ought to be connected with a clear and important fact: the rapid increase of the Latin American population that passed from 60 to 65 million people at the beginning of the Twentieth Century to approximately 210 million in 1960. If from 1900 to 1940 the Latin American population doubled, calculations indicate that from 1950 to 1975—only 25 years—the Latin American population will double again. Countries like Argentina, Brazil and Uruguay experienced great immigration during the first third of this century which rapidly increased their populations. This was not the case in countries like Mexico and other Central and South American nations, which with predominantly indigenous populations received few immigrants and which with both high natality and mortality rates registered minor increases in their population. This relatively slow demographic growth in the mestizo countries of Latin America in the first third of this century was worrisome not only as a factor in their slow political and economic development but also because low population density encouraged foreign expansionary forces which took advantage of any opportunity to occupy new territories. From 1930 to 1940 growth rates increased in Latin American regions of low immigration, and from 1940 to 1960 growth rates increased in Central America and in the so-called Tropical South America. As immigration to Latin America notably decreased in the second third of this century, the ethnic and social structures in each group of countries were more precisely defined with demographic increase coming from consistently high birth rates and notable decreases in mortality.

During the nineteenth and twentieth centuries the technological, economic, political, and social progress that was taking place in Western Europe and the United States was both weak and delayed in the underdeveloped countries of Latin America. A few of these countries, like Argentina, Uruguay and Chile, suffered less delay. But in most of the Latin American countries, mortality decreased only slowly until the end of the World War II. Since then the decline has accelerated as may be observed in spite of good statistical records.

Latin America grew an average of 1.8 percent per year from 1920 to 1930 and an average of 2.8 percent from 1960 to 1965. In Argentina, Uruguay, Chile and Cuba, which share characteristics, and Puerto Rico, due to factors somewhat different, the birth rates are not very high. In the meantime the rest of Latin America maintains high birth rates which exceed 40 births per 1000 inhabitants per year, even reaching 45 per 1000 or more.

The countries that received greater European immigration in the first third of this century are naturally those that have registered a decrease in their birth rates because of cultural, social, and even economic factors. Factors generating rural-urban migration in the second third of this century in Latin America and the effects of this urbanization on mortality, marriage, and birth rates have not been studied in most parts of Latin America. Until recently there has not been much attention given to scientific studies of demographic phenomena at all. As a matter of fact, in the 1930's and the beginning of the 1940's, it was not even common among sociologists, anthropologists, and economists to use the word "demography." Many people confused it with the term "vital statistic."

In the first third of this century, the predominantly mestizo countries without immigrants from Europe were jealous of the neighboring nations where immigration was abundant. Those with growing European populations and without the problems of backward indigenous communities showed a certain superiority and even scorn toward the mestizo countries. The relative political stability of the first group and their advanced political institutions were attributed to absence of indigenous population. Likewise the low standards of living, the high birth rates, the higher mortality rates, and frequent political instability were attributed to the large proportions of Indians and mestizos in the other countries. The incipient forms of a Latin American consciousness were very different from one country to another but these differences have diminished.

The rapid vigorous growth of large cities in Latin America plus acute housing, drinkable water, educational, medicine, and other social services problems along with the political tensions which have sprouted up in these large urban areas have notably increased the economic and cultural differences between urban and rural areas. Together they work to undermine national unity. The economic and social differences between urban and rural areas and between the social classes have greatly increased. These facts have awakened interest in recent years in the complex problems generated by urbanization. Rural-urban migration is not adequately studied in most of these countries as few resources are dedicated to demographic research.

Most of the Latin American countries with rapidly growing populations, high proportions of young people, and strong rural-urban migration are determined to improve their standards of living, but they suffer with growing non-conformity from economic and social structures that aggravate the unjust distribution of the national income. There is debate among the restless and non-conformists who look to violence as the answer and those who desire basic reforms of the social and economic order.

Latin America is a region in the world with the highest rate of population growth. Its age composition is similar to that of underdeveloped countries on other continents with a pyramid that features great numbers of children, adolescents and young people. This rapid increase and age structure generate great social and economic investment demands because of housing requirements, educational and social service requirements. They also demand investments that would both create jobs with increasing salaries for the growing number of young people appearing each year on the job market, and elevate agricultural and industrial production. Rapid population growth necessitates increased productivity and reduction in the uneven distribution of national income in order to reduce economic and social differences. There is a need also for reforms in the educational system at all levels. The process of urbanization, which is stronger in Latin america because of its Western cultural and economic ingredient than in other underdeveloped countries, intensifies and complicates socio-economic tensions and renders important changes in the political and administrative systems urgent and indispensable.

Because of cultural and economic ties with the United States and Western Europe as well as for other reasons, the popular consciousness which demands rights—effective ones, not just promised ones—to education, health, employment, and better standards of living continues growing. During the rest of this century the objectives and responsibilities of the Latin American peoples and governments are great, greater in fact than those in the underdeveloped areas of Asia and Africa because of the cultural proximity to the West and because independence came to Latin America long before it came to Asia and Africa. With a population of nearly 87 million people in 1920, 240 million in 1965, probably 275 million in 1970, and 365 million in 1980, Latin America, if it accomplishes structural reforms and development during the next 15 years of demographic transition, could in 1980 accelerate its progress for the last 20 years of the century. In order to do this there must be significant advancements in the fundamental aspects of economic and social planning, in the process of Latin America economic integration, and in family-planning programs.

Part III

National Policies

Chapter Eleven

Family-Planning Programs and the Dynamics of Agenda-Building in Costa Rica and Chile

Vivian Epstein-Orlowski*

INTRODUCTION

Myron Weiner suggests a new field of social inquiry, "political demography," that can be approached from two directions: (1) studying "the political consequences of population change," and (2) analyzing "the political determinants of population change."[1] This chapter seeks to contribute to the study of political demography in terms of the second approach.[2]

      In this case we are *not* going to analyze policies that were *expressly* designed to achieve demographic change. Instead, we will be focusing on government programs that provide family-planning services in public health facilities and coordinating these with services in the private sector. Family-planning programs are often perceived as tools for controlling population growth, but there is nothing intrinsic to them that necessarily implies that a government implementing such programs has formulated an overall demographic policy for the nation. The provision of contraceptives and family-planning education could be in response to the problem of widespread voluntary abortion or a public health measure to reduce high rates of maternal and infant mortality. It could also be in response to women's demands for the right to control their own reproductive functions or a measure designed to promote responsible parenthood. Costa Rica and Chile, the two countries that are the subjects of this study, have taken the non-comprehensive approach to provision of family-planning services. The programs in these two countries were apparently designed

      *Research for this chapter, which was prepared originally for this volume, was conducted in Costa Rica in 1968 and 1970, and in Chile in 1970. The author made the 1968 trip as a member of the University of Wisconsin's Interdepartmental Field Seminar in Costa Rica. Subsequent dissertation research was undertaken with financial assistance from the Doherty Foundation (1969–1970) and from the Population Council (1970–1971).

primarily as public health measures rather than as attempts to achieve specific demographic goals at the national level, although aggregate population trends are presumably affected by public family-planning programs and national decision-makers are undoubtedly aware of this fact.

Costa Rica and Chile were selected for this study precisely because the two countries have pioneered public family planning and related activities in Latin America and have to date developed some of the most extensive public programs. The primary purpose here is to determine how such programs with a high potential for controversy were adopted and the extent to which they constitute integral national policies.

Our analysis will seek to show the influence of elites on decision-making (especially physicians), and we will trace the resources and participation provided by international and foreign linkage groups.

The Agenda-Building Framework

Theoretically, we are conducting an inquiry into the dynamics of what Cobb and Elder call "agenda-building": "How does an issue come to be viewed as an important and appropriate subject of attention? How does it come to command a position on the agenda of legitimate political controversy?"[3] They postulate that within a context of relatively open political competition (in their case, the United States, and in our case, Costa Rica and Chile before September, 1973) access to governmental agendas is achieved by expanding group conflict in scope, intensity, and visibility. Yet in Costa Rica and Chile, the issue of family planning emerged from obscurity and achieved agenda status without triggering widespread conflict expansion.[4] In our analysis we shall focus on two important, interrelated questions in an attempt to comprehend this apparent paradox:

1. Which groups and individuals defined the issues related to family-planning programs and with what symbolic connotations?
2. What were the sources and levels of resource allocation (in both symbolic and tangible rewards) required to manage the issue?

While Cobb and Elder separate their propositions about *agenda-building* from what happens *after* an issue is placed on the governmental agenda, we will find that there is an interdependence between the two. Attainment of agenda status is certainly a prerequisite to policy response, but the *types* of policy options associated with an issue will influence the receptivity of governing elites to allowing agenda access in the first place. Consequently, we shall see in the Costa Rican and Chilean cases that group conflict may be necessary to gain governmental agenda status for an issue that has few supporters in key decision-making positions; however, such open conflict is neither necessary nor desirable when program initiators have access to national governing elites and influential international or foreign linkage groups.

Our discussion of these topics will proceed with, first, brief background information on Costa Rica and Chile. Next we will look at the evolution of family-planning programs in Costa Rica and Chile—a selective history focusing on the first two stages of issue definition and institutional formation. Stage I covers initiation of individual efforts, achieving systemic and institutional agenda status, and initial inclusion in official government health services. While it is most difficult to pinpoint the initiation dates, Stage I for Costa Rica covered the approximate period of 1962 to 1967 and for Chile, 1959 to 1966. Stage II is characterized by further institutional diffusion; additional involvement of government officials that include attempts to define policy and program guidelines; increased foreign assistance and more international involvement; and a sense of legitimacy and momentum engendered by the routinization and expansion of population related programs. Stage II covered the years 1967 to 1970 for Chile and 1968 to 1970 for Costa Rica. Stage III, which involves further program growth but with increasing self-analysis and self-awareness, includes the period from 1970 through 1973 in both countries. Since the emphasis of this article is on early program attainment of agenda status and because my field research only reaches until late 1970, I will not attempt a detailed outline of this last stage. Finally, the chapter concludes with an analysis and comparison of Stage I and Stage II in Costa Rica and Chile, which focuses on leadership patterns, policy orientations, symbolic connotations, resource allocation, and role of international and foreign linkage groups.

Background

While this study seeks to compare family-planning policies in Costa Rica and Chile, it does not wish to blur the many disparities between the two nations. When we are analyzing the development of family-planning programs in these two countries, disparities as well as similarities in fundamental environmental attributes should be kept in mind. (See Tables I-1 and I-2 in the Introduction of the volume for their demographic characteristics.) Likewise, subtle differences in policy-making systems should also be recognized.[5] However, in comparison with the authoritarian trend in current Latin American politics, Costa Rica and Chile, (at least up until September, 1973) do offer policy-making systems that are *relatively* open. This is especially true in terms of ability of a group to block key decision-makers from adopting a particular policy, rather than in any broad-based participation in decisions. These two countries share traditions of free elections with little military intervention, a choice of political parties including those of Marxist orientation, and active interest groups. Of course, the relativity of this political openness has been pointed out by critics who show how the distribution of economic resources pre-determines to a large degree who can manipulate the political system to further their own interests.[6]

The pace of change in public attitudes, policies, and institutions

has been very rapid in dealing with the family-planning issue. In 1960 the
University of Costa Rica did not have a medical school; it was established the
following year. The question of family-planning programs was a non-issue
within the realm of public policy. In 1960 Chile did have medical schools;
it also had a few pioneering scientists doing research on contraceptives and
demography. Nevertheless, in Chile as in Costa Rica and in most of the Western
Hemisphere, family-planning programs were not even on the systemic agenda.
Yet ten years later, in 1970, Chile and Costa Rica had both adopted family-
planning programs within their systems of public health care. Furthermore,
within each nation, there was a network of organizations in the private and
public sectors involved in various aspects of the population issue. Table 11-1
provides a skeletal outline of the principal agencies active in the two countries
classified according to principal function and sector of origin.

For the sake of clarity, let us trace the development of the
programs in Costa Rica and Chile separately. Then we can identify similarities
and differences in each country's dynamics of agenda-building.

COSTA RICA [7]

Stage I

In 1962, several of the men who were to become the early organizers
of the Asociación Demográfica Costarricense (Costa Rican Demographic
Association) had already begun activities in the area of family planning. In San
José, Dr. Arturo Cabezas was providing contraceptives to patients at the privately run, Protestant-sponsored Clínica Bíblica. At this time, a majority of the
patients came from the middle and upper socio-economic levels.[8] In addition, concurrent family-planning activities were also beginning in the more
rural town of Turrialba; under the direction and initiative of several people, a
pilot program was providing contraceptive pills to the wives of workers at
the Interamerican Institute of Agricultural Sciences (IICA). This was in contrast to the experience of most Latin American nations where family-planning
services did not reach out from the capital city area for a while.

At this time, the prevailing climate of opinion in Costa Rica toward
such projects was very wary. For example, in an interview one of these pioneers
related how he wrote to the Ministry of Public Health to get more information
about fertility control but never received a response. Subsequently, it was dis-
closed that the Ministry did not answer for fear of having the subject of contraception in the correspondence records.[9] During the early 1960's, the Costa
Rican government appeared more supportive of family planning in international
agencies than it was within its own country. Thus, when its ambassador to the
United Nations supported the December, 1962, General Assembly resolution
to give UN assistance in establishing family-planning programs to those countries requesting it, he took his position without asking for explicit instructions

Table 11-1. Principal Organizations Active in Family-Planning Programs or Population Research in Costa Rica and Chile, 1970

Sector of Origin and Major Functions	Name of Agency* Costa Rica	Chile
I. Governmental Sector: 1. Family-Planning Clinical Services	Ministry of Public Health (MSP) Costa Rican Social Security Administration (CCSS)	National Health Service (SNS) National Medical Service for Employees (SERMENA) Military and Police Hospitals
2. Sex Education	Ministry of Public Education	Ministry of Public Education
II. University Sector: Research Training Evaluation	University of Costa Rica Medical School Center for Social and Population Studies (CESPO)	University of Chile Medical School Dept. of Public Health Catholic University of Chile Medical School
III. Private Sector: 1. Information Education Distribution Coordination	Costa Rican Demographic Association (ADC)	Chilean Association for the Protection of the Family (APROFA)
2. Sex Education	Family Orientation Center (COF) Family Integration Center (CIF)	
IV. Mixed Sector: Coordination and/or control of major activities	National Committee on Population (CONAPO)	National Health Service (SNS)
V. International and Foreign Sector: 1. Research Training	Latin American Demographic Center Sub-center (CELADE)	Latin American Demographic Center (CELADE) Latin American Center for Population & Family (CELAP)
2. Grants	International Planned Parenthood Federation (IPPF) Pan American Health Organization (PAHO) U.S. Agency for International Development (USAID) Ford Foundation Pathfinder Fund	IPPF PAHO USAID Ford Foundation Rockefeller Foundation Population Council Pathfinder Fund

*When an agency's original name is in Spanish, the English translation is given, plus Spanish initials or abbreviations used in the text.

from his government. He feared that to specifically raise the issue of family planning could arouse opposition back in Costa Rica.[10] Interestingly, Chile's representatives to the UN were the only other delegates from Latin America to also support this resolution.

Beginning in the early 1960's, various external groups began to study population trends to help development of family-planning programs in other countries. These organizations functioned as linkages between the evolution of programs in the domestic political environment of Costa Rica and their sources of international and private North American foundation support. The pattern of behavior follows James Rosenau's general definition of linkages, "any recurrent sequence of behavior that origmates in one system and is reacted to in another."[11] Three of the foreign organizations that entered the Costa Rican arena at the earliest stage were: the Pathfinder Fund, the International Planned Parenthood Federation (IPPF) and the American International Association for Economic and Social Development (AIA).

The Pathfinder Fund is a small private association located in Boston and founded in 1958 by Clarence Gamble, a physician who had begun to campaign for birth control in the United States in 1929. Between 1953 and 1961, Pathfinder representatives had visited 50 countries in Africa, Asia and Latin America with a personal approach to aiding local family-planning groups.[12] Costa Rican contact with this organization was established in 1964 at the initiative of Dr. Cabezas who wrote for information and supplies. In following years, the Pathfinder Fund would continue to provide this type of small scale assistance to the Costa Rican program.

IPPF's first contacts with Costa Rica may have well started at the informal level back in 1960 when Dr. Cabezas met Dr. Ofelia Mendoza, Field Representative for IPPF, at a Central American Medical Congress.[13] Beginning in 1962, Dr. Mendoza made exploratory visits to Costa Rica to establish local contacts.[14] According to one account, the climate of opinion towards family planning at that time was so unfavorable (the government was especially hostile) that Dr. Mendoza had all of her family-planning literature taken away by the authorities on one of these early visits.[15] Nevertheless, IPPF helped found the local private family-planning association or Costa Rican Demographic Association (ADC). As of 1966, it had contributed about $10,700 to the fledgling ADC, and in April, 1967, the Asociación Demográfica Costarricense became an official national affiliate of IPPF. While IPPF's initial financial and technical support was vital to promoting the growth of the ADC, several interviews revealed that IPPF and ADC did not develop the close initial working relationship characteristic of IPPF affiliates in other Latin American nations, including Chile. Although the relationship may not have been as close, it was rewarding; IPPF donated about 40 percent of ADC's budget in 1970.[16]

One of the first systematic attempts to overcome the initial barriers of government hostility and public doubts was the American International

Association's *Survey of Attitudes Related to Costa Rican Population Dynamics.* The basic supposition of the study was that there was a large bloc of latent support for family-planning practices among the Costa Rican public. Accordingly, if a survey would articulate the widespread acceptance, it would help dissipate governmental reluctance to become involved and move this formerly taboo subject on to the agenda of the Costa Rican system.

The findings of the AIA study strongly confirmed these expectations. The results of the national probability sample of 1500 interviews showed that

> 64 percent believe family planning (or birth control) does not threaten the health of those who practice it, and 60 percent hold that it is morally right. Similarly, 68 percent believe that birth control is not financially costly, and 60 percent believe that it is necessary for the social and economic development of Costa Rica.[17]

On a more personal level the response was somewhat less favorable. In response to the question—"What is your feeling about a married couple practicing birth control?"—43 percent answered that birth control was always or sometimes justified. However, the AIA study places this 1965 favorable response in very optimistic light by comparing it with the only 39 percent who answered favorably to the same question asked in a 1963 survey by AIA.[18] It is these optimistic results that help us understand how family-planning programs attained systemic and institutional agenda status in Costa Rica. The taboo is supposedly exorcised when the press reports the principal findings of such a survey, or when government officials read the findings.

The AIA survey marked the introduction of a major United States private foundation and large amount of foreign funds spent on the population issue in Costa Rica.[19] It was also one of the first population related projects that received support from the United States Agency for International Development (USAID). The preface to the AIA study specifically acknowledges "the early interest and professional counsel" of the "population officer" USAID Mission Costa Rica. (It is more probable that this "population officer" was the Health Officer because the first such specially designated USAID official did not arrive in Costa Rica until 1968.) Support for the AIA study and a comprehensive study by the Ministry of Public Health were the first two projects of a specific population nature that were financed in by USAID. The agreement with the Ministry of Public Health, signed on February 15, 1965, did not come to fruition until late 1967. Therefore, in order to convey a chronological sense of these early formative events, let us proceed to the major developments of 1966.

The year 1966 in Costa Rica began with the excitement of a closely contested presidential election and a narrow upset victory for Professor José

Joaquín Trejos.[20] The campaign of this compromise candidate of the Partido Unificación Nacional (PUN—National Unification Party) against the charismatic Daniel Oduber, favored choice of the Partido Liberación Nacional (PLN—National Liberation Party), had many aspects of bitter contention. However, one issue that received no attention or contention was the recommendation for family-planning services related to Oduber's proposed health program.[21]

Oduber, who lost in 1966 but won the presidency in 1974, had become concerned with the population issue during his term as Costa Rica's Foreign Minister from 1962 to 1966 through his contacts at the United Nations and abroad. It is perhaps understandable then that in consultation with his public health advisor, a family-planning activist, he would include the idea of family planning in his health proposals. What was not quite so understandable, in a very closely fought campaign, was the lack of attempt by the opposition to promote polarization on this issue. There are several possible explanations. First, as one prominent Costa Rican political leader indicated in a confidential interview, there seems to be a tacit "gentleman's agreement" among most politicians not to become embroiled in such a potentially sensitive issue. Second, some politicians were aware of the AIA survey or of the underlying mood of latent popular support for family planning; thus there seemed little to be gained by an attack. Finally, there were not many politicians who actually opposed family-planning services. President Trejos, after his election, approved initial government support of family-planning programs by establishing a Population Office in the Ministry of Public Health.

While these more dramatic political events were occurring, the small group of pioneering population activists continued their endeavors on a modest scale in Turrialba and in San José. On March 18, 1966, they established the Asociación Demográfica Costarricense as a "scientific, cultural and research entity."[22] Of the 17 founders, there were 3 women and 14 men; 7 physicians, 1 nurse, 2 agronomists, 2 lawyers, 2 Episcopal priests, 1 housewife, 1 ecologist, and 1 professor. The Association was founded on the principle that "parents have the human right to determine the number of children they want," and therefore the Association would "assist their aspirations."[23] While this reflects the type of family orientation that is common in Latin American family-planning groups, the ADC differentiated itself somewhat from the general trend both on the symbolic and on the leadership levels. Most private family-planning associations in Latin America include the term "family" in their titles and have physicians as executive directors. In Costa Rica, the founding group sought to emphasize the scientific research of population as well as the rights of the family. Furthermore, it chose a young agronomist as full-time executive director.

By July, 1966, a team of visiting observers from the Ford Foundation noted that the Association's membership had grown to about 50 (half of them physicians), but that there were no direct clinical facilities sponsored by the Association. There was fear of the church and of the possible political consequences of taking a stand related to population policy. The visitors further observed that no one person in the government was responsible for population and the new president's position was as yet unknown. They suggested that insufficient knowledge about the population issue could be remedied by travel grants to international seminars and conferences.[24] Just at the time, several Costa Rican delegates were taking part in the Central America and Panama Conference on Population, Economic Development and Family Planning in Tegucigalpa, Honduras. This conference, the first of its kind to be held at the Central American level, was sponsored by Honduran government agencies with financial support from IPPF. Included in the Costa Rican delegation was the Vice-Minister of Public Health who was sympathetic to placing family planning on the government's agenda.[25]

These events summarize the principal activities that were effectively placing the topic of family planning on the institutional agenda. The taboo was being broken. People were talking, and the issue now had spokesmen. The Costa Rican press also started to reflect an awareness of this issue partially through pressure from ADC and partially in reflection of the changing attitudes of the foreign press and international opinion.[26] The recognition of family planning came quietly and gradually through internal ministerial decisions, personal contacts, research, and seminars, not through any initial legislative decision nor presidential proclamations.

Toward the end of 1966, the Ministry of Public Health published its first public document related to population, a 27-page study entitled *Nuestro problema demográfico (Our Demographic Problem)*. It was written by two professors of Preventive Medicine at the University of Costa Rica, the Director of the Maternal-Child Department of the Ministry of Public Health, and the Director of the Office of Demographic Studies, Ministry of Public Health. In accordance with the demographic theme suggested by the title, the cover of the booklet had a graphic representation of the increasing population density of Costa Rica from 1935 to 1980. The authors identified several causes of this "population explosion" in Costa Rica and then discussed how high population growth rates affected the economic and social development of Costa Rica. Five relationships they underlined were: (1) economic imbalance within the family and in the nation due to the large proportion of dependent population (over 40 percent under 15 years of age); (2) the growing demand on the state for schools and hospitals; (3) increased pressure on usable lands and consequent reduction in agricultural productivity; (4) increased number of disease-weakened individuals that resulted in less productivity; and (5) lack of savings and investment. Finally, a major section of the study was devoted to the subject of induced abortion, or as the authors also referred to it, "criminal abortion," although Costa Rica compared favorably to other Latin American nations on induced abortion rates insofar as they can be determined. Nevertheless, *Nuestro problema demográfico* alerts the reader to the large costs in hospital care and blood transfusions that abortions (which are the third cause of hospitalization) are placing on the system.[27]

Through this rather traditional and unsensational method of sponsoring a study, the Costa Rican government first addressed the population issue. While *Nuestro problema demográfico* took a predominantly "macro" approach to population (stressing the impact on the entire Costa Rican nation rather than just on the "micro" family level), the first Ministry of Health action project was to provide medical training on contraceptives to doctors. The Ministry sent approximately 40 physicians to a three-day intensive course in late 1966.[28]

These first steps toward establishing a family-planning program in Costa Rica did not elicit any overt opposition from Roman Catholic Church leaders. However, many public officials still feared moving too quickly in the implementation of actual contraceptive services because of possible confrontation with some Catholic religious leaders. The controlling factor was the anticipated response in the minds of government officials. By early 1967, when the population issue was now entering the systemic and institutional agendas, the Costa Rican Catholic hierarchy chose to recognize the status of the issue and to clarify its own position.

The bishops of Costa Rica issued a Pastoral Letter that took a firm position against any type of "artificial means which would frustrate the natural effect of the matrimonial act."[29] However, the bishops elaborated that while they opposed artificial birth control, regulation of children was admissible as part of responsible parenthood that can only be reached through total or periodic abstinence.[30] The very fact that the Costa Rican hierarchy felt the need to take a strong stand against "artificial" contraception may have been an indication that an awareness of such methods was now becoming more widespread in Costa Rican society; it was now on the agenda. While the Costa Rican bishops were seeking to reaffirm the anti-birth control outlook, Pope Paul VI's 1967 encyclical (*On the Development of Peoples*) seemed to open the door for national family-planning programs with the admission that "public authorities can intervene within the limits of their competence by favoring the availability of appropriate information and by adopting suitable measures, provided these be in conformity with the moral law."[31] In addition, a majority of the Pope's Commission on Birth Control (report issued in June, 1966) seemed to favor the use of artificial contraceptives.

To publicize the more liberal international Catholic position on fertility regulation, ADC sponsored a visit in January, 1967, by a Mexican priest who was a strong supporter of family-planning programs. His viewpoints were widely diffused through public lectures to a variety of groups, television appearances, and a series of newspaper articles about his activities.[32] In

June, 1967, the Association published a booklet on *La Iglesia y la planificación familiar* (*The Church and Family Planning*) that examined the variety of opinions among Catholics, which ranged from the conservative Pastoral Letter to articles and interviews with a well-known Costa Rican Catholic philosopher to extracts from the Papal Commission on Birth Control. What emerged was a stress on *"paternidad responsable"* (responsible parenthood) and a sense of leeway on the means used to achieve this common goal.

In April, 1967, after only a year in operation, ADC witnessed a major breakthrough in its efforts to obtain official support for family-planning programs and to incorporate such services into existing national health programs. It came in the form of an executive decree that created the Office of Population within the Ministry of Public Health. The functions of this office included: (1) to promote research in the health field related to population; (2) to lend technical assistance to the Ministry and to public and private agencies in aspects related to population; (3) to adopt the pertinent technical and administrative means which will place all operative action in population under the Ministry of Public Health, using scientifically rigorous methods which guarantee the respect of individual conscience and the dignity of the family; (4) to provide agreements for necessary collaboration with national or international training and philanthropic organizations; and (5) to incorporate the health measures derived from population growth into the regular Maternal-Child Care Program of the Ministry.[33] This decree justified the proposed action entirely in terms of the protection of health and welfare of the individual. It argued that numerical and structural variations in the population influence community health conditions and the need to protect the basic sanitary conditions of the nation.[34] The Office of "Population" implies demographic duties, but it was located in the Ministry of Public Health, which was *not* empowered to treat the larger issue of population growth in Costa Rica. The first major project of the office was to formulate a plan for a national family-planning services. It was prepared by the director with the assistance of two advisors from the Ford Foundation and the Pan American Sanitary Bureau. The 66-page report was issued in November, 1967, under the title of *Programa Nacional Sobre Política de Poblacion* (*National Program for Population Policy*).

The title of this report and its initial five pages, which analyze national demographic developments and their consequences in terms of various national problems, seemed to augur for a macro, population policy approach, despite the terms of the original decree. However, instead of integrating the issue of fertility reduction into an overall development policy, the 1967 document focuses entirely on the establishment of family-planning services stressing public health goals without any defined aims of reducing the population growth rate.

Within this family-planning framework, the purposes of the Costa

Rican program can be summarized as follows: (1) to diminish the risk of maternal and infant deaths; (2) to develop an educational campaign about means of voluntarily spacing births and to form a consciousness about responsible procreation; (3) to provide diagnosis and treatment for uterine cancer; (4) to train doctors, medical students and paramedical personnel in family-planning methods; (5) to promote research in family planning among medical personnel.[35] The specific objectives of the program include the goal of reaching 5 percent of the female population of fertile age during the first year of the program. Other goals specify the percentage of couples to be reached with educational programs and types of research to be undertaken in the bio-medical, psychological and sociological fields. They *do not* encompass an overall decline in national fertility and growth rates.

The narrowness of the program reflected the constraints on policy options perceived by decision-makers in 1967. Even advocates of family-planning programs felt that a national population control campaign was not appropriate to the Costa Rican situation.[36]

In 1967, an increasing number of international contacts had helped raise information levels among elites and build momentum into the government's growing commitment to family planning, if not population control. Several short-run inputs should be mentioned: the Eighth International IPPF Conference in Chile, a visit to Costa Rica by a Chilean Advisory Mission on family planning, and a seminar for Costa Rican medical, religious, and intellectual leaders. In terms of longer-run institution-building programs, the UN's Latin American Demographic Center's (CELADE) establishment of a sub-center for Central America at the University of Costa Rica and the formation of the Center for Social and Population Studies (CESPO) also at the University were important developments.

IPPF's meeting in Santiago, Chile, in April, 1967, was the first such worldwide conference on family planning to be held in Latin America. It played an important role in consciousness-raising throughout the continent. The attendance of over a thousand delegates from throughout the world, including an impressive delegation from Costa Rica. Newspaper coverage in Costa Rica helped alert public opinion to a global concern for family planning. The impact of the IPPF meeting was soon reinforced and made more immediate to Costa Ricans by a three-day visit by a team of Chilean family-planning experts. The Chileans spoke before more than 1,000 people, mainly professionals and university students, during their stay, which also included an interview with President Trejos and television appearances.[37]

Reinforcing this momentum towards agenda-building in 1967 was a course on population and family in Costa Rica given by CELAP (the Latin American Center of Population and Family), a Catholic-related research institute located in Chile and financed by USAID. The 37 Costa Ricans who participated in this course were a carefully selected cross-section of policy-makers and influentials.[38] It was the first such occasion in Costa Rica when a broad cross-section of decision-makers were officially assembled to discuss family planning. Perhaps most noteworthy was that the Jesuit-founded CELAP chose to invite Catholic clergy at a time when the Catholic position on family planning was increasingly being discussed. The course served an educational function for many of those leaders who would be making key decisions in relation to family-planning programs in Costa Rica.

While these activities were having immediate short-term impact on the climate of opinion among Costa Rican leaders, institutions were being established that would provide the framework for effective program implementation. In 1967, a demographer from CELADE's Santiago staff came to Costa Rica to establish a branch that would concentrate on demographic research and training for Central America and Panama. Since CELADE is a United Nations organization (although it also receives direct financial support from USAID, the Ford Foundation, and the Population Council), its creation of a sub-center in Costa Rica was not a direct component of Costa Rican national policy. However, its presence at the University of Costa Rican indicated local receptivity to demographic research and established another source of population policy inputs, even if it was only an indirect one. In addition to its work with the University of Costa Rica, its primary relations with Costa Rican agencies have been with the General Directorate of Statistics and Census and the Statistical Department in the Ministry of Health since CELADE concentrates on demographic research and instruction.[39] Personal contacts also can play an important role in agenda-building, especially in a country of Costa Rica's size where most professionals interested in population and family planning do get to know one another. For example, the Director of the CELADE sub-center (acting as an individual, *not* as a representative of his organization) served as Vice President of the Costa Rican Demographic Association in 1968.

As the institutional agenda began to include family planning, the provision of trained human resources on a broader scale became the focus of concern. The method of sending doctors to other Latin American countries for training in family-planning skills would become increasingly expensive once the national program went into operation.[40] A working committee headed by the Dean of the Medical School (and composed of officials from the Ministry of Public Health, CELADE, and ADC) suggested the creation of an interdisciplinary training organization with the University of Costa Rica.

In November, 1967, the committee's suggestions were presented in a report entitled "Program for the Economic and Social Improvement of the Family." This report proposed four principal projects for the Center for Social and Population Studies: (1) institutionalizing the teaching of demography and family planning as an integral part of the medical and nursing school curricula at the University of Costa Rica; (2) training medical professionals and social workers in family-planning services; (3) motivational education of community leaders to promote grass-roots attitudinal changes needed for socio-economic development and for utilization of family-planning services; (4) social research surveys. This detailed proposal, including budget estimates, was then presented to the Ford Foundation representative in Costa Rica. As early as 1966, the Foundation's representatives felt that its assistance to Costa Rica in the population area would be best directed by establishing training programs.[41] Furthermore, the Ford Foundation was more concerned with helping to create a long-term popular consciousness of the population issue and of family planning than with the short-term "pill-pushing" strategy favored by some family-planning advocates.[42] Accordingly, the Foundation responded relatively quickly with a contribution of $136,000, which provided 40 percent of the budget for the first two years of CESPO's operations.[43] This contribution, combined with support from the University of Costa Rica, ADC, Ministry of Public Health, and USAID, permitted CESPO to start functioning by May, 1968.

Stage II

The transition from Stage I to Stage II was not an abrupt occurrence. It was a gradual transition to more certain agenda status signified by increasing institutional diversification and implementation. Thus, from 1968 through 1970, family-planning programs in Costa Rica were reaching a "take-off" level that we can identify as Stage II. This period of approximately three years was characterized by institutional diversification and implementation; increases in foreign assistance and involvement; routinization and proliferation of population-related activities like conferences, seminars, research projects and media coverage; and confirmation of the legitimacy on the institutional agenda of public programs in family planning.

The timetable of increasing specialization of functions from Stage I through the Stage II period can be broadly outlined as follows. ADC, established in 1966, performed all major functions related to family planning in Costa Rica up to 1968. It served as a source for medical training grants, contraceptive supplies, educational materials, publicity, research, and lobbying. In 1967, the University of Costa Rica created CESPO, which in 1968 took over prinicipal responsibility for training programs and research. In 1967, Presidential decree established the Office of Population in the Ministry of Public Health, which by 1968 had started to integrate contraceptive services into its health clinics and also to coordinate educational and other population activities in Costa Rica. In 1968, the Family Orientation Center (COF) began instruction. In 1969, the Costa Rican Social Security Administration (CCSS) approved integration of family planning into its programs that service 42 percent of the Costa Rican population.[44] That same year, the Minister of Education and President Trejos decreed the creation of the Advisory Board and General Supervision of Family Planning and Sex Education within the Ministry of Education. It soon began to oversee the establishment of programs to train teachers in these fields.

With different aspects of program implementation diffused among various organizations, the need for organized coordination became evident. Thus, in late 1968, on the basis of informal agreement the National Committee on Population (CONAPO) was created. Although the committee still has no legal status, it continues to meet usually every two weeks with the chairmanship rotated among representatives from ADC, Ministry of Health, CESPO, COF, CCSS, and CIF. CONAPO's utility is enhanced by the general spirit of cooperation among the directors of family-planning and population agencies in Costa Rica.[45]

The initiative for developing a new dimension of family-planning programs came from the private sector—the Episcopal Church. Although leaders of the Episcopal Church in Costa Rica were founders of ADC, they soon felt a need to broaden the educational approach beyond that of only family-planning information to also include humanistically oriented sex education. The preoccupation of the Episcopal Church in Costa Rica was to put a "Christian emphasis" on the person, not on numbers of contraceptives acceptors.[46] They felt that the international climate tended to equate the salvation of the nation with fertility reduction and did not take the more long-term view of human development and education. The first courses of the Family Orientation Center in January, 1968, were favorably received. For the first two years the program was financed on a pilot basis by the Demographic Association (with USAID funds) and by the Episcopal Church. Eventually more local sources of support were sought so as to be totally independent of non-Costa Rican influence if possible.[47] In contrast to the government's family-planning program efforts that were directed toward a female audience, COF insisted on the attendance of both mates and as a result had an attendance of approximately 47 percent men (the first two years of courses).[48]

In contrast to the frequently strong Roman Catholic opposition to sex education in the United States, the original response to COF in Costa Rica was mixed. Some members of the Christian Family Movement were originally quite negative and voiced their opposition. On the other hand, after the first six months of courses, COF received indirect support from some Catholic priests; one even attended for a while although he eventually was pressured into withdrawing from the program.[49] By 1970, the Christian Family Movement received the Catholic hierarchy's approval to give instruction in scientific and Catholic doctrine relating to responsible parenthood.[50] In 1971, it established the Family Integration Center with most of the initial budget provided by a grant from ADC.[51]

In terms of national policy, COF's successful performance helped pave the way for the Advisory Board and General Supervision of Family Planning and Sex Education within the Ministry of Education. This is a specialized bureau whose functions include:

> Planning and directing the gradual and prudent introduction and consolidation of a healthy, balanced concept and policy of integral sex education in public and private education. This policy conforms to a humanistic and integrated vision of sex education and consequently transmits a perspective of the sexual condition of man which is not only physiological and biological, but also above all, psychological, ethical and religious.[52]

In the courses that would eventually reach school children in all Costa Rica, the Ministry of Education would seek to "Spread the concept of responsible parenthood, which, far from being diffused with a simplistic, extremist antinatalist attitude, would be better defined as the necessary and legitimate rationality of the noble generative faculty of man."[53] The Minister of Education played an active role in agenda-building by developing guidelines and bibliographies for teacher training in sex education, and his expertise was recognized beyond partisan considerations. After the change of administrations in 1970, President Figueres appointed a new Minister of Education, but retained his predecessor as a consultant to the sex education program.

Even before sex education had reached institutional agenda status, the diversification of institutions in the clinical aspects of family planning had made a major breakthrough. The Board of Directors of the Costa Rican Social Security Administration voted unanimously in August, 1969, to support the inclusion of family-planning services in the Caja Costarricense de Seguro Social (popularly referred to as the "Caja").[54] The Caja, a semi-autonomous public institution with its own Board of Directors appointed by the President of Costa Rica upon recommendations from the principal national interest groups, provides health coverage for sickness and maternity. It was slow in following the Ministry of Public Health into family planning because of fear of resistance from its interest group constituency. However, the report of a study commission, along with encouragement from ADC and several international organizations, elicited a change of policy in 1969. The commission report stressed the moral obligation of the Caja to face the consequences of the demographic problem, the favorable national attitude toward family planning, and the economic savings for the Caja of a family-planning program. Perhaps the most convincing argument of the commission report for the Board of Directors was the economic savings in the Caja's expenditures that would result from providing family-planning services.[56] For example, the commission estimated that in one year a 25 percent reduction in hospital births would have provided a savings of about $50,000.[57] There would be additional savings on pediatric services and other demands for medical attention.

In view of these factors, the Caja's Board of Directors permitted the beginning of pilot project service in four clinics on the periphery of San José and in the Social Security Hospital in Turrialba in April, 1970. After evaluations of these units, services were extended to the remaining 42 clinics and 3 hospitals operated by the Caja throughout Costa Rica. The Caja is self-financing and only relied on other Costa Rican and foreign agencies for technical assistance.[58]

The financial independence of the Caja was rather an exception among Costa Rican organizations involved in the family-planning program. Indeed, the rapid "take-off" of such programs after the initial achievement of agenda status by 1968 probably could not have been accomplished without financial support from abroad. As of 1970, **92.6 percent** of the total cost of family-planning program activities in Costa Rica was defrayed by international funds.[59]

Figure 11-1 illustrates the principal flow of funds from foreign to Costa Rican organizations in 1970. USAID was the source of the largest sum of funds, a total of $336,120 in *direct* contributions to Costa Rican agencies in 1970.[60] Furthermore, it should be noted that USAID also can be considered an *indirect* contributor through its financial assistance of other external agencies, such as IPPF, that operate in Costa Rica. During 1970, IPPF donated the third largest amount of funds, with $104,613 going to ADC. However, during that same period IPPF (WHR) received $1,750,000 from USAID for its Western Hemisphere work.[61] The second largest contributor in 1970 was the Ford Foundation, which directed all its assistance to CESPO at the University of Costa Rica. These three largest contributors provided *two-thirds* of the financing for Costa Rican family-planning programs in 1970. This proportion captures the key role played by funds from abroad in the Costa Rican family-planning movement; international sources provided the budgetary support needed so the issue could reach agenda status without competing with other Costa Rican agencies for scarce national funds. However, the 1970 funds represent a large increase over the amounts received in earlier stages of program development. For example, from its origins in 1966 to its 1970 level of $271,229, ADC's budget rose approximately 16 times.[62]

Once the family-planning issue was firmly on the Costa Rican agenda and its institutionalization assured by sufficient financial aid, the emphasis turned toward building a broader consensus among high level policymakers and public officials who would be coming into contact with family-planning programs at administrative levels. Family-planning advocates wanted to expand the programs through linking their efforts with the interests of a broad spectrum of groups. Their theme was the confluence of interests not confrontation politics.

The Primera Asamblea Centroamericana de Población (First Central American Assembly on Population) was the first large-scale conference in Costa Rica that sought to sensitize influential figures to the relationships

222   National Policies

Key:
SOURCES OF FUNDS

International or Foreign Institution

CWS   = Church World Service
EPISCOPAL = Episcopal Church
IPPF   = International Planned Parenthood Federation
USAID   = U.S. Agency for International Development
B. Gray   = Bowman Gray School of Medicine, Wake Forest University
Ford Found. = Ford Foundation

Costa Rican Institution

Univ. C.R.   = University of Costa Rica
Govern. C.R. = Government of Costa Rica

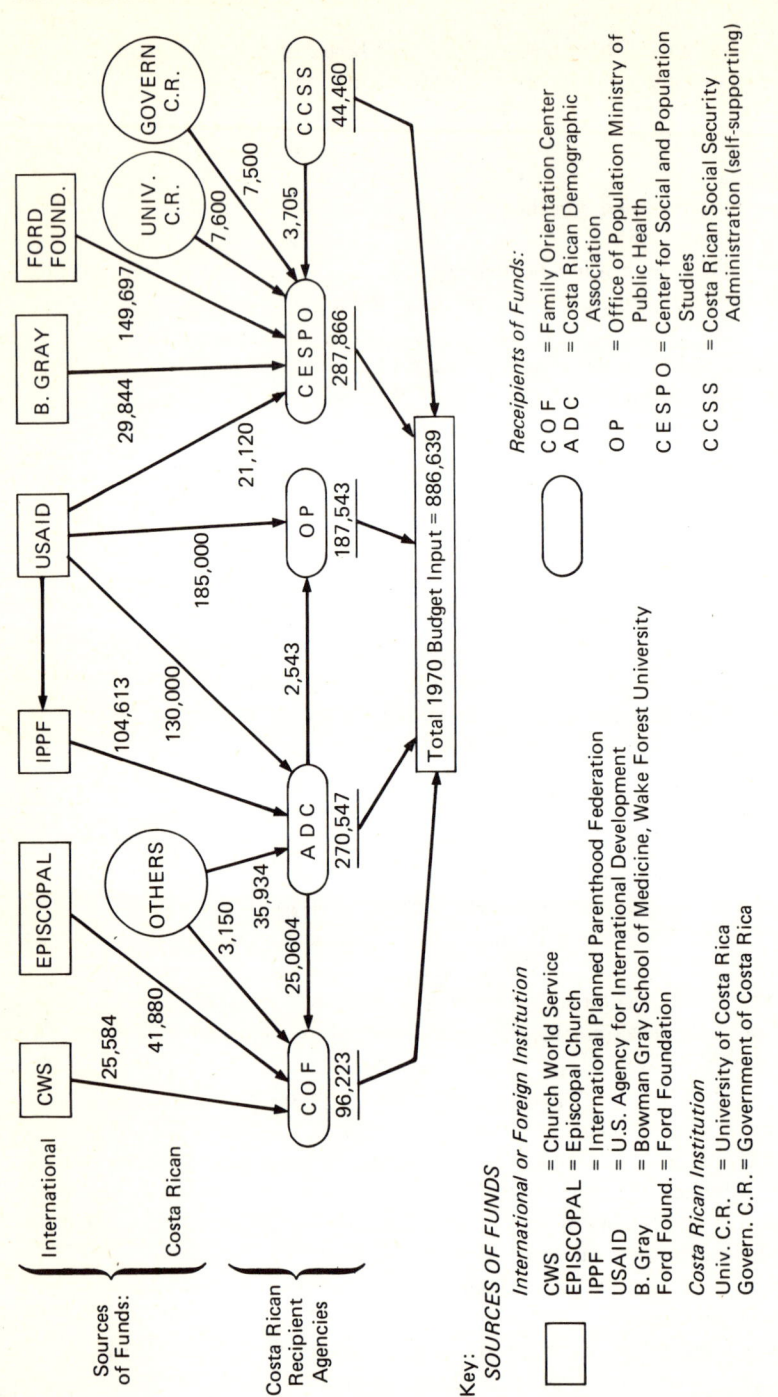

Recipients of Funds:

C O F   = Family Orientation Center
A D C   = Costa Rican Demographic Association
O P   = Office of Population Ministry of Public Health
C E S P O = Center for Social and Population Studies
C C S S = Costa Rican Social Security Administration (self-supporting)

Figure 11-1. Principle Sources of Costa Rican Family-Planning Program Financing, 1970 [in U.S. dollars]. Source: United Nations Mission, *Informe de la evaluación del Programa Nacional de Planificación Familiar de Costa Rica.*

between socio-economic development and population. From July 24–26, 1968, 115 persons—including 39 host country participants, various Costa Rican guests, and the delegates from six Central American nations—participated in a series of panels and discussion groups at the University of Costa Rica.[63] The topics covered by the panels ranged from the population-ecological balance in Central America to social welfare policies, to economic integration, to industrialization. An analysis of the current situation and perspectives for family planning in Central America was also included as one of the 10 themes, but the focus was generally on the broader aspects of development and their links with demographic changes. The Assembly concluded that population growth itself could not be considered beneficial or harmful without analyzing its relation to economic, social, and political structures, but that under current circumstances in Central America such accelerated demographic growth "could have" negative repercussions on economic growth.[64] The Assembly made a distinction between a "population policy" (which had to be based on further research and would eventually involve structural reforms of national, social, and political systems) and the fact that "regulation of the number of children is the exclusive right of those who procreate them." [65] On the latter issue, the Assembly asserted that the government had the responsibility to offer the people the means to achieve a better formation and integration of the family. But such information and assistance should be offered without any pressure that would impinge on the dignity of the person. The Assembly specifically rejected any coercive or compulsory means that national and international agencies might seek to impose.[66]

What was the impact of the conference among the Costa Rican participants? In order to probe this question, four of the party leaders in the Legislative Assembly who attended the conference were interviewed. However, it is difficult to isolate the effects of the conference because in the intervening time the *Humanae Vitae* encyclical was proclaimed. Of these four politicians (representing all the major Costa Rican parties at the time), two had previous contact with the population issue through reading and/or conferences, while the other two said that the Central American Population Assembly was their first contact with this issue. Three of the four said they would vote for funds to support increased family-planning services in Costa Rica.[67] One of the four would only favor further study on the relation of population to development. He strongly supported the encyclical because he saw a need for population growth in order to generate economic development.[68]

The feedback from the 1968 First Central American Assembly on Population as well as other activities was sufficiently favorable to encourage further seminars and conferences on the national, regional, and hemispheric level. By 1970, the calendar included the 15 major gatherings enumerated on Table 11-2.

Along with routinization and proliferation of population-related

224 National Policies

Table 11-2. 1970 Calendar of Family-Planning and Population Conferences in Costa Rica

Date	Activity	Sponsoring Agencies
February 16-March 28	International Course of Communication Applied to Family Planning	ADC
March 14-15	Seminar for Evaluation of the Family-Planning Program for Doctors and Nurses Graduating from CESPO Courses	ADC CESPO
March 29-April 4	Latin American Congress of Gynecology and Obstetrics	ADC Support
April 20-25	First Regional Seminar of Parent Orientation	ADC DGBS*
April 24-25	International Seminar for Newspaper Editors	ADC
July 3-7	Regional Seminar on Population and Sex Education	PRB*
July 8-10	Regional Seminar on Demography and Sex Education	DGBS
July 13-17	Sex Education Seminar for Teachers of Adults	MEP,* COF, CESPO, ADC
August 23-26	Second Seminar for Population Leaders of the Central American Isthmus	ADC
September 1-5	Seminar on Maternal and Child Health and Family Welfare	MSP*
September 24-25	Fifth National Demography Seminar	ADC
October 16-17	Second Seminar of Social Workers	ADC
November 4-6	First Seminar for Public and Private High School Directors	MEP, COF, CESPO, ADC
December 3-5	Seminar for Labor Union Leaders	ADC
December 2-4	Seminar for School Supervisors	MEP, COF ADC

*Abbreviations not previously identified:
DGBS = Dirección General de Bienestar Social (General Directorate of Social Welfare)
PRB = Population Reference Bureau, located in Washington, D.C.
MEP = Ministerio de Educación Pública (Ministry of Public Education)
MSP = Ministerio de Salubridad Pública (Ministry of Public Health)
Source: ADC, *Programas de planificación familiar en Costa Rica: Informe de la Asociación Demográfica Costarricense 1970* (San José: ADC, 1971), pp. 6-15.

activities as illustrated by the 1970 calendar of meetings, Stage II also involved confirmation of institutional agenda status for the public program in family planning. The potentially greatest challenges to the gathering momentum of population oriented programs came from religious opposition and also from political and ideological differences.

Probably the most dramatic negative development was with the encyclical *Humanae Vitae*, which was promulgated by Pope Paul VI on July 29,

1968. In the short run, the effects of the encyclical were measurable in two areas: a large increase in mass media attention to population issues and a brief decline in new cases at government family-planning clinics. For example, in June, 1968, with 18 clinics in operation, there were 456 new cases. In July, with 28 clinics working, there was a climb to 705 new cases. In August, after the Pope's proclamation, there was a drop to 623 cases entering 29 clinics. In September, with 32 clinics, the entries picked up to 647 cases, and in October, with the same number of clinics, there were 726 new cases. In November and December, there was another decline in new acceptors that was difficult to relate directly to the encyclical. The encyclical did not seem to have even temporary impact on control cases—contraceptive users returned in increasing numbers for their checkups.[69]

On the other hand, the increase in newspaper coverage was immediate and noticeable in Costa Rica as in many other Latin American countries. In the two months prior to *Humanae Vitae,* Costa Rican newspapers averaged just over one article per day per newspaper on population matters. During the period following the encyclical, there was over an 800 percent increase in foreign-originated articles on population and nearly than a 300 percent increase in locally originated articles. Of these clippings, 63 percent of the local items had favorable views toward the encyclical while only 44 percent of the foreign dispatches saw the encyclical in a favorable light.[70]

Costa Rican family-planning leaders accurately gauged that the long-run positive effects of the massive publicity would probably outweigh the short-run negative response to contraception. Accordingly, none of the principal agencies evidenced undue alarm with direct attempts to counteract the encyclical or confront Church leaders.[71] However, in personal interviews shortly following the encyclical, three well-known priests who had previously given public support to family-planning programs in Costa Rica indicated a much greater sense of uneasiness. They sought to accept the Pope's instruction, yet reconcile it with "individual conscience" and "exceptional cases."[72]

On the political level, the reaction was cautious and low-keyed. The day after the encyclical, the Minister of Health told the press that it was necessary to study the document thoroughly and that he had called on his advisors (including a prominent priest) to begin the analysis.[73] Ten days later, President Trejos stated that public response to the encyclical "is a matter of conscience which concerns the Church more than it does the State."[74]

The overall effect of *Humanae Vitae* in the long run appears to be somewhat mixed. The ensuing publicity certainly served to acquaint thousands of Costa Ricans with the concept of family planning, but while the government was not intimidated into cutting back on its programs, neither was development of future public programs stimulated. More than two years after the encyclical's promulgation, a high level government advisor indicated that Costa Rica (while maintaining family-planning programs) does *not* have an official population policy.[75] One reason for this lack of an officially defined broad population policy is the need for church cooperation in other policy areas that makes government officials hesitant to alienate this sector of elite opinion. While there are no direct controls by the church, its influence operates through a sense of anticipated response felt by government officials who might otherwise contemplate more extensive policies in relation to population growth. Thus, the encyclical provided both publicity for the concept of family planning and definite constraints that presumably would not have existed if the Pope had welcomed all safe contraceptive procedures instead of condemning them.

In the political sphere, the challenge of possible partisan polarization on the population issue has not materialized despite two occasions during Stage II of heightened political discussion and competition: the Democratic Manifesto for a Social Revolution in 1968 and the Presidential and National Assembly election campaign in 1970.[76]

In July, 1968, a few days before the encyclical was released, the two largest daily newspapers in Costa Rica obtained copies of the Democratic Manifesto for a Social Revolution. The "Patio de Agua Document," as it was immediately labelled in reference to the site of its formation, sought to serve a consciousness-raising function. According to the Patio de Agua coordinating committee:

> The document is directed to all groups and citizens who sincerely want to confront the challenge of communist totalitarianism and of conservative groups, by the positive recourse of social transformation conceived in liberty and dedicated to human dignity.[77]

The Manifesto covered statements of ideals for a broad spectrum of social policies including such areas as education, health, work, property, social security, financing of development, agrarian programs and international relations. The section on population policy presents forthright explanation of basic family rights and national goals for achieving equilibrium between resources and population and between rural and urban population distribution. To paraphrase the statement relating to family planning:

> The decision of the number of children belongs exclusively to the parents to whom adequate information and medical assistance must be made universally available on the planning of their family.[78]

The publication of this Manifesto aroused widespread reaction among the politically aware sectors of Costa Rica. The newspapers were filled with editorials, commentaries, and letters in response and rebuttal. The immediate responses criticized the "utopian" approaches of the Patio de Agua group and the internal contradictions in the document. A very strong polemic against the Manifesto was published by the "Liberationist Group of 1970." This "Grupo 70" was especially vehement in rejecting the Patio de Agua group as ideological spokesmen for the entire National Liberation Party.[79] However, its criticism was never specifically directed at any of the provisions on population and family planning. Despite this early attempt by the "Grupo 70" to disassociate the PLN from Patio de Agua, the 1970 elections witnessed the resurrection of the controversial document.

The 1970 campaign was principally oriented toward personalistic appeals of two former Presidents (PLN's José Figueres and PUN's Mario Echandi) who were competing for a second term. The discussion of policy issues was minimal. Figueres did present an outline of his program, but Echandi's approach was to associate Figueres with communism—a tactic that worked successfully against Oduber in 1966. Since Figueres' own background is strongly anti-communist, an attempt was then made to link him with the Patio de Agua group that was portrayed as very leftist oriented. But the PUN campaign did not focus on the population section of the Patio de Agua Manifesto. This willingness to keep the family-planning issue out of partisan debate was reinforced by the fact that the Trejos administration had fostered the growth of government involvement in family-planning services and sex education. On the other side, PLN would have been able to use this as grounds for opposition except for the fact that most PLN leaders including Figueres personally favored such programs for Costa Rica.

Several days after the February election landslide victory for Figueres, *La Nación* headlined: " 'It is Necessary to Practice Birth Control'— The President-Elect Declares Himself Totally in Agreement with Birth Control."[80] That reaction to this strong declaration by Figueres was limited could be seen as a barometer of the legitimacy attained by family planning. Most publicity went to criticism of Figueres' approach by Dr. Rodrigo Gutiérrez, Dean of the Medical School, Director General of CESPO at the University of Costa Rica, and Board Member of ADC. First, the Dean disagreed with "those who believe that it is possible to combat the misery in which two-thirds of the Costa Rican people live by intensifying an antinatalist campaign.[81] Secondly, he corrected the President-elect's use of the term "birth control." Dr. Gutiérrez distinguished "birth control" from "family planning" or "responsible parenthood" and pointed out that neither the ADC nor CESPO have sponsored "birth control."[82] The Dean's critique was thus directed more toward the issue of goals for Costa Rican population policy than to the basic legitimacy of family-planning programs that he himself was a leader in developing.

Several months after the 1970 elections, the sense of political acceptance had advanced to such a degree that major public figures were presenting television testimonials (produced by ADC) giving their personal and professional support for family planning in Costa Rica. Shortly before the end of his term in May, 1970, President Trejos in a television address on the Costa Rican family cited the achievements of his administration in establishing family-planning services within the Ministry of Health and Social Security and sex education under supervision of the Ministry of Education.[83] In July, 1970, President Figueres announced on television his advocacy of a moderate number of children for each Costa Rican family. He explained that educational, medical, housing services were not keeping up with the rate of population growth. In the same address, he announced the intention of beginning family subsidies, which he stressed would be so small that they would only provide the basic needs and not be an incentive for more births.[84]

Thus, in less than a decade, the family planning and population issue in Costa Rica had emerged from the taboo level to institutional agenda status and a high degree of bi-partisan support as evidenced by the 1970 television declarations by prestigious public officials. By 1970, the initial political barriers to the access of family planning to the governmental agenda had been overcome. However, after this take-off stage, issues of implementation and goals were still objects of differences of opinion. Furthermore, after gaining legitimacy for the initiation of programs, family-planning advocates still faced the challenge of extending the impact of their initial programs. Success in increasing the scope of services in Costa Rica can always mean the possibility of negative feedback and new political opposition. However, after tracing Costa Rica's evolution of Stages I and II in family-planning policy-making, one can project that as long as the political system in Costa Rica continues within the framework maintained since the Constitution of 1949, family-planning policy and related issues of sex education and population growth are likely to remain on the systemic and institutional agendas of the nation.

CHILE [85]

Stage I

The Chilean government has never attempted to sponsor a population policy to cope with problems of population growth. The earliest formal statements by the National Health Service on family planning explicitly state that its program is not aimed at birth control.[86]

Nevertheless, the Chilean government was one of the first in Latin America to activate programs providing contraceptive services and thus open the institutional agenda to population issues. At both the systemic and institutional levels, Chile experienced a wide range of programs and policies that were not only more diverse than those in Costa Rica but also seemed to evolve with less internal coordination and cooperation among agencies than was managed in the smaller country.

From 1959 through 1966, the mobilization of bias in most countries generally favored inertia and "non-decision-making" concerning population and birth control.[87] Yet during this same period (Stage I), Chile was experiencing pioneer research activities and governmental initiatives. The abortion issue first sparked medical and demographic research—the results of which helped motivate official public health response. During this stage, two centers of programming emerged: the Asociación Chilena de Protección de la Familia (The Chilean Association for the Protection of the Family, APROFA) and the Servicio Nacional de Salud (The National Health Service, SNS). In contrast to Costa Rica, where the private association served as a catalyst to stimulate government participation, official initiative fused an advisory committee onto the National Health Service structure in Chile. Subsequent public leadership changes led to administrative reconsideration, reaction, and fission of these efforts into public and private organizational spheres. In addition, the first stage of population agenda-building in Chile also relied upon the inputs of training and research agencies (which were mostly supported by North American foundations or international organizations).

The antecedents in Chile that set the stage for initial agenda-building encompass three principal areas of activity: clinical services, contraceptive research, and surveys of the incidence of abortion.

Clinical services available to the public (albeit on a restricted basis) can be traced back to 1938 in Chile. From that date until 1961, patients for whom pregnancy was forbidden because of critical health reasons and who did not have access to a private practitioner were able to receive contraceptives (diaphragms) at one clinic in Santiago.[88] This clinic was subsequently annexed by the fertility service of the Department of Gynecology, University of Chile. Given its unique service to the public, the work was performed as unobtrusively as possible, but it existed. Since 1961, advice and a variety of contraceptives have been provided free to anyone requesting them; between 1961 and 1965 the clinic averaged over 3,500 cases per year.[89]

In 1959, contraceptive research began in Chile with the aim of developing an IUD (inter-uterine device) that could be both made and inserted by medical and paramedical personnel.[90] This research, headed by Dr. Jaime Zipper of the Institute of Physiology at the University of Chile, resulted in a nylon ring ("Zipper ring") that was test inserted into 3,000 women at the Barros Luco-Trudeau Hospital between late 1959 and mid-1963.[91] The creation of indigenous contraceptive technology brought considerable attention to Chilean medical research as well as developing effective contraceptives for public programs.

While these early research and clinical activities in Chile provided the means for implementing family-planning programs, surveys of growing abortion rates provided the motivation for confronting the issue at the institutional agenda level. The incidence of voluntary abortions was systematically investigated in Chile for the first time in 1950. A survey of 3,038 women indicated that 26.5 percent of them had terminated one or more pregnancies through voluntary (illegal) abortion.[92] The repercussions of this pioneering study on the systemic agenda remained rather limited until the late 1950's and early 1960's when the revelation of new research results had major impact. The cumulative effect of these new abortion studies was to raise the issues of abortion and family planning in public health circles and create the pre-conditions for their emergence on the institutional agenda.

The Tabah and Samuel survey of 2,000 women of fertile age in Santiago revealed the proportion of abortions to live births was 1:3 for married women and 1:2 for those in common law arrangements. Furthermore, even at that time, less than 20 percent of those interviewed opposed birth control in principle, and some of those who objected practiced it. Armijo and Monreal interviewed 4,000 women of fertile age in their survey of Santiago. Around one quarter of the sample admitted having at least one abortion while 75 percent favored legalizing both family-planning services and abortion. Less than 10 percent opposed family limitation on religious grounds. The data from this survey indicated that an estimated 50,000 induced abortions occurred in Santiago per year.[93]

The policy impact of these personal decisions by a high proportion of women to risk illegal abortion was reinforced by a study of abortion as a hospital problem. In 1963, Plaza and Briones showed that in Chile abortions accounted for 8.1 percent of all hospital admissions, 27.3 percent of all admissions in obstetric services, and 29.4 percent of bed days in these sections, thereby exacerbating a shortage of obstetric beds available. For Santiago the figures were even more urgent. Abortions were calculated as 41.5 percent of all admissions, and they were responsible for 26.7 percent of the volume of blood dispensed. From 1937 to 1960, admissions for cases of post abortion complications increased from 12,963 to 51,368. The cost in terms of human suffering, maternal mortality, and public health expenditure was so high that it inevitably became a public issue.

In May, 1962, the Director General of the National Health Service assembled the heads of the SNS services in Obstetrics, Gynecology, Maternal and Child Health, and Preventive Medicine (most of whom were also professors of these specialties at the University of Chile) for the purposes of creating an advisory committee to the Office of the Director General on the question of criminal abortion and its prevention. The catalyst for this activity had been a visit by a representative of the International Planned Parenthood Federation (Dr. Ofelia Mendoza, the same person who played a key role in Costa Rica) who met with a group of physicians concerned about the epidemiology of abortion. This meeting was the base for informal organizing of further efforts that then led to the SNS initiative.[94]

Dr. Luisa Pfau, director of the SNS Sub-Department of Health

Development, became President of the Comité Chileno de Protección de la Familia (Chilean Committee for the Protection of the Family). The nine founding members of the Committee (who comprised its first Board of Directors) included four women and five men—all of them physicians.[95] This group defined the main purposes of the Committee as follows:

> —Investigation of abortion as a clinical, social and health problem;
> —Prevention of criminal abortion and combating its disastrous consequences through education and the use of acceptable and effective contraceptives;
> —Information to the community on demographic problems especially those related to the socio-economic, and cultural development of the country.[96]

The launching of the Committee's activities in 1963 was assisted financially by a small grant of US $12,000 from IPPF.[97] By the second half of their first full year in operation, the Committee had begun distribution of contraceptive information in various Santiago clinics. Despite, or perhaps because of, these initial efforts at implementation of contraceptive services the Committee was required to cut its formal ties to SNS at the end of 1963. The split resulted from the departure of the Director General who helped initiate the Committee; his replacement requested the termination of its official status as an advisory committee formally within the structure of the National Health Service.[98]

The Committee became a private entity but maintained close cooperative links with SNS through the official positions within the National Health Service, which were also held by some Committee leaders.[99] By June, 1965, increased membership and a broader role with national scope prompted the transformation of the Committee into the Asociación Chilena de Protección de la Familia. In September, 1965, the Association became an affiliate of IPPF. Finally, a year later the Ministry of Justice granted *"personalidad jurídica"* to the Association. This act, which was the result of considerable lobbying by the group's leadership, officially formalized the legal existence of the organization—over three years after its actual formation.[100]

The Committee's early years were devoted to organizing within Chile and developing contacts in the international sphere, which also had feedback into national agenda-building. In 1963, Chilean delegates attended the Seventh International IPPF Conference held in Singapore. This was the first international IPPF conference attended by representatives from Latin America.[101] In both 1962 and 1964, Chilean researchers attended meetings on the IUD, which were sponsored by the Population Council in New York. In 1964, six Chileans participated in the IPPF Western Hemisphere Regional Conference in Puerto Rico. As a result of personal contacts made at this meeting, the possibility of designating Chile as the site for the Eighth International IPPF Conference was first raised.[102] Other conferences and international contacts followed, and in March, 1965, Chile's selection as conference location was confirmed by a visit from an IPPF representative. In addition to sending delegates to international meetings, the Chilean Association also hosted an increasing number of visitors from abroad, especially from private North American foundations concerned with population and family planning (included among these visitors were such prominent and powerful individuals as John D. Rockefeller III, founder of the Population Council, who devoted three days to inspecting Chilean program activities in 1966).[103]

During this initiation stage, the Asociación Chilena de Protección de la Familia (or APROFA as it would come to be called by 1969) was instrumental in creating an infrastructure for the national family-planning program. In order to provide a supply of trained medical manpower for the hoped-for national programs, APROFA created a subcomittee in 1964 to push for the inclusion of family-planning and population studies in the medical school curricula. This was accomplished by 1967 when the University of Chile and the Catholic University began to include the teaching of contraceptive techniques in their medical and nursing schools.[104] In 1965, APROFA began its sponsorship of the Latin American Training Center in Family Planning located at Barros Luco Hospital. The Center was established through grants from IPPF (US $40,000 in 1965-66 and $42,000 in 1966-67).[105] The month-long course, given five times per year, trains doctors and nurses from all over Latin America with the collaboration of the University of Chile School of Medicine and CELADE.[106] Although the course was originally not open to Chileans, since 1967 they too have frequently participated as trainees.[107]

Along with providing the mechanisms for program operation, APROFA sought to spread awareness of the abortion and family-planning issues and to generate support for its approaches for dealing with these problems. The Association's information program included publishing its monthly *Boletín*, writing and distributing educational pamphlets, and producing and disseminating a movie on abortion.[108]

APROFA's membership grew rapidly (from the original nine in 1964 to 500 in 1967), but, since the income from annual dues was certainly not sufficient to sustain its expanding activities, the contributions of IPPF were a necessary input.[109] From its 1963 contribution of US $12,000, IPPF's assistance rose to $50,000 in 1964, $86,000 in 1965, and $130,000 in 1966 (over a tenfold increase in the four "take-off" years of Stage I).[110] These funds, in addition to supporting information, training, and educational activities and providing the administrative expenses necessary to sustain them, were used for contraceptive supplies and medical equipment for the National Health Service.

The Chilean government's involvement with family-planning

programs began in May, 1962, (under the regime of President Jorge Alessandri) when SNS established the advisory commission on criminal abortion. However, the Chilean Committee for the Protection of the Family left the direct SNS auspices in 1964 with the advent of a new Director General "so that the government would not be responsible for having a family-planning policy."[111] Despite the change in status, the Committee continued to use SNS facilities made available by members with official SNS positions.

By 1965, under the new Christian Democratic government of Eduardo Frei, SNS authorities were faced with the fact that contraceptive services were being provided as part of an abortion control program that did not have their official authorization and leadership. Accordingly they sought to re-exert their control and take charge of the management of the issue on the institutional agenda. In August, 1965, the Ministry of Health designated an Advisory Commission on Population and Family whose objectives were: (1) to give technical advice in the areas of population and human reproduction; (2) to sponsor and carry out research; and (3) to contribute to the determination of standards of coordination between public and private initiative in this field in order to facilitate the determination of the bases of population policy.[112] However, it was made clear that the recommendations of this permanent ministerial commission would refer exclusively to public health issues and that a global policy, which would comprise all the diverse factors related to population, would have to be settled at a higher political level.[113] Such a national population policy has yet to occur. A few days later in August, 1965, SNS named a temporary Director General's Advisory Commission composed of the members of the permanent advisory commission to the Ministry of Health, plus the head of the SNS Sub-Department of Development, professors at the University of Chile, and a delegate from APROFA.[114] This provisional commission was charged with providing the SNS Technical Council with the fundamental information needed to define the institution's policy in population and family-planning issues.

In November, 1965, the SNS Technical Council approved a report based on the Director General's Advisory Commission's recommendations for a "Política de Regulación de la Natalidad" (Birth Control Policy).[115] The Commission report begins with a survey of Chile's demographic growth, high prevalence of provoked abortions, and high rates of maternal and infant death. It also refers to world concern for these issues—citing the 1965 Geneva International Conference on Family-Planning Programs and the 1965 United Nations in SNS, the Commission recognized that birth control services were aimed at lowering the rate of clandestine provoked abortion. Such services had been offered in its clinics and were becoming more widespread: 15,094 women received contraceptives from SNS.[117] Despite the growing services dispersed through SNS facilities, the report observed that these services were not part of the permanent SNS administrative structure and recommended that this situation be changed by considering contraceptive services as part of the maternal care program and thus subject to administrative supervision of the SNS hierarchy.[118] The report also urged that SNS supervise agreements with other national and international training, service or philanthropic organization in order to coordinate collaboration and formalize SNS as the final arbiter of program execution.[119]

In September 1966, responding to these recommendations, the SNS Director General issued the "Basic Standards for Birth Control." These were the first official guidelines to be articulated by the government for its health services and they emphasized the free selection of effective contraceptive methods for the principal goals of reducing maternal mortality from provoked abortion, lowering infant mortality, and promoting family welfare favoring responsible procreation.[120] The SNS directive went beyond these generalities and (without indicating how specific percentages were decided) set quantitative priorities for its family-planning and abortion control program:

1. 100 percent of the women who are hospitalized for abortion;
2. 40 percent of the women attended for birth—with special attention to multi-parous women, those with chronic illness or severe socio-economic difficulties;
3. Up to 10 percent of the women of fertile age who come for consultation will also receive the same priority attention as the first two groups.[121]

Reviewing the transition process through which the issue of family planning gained access to the Chilean institutional agenda, we can delineate three steps during Stage I (1959 through 1966). One, as a result of its attaining systemic agenda status among a limited but highly salient group of public health leaders, the government sought to meet the abortion problem and established an advisory committee. Two, a change in public health leadership prompted the separation of the family-planning program from official sponsorship; however, the issue continued to attract attention and concern at the systemic agenda level among certain sectors. Three, a small group of dedicated physicians continued to work through government facilities; this led to a re-recognition of the abortion and birth control issues by the policy-making authorities. In this manner institutional agenda status was achieved by presenting the government with a *fait accompli* that they had to place on the formal agenda in order to control.

The Chilean Association for the Protection of the Family and the National Health Service were the principal actors in attaining agenda status for family-planning programs during the Stage I period. However, the leaders of these groups did not act in a vacuum. Indeed, an infrastructure of training, research, and action programs preceded agenda status for family-planning programs, and once family-planning and population issues became matters of concern, these other activities continued to grow and help expand the narrowly defined agenda outlook.

As a transition to Stage II of agenda-building, let us briefly overview some institutions and projects that helped create the climate of opinion during Stage I and whose leaders continued to have increasing intellectual and policy impact during Stage II. CELADE (Centro Latinoamericano de Demografía), founded in 1957, concentrates on demographic training and research and has provided a major input to such activities in Chile as well as other Latin American nations.[122] Training of Latin American students is conducted at elementary, intermediate, and advanced levels and also through technical meetings, special seminars, and workshops. Research, which takes place at the headquarters in Santiago and throughout Latin America, covers such topics as urban migration, comparative fertility rates in large urban areas, smaller cities, and rural areas, and surveys of induced abortion and birth control. CELADE was established by a United Nations resolution through which the Chilean government and the UN agreed to a pact providing that from 1957 to 1966 CELADE would function as a UN Technical Assistance project under the aegis of the University of Chile. CELADE's operation began in 1958 with a modest budget of $106,500.[123] The initial financial support came from the Population Council, Ford Foundation, and also USAID (beginning in 1964 with a $100,000 grant). In 1966, CELADE separated from the UN Office of Technical Assistance, instead funding continued from private foundations, USAID, as well as from the UN Development Programme (Special Fund, with contributions from 13 Latin American nations). The budget increased from $333,000 in 1966 to $899,000 in 1970 along with the range of activities undertaken.

Another research organization that is also international in character, Latin American in focus, and Chilean in location is the Centro Latinoamericano de Población y Familia (Latin American Center of Population and Family or CELAP). CELAP was founded in 1965 by Father Roger Vekemans, a Belgian Jesuit sociologist, as a branch of the Latin American Center for Economic and Social Development of Latin America, which he also headed. [124] CELAP's orientation and impact has been quite different from that of CELADE. CELAP is dedicated only to research and seminars and, not to teaching. Its research is chiefly designed to understand the values that condition fertility. Instead of concentrating on solely demographic methods, its research teams include sociologists, anthropologists, psychologists, physicians, social workers, legal experts, philosophers, and theologians as well as demographers. Two of their studies most relevant to Chile were a study of family and fecundity in marginal populations of Greater Santiago and a survey of attitudes toward birth control on the part of gynecologists and obstetricians in Santiago.[125]

CELAP directs its attention toward two principal audiences: (1)

researchers and policy-makers concerned with development, population, and family planning and (2) church officials whom it hopes to influence on population matters. According to one analyst: "CELAP acts not only intellectually, but also tries to use its influence as the leading Catholic agency in the region concerned with population in guiding the Church in various countries toward a more open line."[126] Taking an innovative and provocative intellectual approach, CELAP sought to push on to the agendas of both the Church and the government the theme of *"Promoción Popular"* (Popular Participation) in relation to development and population.[127]

CELAP's early impact on policy-making agenda-building within the church and the Christian Democratic administration was made financially feasible by considerable support from USAID. During the Stage I period of 1965-66, USAID contributed $400,000 to the fledging CELAP.[128] Although the reports from CELAP and its associated organizations were quite critical of United States development and population policies, USAID continued to support CELAP throughout Stage II with $160,000 in 1967, $200,000 in 1968, $230,000 in 1969, and $350,000 in 1970.[129]

In addition to inputs from these two regional research institutions, the systemic and institutional agendas also felt the impact of action-oriented research projects in the western area of Santiago and the San Gregorio neighborhood of the capital. These two pioneering programs were designed by Chileans, implemented by Chileans, and directed toward Chileans, but were financially assisted by grants from private North American foundations from the United States.

A 1964 grant from the Rockefeller Foundation to the University of Chile enabled Dr. Benjamín Viel, Professor of Hygiene and Preventive Medicine, to undertake an intensive birth control program in the western area of Santiago.[130] The primary objective of the program was to reduce the high frequency of illegally induced abortions as well as reduction of high rates of birth and infant mortality.[131] This program was the first in Chile to offer both post-abortion and postpartum insertion of the IUD in addition to regular community family-planning services.[132] By 1968, 20 to 22 percent of the women of reproductive age were using contraceptives and, the number of hospitalized abortions in the area had dramatically decreased by 31 percent while birth rates declined 40 percent.[133]

The other major action and research program was undertaken in San Gregorio, a low-income, working-class area with about 36,000 inhabitants in the South Santiago Health Area.[134] The purpose of the study was to study the possible effects of a family-planning program on abortion and birth rates and to see whether or not the program (either by itself or through its possible demographic effects) was capable of inducing sociological and psychological changes in that population.[135] Supported by a grant from the Population Council, the project got underway in early 1965 with a sample of 20 percent of the households.[136] As a result of its intensive educational and service program aimed at women with the highest risks of induced abortion, both the fertility and the abortion rates declined significantly between 1964 and 1966. Total fertility declined 19.4 percent and total abortion was reduced 39.4 percent.[137] The pregnancy history method demonstrated that the San Gregorio Program was, "the main—and almost the only—factor responsible for the decline in observed fertility," and comparing San Gregorio with neighboring communities the study was also able to support the hypothesis that the reduction in abortion was also an effect of the program.[138]

The activities of these research programs and services gave impetus to the agenda-building efforts during the Stage I period. The evidence from the surveys and clinical work helped buttress the legitimacy of government sponsored services and the expansion of family-planning related issues and research on the agenda during the Stage II period.

Stage II

As in Costa Rica the transition to the second period of agenda-building was *not* abrupt. Instead, it was more a question of the degree of recognition and involvement—a progression along a continuum—not an introduction of entirely new agenda items. However, while Chilean family-planning programs and population research expanded and legitimized their institutional agenda status from 1967 to 1970, more elements of controversy and conflicting views were present than was the case in Costa Rica. This period of three years was characterized by: (1) increased foreign assistance and involvement (highlighted by the Eighth International IPPF Conference), (2) additional participation of government officials in defining (and sometimes limiting) policy and program guidelines, (3) routinization and proliferation of population-related activities like conferences, seminars, research projects and media coverage, (4) reinforcement of agenda status by meeting challenges to legitimacy of family-planning programs on the governmental agenda. By 1967, SNS statistics showed that 67,677 women had sought contraceptive services at National Health Service centers during 1966.[139] Furthermore, in 1967 the Chilean government made its first allocations (approximately US $400,000) to provide contraceptives and related medical treatment to an additional 100,000 women.[140] This increase in governmental activity, plus the forum presented by the Eighth International IPPF Conference, helped generate a public proclamation by Minister of Health Valdivieso on family planning and population in relation to Chilean development.

At a time when most Latin American governments were still maintaining a passive or hostile position vis-a-vis family planning, the seven day IPPF conference in Santiago represented a major symbolic breakthrough in Chile. The descent on Santiago of 1,126 delegates and 500 observers from 87 countries, plus the widespread media coverage, helped engender a sense of legitimacy for family-planning programs on the institutional agenda.

Naturally, Chileans played a prominent role in the organization and leadership of the conference. The Executive Secretary and Co-President were both Chileans, and over 15 papers and speeches were presented by Chileans. President Frei's inaugurated the conference in the name of the Chilean government, and Minister of Health Valdivieso's opening address presented a detailed examination of the Chilean government's birth control and population policies. Dr. Valdivieso first outlined the tremendous human and financial toll suffered by Chile from induced abortions. On the basis of this evidence the Ministry of Health "established birth control attention as one of the features of its mother and child health programme, oriented solely to the purpose of preventing and combatting criminal abortion."[141] He differentiated these birth control programs in the health domain from the concept of population policy in relation to social and economic planning and the development of Chile. Basing his reasoning on the definition of population policy proposed by the 1967 Organization of American States Seminar on "Population Policy in Relation to the Development of Latin America," Valdivieso stressed that the establishment of such a policy is a complex procedure that calls for prudence. Citing calculations made by the Chilean Office of National Planning, he indicated that "a policy of rigorous braking of the birth rate," which would reduce it by half in 25 years, would only hasten the doubling of per capita income three years sooner than without such a birth control policy. Thus, he characterized such a policy as "a question of very slight advantage."[142] Besides expressing these doubts about the effects of population growth rate reduction on per capita income, the Minister of Health also voiced his skepticism about the "efficacy of the instrument of family planning to secure a reduction of the birth rate."[143] He reasoned that while it is the poorest Chileans who most need family-planning programs, these are the people who are least willing to accept contraceptives. The policy response of the government to this vicious circle of poverty-ignorance-demographic explosion-poverty is to make a massive investment in education for the benefit of the poorest part of the population.[144]

Thus, the Minister of Health confirmed the legitimacy of family-planning programs on the institutional agenda in response to maternal and infant health needs. However, at the same time he sought to *confine* the family-planning issue only to the health agenda and to indicate its limitations in respect to the government's priority agenda item—economic development.

The international contacts and publicity resulting from the IPPF conference gave an impressive boost to the place of family planning on the institutional agenda. In addition to increasing the esteem of family planning in the Chilean climate of opinion by means of this one prominent event, IPPF also provided financial support to on-going efforts during the Stage II period. From its 1966 level of US $130,000 in assistance to APROFA, IPPF's contribution almost doubled in 1967 to $250,000 (partially to help finance efforts in behalf of the 1967 International Conference.)[145] In 1968, the

APROFA grant was somewhat reduced to $200,000, but in 1969 it jumped up to $290,000 and reached $300,000 by 1970.[146]

Along with IPPF, there were other external organizations whose grants were vital to the growth of family-planning services, sex education, and population research in Chile. Indeed, as in the Costa Rican case, such rapid and diverse undertakings could probably not have been accomplished without financial support from abroad. By 1970 in Chile, USAID was the principal source of outside funds. In 1968 USAID entered into agreements with the National Health Service, the Ministry of Public Education, and the Department of Public Health and Social Medicine of the University of Chile. [147] The total amount of these bi-lateral grants from the United States totalled $968,000 in FY 1968; $444,000 in FY 1969; and $465,000 in FY 1970.[148] The Population Council, the Rockefeller Foundation, and the Ford Foundation were also important sources of the external assistance that flowed into Chile during Stage II. As of 1970, the Population Council had provided a total of $637,000 for research in human reproduction at the University of Chile, the Catholic University, the Austral University, and two SNS hospitals.[149] The Ford Foundation provided grants of $535,000 to Chilean groups for research, professional training, institution-building in demography, reproductive biology, and social science research on population.[150] Ford also donated $750,000 for the Latin American Postgraduate Course in Reproductive Biology and Population Dynamics conducted by universities in Argentina and Uruguay as well as in Chile.[151]

The Rockefeller Foundation gave $450,000 to the University of Chile School of Medicine for the continuation through 1970 of projects begun during Stage I by Dr. Benjamín Viel. They included the family-planning program in the Western Health Area of Santiago, a study of expanded family-planning programs outside Santiago, and research on contraceptive application in the post partum period.[152] These projects directed by Dr. Viel and funded by the Rockefeller Foundation were so noticeable that they aroused opposition from some government health officials. The magnitude of the effort was very large in proportion to the total Chilean effort; it has been estimated that as of December 31, 1969, 100,653 IUD's (44 percent of all those inserted in Chilean women) were inserted under the programs sponsored through Dr. Viel's Rockefeller grant at the University of Chile.[153] According to the assessment of a foreign advisor, as of 1970 Dr. Viel's program had provided approximately 35 percent of all family-planning services in Chile while APROFA had provided salaries and materials for another 50 percent, with the government accounting for the remainder.[154]

In addition to the reaction to this program in particular, opposition to the expansion of family planning during Stage II was predominantly based on two rationales: (1) family planning was seen as overshadowing the importance of other health services and absorbing too much time of medical personnel and

(2) the distribution of contraceptives could help reduce the national rate of demographic growth despite the absence of explicit demographic objectives. Thus, in 1968, the SNS program goals, which had been established in 1966 to deal with abortion and maternal and child health through contraceptive services, were modified. The SNS Directive of October 8, 1968, warned that the program *as a whole* should not cover more than 15 percent of all Chilean women of fertile age.[155] In addition to the 1968 15 percent limitation on contraceptive treatment, SNS took steps to curb the family-planning services that were being extended under the auspices of the University of Chile Rockefeller-funded program.[156] Thus from 1968 to 1970, the increased participation of the government in attempts to define policy guidelines confirmed institutional agenda status for family planning, but also limited specific programs in practice.

The proliferation of population-related research continued so rapidly during the Stage II that by 1970 a knowledgeable observer could identify the lack of communication among the various population and family-planning projects as a major problem.[157] Although SNS sought to exercise its control over all clinical services offered, it did not have, nor did it create, the mechanisms to coordinate research work. Therefore, Chile did not have the equivalent of the mixed sector close coordination and cooperation fostered in Costa Rica by the National Committee on Population.

Along with the growth of research endeavors during Stage II that helped open new ground on the systemic agenda among the scientific and public health community, there were also other non-research oriented conferences and seminars for other elements in Chilean society. By reaching out to new sectors of the community, advocates of family planning could push their concerns onto the agendas of specific interest groups and broaden the supportive coalition. One such outreach was a National Seminar for Labor Union Leaders on "The Worker and His Responsibilities as Head of the Family." This seminar was organized by APROFA and PRB for the leaders of the Central Unica de Trabajadores (National Confederation of Chilean workers or CUT) in August 1969.[158] CUT leaders not only demanded that an effective means of combating criminal abortion be found, but they, unlike most officials, admitted the possibility of accomplishing this through legalizing abortion for special cases as well as through the more generally acceptable means.[159] While stressing the fact that family-planning services should be facilitated for all couples, they nevertheless also called attention to "the danger entailed by the creation of birth control programs with respect to which, in present circumstances we declare our repudiation and irrevocable opposition."[160] CUT leaders, many of whom were Marxists, reinforced the prevalent trend to distinguish between family planning and birth control. The difference could not be clearly distinguished by terminology (because SNS frequently used the term "birth control" for its official program) but more by the implied meaning that voluntary programs were permissible for health purposes, whereas "birth control" as a national policy aimed at reducing the birth rate was not.

Press coverage, which also serves as an instrument of agenda-building, evolved a division of labor between the major newspapers and the popular women's magazines in coverage of population and family-planning stories. The former lconcentrated on extensive coverage of national and international news like the 1967 IPPF International Conference and the 1968 *Humanae Vitae* encyclical, while the latter emphasized articles on legalizing abortion, male sexual attitudes, and sex education.

In 1969, a radical party congressman introduced a bill to legalize abortion in Chile. Even though the bill would restrict the circumstances under which abortion could occur, it still stood little chance of being passed. The effort was made mainly to help get the issue on the systemic and institutional agendas. On the systemic level, the discussions and interviews published by the women's magazines in a series of articles certainly helped to bring the issue to the attention of a broad public.[161] These periodicals also publicized the results of an opinion survey of over 800 men from greater Santiago. Although treated somewhat sensationally by the magazine, the study found that 61 percent of the respondents admitted infidelity, that 58 percent approved of abortion when necessitated by economic conditions, and that the men felt that they should be more informed about contraceptives than women. They saw birth control knowledge in the hands of women as a threat to female fidelity. The study also reported that 80 percent of the men interviewed agreed that sex education (in the home and then in the schools) was necessary for adolescents.[162] With a program on "Family Life and Sex Education" scheduled for its first inclusion in Chilean public schools in 1970, the magazines also reflected the sex education theme in many articles.

Open coverage of family planning, legalized abortion, and sex education in the popular Chilean magazines occurred only about a year after the proclamation of the *Humanae Vitae*. At the time of Pope Paul's proclamation, it first appeared to observers as if the encyclical restrictions would set family-planning programs back many years, and the papal decision came as quite a shock to most informed people. A 1967 survey in Chile found that only 9 percent of the clergy and 14 percent of the laymen interviewed expected the Pope to allow *only* the rhythm method.[163] In the two months following *Humanae Vitae,* there was more than a tenfold increase in foreign-originated articles on family planning and population and a fivefold increase on locally originated news in major Chilean newspapers.[164] Considering that 76 percent of the local articles and 38 percent of foreign dispatches were *favorable* to the encyclical, it seems as if public opinion might be influenced to oppose public family-planning programs.[165] But, ironically such challenges helped reinforce agenda status because greater attention was focused on population-related issues than ever before by the mass media. Government and church leaders had to publicly confront the Pope's position. President Frei commented that "Latin American governments can carry out family planning in any way, and no one can escape that responsibility."[166] Cardinal Silva Henriquez of Chile interpreted the encyclical as placing chief emphasis on "responsible parenthood."[167]

In the wake of these ambiguous statements, more women were admitted as new patients to family-planning clinics in Chile in the months directly after the encyclical. The monthly mean of 1,410 new cases during the period of April to June, 1968, increased to a mean of 1,729 for the period of July to September, 1968.[168] This lack of congruence between papal proclamation and personal behavior regarding family planning was shown in a 1968 study of lower-income women:

> The results of the study of religious influence serve to confirm that neither the type of religious creed, nor its greater or lesser practice, are factors of real weight in the decision to use contraceptives.[169]

Thus, the official Catholic position helped keep family-planning programs in the public eye, while in practice these programs had attained legitimacy.

Perhaps in a country that was as highly politicized as Chile was in 1970, the threat of *political* opposition to family planning udner government sponsorship should have been greater than even religious opposition. Although there was political criticism of the government's family-planning program, it never became a major issue in the bitter 1970 election. Costa Rica avoided political polarization over the issue because there was a general consensus between the major candidates on support for family planning. In Chile during the campaign, family planning and population remained in the background, greatly overshadowed by more controversial issues. Nevertheless, let us briefly review the positions of the major candidates on population-related topics.

Radomiro Tomic, the Christian Democrat, was in difficult position. Family planning had strengthened its hold on the institutional agenda under Eduardo Frei's Christian Democrat regime, yet opposition had been aroused from within the administration itself. Tomic's own views, expounded in most detail while he was Chilean Ambassador to the United States in 1967, stressed the necessity of avoiding over-emphasis on the population issue within the total development picutre. Instead, he advocated more equilibrium among family planning, economic development, and respect for the individual as inseparable elements in a demographic policy.[170] His few statements during the campaign in 1970 reflected acceptance of family planning as a government program but hostility towards its expansion.

Jorge Alessandri, a conservative independent, had supporters who were bitter opponents of family-planning programs as well as outspoken proponents such as Dr. Benjamín Viel. Since family planning was first introduced to the institutional agenda under the Alessandri's administration (1958 to 1964) and since Dr. Viel had published many newspaper articles defending Chile's need for public access to birth control and other articles supporting Alessandri, it seems likely that Alessandri would have permitted more government support for such programs if he had won.

However, Socialist Salvador Allende, backed by a leftist coalition, won the presidency. Allende's position was also ambivalent. On one hand, as a physician, a Socialist, and an advocate of women's rights, Allende personally supported the idea of public health programs providing free access to birth control. On the other hand, as a Marxist and as the leader of a coalition that included severe critics of family-planning programs, Allende did seek to remove the influence of direct United States financial support for Chilean family-planning programs and population research. Furthermore, his government was careful to disassociate family planning from population control.

Chile was one of the pioneering countries in Latin America to develop access to family planning through public health services. The birth control question and related population issues entered its systemic and institutional agenda early in the 1960's. However, by the 1970's, while the principal of providing family-planning services remained a legitimate item on the institutional agenda, the differences of policy approach to practical implementation reflected the polarization of the larger political arena.

CONCLUSIONS

Policy-making has been described as "an extremely complex analytical and political process to which there is no beginning or end, and the boundaries of which are most uncertain."[171] In our study of the formation of family-planning policies in Costa Rica and Chile, we have tried to delineate the *beginning*: how and in what form policies related to population growth achieved systemic and governmental agenda status. The boundaries of this many faceted issue, while temporarily defined as family planning, remain uncertain and future policy developments have yet to be determined. To conclude this chapter, let us try to articulate more explicitly what these two case studies have told us about the dynamics of agenda-building in relation to population policy. Then, hopefully these insights will help us interpret some recent events in Costa Rica and Chile in terms of their implications for policy-making in this sector.

In their study of agenda-building, Cobb and Elder postulate that within a context of relatively open political competition, access to the governmental agenda is usually achieved by expanding group conflict in scope, intensity, and visibility. Yet in Costa Rica and Chile, family planning—an issue with apparent potential for controversiality—came to be "perceived as legitimate subjects of governmental concern" and also "to be explicitly scheduled for the active and serious consideration of a decision-making unit" without broad expansion of conflict.[172] There are three major interrelated variables that help to explain why the non-antagonistic model of agenda-building characterized the Chilean and Costa Rican experiences with family-planning programs: (1) sources of leadership, (2) issue definition and symbolism, and (3) sources and allocation of resources.[173]

Sources of Leadership

> The bulk of the demands made on the Latin American nation-state, presented in such a way as to elicit the recognition and response of decision-makers, derive from a small proportion of the total population.[174]

The Latin American political system functions as it does not because the majority of the people do not have demands to make on the state, but because "differences in accessibility to decision-makers are a function of the relative legitimacy of various groups."[175] While a latent demand for family-planning services could be considered as coming from a large proportion of the female population, only a minute fraction of the total population was able to articulate these demands in such a way as to elicit the recognition and response of decision-makers. In both Costa Rica and Chile, it was a small group of physicians along with a few other supporters—domestic and foreign—who defined a new problem and placed a policy response to that problem on the agenda.

The effectiveness of these activist physicians (along with their avoidance of a high degree of conflict) was facilitated by the climate of opinion in their respective medical circles. Two separate surveys of the medical professions in both countries show that professional attitudes were highly favorable to including family-planning programs on the systemic and governmental agendas.[176] While the surveys were made in different years (1966 in Chile, 1968 in Costa Rica they were at equivalent periods in each country's stage of agenda-building, right after institutional agenda status had been reached and the transition from Stage I to Stage II was occurring. The crucial question on whether government should support national family planning elicited a favorable response from 94 percent of the doctors in the Chilean sample and 86 percent of the Costa Rican physicians surveyed. The overall impression conveyed by the surveys that in each country an overwhelming majority of the medical profession was concerned about adequate birth control services, favored government support of family-planning programs, and took the initiative in introducing contraceptives to their female patients or at least reacted positively to patient requests for birth control assistance. Thus, insofar as the issue was defined as a medical problem, there were relatively few professionally qualified individuals who opposed agenda status, and furthermore opponents did not have a sympathetic audience among the medical profession.

Another similarity between the Chilean and Costa Rican leadership pattern was the indirect, but nonetheless influential role played by foreign advisors from external organizations with large financial commitments to local population family-planning activities. To the extent that some of these foreign agencies entered the picture in Chile after the initial pathbreaking had already been accomplished, they were less leaders in agenda-building and more supporters in implementation. Furthermore, since the policy-making arena and research resources were more diverse and diffuse in Chile the leadership input from foreign linkages appeared more diluted than in Costa Rica.

While the financial role established external linkages, variations in personality and qualifications resulted in real differences in the actual influence of foreign participants. In some cases, a foreign consultant was instrumental in formulating a new initiative for inclusion in the systemic or institutional agenda. In other cases there was only pro-forma consultation. As with the physicians, the high degree of consensus among the external linkage groups was crucial in promoting non-antagonistic introduction of public family-planning programs to the agenda. The exceptions to this of course were the church and some Marxist groups that did present diverse, competing viewpoints while the issue was gaining access to the agenda.

One feature of the leadership that was more evident in Costa Rica than in Chile was the predominance of men. The fact that men introduced and implemented programs that were oriented almost entirely towards influencing the behavior of women (except for sex education courses) reflects both the prevailing trends in family-planning throughout Latin America and the distribution of political and economic power in the region. According to Stycos the most important difference between the Latin American family-planning movement and that in North America has been its domination by males rather than females:

> The movement assumed a professional character from the beginning and never went through a significant period of women crusading for female liberation. Thus, in 1969, of the eighty-two top positions in seventeen family planning associations, seventy were occupied by males.[177]

Whereas family planning might be considered as a field where female leadership would be especially appropriate, men have assumed (except for the Stage I period in Chile) much of the initiative in both Chile and Costa Rica. [178]

To summarize the influence of leadership on the politics of agenda-building, Cobb and Elder point out that

> The content of a formal agenda will tend to reflect structural and institutional biases found within the system. These biases

arise from differential resources among individuals and groups and concomitant differences in access.[179]

When access to family-planning services was just a felt need among women (as evidenced by their recourse to abortion and to ineffective birth control techniques), it did not get on either the systemic or institutional agenda. The reason was that the women who needed the public programs the most were also the least articulate, the least organized, and the least visible. However, when physicians began to expose the extent of the problem and subsequently received support from foreign and international agencies, leadership became organized and access to the systemic and governmental agendas opened rapidly. Since the leadership was assumed by groups that were "held in greater esteem by the public . . . and thus can command greater access to decision makers," there was no need to resort to conflict expansion or to seek mass involvement.[180]

Issue Definition and Symbolism

The similarity between the Costa Rican and Chilean experiences in issue definition was that in neither country did advocates of family planning relate their proposals to formulation of a population control policy for the entire nation. In 1968, Chilean Minister of Health Valdivieso succinctly summed up the situation to a meeting of Ministers of Health of the Americas when he stated:

> In our country a birth control program exists, but we do not have a population policy. This program is integrated into the maternal-child health plan and has the precise objective of preventing induced abortion.[181]

In Costa Rica, a similar definition prevails:

> As is true in most countries, a systematized population policy does not exist in Costa Rica; that is to say, there is no integrated and comprehensive policy to cover all the distinctive aspects of population—both the demographic aspects (fertility, mortality, migration, marriage age, etc.) as well as the socio-economic aspects (level of income, sources of employment, education, etc.).[182]

Thus, despite a somewhat broader focus in Costa Rica, in both countries the terms chosen to define the issue had a reassuringly limited scope rather than symbolic connotations of a sweeping social policy.

In their analysis of symbolism in building agendas, Cobb and Elder rely on Murray Edelman's differentiation between referential symbols (those with a factual base) and condensation symbols (those with an emotive base).

[183] In Latin America where the emotive reactions to the symbol of the family may be even stronger than in other contemporary cultures, the concept of "family planning" seeks to convey protection and strengthening of family life. The implied morality in this symbolic reference helped open agenda access since few politicians will put themselves in a position of opposing the welfare of the family. In Costa Rica, for example, "the emphasis on the moral dimension of family planning is believed superior to the 'materialism,' 'individualism,' and 'technicism,' which they think characterizes the perspective of the developed world."[184]

Terms like "birth control" have been used as referential symbols to refer to the application of contraceptives without causing any negative reaction. However, non-family-directed program descriptions such as "birth control" or "population control" can also be condensation symbols and have triggered hostility in both the Costa Rican and Chilean contexts. These terms assume additional negative connotations in some circles due to their use by foreign leaders whose motivations are greatly mistrusted. For example, one such statement, which antagonized Latin Americans with its arrogant implications, was President Johnson's exhortation in 1965: "Let us act on the fact that less than five dollars invested in population control is worth a hundred dollars invested in economic growth."[185] It is rare *not* to find Johnson's statement cited by those opposing family-planning programs as instruments of population control. It was, for example, referred to by medical students at the University of Chile when they demanded restriction of activities related to birth control conducted by the university.[186]

Inadvertent inflammation of the symbolic connotation of population control was a very visible way that foreign influence affected issue definition. As Douglas Chalmers points out, "one of the striking things about Latin American politics is the extent to which prominent issues are loaded with international overtones."[187] Most foreign influence was of course less blatant, and less counterproductive, than President Johnson's declaration, but it was there, even when not highly visible. As Chalmers points out the very "methods of collecting data, problem identification and diagnosis, and the programs and policies used often derive from experience in other countries." [188] In spite of this argument, it would not be fully accurate to imply that issue definition for family-planning programs was something that seeped in from abroad to be gradually soaked up by the agenda blotter. If this were the case, issue definition in Costa Rica would have been almost a carbon copy of the Chilean agenda. It was not. Costa Ricans shared the Chilean aversion to a national policy of population control; nevertheless, they framed the family-planning issue to include more concern with demographic pressures in Costa Rican society. In the 1968 survey of Costa Rican doctors' attitudes, 96 percent of those interviewed thought that Costa Rican population was growing rapidly, 83 percent considered that the best path for the future would be no or low growth, and 81 percent thought that the majority of couples have more children than they desire.[189] Presumably this alarm with the population explosion in part reflected Costa Rica's extremely high growth rate in the 1960's.

While the Costa Rican agenda was thus able to define the issue in terms of demographic stresses as well as health care, the *response* to the issue was similar to the Chilean emphasis on family planning integrated into public maternal-child health services. Of course, this low profile policy response helped the dynamics of agenda-building to "accumulate consensus without conflict, through persuasion, influence and personal contacts."[190]

Sources and Allocation of Resources

To further resolve the apparent paradox of how an issue with a seemingly high potential for controversy achieved agenda status without triggering widespread conflict, let us briefly examine one more factor—financial resources. In both Costa Rica and Chile family-planning programs did not have to seek most of their financial support from scarce national or government funds. Consequently they were able to sidestep the problem of scarcity—the "fundamental condition of social conflict."[191] We have already enumerated the sources and amounts of financing for research and action programs coming from a wide spectrum of external organizations. As the reader is well aware, this condition of abundant international support characterized population and family-planning throughout Latin America.

> Indeed, that family planning programs exist at all is largely due to the fact that foreign financing has made it possible. Few are the national funds, private or public, which have been utilized for family planning in Latin America.[192]

Foreign financial assistance was not an unmixed blessing, however. On one hand it was instrumental in avoiding conflict while helping family-planning programs achieve agenda status rapidly in Costa Rica and Chile. On the other hand, the symbolic significance of a large influx of foreign funds also helped arouse opposition from those who resented outside interference in national policy-making. This resentment was greater in Chile than in Costa Rica although the $5 million that Chile was estimated to have received in aid for population research and family planning programs since the mid-1960's was *proportionately less* than the total inflow to Costa Rica during the same period.[193] Costa Rica depended more on foreign assistance, but the legitimacy of foreign supported programs was challenged more in Chile due to the higher degree of political polarization in that South American country.

Our case studies seem to indicate the assets provided by the input of foreign resources outweigh the liabilities they entail. To find the reasons for this, we must return to the prestigious medical leadership and narrow apolitical issue definition which influenced the *low priority* that family-planning programs had on the *overall spectrum* of agenda issues. Since these programs were not designed to cause any major changes in the distribution of economic resources, political power or social status, they were able to rapidly attain standing on the systemic and institutional agendas in Costa Rica and Chile without engendering conflict expansion.

Prospects for Program Implementation and Introduction of New Approaches to Family Planning and Population on the Costa Rican and Chilean Agendas

While the purpose of this study has *not* been to evaluate policy implementation, recent estimates of family-planning program output and related indicators should be summarized in order to gain insight to future agenda prospects. A 1969 CELADE evaluation of family planning throughout Latin America estimated that Chilean and Costa Rica clinics had reached the highest percentage of women of fertile age in proportion to their population.[194] Between 1965 and 1969, 37,067 women (9.83 percent of those of reproductive age) in Costa Rica were reported to have received contraceptives from either private or governmental clinics. Costa Rica had 42 government clinics and 10 private, and Chile had 173 government and 8 private clinics in operation by 1969.[195] Other reports show that by 1970 Costa Rica had 91 clinics with family-planning facilities (80 government and 11 private) and Chile had 352 facilities of all types which offered family-planning services.[196] The personnel allocated to family planning services in these facilities included 152 physicians and 385 nurses in Costa Rica and 360 physicians and 479 midwives in Chile (naturally most of these professionals were only spending part of their working time on contraceptive services).[197] While there are many intervening variables to take into consideration, advocates of family planning point to the dramatic drop in the birth rates as evidence of significant program development.[198] According to one source, in Chile, the crude fertility rate declined by one-fourth, from 37.1 births per 1000 inhabitants in 1963 to 26.9 in 1970.[199] In Costa Rica the decline from 47.8 per 1000 in 1960 to 34.4 in 1970 resulted in a 28 percent drop.[200]

Where do these issues stand on the Costa Rican and Chilean agendas currently and what are the prospects for the future? In Costa Rica under the Figueres administration, family-planning programs have remained firmly on the systemic and governmental agendas since 1971, while significant, sustained steps were taken toward full implementation. During the 1974 presidential election campaign the legalization of abortion even became visible on the systemic agenda. The largest daily newspaper carried a story with the headline, "Candidates Against Legalization of Abortion," about how all four major presidential candidates had issued strong negative responses to an inquiry made concerning their positions on this issue.[201] Although they rejected the legalization of abortion, at least two of the major candidates (including the victorious Daniel Oduber) had expressed prior approval of government family-planning programs based on contraceptives.[202] Thus, while legalized abortion has been introduced to the systemic agenda in Costa Rica (as it already had been in Chile), it does not seem likely to gain governmental agenda status or policy legitimacy as rapidly as did family-planning programs.

In Chile, under Allende's Popular Unity government, policy development was more erratic due to the clash of proponents and opponents of systemic change. On one hand, Allende was personally in favor of providing contraceptive services and also sought to introduce innovative reforms to the agenda like legalization of abortion and divorce and creation of a Ministry for Protection of Women and Family. On the other hand, for ideological reasons his administration terminated most of family planning's direct financial support from United States sources although they eventually received United Nations funding to replace it.[203] Furthermore, amidst the pressure and turmoil of many more urgent and explosive agenda issues, family-planning implementation received low priority. With the advent of the military junta that overthrew Allende's elected regime, it is difficult to determine the fate of family-planning programs on the Chilean agenda. Interpretation of current trends depends for the most part on one's sources of information. According to an article a conservative Santiago newspaper, the junta's health policies include the extension of family-planning services in order to raise life expectancy at birth and to reduce maternal and infant mortality.[204] However, if one reads news filtering out of Chile that could not be printed in the censored national press, the picture is much grimmer. Arrests, imprisonment, and execution of doctors and other health workers have been reported throughout Chile.[205] Given the possibility that Chile is suffering the most severe repression in recent Latin American history, family-planning programs will obviously not have high priority on the agenda when widescale persecution and hunger become the overshadowing specter for the lower classes.

As we have seen, the successful dynamics of agenda-building without conflict expansion in Costa Rica and Chile has primarily depended on medical leadership, narrow issue definition and foreign support. While this approach has yielded important results it still has limits in the scope of its effect on the welfare of the entire population.[206] Furthermore, the necessity of relying on foreign financing during the early stages of program development has some inherent risks for broadening public participation in future policy formation; as Chalmers says:

> ... linkages contribute to the tendency to develop means of resolving conflicts, aggregating and articulating interests, through traditional

informal means, or through the more or less 'private' representation through the bureaucracy.[207]

This pattern of pre-decision-making by a largely technocratic elite has also been analyzed as a significant characteristic of population policy formation and agenda-building in the United States. While many of the factors related to the population issue in the United States are different from those in the Latin American context, one condition prevails in both settings: in neither case has the dynamics of agenda-building at the national level included the principal consumers of the program (poor women) in policy formation.[208] As long as this pattern of elite policy formation continues, it will be quite probable that family planning will expand and new approaches will be introduced; but if such family-planning programs are to become active, integrated population policies functioning for major social change, then the dynamics of agenda-building will require more control from the population it hopes to effect. According to Ivan Illich, these demands for more widespread participation in agenda-building and implementation will arise from the conscientization caused by family planning itself:

> People who freely decide to control their own fertility have new motivations or aspirations to political control. It is clear that responsible parenthood cannot be separated from the quest for power in politics.[209]

NOTES TO CHAPTER 11

1. Myron Weiner, "Political Demography: An Inquiry into the Political Consequences of Population Change," *Rapid Population Growth*, edited by Roger Revelle (Baltimore: Johns Hopkins University Press, 1971), p. 567.
2. Studies of population and family planning often tend to leave implicit their assumptions about the relation between population policies and socio-economic development or maldistribution. This can lead to unfortunate inferences, especially on the part of Latin Americans who rightly resent an overemphasis on fertility control emanating from United States sources. Thus, I would like to make my own viewpoint explicit.
   I believe that family-planning services, abortion, sterilization, and sex education programs should be made available to all individuals in all countries. Access to such knowledge and means is necessary to promote human dignity, women's rights, humane child-rearing, and family welfare. In most countries, rich people can obtain all these services from private physicians; why should poorer people not have equal rights through public health facilities? Furthermore,

a national population policy that seeks to influence population growth rates and migration patterns as well as to alleviate infant and maternal mortality will probably be a necessary component of overall development planning in many countries.

While such population policies and family-planning programs may be *necessary* for every nation (whatever its economic or political system), they certainly *cannot* be regarded as *sufficient*. Major iniquities in economic distribution, reflected in large differentials in income, education, nutrition, health, housing, and so forth, require changes in the fundamental structures of the system. Or if the political system is rigidified into a narrow network of national elite and foreign exploitation, then the basic economic relationships which reinforce the system must be replaced. Accordingly, within this framework of analysis, I see family-planning programs as having a modest, yet vital, role.

3. Roger W. Cobb and Charles D. Elder, *Participation in American Politics: The Dynamics of Agenda Building* (Boston: Allyn and Bacon, 1972), p. 12.
4. According to Cobb and Elder, "The systemic agenda is not in any sense a formal agenda. It exists only in the sense that popular concerns, priorities, and values will both prescribe and proscribe the type of questions upon which authoritative decisions may be rendered. The systemic agenda is formed through the normal struggle of social forces. At any point in time, it will reflect the existing balance of these forces, or the 'mobilization of bias' within a community."

In contrast, the "institutional or governmental agenda . . . is much more formal and represents those items explicitly scheduled for the active and serious consideration of a decision-making unit." *Ibid.,* pp. 160–161.
5. For a summary of political processes in Costa Rica and Chile during the years of Stages I & II of population policy making, see Charles W. Anderson, "Central American Political Parties: A Functional Approach," *Western Political Quarterly,* XV (March, 1962); Charles F. Denton, *Patterns of Costa Rican Politics* (Boston: Allyn & Bacon, 1971); and James F. Petras, *Politics and Social Forces in Chilean Development* (Berkeley: University of California Press, 1970).
6. For example see: Oscar Arias Sanchez, *Grupos de Presión en Costa Rica* (San José: Editorial Costa Rica, 1971), and Dale L. Johnson, editor, *The Chilean Road to Socialism* (New York: Doubleday & Co. Inc., 1973).
7. My field research in Costa Rica was centered in San José, the hub of primary activity for Costa Rican and foreign agencies involved in formulating and implementing family-planning programs and research. I visited Costa Rica during three separate seasons: the summer of 1968, the winter of 1970, and the autumn of 1970. These intervals permitted time span perspective and also gradual building of mutual confidence.

During these visits, I completed interviews with 55 policy-makers, opinion-leaders, administrators, and researchers. In some cases, I was able to follow-up interviews later with informal discussions on a more frequent basis. I am very grateful to the individuals in Costa Rica who provided access, information, and encouragement and especially to certain members of the administrative staff and Junta Directiva of the Asociación Demográfica Costarricense.
8. Olda María Acuña Bonilla, *Evaluación de la Consulta de planificación familiar de la Clínica Bíblica abril 1967-mayo 1968* (San José: Asociación Demográfica Costarricense, 1969), p. 1.
9. Personal Interview, San José, Costa Rica, August, 1968. Since all my sources were assured of anonymity in the use of the information they provided in interviews, they must remain confidential. Thus, throughout this article in order to indicate an individual as a source, I will only cite "personal interview" and the place, month and year it took place. I realize that this system does not permit the reader to check sources, but it is only fair to the people involved in various aspects of policy-making or research who spoke openly and frankly to me. I have tried to check principal interview statements with published sources or with other interviews, but in some cases where no such verification was possible, I do accept statements in good faith when there seemed no reason to doubt them.
10. Personal Interview, San José, August, 1968.
11. James Rosenau, ed., *Linkage Politics* (New York: Macmillan, 1969), p. 45.
12. Richard Symonds and Michael Carder, *The United Nations and the Population Question* (New York: McGraw Hill, 1973), pp. 106–107.
13. Personal Interview, San José, February, 1970.
14. Luis Fernando Mayorga Acuña and Mayra Gutiérrez Rivera, *Programa national de planificación familiar en Costa Rica* (San José: Universidad de Costa Rica, Centro de Estudios Sociales y de Población, 1972), p. 3.
15. *Ibid.*, p. 5.
16. *Ibid.*, p. 27.
17. F.B. Waisanen and Jerome T. Durlak, *A Survey of Attitudes Related to Costa Rican Population Dynamics* (San José: American International Association, 1966), p. 19.
18. *Ibid.*
19. The American International Association for Economic and Social Development (AIA) was created in 1946 by Nelson Rockefeller to promote infrastructure reforms in Latin America—particularly in the fields of agriculture and health. By 1967, AIA had total assets of $500,000. In addition to direct Rockefeller family grants, AIA receives grants from some corporations including: Creole Petroleum, Shell Caribbean, Mobil, and International Basic Economy Corporation (an organization created by the Rockefeller Brothers). For further information and a critical analysis of the AIA, cf. *NACLA Newsletter* (New York: North American Congress on Latin America), Vol. III, Nos. 2 and 3, April–June, 1969, p. 19.

20. The PUN won the Presidency by only 4,220 votes less than 1 percent of the total 451,490 votes cast. For further information see: Paul G. Stephenson, *Costa Rican Election Factbook, February 6, 1966* and *1970 Supplement* (Washington, D.C.: Institute for Comparative Study of Political Systems, 1966 and 1970).
21. Personal Interview, San José, January, 1970.
22. Asociación Demográfica Costarricense, *Actas,* San José, Costa Rica, March 18, 1966.
23. III Asamblea General de Socios de la Asociación Demográfica Costarricense, *Los estatutos de la Asociación* (San José, 1968), p. 1.
24. "Population Study in Central America," The Ford Foundation, Inter-Office Memorandum, July 12, 1966, pp. 4-8.
25. *Ibid.,* p. 4.
26. For example, as early as 1966, one could find such diverse articles in the Costa Rican Press as follows: in *La Nación,* October 10, 1966, "La tasa de natalidad más alta del mundo" (referring to Costa Rica's having the highest birth rate in the world); and on November 6, 1966, "El Papa consultará a expertos sobre control de la natalidad" ("The Pope will Consult with Experts Concerning Birth Control"); or in *La Prensa Libre,* November 5, 1966 "El crecimiento demográfico del país es un desafío a la acción" ("The Demographic Growth of the Country is a Challenge to Action"); and on June 7, 1967, "Atención médica de abortos en 6 años costó 6 milliones de colones" ("Medical Care for Abortions in 6 Years cost 6 Million Colones").
27. Dr. José Amador, Lic. Augusto Perera, Dr. Miguel Asís, Dr. Charles Chassoul, *Nuestro problema demográfico* (San José: Ministerio de Salubridad Pública, 1966), p. 12.
28. "Médicos analizan la planificación familiar," *Planifamilia* (newsletter of ADC), January, 1967, p. 1.
29. "Carta pastoral sobre paternidad responsable," *La Iglesia y la planificación familiar* (San José: Asociación Demográfica Costarricense, 1967), p. 4.
30. *Ibid.*
31. Encyclical letter of Pope Paul VI "Populorum Progressio . . . ," 1967, paragraph 37. As quoted in Symonds and Carder, *The United Nations and the Population Question,* p. 131.
32. "Sacerdote católico acaparó atención de Costarricenses," *Planifamilia,* February, 1967, p. 4.
33. *La Gaceta, Diario Oficial,* (San José), April 7, 1967, No. 3.
34. *Ibid.*
35. Lic. Augusto Perera, Dr. William J. Moore, Dr. Bienvenido Delgado, *Programa nacional sobre políticade población* (San José: Ministerio de Salubridad Pública, 1967), p. 9.
36. Personal Interview, Washington, D.C., June, 1971. Several interviews with both Costa Rican policy-makers and foreign advisors corroborate this assessment of the climate of opinion in 1967.

37. "Jornada científica realizó misión de expertos chilenos," *Planifamilia,* June, 1967, p. 2.
38. CELAP, "I Curso de Población y Familia de Costa Rica, Asistentes," San José, 1967.
39. Personal Interview, San José, February, 1970.
40. *Programa para el mejoramiento económico y social de la familia, Presentado al representante de la Fundación Ford en San José* (San José: Universidad de Costa Rica, Facultad de Medicina, 1967), p. 20.
41. Personal Interview, San José, February, 1970.
42. Personal Interview, Washington, D.C., June, 1971.
43. Mayorga and Gutiérrez, *Programa nacional de planificación familiar...,* p. 7.
44. "Costa Rican Social Security Institute Accepts Family Planning," English summary of *Establicimiento de un programa de planificación familiar en la Caja Costarricense de Seguro Social.* Informe de Comisión V-1212/1 (San José: Caja Costarricense de Seguro Social), 1969.
45. This assessment is made on the basis of personal observation and various interviews.
46. Personal Interview, San José, January, 1970.
47. Personal Interview, San José, January, 1970.
48. Personal Interview, San José, January, 1970.
49. Personal Interview, San José, January, 1970.
50. Mayorga and Gutiérrez, *Programa nacional de planificación familiar...,* p. 13.
51. *Ibid.,* p. 53.
52. President José Joaquín Trejos, Minister of Education, Victor Brenes, "Poder Ejecutivo Decreto No. 26," *La Gaceta,* March 18, 1970.
53. *Ibid.*
54. Edgar Brealey, Luis Asís, Rafael Ruano, Carlos Campos, *Establicimiento de un programa de planificación familiar....*
55. *Ibid.*
56. Personal Interview, San José, January, 1970.
57. Brealey, et al., *Establicimiento de un programa de planificación familiar...,* pp. 9-11.
58. The Caja Costarricense de Seguro Social was able to remain independent from foreign financial assistance to support its family-planning services because it is in the enviable position of having large budget surpluses most years. Its ample financial resources are reflected in the buildings that house Caja clinics and offices throughout the country; they are consistently some of the most impressive public buildings in Costa Rica. In monetary terms, in 1970 for example, the Caja had a budget surplus of 100,834,384 colones (approximately $15.3 million at the 1970 exchange rate) from its total income of 273,455,136 colones (approximately $41.5 million). Cf. República de Costa Rica, *Anuario estadístico de Costa*

Rica 1970 (Dirección General de Estadística y Censos, Ministerio de Economía, Industria y Comercio, 1972), p. 147.
59. *Informe de la evaluación del Programa Nacional de Planificación Familiar de Costa Rica, Preparado para el Gobierno de Costa Rica por una Misión de las Naciones Unidas,* October, 1970, p. 95.
60. These figures from the United Nations Mission report are based on figures from the Asociación Demográfica Costarricense. However, other sources give somewhat varying amounts and thus these figures should be regarded as approximate. We are using the United Nations Mission report for this analysis because it is generally complete and reliable.
61. Agency for International Development, Bureau for Technical Assistance, Office of Population, *Population Program Assistance* (Washington, D.C.: United States Agency for International Development, 1971), p. 227.
62. Mayorga and Gutiérrez, *Programa nacional de planificación familiar . . .*, p. 27. (My calculations).
63. Dr. Rodrigo Gutiérrez and Dr. Ferdinand Rath, eds., *Población y recursos en Centroamérica: El desafío del siglo XX* (Ciudad Universidad de Costa Rica, 1969), p. v.
64. *Ibid.,* p. 333.
65. *Ibid.,* p. 335.
66. *Ibid.*
67. Personal Interviews, San José, August, 1968.
68. Personal Interview, San José, August, 1968.
69. República de Costa Rica, Oficina de Población, Ministerio de Salubridad Pública, "Casos nuevos y consultas de control en planificación familiar, segun método escogido, por meses—1968," (1968), one page statistical summary.
70. J. Mayone Stycos, *Ideology, Faith and Family Planning in Latin America* (New York: McGraw-Hill: 1971), pp. 375-8.
71. Personal Interview, San José, August, 1968.
72. Personal Interview, San José, August, 1968.
73. *La República* (San José), July 30, 1968, p. 14.
74. *La República,* August 10, 1968.
75. Personal Interview, San José, September, 1970.
76. I was doing my research in Costa Rica when the Democratic Manifesto for a Social Revolution was made public and also during the 1970 Presidential and legislative campaign and elections. Accordingly, the following observations are not only based on documentary and interview perspectives but also on my own observations.
77. *La República,* July 26, 1968, p. 11.
78. "Patio de Agua: Revolución ideológica en el Partido Liberación," *La República* (San Jose), July 24, 1968, p. 6.
79. "El 'Grupo 70' del Partido Liberación enjuicia documento de 'Patio de Agua'," *La Nación,* August 10, 1968, p. 6.

80. Television interview of José Figueres by Jacobo Zabludovsky broadcast on Mexican television and also on Costa Rican Chanel 6 on February 15, 1970. cf. *La Nación*, February 16, 1970, pp. 1 and 59.
81. "Miseria no se combate con una compaña antinatalista," *La Nación*, February 23, 1970, p. 12.
82. *Ibid.*
83. Script for a television program entitled "Dilemma" for guest speaker President José Joaquín Trejos, presented on Costa Rican television during Spring, 1970 (TV script not dated.)
84. Television presentation by President José Figueres. Transcribed as: "El Gobierno y el crecimiento de la población," *La Nación,* July 4, 1970.
85. My research in Chile was centered in Santiago, the locus of activity for Chilean and international agencies involved in family-planning programs and demographic research. I was in Chile from March through August 1970. During this time I conducted interviews with 20 policy-makers, administrators and researchers from Chilean and international agencies. In some cases I was able to follow-up interviews later with informal discussion. I am very grateful to the individuals in Chile who provided access, information, and encouragement, and especially to certain staff members at APROFA and CELADE. Unfortunately, being in Chile during the very intense 1970 Presidential election campaign, while very exciting and educational, also had definite drawbacks. First, the ideological polarization created a general atmosphere of apprehension. Secondly, the memories of Project Camelot directed suspicion toward researchers from the United States. Given this climate, North American foundation and government representatives in the population area warned me that my study could be used to attack family-planning programs and United States assistance to such programs. Furthermore, even some Chileans who graciously cooperated with me resented the fact that the results of my study would be generally more accessible to North Americans than to Chileans. For a more thorough discussion of the risks and ethical dilemmas of field research in Chile, see: Myron Glazer, *The Research Adventure* (New York: Random House, 1972).
86. "Chile," *Country Profiles* (New York: The Population Council, October 1970), p. 4.
87. "While advocates of change must win at all stages of the political process— issue recognition, decision, and implementation of policy—the defenders of existing policy must win only at one stage in the process. It is difficult to avoid the conclusion that all political systems have an inherent 'mobilization of bias' and that this bias strongly favors those defending the status quo." Peter Bachrach and Morton Baratz, *Power and Poverty* (New York: Oxford University Press, 1970), p. 58. For the same authors' view of non-

decision-making cf. "Decisions and Nondecisions: An Analytical Framework," *American Political Science Review* 57 (1963), pp. 632–42.
88. Hernan Romero, "Chile" in *Family Planning and Population Programs*, edited by Bernard Berelson *et al.* (Chicago: University of Chicago Press, 1966), pp. 237–9.
89. *Ibid.*
90. J. Zipper, M.L. Garcia, L. Pastene, "The Nylon Ring—A Device with a Half-Life of Eight Years," *Proceedings of the Eighth International Conference of the International Planned Parenthood Federation Santiago Chile 9–15 April 1967* (London: IPPF, 1967), p. 302.
91. *Ibid.*, p. 303.
92. Romero, "Chile," p. 243.
93. The following discussion of this early research work is based on these studies: Leon Tabah and Raul Samuel, "Encuesta de fecundidad y de actitudes relativas a la formación de la familia: Resultados preliminares," *Cuadernos médico-sociales*, II, 2 (December, 1961); Rolando Armijo and Tegualda Monreal, "Epidemiología del provocado en Santiago," *Revista médica de Chile 92* (July, 1964); Silvia Plaza and Humberto Briones, "El Aborto: Problema asistencial," *Revista médica de Chile*, 91 (April, 1963); Mariano Requena, "Social and Economic Correlates of Induced Abortion in Santiago, Chile," *Demography*, 2 (1965).
94. Personal Interview, Santiago de Chile, July 1970.
95. *Estatutos de La Asociación Chilena de Protección de la Familia* (Santiago de Chile, 1965), p. 13. The original Board of Directors included: Dr. Luisa Pfau, Dr. Onofre Avendaño, Dr. Lucia Lopez, Dr. Eneida Aguilera, Dr. Amalia Ernst, Dr. Hernán Romero, Dr. Benjamín Viel, Dr. Aníbal Rodríguez, Dr. Guillermo Adriasola.
96. *Ibid.*, pp. 1–2.
97. Thomas G. Sanders, *Family Planning in Chile, Part I: The Public Program*, American Universities Field Staff Reports, West Coast South America Series, (January, 1967), p. 11.
98. "Reseña histórica de nuestro Comité," *Boletín del Comité Chileno de Protección de la Familia*, I (June, 1965), p. 1.
99. Mariano Requena, "Chilean Program of Abortion Control and Fertility Planning: Present Situation and Forecast for the Next Decade," *Fertility and Family Planning: A World View*, edited by S.J. Behrman (Ann Arbor: University of Michigan Press, 1969), p. 480.
100. Personal Interview, Santiago, July 1970.
101. Onofre Avendaño, "La Federación Internacional y la VII Conferencia," *Boletín de la Asociación Chilena de Protección de la Familia*, III (April, 1965), p. 3. (The other Latin American countries to also attend the meeting were: Argentina, Guatemala, Honduras and Puerto Rico.)
102. *Ibid.*
103. "John D. Rockefeller 3rd visita Chile," *Boletín de la Asociación Chilena de Protección de la Familia*, II (December, 1966), p. 3.

104. "Chile," *Country Profiles,* p. 7.
105. Pan American Health Organization, Population Information Center, *Population Dynamics: Programs of Organizations Engaged in Pan American Cooperation 1965-66, Document II* (Washington, D.C.: Pan American Health Organization, 1967), p. 44.
106. *Ibid.*
107. "Programa latinoamericano de adiestramiento en planificación familiar," *Boletín de la Asociación Chilena de Protección de la Familia,* IV (March, 1968), p. 6.
108. "Educación y Divulgación," *Boletín del Comité Chileno de Protección de la Familia,* I (July, 1965) p. 3.
109. "Asociación Chilena de Protección de la Familia se constituye en Asamblea General Ordinaria," *Boletín,* III (June, 1967), p. 6.
110. Pan American Health Organization, Population Information Center, *Population Dynamics,* p. 45.
111. Personal Interview, Santiago, July 1970.
112. "Posición del Ministerio de Salud Pública frente a los problemas de población y familia," *Boletín,* II (August, 1966), pp. 5-6.
113. *Ibid.,* p. 5.
114. *Regulación de la natalidad en el Servicio National de Salud de Chile* (Santiago: SNS, 1966), p. 1.
115. "Informe sobre política del Servicio Nacional de Salud para regular la natalidad en Chile," *Revista médica de Chile,* 94 (November, 1966).
116. *Ibid.,* p. 747.
117. *Ibid.*
118. *Ibid.,* p. 748.
120. "Normas básicas del SNS para regulación de la natalidad," *Revista médica de Chile,* Vol. 94 (October, 1966), pp. 663-4.
121. *Ibid.,* p. 663.
122. This background information on the development and functions of CELADE is drawn from: *Las Naciones Unidas en el campo de población* (Santiago: CELADE, 1968), and *CELADE: Origen, actividades, objectivos* (Santiago, CELADE, 1968).
123. The discussion of financial support for CELADE is based on: "Report on Second Meeting of CELADE's Governing Board, San José, June 13-16, 1969,"United States Department of State *AIRGRAM* (unclassified), San José, August, 1969, p. 4.
124. Thomas G. Sanders, *Family Planning in Chile, Part II: The Catholic Position,* American Universities Field Staff Reports, West Coast South America Series, (February, 1967), p. 3.
125. Cf. CELAP, *Fecundidad y anticoncepción en poblaciones marginales* (Santiago: DESAL, 1970), and Guido Solari and Gerardo González, *Los Médicos y el control de la natalidad* (Santiago: DESAL, 1969).
126. Sanders, *Family Planning in Chile,* Part II, p. 4.
127. Cf. *Reportaje DESAL* (Santiago de Chile, Second Semester, 1969, No. 3), pp. 5-11.

128. United States, Agency for International Development, Bureau for Technical Assistance, Office of Population, *Population Program Assistance* (Washington, D.C.: 1970), p. 188.
129. *Ibid.*
130. Benjamín Viel, and Sonia Lucero, "An Analysis of 3 Years' Experience with Intrauterine Devices Among Women in the Western Area of the City of Santiago, July 1, 1964, to June 30, 1967," *American Journal of Obstetrics and Gynecology,* 106 (March 1, 1970), p. 765.
131. *Ibid.*
132. Benjamín Viel, "Results of a Family Planning Program in the Western Area of the City of Santiago," *American Journal of Public Health,* 59 (October, 1969), p. 1900.
133. "Chile," *Country Profiles,* p. 7.
134. "Programa de 'San Gregorio'," *Boletín de la Asociación Chilena de Protección de la Familia* II (June, 1966), p. 4.
135. Pan American Health Organization, Population Information Center, *Population Dynamics,* pp. 41–42.
136. "Programa de 'San Gregorio'," *Boletín,* p. 4.
137. Aníbal Faúndes, German Rodríguez, Onofre Avendaño, "The San Gregorio Experimental Family Planning Program: Changes Observed in Fertility and Abortion Rates," *Demography,* 5 (1968), p. 843.
138. *Ibid.,* p. 844
139. Francisco Mardones, Jorge Rosselot, Lucia Lopez, *Política y programa de regulación de la natalidad en el SNS de Chile* (Santiago: SNS Dirección General, 1967), p. 7.
140. Luisa Pfau, "Programmes: Western Hemisphere Region Report," *Proceedings of the Eighth International Conference of the International Planned Parenthood Federation Santiago Chile 9-15 April 1967* (London: IPPF, 1967), p. 181.
141. Ramon Valdivieso, "Opening Address," *Proceedings of the Eighth International Conference of the IPPF,* p. 3.
142. *Ibid.,* pp. 3–4.
143. *Ibid.,* p. 5.
144. *Ibid.*
145. Pan American Health Organization, Population Information Center, *Population Dynamics,* p. 45 and Sanders, *Family Planning in Chile, Part I,* p. 11.
146. International Planned Parenthood Federation, "Summary of Application for Grant by National Organization," (copies submitted by APROFA, Santiago, 1968, 1969, 1970.)
147. "Chile," *Country Profiles,"* p. 9.
148. Personal Interview, Washington, D.C., June 1972.
149. "Chile," *Country Profiles,* p. 8.
150. *Ibid.,* pp. 8–9.
151. *Ibid.,* pp. 7–8.
152. *Ibid.,* p. 8.

153. Norman Gall, *Births, Abortions, and the Progress of Chile,* American Universities Field Staff Reports, West Coast South American Series (March, 1973), p. 4.
154. Personal Interview, Santiago, May 1970.
155. Director General, Servicio Nacional de Salud, *Resumen de normas básicas sobre regulación de la natalidad en el Servicio National de Salud,* Circular A.2.1., No. 3 (8 October 1968), p. 1.
156. Funds from the Rockefeller Foundation grant were used to pay a significant proportion of medical personnel doing contraceptive work in Chile: 37 percent of specialized physicians, 46 percent of the general practitioners, 38 percent of midwives, 52 percent of the auxiliary personnel, and 50 percent of the administrators and statisticians. Cf. Benjamín Viel and Sonia Lucero, "Analisis del programa anticonceptivo y de control del aborto en Chile (1964-1969)," *Revista médica de Chile,* 99 (July, 1971), p. 486.
157. Personal Interview, Santiago, May, 1970.
158. "Posición de la CUT frente a los problemas de la familia," *Boletín de la Asociación Chilena de Protección de la Familia,* V (October, 1969), pp. 6-7.
159. *Ibid.*
160. *Ibid.,* p. 7.
161. "Aborto legal o control intensivo de la natalidad?" A series of articles appearing in *Paula* from No. 51 (December, 1969) through No. 56 (February, 1970); also "Legalización del aborto: Crimen o solución?" *Eva,* No. 1.284 (December 5-11, 1969).
162. "La Conducta Sexual de los Chilenos," *Paula,* No. 60 (April, 1970), pp. 93-97. This study was also published in a more complete form in *Cuadernos medico-sociales* (Santiago), 1970.
163. Stycos, *Ideology, Faith, and Family Planning in Latin America,* p. 364.
164. *Ibid.,* p. 375.
165. *Ibid.,* p. 378.
166. *Ibid.,* p. 373.
167. *Ibid.,* p. 369.
168. *Ibid.,* p. 385.
169. Josefina Losada de Masjuan, *Comportamientos anticonceptivos en la familia marginal* (Santiago: DESAL/CELAP, 1968), p. 68.
170. Radomiro Tomic, "Planificación familiar, desarrollo económico, y respeto a la persona humana: Tres elementos inseparables de una política demográfica en América Latina," (November, 1967, mimeographed), p. 17.
171. Charles E. Lindblom, *The Policy-Making Process* (Englewood Cliffs, N.J.: Prentice-Hall, 1968), p. 4.
172. Cobb and Elder, *Participation in American Politics,* pp. 160-161.
173. *Ibid.;* for a theoretical discussion of these factors in the dynamics of agenda-building, see especially chapters 5, 6, and 8.
174. Charles W. Anderson, *Politics and Economic Change in Latin America* (Princeton, N.J.: D. Van Nostrand, 1967), p. 126.

175. Cobb and Elder, *Participation in American Politics*, p. 92.
176. The following discussion is based on: Guido Solari and Gerardo González, *Los médicos y el control de la natalidad* (Santiago: DESAL/CELAP, 1969), and Gilda Echeverría Alarcón and Luis F. Mayorga Acuña, *Actitudes y acciones en planificación familiar de los médicos costarricenses* (San José: Facultad de Medicina—Universidad de Costa Rica, Asociación Demográfica Costarricense, 1969).
177. Stycos, *Ideology, Faith and Family Planning in Latin America*, p. 396.
178. For more information on the political limitations on women leaders in Latin America, see Elsa M. Chaney, "Women in Latin American Politics: The Case of Peru and Chile," in *Female and Male in Latin America*, edited by Ann Pescatello (Pittsburgh: University of Pittsburgh Press, 1973).
179. Cobb and Elder, *Participation in American Politics*, p. 89.
180. *Ibid.*, p. 90.
181. "Sobre control de natalidad: Polémica en Reunión de Ministros de Salud de America," *Boletin de la Asociación Chilena de Protección de la Familia*, IV (December, 1969), p. 2.
182. Mayorga and Gutiérrez, *Programa nacional de planificación familiar en Costa Rica*, p. 15.
183. Cobb and Elder, *Participation in American Politics*, pp. 57–60. See also Murray Edelman, *The Symbolic Uses of Politics* (Urbana: University of Illinois Press, 1964), pp. 5–7. "Referential symbols are economical ways of referring to the objective elements in objects or situations: the elements defined in the same way by different people . . . Condensation symbols evoke the emotions associated with the situation. They condense into one symbolic event, sign, or act, patriotic pride, anxieties, remembrances of past glories or humiliations, promises of future greatness . . ."
184. Thomas G. Sanders, *Population Perception and Policy in Costa Rica*, American Universities Field Staff Reports, Mexico and Caribbean Area Series (January, 1973), p. 14.
185. From Lyndon B. Johnson's address to the 20th anniversary celebration of the United Nations in San Francisco (June 25, 1965) quoted in: Phyllis Tilson Piotrow, *World Population Crisis; The United States Response* (New York: Praeger, 1973), p. 90.
186. Francisco Mardones, *Proposiciones para un pronunciamiento de la Facultad de Medicina sobre el control de la natalidad* (Santiago: Universidad de Chile, Facultad de Medicina, April, 1970) (mimeographed), p. 7.
187. Chalmers, "Developing on the Periphery," in *Linkage Politics*, p. 80.
188. *Ibid.*, p. 83.
189. Echeverría and Mayorga, *Actitudes y acciones en planificación familiar de los médicos costarricenses*, pp. 10–11.
190. Sanders, *Population Policy in Costa Rica*, p. 13.
191. Cobb and Elder, *Participation in American Politics*, p. 39.
192. Stycos, *Ideology, Faith and Family Planning in Latin America*, p. 405.

193. Gall, *Births, Abortions, and the Progress of Chile*, p. 2.
194. María Luisa García, *Programas de planificación familiar en América Latina: 1969* (Santiago: CELADE, 1970), p. 6.
195. *Ibid.*
196. Dorothy Nortman, "Population and Family Planning Programs: A Factbook," *Reports on Population/Family Planning,* September, 1972, p. 41.
197. *Ibid.*
198. For an example of impact evaluation, cf. Jack Reynolds, *Costa Rica: Midiendo el impacto demográfico de los programas de planificación familiar* (San José: Universidad de Costa Rica, CESPO, 1972).
199. Gall, *Births, Abortions, and the Progress of Chile,* p. 1.
200. Sanders, *Population Perceptions and Policy in Costa Rica,* p. 4.
201. "Candidatos contra la legislación del aborto," *La Nación,* January 15, 1974, p. 1 and p. 6.
202. Personal Interviews, San José, August, 1968 and January, 1970.
203. Gall, *Births, Abortions, and the Progress of Chile,* p. 5.
204. "Nuevas políticas de salud analizan Directores Zonales del SNS," *El Mercurio,* November 14, 1973, p. 22.
205. "In Chile, The Doctors had a Dream of Life . . . Now they Face Death," (Advertisement by Emergency Committee to Save Chilean Health Workers) *The New York Times,* January 27, 1974, p. 5.
206. For a critical analysis, cf. Stycos, *Ideology, Faith, and Family Planning in Latin America,* p. 397.
207. Chalmers, "Developing on the Periphery," p. 89.
208. Peter Bachrach and Elihu Bergman, *Power and Choice: The Formulation of American Population Policy* (Lexington, Mass.: D.C. Heath, 1973), p. 97.
209. Ivan Illich, "Sexual Power and Political Potency" in *Population Policies and Growth in Latin America,* edited by David Chaplin (Lexington, Mass.: D.C. Heath, 1971), p. 179.

Chapter Twelve

National Planning and Population Policy in Colombia*

Germán A. Bravo

EVOLUTION OF CONCERN WITH POPULATION

Colombia shares with other developing countries certain well-known demographic and socio-economic characteristics: rapid population growth (3.2 percent per year) due to sustained high fertility (47.2 births per 1,000) in the face of a rapid reduction in mortality (15 deathers per 1,000). Consequently, the age structure features a high proportion of young people (46.6 percent is under the age of 15), and the demographic dependence ratios have been increasing (from 84.2 in 1918 to 106.6 in 1964). The country also exhibits an accelerating redistribution of its population which tends to concentrate itself in the biggest cities; in fact some of these, such as Bogotá, Cali and Medellín, are doubling in size every nine to ten years.[1]

Growing Awareness of the Demographic Situation

Scientific interest in the study of the demographic situation of the country is very recent. Difficulties in obtaining accurate information, the lack of skilled professionals, and the small interest manifested on the part of the academic, private, and official sectors explain the "procrastinated" awareness

*Prepared originally for this volume, this chapter summarizes the background, dynamics, obstacles, results, and planning context of Colombian population policy. The Colombia case is of interest because the country used to be considered one of the most traditional in Latin America, especially in the realm of population where its political and religious leaders manifested strong pronatalist tendencies. But the situation seems to have changed radically. At present, Colombia is the only Latin American nation to have integrated population policy into a general strategy of planned development. Colombia's experience to date seems to indicate that national planning structures are important to population policy-making in a democratic, developmental context.

accorded the "demographic explosion."[2] While such ignorance was found at the societal level until recently, it was not exhibited within the family where perception of the demographic problem was manifested in the preference for smaller families. Contraceptive practices and the use of abortion grew alarmingly over recent decades, a situation perceived first by priests and physicians. As the latter, some of whom were concerned about the social function of their profession, came to see the "demographic explosion" as a family problem of societal dimensions, they started to study its causes and consequences. A former Minister of Public Health, Antonio Ordoñez-Plaja, describes the pioneering role of the medical profession in these terms:

> Demographers were not available in the country, and other professionals, possibly because they were not exposed to a dramatic stimulus as we received it, did not concede any attention to the family problem. Physicians recognized it, we started studying the problem, reaching solutions, looking for the advice of sociologists, psychologists, economists, and in this way interdisciplinary groups began to study population problems.[3]

Other groups contributed to the general awakening in Colombia on population growth. For more than 20 years foreign technical missions came to Colombia invited by the government to study the social and economic conditions and advise the public sector of the possible solutions. Every one of these missions mentioned the demographic situation of Colombia; however, none of them dared to suggest direct public action. Most simply affirmed that the level of fertility was very high, and that the persistence of this situation could produce some disadvantages. The following are excerpts from some of their reports:

> At the present time, population is completely out of balance with other factors in Colombia. If it were merely a question of utilizing existing resources, including land, more efficiently and increasing capital equipment, especially power-generating facilities, the problem would be relatively simple. The difficulty arises from the fact that while these other things are being done, population itself continues to increase. . . . Thus an increase in the rate of population growth for a time must probably be assumed as one of the conditions of our problem. It is not an insuperable obstacle over the near term to a substantial improvement of living conditions, though it acts as a drag on the rate of improvement. On the basis of experience in some other countries, it is possible that the process of economic advance will itself bring about a reduction in the birth rate and a slowing of population growth. Failing such a development, however, the prospects for a continued rise in the standard of living would be gravely jeopardized indeed.[4] (1950)

It is possible that urban concentration and industrialization will produce lower fertility rates in the urban areas, however, there are no reasons to affirm that the same will happen in the rural areas.[5] (1958)

A rapid reduction in fertility . . . requires radical changes in the attitudes toward family formation. Because there is no evidence that the population desires small families, it is difficult to imagine any kind of public action which could diminish effectively the rate of population growth. . . . The growth of population, as such, is not susceptible to any direct public action, as far as there will be clear evidences of a generalized collective attitude toward a limitation of family size.[6] (1962)

A demographic policy poses important ethical and social problems, and we are not going to try, obviously, to recommend the way to solve them to the Colombian government. . . . In any case, we have been asked to suggest ways of reducing unemployment, but we have to affirm the existence of strong relationships between a demographic policy and the problem of a chronic unemployment.[7] (1970)

[The chapter on population policy, included in the recent plan of social and economic development] is highly sensitive to the cultural, religious and political framework in which the government of Colombia must function and also takes into critical account the vast array of economic and social consequences of uncontrolled population growth in a developing society. . . . It can be stated, without reservation, that no single developmental problem basically identified with health and medical services has received so comprehensive a consideration from a multi-sectorial vantage point. It is of interest, however, that the major burden of effort to alter the rate of population increase still rests on the shoulders of the health sector which . . . is seriously handicapped by severly limited financial, physical, manpower, organizational and even political resources.[8] (1972)

This overview of the contributions made by foreign missions reveals that for more than 20 years Colombia received clear statements on the relationships between population and development, but none of them have directly asked the government to adopt any particular measure. One does notice, however, that over this period of time perception of a demographic problem and its implications has become more pronounced.

In the early 1960's, several private organizations became interested in studying the demographic situation of the country. The first results were the organizing of interdisciplinary research groups and the teaching of demography in medical schools. Since the first studies had to confront the problem of inaccurate or non-existent statistical information, their efforts centered on small urban samples, using techniques of research imported from other countries (especially from the United States), which in some cases were inappropriate. But as these research centers became equipped with better human and technical resources, they produced better reports.[9]

In 1959 the different schools of medicine created the Asociación Colombiana de Facultades de Medicina (Association of Colombian Medical Schools or ASCOFAME), and in 1964 the División de Estudios de Población was added to the Association. With assistance from various international organizations (Ford Foundation, Pathfinder Fund, USAID, Population Council, International Planned Parenthood Federation, and others) the Association became the pioneer in modern demographic awareness of a wide range of activities such as demography, urban problems, obstetric and gynecologic research, family planning, training of human resources, and sexual and population education.

In 1965 another private organization emerged: the Asociación Pro-Bienestar de la Familia Colombiana (The Colombian Family Welfare Association or PROFAMILIA). Its activities centered on providing family-planning services, particularly to poor families. At present, it also offers sexual and family education through 32 clinics located in the largest urban centers. Other important centers and organizations were part of this pioneer effort, such as the Asociación Colombiana para el Estudio Científico de la Población (Colombian Association for the Scientific Study of Population), the Instituto Colombiano de Desarrollo Social (Colombian Institute of Social Development), the Centro de Estudios Sobre Desarrollo Económico, and several interdisciplinary research groups in the universities.

The Position of the Catholic Church

Since colonial times Colombia has been a Catholic country. The strong links between the Catholic Church and the government became formalized at the end of the last century with the "*concordato*." More than 95 percent of the population is considered Catholic, and given the wide range of Church activities (schools, hospitals and charity organizations), the support of the Catholic hierarchy has been a condition for the success of most important public policies. The Church has been an important political power, perhaps more so than in most other Latin American countries.

Colombia suffers from a kind of intellectual isolationism—except in the arts—which is especially strong in the realm of religious, social and political ideas.[11] Traditional values, combined with religious beliefs to produce a providentialist, even fatalist view of the world. Responding to the misery of the poor people, priests used to offer "spiritual abundance," and preach resignation. Drawing upon the Spanish belief that the best way of expanding Catholicism was by increasing the population, the Colombian Church argued that the country needed more people to settle its territory. Within this framework the Church was the first to oppose the early suggestions by physicians that family size be planned. The first governmental action—an agreement between the Association of Medical Schools and the government for training and research in the diagnosis of genital feminine cancer and family planning—was denounced by *El Catolicismo* (a meddlesome newspaper of the Church) in a red letter headline: "BIRTH CONTROL: With American Dollars the Government Launches Artificial Birth Control; Methods Forbidden by the Church Will be Used." The same issue contained the following editorial:

> These facts are even more seriously disrespectful of Church authorities. . . . One of the most regrettable aspects of the campaign is the fact that it amounts to playing into the hands of President Johnson, who is determined to sterilize underdeveloped countries in an effort to stop a population growth that implies so many political and financial difficulties for his own country.[12]

For more than two months the nation was subjected to an extraordinary battle of ideas, figures, facts, complaints, and solutions to the demographic problem carried on by priests, bishops, journalists, statesmen, politicians, officials, social scientists and demagogues. On May 11, 1967, the daily newspaper, *El Espectador,* published some of the conclusions of the Papal Commission on Birth Control. Two months later the Colombian Episcopate declared: "Sometimes married couples find themselves in such circumstances that they have to limit the resulting fertility of their amorous donation," however, ". . . not all the work done by the Division of Population Studies [of ASCO-FAME]. . . and the Colombian Family Welfare Association can be accepted; every kind of undiscriminating campaign centered on antinatalist propaganda and the diffusion of immoral methods must be rejected."[13]

Meanwhile, the diffusion of the conclusions of the Papal Commission as well as the presentation of the texts from the Vatical Council II on paternal responsibilities gave hope for a more liberal position on birth control by Pope Paul VI. But in July 1968 *Humanae Vitae* was issued. A month later Paul VI visited Bogotá for the International Eucharistic Congress where he affirmed that "His word in defending life was not a limitation to a wise freedom on the part of married couples."[14] These kinds of ambiguous statements after *Humanae Vitae* put more pressure on the local hierarchy to define the proper Catholic position on birth control.

The Plenary Assembly of the Colombian Episcopate met in July, 1969, in order to present the nation with a set of clear pastoral directions. A group of laymen and priests was asked to advise the Church. After five months of work, the Assembly approved the final document *La Iglesia ante el cambio* (*The Church in Presence of Change*) which became the pastoral platform for the Church. The first part of this document is concerned with the problem of "Human Advancement" with three important subdivisions: "Justice and

Peace," "Youth and Education," and "The Family." The chapter on "Justice and Peace" summarizes the socio-economic conditions of the country (education, levels of living, health, unemployment, concentration of wealth and opportunities, external economic dependence, "brain" and capital drain, immaturity of political parties, and other related matters) and then refers to the population situation as follows:

> The present economic, social, cultural, and spiritual situation of the country becomes worse given the demographic reality. . . . In such circumstances, the possibilities of obtaining integral human development are far and away from accompanying the rapid population growth.
> In the presence of this difficult situation we believe that it is noxious to ignore it as well as to fall into a deep pessimism or to think that an indiscrimate reduction of natality . . . will be the only available instrument to achieve the development of our country.
> As pastors dedicated to service . . . we reiterate our deep concern and we give our approval different measures tending to find an integral answer centered toward development. We recall also the Mastery teachings about responsible parenthood, which make it clear that parenthood is not a simple biological fact but implies a serious commitment to the family, to society, and to the Creator. Likewise we manifest our concern on foreign interventions in these matters and the conditioned aid to antinatalist campaigns.[15]

The chapter devoted to the family affirms the necessary complementarity of love and sex in order to "understand marriage problems due to difficulties inherent to population problems or childhood education."[16] It concludes:

> . . . marriage is not only an institution for procreation, it is also for achieving and manifesting love. Any Pastoral which ignores this excludes the core.
> Married couples must have a paternal responsibility which, out of home implies the required continence inherent to matrimonial fidelity; and among couples, demands wise family planning according to the conditions indicated at the Council.[17]

One year later, the Assembly created the agencies necessary to achieve its proposals. Among them is the Population and Family Office of the Episcopate which advises the hierarchy, diffuses the teachings of modern theology and social sciences at different levels (bishops, urban and rural clergy, laymen leaders), and provides private and public organizations concerned with family and population issues with religious advice. With these important changes, the Colombian Catholic Church shifted from outright opposition to sympathetic openness on the population question as it affects families. Its leaders are making important efforts to understand the complicated modern world in order to help it to become better.

Position of the Colombian Government

The Colombian government moved overtly into population matters under the Liberal government of President Carlos Lleras-Restrepo. In 1965 on becoming the National Front or official candidate for the presidency, he affirmed his interest in dealing with the demographic problems. As president, he nominated Antonio Ordoñez-Plaja, M.D., who was the president of the Colombian Association for the Scientific Study of Population, to be his Minister of Public Health. Some months later, the government signed the contract with the Association of Medical Schools to initiate family-planning research and training. President Lleras-Restrepo was the only Latin American among the eleven Chiefs of State who originally signed the Declaration on Population presented to Secretary-General U Thant of the United Nations on Human Rights Day, December 10, 1966. In an early presidential message to Congress, referring to the opponents of family planning, he complained:

> What can they say to us of the promiscuity, the prevalence of incest, the primitive nature of sex education, the children sold into white slavery because of poverty, the child prostitution that exists among both sexes, the frequency of abortion, the almost animal-like mating in the mindlessness of alcoholic excess? . . .
> I cannot stop to consider the morality or immorality of contraceptive practices without thinking at the same time of the immoral, often criminal, circumstances of the act of human conception and the situations it creates and perpetuates.[18]

In Caracas, Venezuela, in September 1967, the Organization of American States, with the support of other regional agencies and organizations, held the Meeting on Population Policies in Relation to Development in Latin America, which was attended by ministers and other high officials. Conclusions of the meeting included the necessity of considering population variables within a general framework of development, the adequacy of action policies, the democratization of family-planning services, and the encouragement of dialogue and interdisciplinary approaches.[19] That same year the Colombian government began to study the feasibility of some important reforms, such as the incorporation of women into the civil service and the elaboration of measures on responsible parenthood. After long discussions, Congress passed Law 75 on responsible parenthood in 1968 and established the Colombian Institute of Family Welfare. After the reform of the constitution (which will be discussed shortly), the president reorganized the public administration and institutionalized the planning process under which the National Planning Department became responsible for the preparation of a national population policy. In July 1969 the Planning Department presented the president and members of the National Economic and Social Council the first document on population policy, which became a chapter of the Plan of Social and Economic Development. This plan went to Congress five months later.[20]

In 1970 Conservative Misael Pastrana-Borrero was elected president. As the last candidate of the National Front—the Liberal-Conservative coalition that had ruled for 16 years—he declared his personal concern for population problems along with an interest in achieving important social and economic reforms aimed at their solution. He created the National Population Council with representatives from both the public and private sectors as well as the Episcopate to advise the government on population matters. The basic document elaborated by the Planning Department was finally incorporated into the general Plan of Development which was submitted to Congress.[21]

Recent Developments

Over the last few years there have been intensified studies of the so-called "demographic explosion," its repercussions, and public attitudes toward it. These studies conclude that there is an increasing perception of rapid population growth although most of the concern is at the family level. Between 70 and 80 percent of the respondents do not want more children, usually for economic reasons. Some claim to have knowledge of contraceptive methods; however, in many cases this "knowledge" is no more than vague familiarity.

Under these circumstances ASCOFAME and PROFAMILIA came to satisfy a general demand. But they also became scapegoats. Physicians, who were the first to show concern, organized rapidly, but did not find other professionals interested. Some supporters sincerely believed that educational, employment, housing, or other problems were the consequence of population pressures with the only solution being birth control. This exaggerated position has been characterized as the "animal science approach." On occasion, ethical considerations were absent in the care of patients. Given such excesses, there were reactions from opponents. Family planning became a synonym of genocide, imperialism, violation of private life, and family disintegration. For instance, it was reported by a high official of the Ministry of Public Health that a group of vaccinators were physically attacked by members of a community after a local priest claimed that that they were there to sterilize women in order to make them prostitutes. In addition, some organized groups not only attacked the government and private organizations but even the Catholic hierarchy for failing in its responsibility to denounce "massive genocide." Leftist and anticlerical groups began to use traditional Catholic arguments against family planning, while traditionalist sectors used Marxist jargon.

Two months after the government included the chapter on population in its development plan, the Colombian Institute of Social Security began a family-planning program in its clinics and hospitals with the assurance the religious values and freedom of choice would be respected. The rationale for the program was the problem of illegal abortion, but the announcement rekindled public controversy and debate in congress. The Minister of Public Health declared before the Social Affairs Commission of the House of Representatives that:

> There have been contraceptive practices in Colombia for a long time. But who has been planning? There are many who are able to do it; but planning must be done by those who desire it and not only by those who have money to do it. Similar to vaccination, we believe that this service must be available for everybody and under the idea that physicians must practice their profession according to the advancements in science but considering the free decision on the part of their patients. . . .[22]

Following the debate, the Commission passed this resolution:

> The Congress of the Republic, Fifth Commission of the House of Representatives, having heard the explanations of the Ministers of Public Health and National Education and of the representatives of the Colombian Association of Medical Schools regarding the official policy on family planning, support the stand which the Government has taken on this important matter and hope that the respective plans are implemented and expanded as necessary in order to improve the standards of living of the Colombian society.[23]

During the debate over family-planning policy critics charged that Robert McNamara of the World Bank was trying to tie Bank assistance to the adoption of birth control programs. But questioning such speculation the Colombian Minister of Finance declared at the 1969 World Bank meeting, that "we are sure that . . . there are no reasons to suspect that the World Bank is trying to impose conditions of adoption of family planning which, given its character, must be a matter reserved to autonomous decision of each State. A new tying of this kind will not be acceptable."

Public controversy helped increase the level of awareness of the population problem. Public debate became an informal plebiscite which facilitated the adoption of important reforms. Today nobody questions the existence of a population problem; rather discussion is centered on technical issues, such as the relationship of family planning to maternal and child care programs.

However, these general reforms and commitments are not a guarantee that the effort will continue to be successful over the long run. In fact, any public policy depends on the degree of commitment manifested by the heads of the government, particularly by the president and his ministers, which in the case of Colombia is considerable. Beyond the increasing awareness by the public and the position of national leadership, the success of Colombian population policy rests on its incorporation into the national planning process.

THE INSTITUTIONAL FRAMEWORK

In contrast to traditional liberal, interventionist, and welfare notions of the state, the modern state "can be explained as an effort to make the 'invisible hand' as visible as possible."[24] This effort is based on the conviction that the public sector should modify the general social and economic trends of the nation and induce the private sector into a set of desired actions. Such ideas opened the door to the planning state:

> No longer is government either the simple arbiter of conflicting interests between business, labor, farmers, or whatever, or the agent to whom all social action should be delegated. Instead, government . . . is taking on the function of social pioneer and leader of a team; it seeks to identify opportunities over the horizon and problems before they are upon us and to marshal the forces, public and private, needed to deal with both.[25]

Colombia experienced this evolution in a very short time.

The country declared its independence from Spain in 1810. After a long period of instability, the nation adopted its present constitution in 1886 which declared Colombia a centrally ruled republic.[26] Legislative public power lies in a bicameral congress which is vested with the power of making the laws. Laws may originate in either house, although in 1968 an amendment was enacted which gives the president and his ministers responsibility for initiating legislation having to do with the budget, developmental plans, public administration, and other matters. This meant that control over public expenditures, which used to be the principal concern of congressmen because of its political power, shifted into the hands of the executive. The executive branch is composed of the president, 13 ministries, and five administrative departments. One hundred decentralized agencies are attached to the different ministries and constitute the operative branches of the executive.

National Planning

Various laws and amendments enacted in the 1920's and 1930's established the state's right to intervene in the economy for purposes of rationalizing it. In 1931 a law led to the creation of the National Economic Council. In 1945 congress was given the power to draw up "plans and programs for the improvement of the national economy as well as plans and programs for all public works which are to be built or continued in operation . . ." Or, in other words:

> The power to establish overall plans for public works and in the interest of the national economy is a logical adjunct to the power of the State to intervene in public and private business for the purpose of rationalizing production, distribution, and consumption. The planning power rounds out the power to intervene.[27]

Decree No. 1928 (1951) replaced the National Economic Council with the Planning Office of the Presidency. Then in 1958, the latter was reorganized into the National Council of Economic Policy and Planning and the Administrative Department of Planning and Technical Services.

At the end of the 1940's the United Nations created the Economic Commission for Latin America (ECLA). Its first decade was devoted to studying the economic conditions of the area and to developing the planning techniques and human resources needed to modernize Latin America.[28] The Conference Punta del Este in 1961, which created the Alliance for Progress, had as one of its most important conclusions the recognition on the part of the Latin American governments and the United States that planning was a basic instrument of development policies. Each country was to redefine their policies within a planning framework in order to comply with the Alliance for Progress. An ECLA mission visited Colombia to assist in the elaboration of a plan of social and economic development for the period 1961 to 1970. Unfortunately, this plan was not implemented because of a variety of factors: the industrial component was the only part given special study; the general goals were overly optimistic; the instability of international prices affected the country's monetary reserves; part of the promised foreign aid did not come; and, what seemed to be most crucial, governmental support decreased. Given this experience, important new amendments were adopted in the constitutional reform of 1968 which tended to strengthen the commitment to planning.

> Freedom of enterprise and private initiative are guaranteed within the limits of common good, but the general direction of the economy will be in the hands of the State. By means of legislation the State shall intervene in the production, distribution, utilization, and consumption of public and private services for the purpose of rationalizing and planning the economy in order to achieve an integral development.
> The State shall also intervene, through use of the law, to give full use of human and natural resources within a policy of incomes

and salaries under which economic development will have as its principal objective the improvement of the community and of the proletarian classes in particular.[29]

After the constitutional reform the president was vested with extraordinary powers (according to Art. 76, No. 12 of the Constitution) to reorganize the public administration among other things. (Under extraordinary powers presidential decrees have the same status as congressional legislation, thus they are called Decretos-Leyes or Decree Laws.) He issued two important decrees. The first one required that each ministry and administrative department elaborate its own plans and programs through its planning offices working together with the Planning Department and, in some special cases, with representatives of other agencies and the private sector. The second spelled out the functions of the National Council of Economic and Social Policy and reorganized the National Planning Department. The Council (composed of the Ministers of Foreign Relations, Finance, Economic Development, Agriculture, Public Works, Labor, and the heads of the Planning Department, the Colombian Institute of Foreign Trade, the Bank of the Republic, the National Federation of Coffee Producers, and the Secretary of Economic Affairs of the Presidency) is the governmental advisory agency on planning matters, and its executive secretary is the Planning Department.

When Carlos Lleras-Restrepo assumed office in 1966, the Council of Economic Policy, which became the Council of Economic and Social Policy, began to meet each week with the President. The Council aided by the Planning Department was guided by the following philosophy:

> ... Governmental intervention in the social and economic development is a dynamic process; consequently, planning this intervention must answer with the same dynamism in order to prevent a gap between planning and execution. Under these considerations there has started in Colombia a process of planning called "circular"; it consists in the periodic evaluation of the economic and social reality of the country in order to identify the required adjustments which must be introduced to orient policy towards the fundamental objectives of development.[30]

Results of economic and social activities are measured, studied, and evaluated in order to identify their implicit (hidden) policies and their possible future results (Figure 12-1). These results are also evaluated with respect to the proposed objectives. The sectorial dimension is compared with the regional one, and both are confronted with such aggregate concepts as growth of gross national product, employment and balance of payments. This step leads to the forumlation (sometimes re-formulation) of new policies which, once adopted, produce a direct obligatory implementation on the part of the public

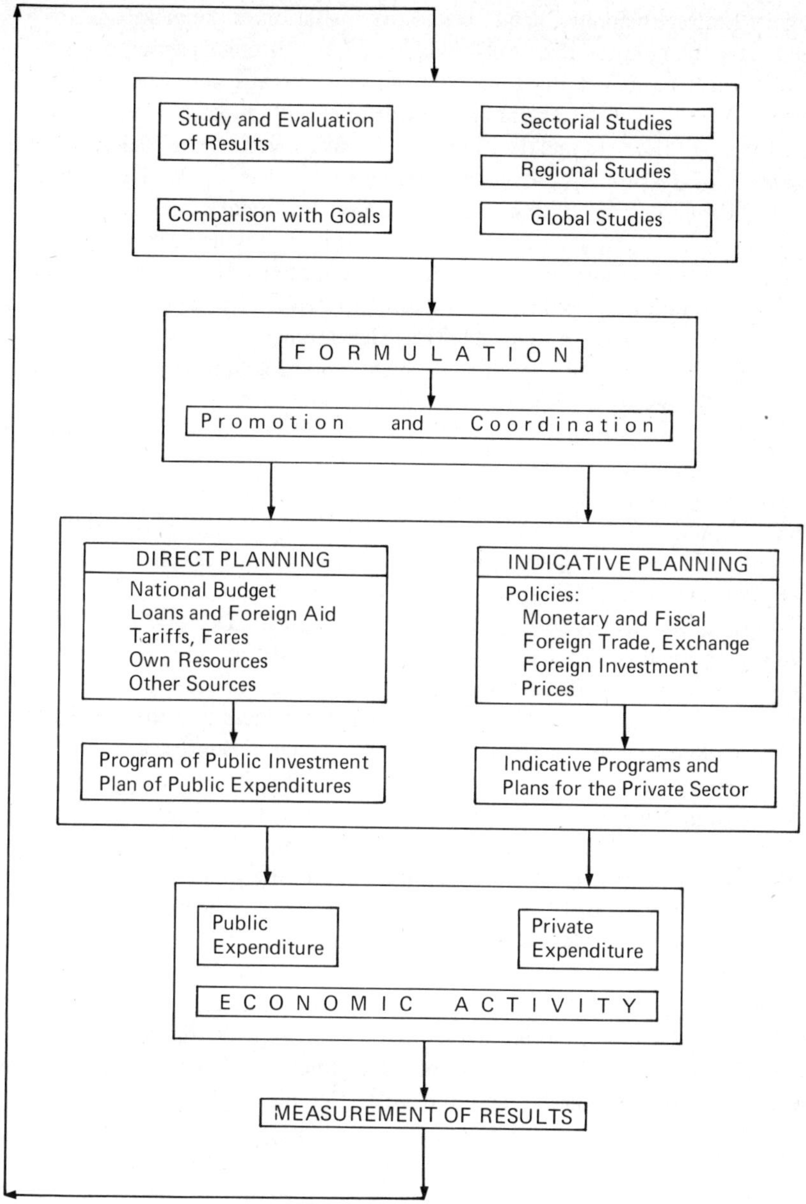
Study and Evaluation of Results
Comparison with Goals
Sectorial Studies
Regional Studies
Global Studies
FORMULATION
Promotion and Coordination
DIRECT PLANNING
National Budget
Loans and Foreign Aid
Tariffs, Fares
Own Resources
Other Sources
INDICATIVE PLANNING
Policies:
Monetary and Fiscal
Foreign Trade, Exchange
Foreign Investment
Prices
Program of Public Investment
Plan of Public Expenditures
Indicative Programs and
Plans for the Private Sector
Public Expenditure
Private Expenditure
ECONOMIC ACTIVITY
MEASUREMENT OF RESULTS

Figure 12-1. Colombian Planning Process. Source: Colombia, Departamento Nacional de Planeación *Planes y programas de desarrollo, 1969/72*, Doc. 417–J (Bogotá: DNP, 1969), p. 8.

agencies ("direct planning") and a suggestive invitation to the private sector ("indicative planning"). Direct planning is achieved through a series of instruments (tariffs, national budget, internal and foreign loans, and other available resources) while indicative planning consists of stimuli directed at the private sector through fiscal, monetary, foreign trade, and investment policies. Given the circularity of the process, policies are constantly being confronted with the social and economic results which facilitate a readjustment of general goals by the government. Sometimes one goal, such as full employment, may not necessarily serve other important goals, such as growth of gross national product. In such cases important political considerations defined by the government determine which goals are followed. Thus, development conceived as an objective becomes operative in a set of goals, plans, and programs, and circularity facilitates the passage from purposes to performances.

Population and Planning

Efforts to discover the effects of governmental actions on demographic variables made it clear that population constantly interacts with the other dimensions of socio-economic reality. Therefore, any explicit population policy must be conceived as part of a larger policy which both affects population and is affected by specific demographic measures. Decree-Law 2996 (1968) gave the Planning Department the function of "studying the population phenomenon and its economic and social repercussions in order to define the basis of the population policy." The Planning Department had already created the Socio-Demographic Division in its Unit of Human Resources and charged it with "coordinating the programming activities of other public agencies in population matters and collaborating in their evaluation." Experience had demonstrated that the interdisciplinary approach had to complement an interinstitutional arrangement which would incorporate the views of different groups and interests. In 1970 President Pastrana-Borrero accepted the suggestion presented by the Planning Department of creating the National Population Council as a governmental advisory committee on population matters. It is attached to the Planning Department and is composed of representatives of the ministries of Agriculture, Labor and Social Security, Public Health, Education, Economic Development; of the Planning and Statistics Departments, the Office of Family and Population of the Colombian Episcopate, the Association of Medical Schools and of population research groups.

Figure 12-2 is a diagramatic representation of the relationship between population policy and national planning. The study of the standard demographic variables accompanies the analysis of the interaction between population and other socio-economic factors—family allowances and fertility, for example. The Council serves as a forum where the different representatives present their points of view based on the conclusions of the studies made in their respective institutions. Drawing on these inputs, the Planning Department

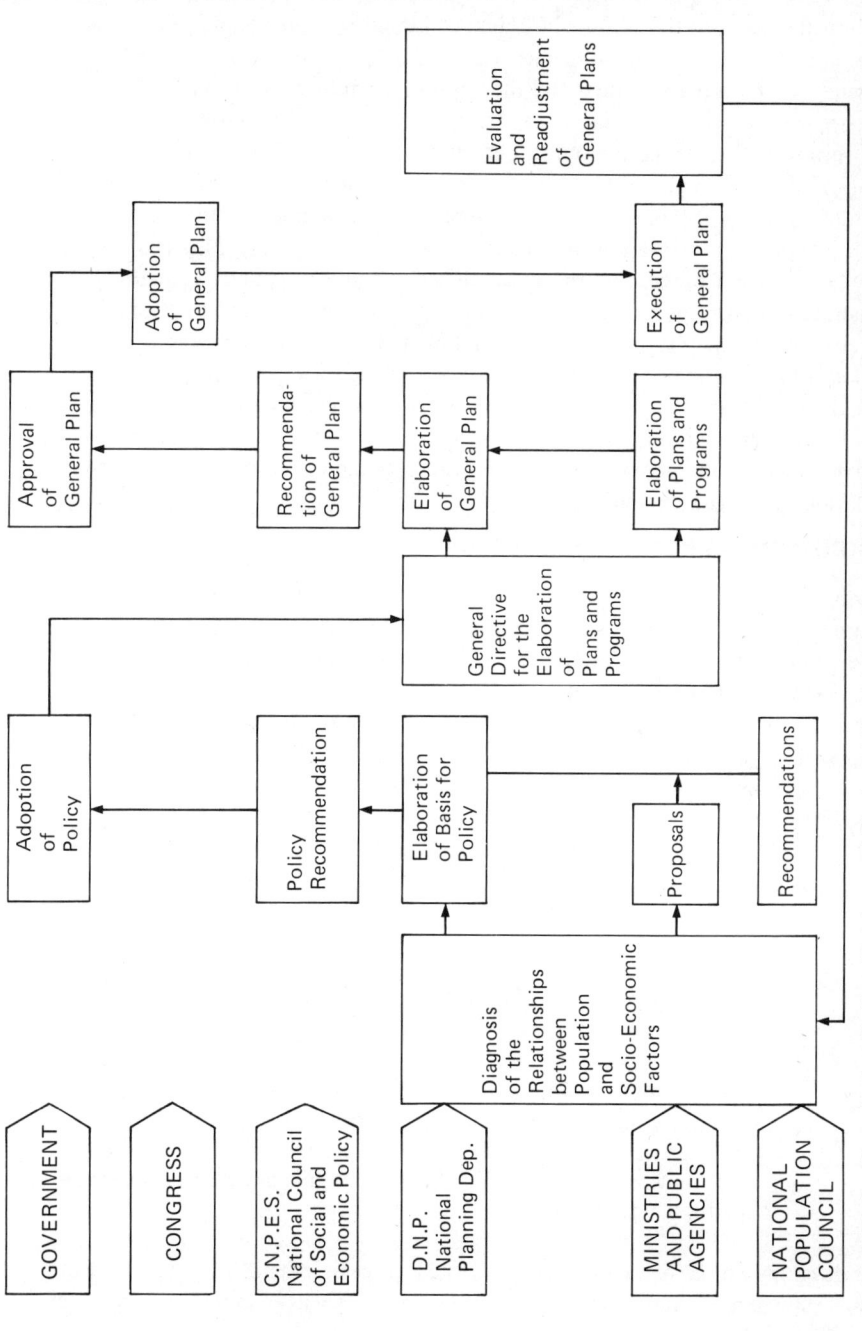

Figure 12-2. Population Policy-Making and National Planning in Colombia. Source: Colombia, Departamento Nacional de Planeación, *Plan de desarrollo económico y social 1970–1973* (Bogotá: DNP, 1970), p. IV. 26.

proceeds to elaborate the basis for policy, which—once approved by the Council—passes to the National Council of Economic and Social Policy which, in turn, studies it and recommends action to the government. (The "government" refers to the president and the appropriate ministers, who in population matters are those with economic and social concerns.) Once adopted by the government the population policy becomes a "general directive" for the elaboration of plans and programs at the national (Planning Department) and sectorial (ministries and other public agencies) levels. In this manner population policy is tied into other relevant government actions through the planning process.

The process continues as ministries and other public agencies elaborate their respective plans and programs with the advice of the Planning Department which supervises the general plan. This plan is then presented to the National Council of Economic and Social Policy and passes to the government for its approval. The government presents the general plan and its budget to Congress which must finally approve it. The circularity of the process is maintained by the periodic evaluation of results and the formulation or reformulation of the adjustments.

GOVERNMENT POPULATION POLICY

Population statistics used to be considered as additional data on national reality, serving as an indicator for calculating present and future needs and also as a denominator for gross national product, number of physicians, and the like. It goes without saying that the educational, health, and agricultural programs of the country influences the behavior of the demographic parameters, but these implicit or "latent" effects were not pursued with much interest. The first efforts in industrializing the country made it clear that social welfare did not necessarily flow from economic growth and that there was no automatic decline in fertility as a consequence of urbanization and industrialization. Therefore, Colombians came to see that development was more than economic growth.

> Development is the sum total of changes of the mental, social, political, economic, and cultural structures of the society, which allow the nation to perform simultaneously both a sharp increase in its global real product and to define the kind of society it would like to become. To achieve this goal, it must choose, in the context of its real limitations and availabilities, the means and necessary strategies so that its members could have more, be more, relate and participate more, not only in the production, but also in the distribution of the benefits of the economic, political, social, and cultural activities.[31]

If development is then conceived as a global process, it is not legitimate to exclude the demographic dimension as one aspect of socio-economic reality which should be the object of wise planning. The Colombian government gradually accepted the desirability of integrating demographic considerations into developmental planning. It still faced the question of how to manipulate demographic variables.

At the beginning of the 1960's it was believed that the availability of modern contraceptive technology alone would lead to rapid fertility reduction. Two facts challenge this assertion. First, European countries reduced their fertility without modern contraceptives. And second, current family planning programs in developing areas, where important official efforts have been made with foreign aid and advanced contraceptive devices, have had little impact.[32] The diffusion of tools and instruments seems to be running up against the diffusion of cultural patterns. Reproductive behavior, like most human behavior, is the result of the interaction between inherited tendencies and patterns learned through the process of socialization which, in turn, reflects social structures. Therefore, "sexual behavior is regulated by social institutions."[33] From this perspective, the use of a particular method follows the decision to plan or not, and this decision depends on current conceptions about sex and the family.[34] Within these and the additional consideration that a population policy is not a panacea, but rather only one important element in a general strategy of development which emphasizes structural changes, the Colombian Planning Department defines population policy as:

> ... the coherent set of principles, objectives, and decisions adopted by the public sector according to the rights, needs, and aspirations of the community for the specific purpose of orienting the rate of growth and the size of the population, its age composition, its degree of concentration and regional and spatial distribution through the creation of conditions that facilitate a more rational behavior on the part of the members of the community towards themselves, society and their ecological resources.[35]

The above definition contains the following elements of importance: (1) "set of principles" meaning the rationale of the policy, the role of the state, the main objectives of development, the rights of individuals and families, and interdependence with other policies; (2) "objectives" or specific goals of the policy in regards to the orientation and modification of the demographic variables of size, rates, compositon, and distribution; (3) "decisions" or the different plans and programs which create the "conditions" through which individuals, families, groups, agencies, and the whole nation will be able to behave more rationally and through which the community gets a better picture of itself and assumes responsibility for its development; and (4) "according to the rights, needs, and aspirations of the community" or the ethical, social and political aspects of policies.

Objectives and Instruments of Colombian Population Policy

The population policy of the Colombian government has two main objectives: to achieve a territorial redistribution of population and to reduce the present rate of population growth. What follows is an elaboration of these objectives and the corresponding policy instruments as presented to Congress in 1970:[36]

I. Territorial Redistribution of The Population

    A. Principal Goal: "To achieve a more equal and harmonious development among the different regions so that it will be possible to obtain full employment of human and natural resources."[37]
        1. Existing Instruments: National budget, monetary policy, other specific policies, funds for regional and urban development, rules concerning creation of municipalities, land reform, and the like.
        2. Recently Proposed Measures: Organization of regional planning offices, creation of the regional development committees, fiscal reform, delimitation and creation of metropolitan areas, special regional funds, and urban reform.

    B. "Push" Factors
        1. Community Level
            a. Goal: To increase community participation through association.
            b. Instruments: Institutionalization of community development within a general direction which could coordinate the present dispersed action.
        2. Public Sector Level
            a. Goal: To achieve a better distribution of land and income through forms of community ownership, opening of credit, marketing facilities, technical assistance, and "service centers" (education, health, recreation).[38]
            b. Instruments: Land reform, coordination of the diverse programs, and better use of available policies.

    C. Reorientation of Migration Streams [39]
        1. Intermediate Cities
            a. Goal: To revitalize cities between 30,000 and 200,000 inhabitants.
            b. Instruments: Promotion of intensive labor enterprises, enlargement of public investments, and design of urban and housing plans.

2. Big Cities
      a. Goal: To achieve a better equilibrium between the six largest cities and the national capital.
      b. Instruments: Creation of big industrial complexes, and achievement of self-financing of public services which have to serve all of their areas of influence.
   3. Settlement
      a. Goal: Reorientation of part of the migration stream towards less developed but rich zones.
      b. Instruments: The plan of development has defined three main zones of settlement: rights to possession of land will be accompanied by other measures such as road construction, credit and market facilities, social and public services.
   4. Seasonal Movements
      a. Goal: To achieve a permanent settlement of seasonal workers.
      b. Instruments: Training of seasonal workers and diversification of cultures.

II. Reduction of The Present Rate of Population Growth [40]

   A. Principal Goal: To achieve a significant reduction in the rate of population growth through decreasing the level of fertility. The plan does not mention any quantitative goal since it would be futile under the present national situation.

   B. The Societal Level
      1. Socio-Cultural factors
         a. Goal: To create a new "mentality" which could produce a more favorable climate for development, a better participation in social and political life, paternal responsibility, a better valuation of life, and a more rational use and care of natural resources.
         b. Instruments: Increasing the efficacy and coverage of the educational system, introducing themes pertaining to population, family, and sex education, and utilizing existing programs to reach the adult population with similar ideas.
      2. Age at Marriage
         a. Goal: To raise the age of marriages.
         b. Instruments: Longer retention in the educational system, youth movements, and so forth.[a]
      3. Status of Women
         a. Goal: To achieve equal opportunities for women in

---

[a]The role of the Catholic Church is particularly important here since a civil marriage is virtually impossible. The Church is studying the problem.

socio-economic and political life.
   b. Instruments: The voluntary or obligatory incorporation of women in social services and supervision of the fulfilment of equality in job and salary opportunities.
4. Protection of Children
   a. Goal: To improve family conditions so that each member, especially children, can achieve their full development.
   b. Instruments: Enforcing Law 75 (filial relationship and family welfare), maternal and child care programs, rehabilitation of youth, and special treatment of exceptional children.
5. Other Conditioning Factors: At present it is clear that there are certain relationships between fertility and certain socio-economic variables such as education, feminine participation, age at marriage, legitimacy, and socio-economic class. However, there is no consensus about the nature of other relationships between fertility and family allowances, taxes, housing, and level of consumption, for example.[41] Current research is trying to discover not only the existence and direction of possible relationships but also the "mechanisms" by which these conditioning factors operate in order to transform them into programs and policies.

C. The Family Level
   1. Goal: To create the conditions for the fulfillment of the basic human right of "deciding the number and spacing of children."
   2. Instruments: Raising the educational level with the purpose of developing greater responsible parenthood and making available information and medical services which facilitate free decisions, proper care, and respect.[42]

CONCLUSION

Different schemes are available to classify the objectives and instruments of national population policies.[43] Lowi's "arenas of power" paradigm seems useful for the present case not only because of its analytical power but also because it permits one to compare policy-making processes of different regimes or of different times for the same regime. Coercion, which is implied in every social and political action, is dichotomized according to target (individual conduct or environment of conduct), and likelihood (remote or immediate). The resulting cells correspond to four types of policies: distributive, constituent, regulative,

Table 12-1. **Coercion and Population Policy Types**

The Applicability of Coercion (works through:)

	Individual Conduct	Environment of Conduct	
Likelihood of Coercion:			
Remote	Distributive	Constituent	log-rolling party (electoral organization)
Immediate	Regulative	Redistributive	bargaining interest organization
	decentralized disaggregated local interest identify (person)	centralized "systems" level cosmopolitan ideology status (type of person)	

Source: Adapted from Theodore J. Lowi, "Population Policies and the American Political System" in *Political Science in Population Studies*, edited by Richard L. Clinton, William S. Flash, and R. Kenneth Godwin (Lexington, Mass.: Lexington Books, 1972), pp. 30 & 32.

and redistributive (See Table 12-1). Each one of them has its own characteristics, procedures, levels of effectiveness, and implies a greater or lesser degree of democratic participation.[44] According to Lowi, remote or indirect coercion tends to produce policies which are usually elaborated within congressional committees where "log-rolling" is a dominant pattern; in contrast, immediate or direct coercion produces such policies which tend to be elaborated in the "floor" with an important participation of the executive and with an important amount of "bargaining." Coercion may refer to the individual conduct; in this case, policies tend to be decentralized, disaggregated, local, and concerning the person as an individual. But coercion may refer also to the environment of conduct; here, policies tend to be centralized, aggregated (systematic level), cosmopolitan, guided by ideological considerations, and concerned with 'types of persons' (categories of social actors).

Although Lowi's paradigm was developed with specific reference to the United States, it can profitably be applied to the evolution of Colombian population policy. In general, Lowi sees that policy-making has been evolving from simple distributive policies to complex policies in which coercion is more immediate and direct. The exercise of power is becoming more visible, more immediate, and more concerned with society as a whole. Or in his own words, "So, as modern liberals and humanitarians would have it, the policy has finally been allowed to intervene without being required to wait for the long run to arrive."[45] The same general process of "making coercion more visible" has occurred in Colombia. The porkbarrel procedure within congress and mere "patronage" evolved toward a more clear intervention of the state in economic and social affairs and the formulation of the base for a "planning state." This evolution took place in the planning process itself. From the simple evaluation of isolated projects, planning became concerned with complex programs and with the formulation of sectorial, regional, and global plans of development. Unfortunately, as is understandable at the beginning of the process, these new formulations were not perfectly implemented by the different agencies, groups, and procedures charged with their execution. This situation required strong presidential leadership to overcome the institutional jealousies triggered by the planning process and newly acquired status of the planners. President Lleras-Restrepo provided this leadership to a certain extent.

Distributive Policies

The first governmental actions dealing with population were distributive in nature although they resulted from executive action rather than congressional as Lowi predicts. "One of the synonyms for this kind of policy is 'patronage' . . . in the generic sense of 'to patronize'." [46] Although they are easy to adopt because distributive policies "work entirely on the benefits side and coercion is displaced onto the general revenue system or to all who have no access to the program in question, it is possible to disaggregate the available resources and to treat each decision in isolation from other decisions." [47] In the case of Colombia, these policies include land grant programs, the establishment and expansion of family-planning services, funds for regional and urban development, funds for private social welfare organizations, payments to physicians who work in family planning, grants and loans to research organizations, urban and regional development, and other subsidies to the private sector. However, most of these policies, as they work today, have become regulatory insofar as the procedures are stipulated. In fact, when a system of incentives is established with efficacy, it has to determine who shall be a beneficiary, within which conditions, in what amount; that is, there must be some "rules of the game" which make coercion more direct.

Constitutent Policies

Included here are those policies which are also indirect or remote but refer to the conditioning factors of individual conduct. Given their universalism and ideological ingredients, they refer to basic changes which in most cases are nothing else than the call to change since they do not specify the ways in which coercion has to be exerted. Constituent policies do not produce important changes if they are no more than declarations, but, when they inspire programs, projects and plans which require direct and immediate coercion, their impact on political life "could be profound, even if their impact on population growth rates were not felt for a very long time," and therefore, "[they] may be particularly attractive to policy-makers because [they] might produce a kind of national referendum."[48] Colombian constituent policies affecting population include executive proposals calling for the creation of a "new mentality" which shall go hand in hand with the requirements of development, the creation of agencies, recognition of family rights in deciding the number and spacing of children, introduction of population, and family and sexual education in the normal curriculum. In this arena of power, the change on the part of the Catholic Church has been decisive, and agitation of public opinion during the controversial years made it possible to get a positive response to the informal referendum which the different proposals of the government represented.

Redistributive Policies

Those policies which exert direct or immediate coercion upon the factors conditioning individual conduct are called "redistributive" policies. In this case, the executive tends to be the center of policy-making, and ideological considerations turn these policies into class-oriented actions. According to Lowi, their centralism and bureaucratic traits expose these policies to the public eye and the sources of disagreement and tensions are activated. Redistributive policies are best represented in the detailed budget figures of the plan of development (at the sectorial, regional, and program levels), the Internal Revenue Code, the legislation and decrees on social security and welfare (i.e., family allowances, filial relationships and responsible parenthood, accessibility to certain programs—housing, credit), "self-financed public services" in the big cities, and agrarian reform. Given the family-centered character of the family-planning programs, there are no compulsory policies dealing directly with fertility control.

Regulatory Policies

Regulatory policies consist of the direct and immediate application of coercion to the individual. Lowi contends that the United States case demonstrates that, because of their decentralism and the domination of different interest groups, these policies tend to be highly effective if adopted, but when this does not happen, and a decision is needed, there exists the enormous risk that regulatory policies become simple distributive policies, or even worse, policy-making is delegated to bureaucracies. Regulatory policies, in which coercion is established in the statute, are illustrated in Colombia by Law 75 (1968), usually called the "Law of Responsible Parenthood," the medical and labor codes, the rules concerned with the creation of municipalities, and the rules concerning foreign aid and technical assistance. Other actions mentioned in the plan, but not yet sanctioned, refer to the creation of a social service for women, the establishment of rules concerning private medical practice in family planning, determination of a new age of marriage, and the establishment of the new forms of community property.

Concluding Remarks

Colombia has made an effort to adapt its institutions to the requirements of development. In the population area, Colombia is the only Latin American country which has attempted to integrate population policy into developmental planning, or that in fact has a "policy."[49] However, it is an exaggeration to affirm that it is "the Latin American country which might have put the greatest effort in demographic research and family planning" when less than seven percent of the women of reproductive age attend family-planning clinics.[50] This means that only the first steps toward "demystification" and awareness have been taken. If they are successful, it does not necessarily mean that the implementation of these and future proposals will be automatic.

In spite of the fact that the Colombian population policy features neither spectacular actions nor compulsory control, it has made progress within a democratic context in providing the basis for a more meaningful participation of its citizens in national life and development. Certainly there is the risk that policies based on free choice will not produce significant reductions in fertility in the short run. However, Berelson points out that population policies "must compete in the arena with other claims and values, and that kind of competition accords with the political bases of an open society."[51] Within these considerations, the central issue turns to be "whether or under what conditions the 'population problem' is sufficient to justify intervention." [52] This central issue is crucial, given the fact that:

> Any policy which aims at limiting the number of children born, for instance, will inevitably affect the future distributions of ethnic, class, religious, and age groups in society and consequently the relative power and other kinds of relationships among these groups ... for seldom is the central dilemma of politics so clearly encountered as in trying to reconcile *the right of the individual* to determine how many children he will have with *the need of the community* to regulate its population size and rate of growth.[53]

Taking for granted the need for population policy as a component of the general strategy of development, it appears clear that in a democratic process of planning, the population problem is a particular arena where technicians and politicians must confront each other, the former with diagnoses, forecastings, and the technical feasibility of proposals and the latter with their abilities to understand the real issues and their commitment to serve the interests of the community they represent.

NOTES TO CHAPTER 12

1. Vital statistics are not accurate in Colombia. Fertility and mortality estimates are taken from Alvaro López, *Análisis demográfico de los censos*

colombianos: 1951 y 1964 (Bogota: CEDE, Universidad de los Andes, 1968), chap. 5.
2. For background see Germán A. Bravo, "Antecedentes sobre políticas de población en Colombia" (Bogotá: Secretariado Permanente del Episcopado Colombiano, 1970);Hernán Mendoza, "The Colombian Program for Public Education, Personnel Training and Evaluation," *Demography,* 5 (1968): 827–835; Antonio Ordoñez-Plaja, "A Case Study in Population: Colombia," in P.B. Taylor, and S. Schulman, *Population and Urbanization Problems of Latin America* (Houston: University of Houston, 1971), pp. 50–55; and Thomas C. Sanders, *Family Planning in Colombia,* Fieldstaff Reports, West Coast South America Series, XVII, No. 3, 1970.
3. Antonio Ordoñez-Plaja, "Palabras en la Sociedad de Obstétricia y Ginecología," quoted in Bravo, "Antecedentes sobre políticas . . . ," p. 2.
4. International Bank for Reconstruction and Development, *The Basis of a Development Program for Colombia* (Baltimore: The Johns Hopkins Press, 1950), pp. 358 and 359.
5. Colombia, Presidencia, *Estudio de las condiciones del desarrollo de Colombia* [report of the mission "Economie et Humanisme", directed by J.L. Lebret] (Bogotá: Cromos, 1958), p. 220.
6. United Nations, ECLA, *Algunos aspectos del crecimiento demográfico de Colombia.* Series E/CN.12/618 (Santiago de Chile: ECLA, 1962), pp. 74 and 81.
7. International Labour Office–ILO, *Hacia el pleno empleo. Un programa para Colombia* (Bogotá: Banco Popular, 1970), p. 49.
8. International Bank for Reconstruction and Development, *Economic Growth of Colombia: Problems and Prospects* (Baltimore: The Johns Hopkins Press, 1972), p. 460.
9. A good collection of studies has been published by the Asociación Colombiana de Facultades de Medicina (ASCOFAME): *Planificación familiar, motivación-comunicación-valoración* (Bogotá: Antares, 1966); *Regulación de la fecundidad,* 2 vols. (Bogotá: Tercer Mundo, 1968); *Urbanización y marginalidad* (Bogotá: Tercer Mundo, 1968); and *Migración y desarrollo urbano* (Bogotá: Tercer Mundo, 1970).
10. See Benjamin Haddox, "A Sociological Study of the Institution of Religion in Colombia" (Unpublished Ph. D. dissertation, University of Florida, 1962); and Gustavo Pérez, *La Iglesia en Colombia* (Bogotá: Centro de Investigaciones Sociales-CIS and FERES, 1961).
11. See Thomas K. Burch and Gail A. Shea, "Catholic Parish Priests and Birth Control: A Comparative Study of Opinion in Colombia, the United States, and the Netherlands," *Studies in Family Planning,* 2 (1971): 121–136; Luís Leñero (ed.), *Población, Iglesia y cultura: Sistemas en conflicto* (México: Instituto Mexicano de Estudios Sociales-IMES and FERES, 1970); Thomas G. Sanders, "Population Planning and Belief Systems: the Catholic Church in Latin America," in *Are Our Descendants Doomed? Technological Change and Population Growth,* edited by H. Brown and E. Hutchings (New York: Viking Press, 1972), pp. 306–329; and J. Mayone Stycos, *Ideology,*

Faith, and Family Planning in Latin America (New York: McGraw-Hill, 1971), chaps. 6 and 9.
12. *El Catolicismo*, January 22, 1967.
13. *El Espectador*, July 29, 1967.
14. Colombia, Secretariado Permanente del Episcopado, *La Iglesia ante el cambio* (Bogotá: Ediciones Paulinas, 1969), p. 80.
15. *Ibid.*, pp. 37–38.
16. *Ibid.*, p. 78.
17. *Ibid.*, p. 80.
18. Colombia, Presidencia, *Mens*ª *je del Señor Presidente de la República de Colombia, Dr. Carlos Lleras Restrepo al Congreso Nacional* (Bogotá: Imprenta Nacional, 1967), Vol. 1, pp. 305 and 306.
19. Organization of American States, *Latin America: Meeting on Population Policies in Relation to Development in Latin America* (Washington, D.C.: OAS, 1967).
20. Colombia, Departamento Nacional de Planeación–DNP, *Planes y programas de desarrollo, 1969/72*. Doc. 417-J (Bogotá: DNP, 1969), pp. I. 132-I. 145. The extended version was published as "La población en Colombia: Diagnóstico y política," *Revista de Planeación y Desarrollo*, 1, No. 4 (December, 1969): 20–81.
21. Colombia, DNP, *Plan de desarrollo económico y social 1970–1973* (Bogotá: DNP, 1970), chap. IV.
22. Antonio Ordoñez-Plaja, Minister of Public Health, "Palabras del Señor Ministro de Salud Pública," quoted in Bravo, "Antecedentes sobre políticas . . . ," p. 11.
23. Colombia, Congneso, Comisión V de la Cámara de Representantes, *Actas* (quoted in *Ibid.*, p. 11).
24. Theodore J. Lowi, *The End of Liberalism* (New York: W.W. Norton & Co., 1969), p. 19.
25. Emmanuel G. Mesthene, *Technological Change* (New York: New American Library, 1970), p. 69.
26. Good political histories of Colombia are found in José M. Henao and Gerardo Arrubla, *History of Colombia*, translated by J.F. Rippy (Chapel Hill: University of North Carolina Press, 1938); William M. Gibson, *The Constitutions of Colombia* (Durham: Duke University Press, 1948); and John D. Martz, *Colombia: A Contemporary Political Survey* (Chapel Hill: University of North Carolina Press, 1962).
27. William M. Gibson, *The Constitutions of Colombia*, p. 401.
28. See United Nations, ECLA, *El pensamiento de la Cepal* (Santiago de Chile: Editoral Universitaria, Col. Tiempo Latinoamericano, 1969).
29. Colombia, *Constitución política de Colombia* (Bogotá: Imprenta Nacional, 1968), art. 32.
30. Colombia, DNP, *Planes y programas de desarrollo*, p. 8.
31. Colombia, DNP, *El desarrollo socio-económico colombiano, diagnóstico y política*, Doc. DNP-472-URH (Bogotá: DNP, 1970), p. 121.

32. See Bernard Berelson, "Beyond Family Planning" *Studies in Family Planning,* No. 38 (1969); Judith Blake, "Population Policy for Americans: Is the Government Being Misled?" *Science,* 164 (1969), pp. 522-529; Kingsley Davis, "Population Policy: Will Current Programs Succeed?" *Science,* 158 (1967), pp. 730-739; and J. Mayone Stycos, "A Critique of the Traditional Planned Parenthood Approach in Underdeveloped Areas," *Research in Family Planning,* edited by C.V. Kiser (Princeton: Princeton University Press, 1962), pp. 477-501.
33. Judith Blake, "Population Policy for Americans," p. 238.
34. See Ronald Freeman, "Norms for Family Size in Underdeveloped Areas," *Proceedings of the Royal Society,* Series B, Biological Sciences, Vol. 159 (1963), pp. 220-245; Norman B. Ryder, "The Character of Modern Fertility," *The Annals,* 369 (1967), pp. 26-36; J. Mayone Stycos, *Human Fertility in Latin America* (Ithaca: Cornell University Press, 1968); and Jean Sutter, "Sur la Diffusion des Methodes Contraceptives," in H. Bergues, pp. 341-359.
35. Colombia, DNP, *Plan de desarrollo . . . 1970-1973,* p. IV. 13.
36. Although a new Plan was submitted in December 1971 (the second under the present administration), the chapter on population remains the same in its structure, objectives, and means. See Colombia, DNP, *Plan de desarrollo.* 22 vols. (Bogotá: DNP, 1971).
37. Colombia, DNP, *Plan de desarrollo . . . 1970-1973,* p. 13.
38. *Ibid.,* p. III.9. and p. IV.15.
39. *Ibid.,* pp. IV.15 - IV.16.
40. *Ibid.,* pp. IV.16 - IV.19.
41. It is affirmed that family allowances have a pronatalist bias. However, such a bias is not clear; in Bogota, it was discovered that those who receive this subsidy are more aware of family planning than other similar socio-economic groups who do not receive it. Subsidy for them was the opportunity to think about the costs of rearing children (which was greater than the amount of the subsidy); therefore, they decided to start planning (see Beatríz de Bravo, "Subsidio familiar y fecundidad en Bogotá," [Bogotá: Instituto Colombiano de Desarrollo Social—ICODES, 1967, mimeographed]). Similar conclusions are found in Luke T. Lee, "Law and Family Planning," pp. 88-89; and U.S. President, Commission on Population Growth and the American Future, *Population and the American Future* (Washington: Government Printing Office, 1972), pp. 94-96.
42. The ethical issue, which sometimes is not taken into account, seems to be solved when family and governmental actions "satisfy the following criteria: knowledge of facts; vivid imagination of how others are affected by our actions; and impartiality with respect to both our interests and our passions." Arthur J. Dyck, "Population Policies and Ethical Acceptability," in *Rapid Population Growth,* p. 620.

43. See, for example, Bernard Berelson, "Beyond Family Planning" and "Population Policy from Personal Notes;" and A.E. Keir Nash, "Going Beyond John Locke? Influencing American Population Growth," *Milbank Memorial Foundation Quarterly*, 49 (1971): 7–31.
44. Theodore J. Lowi, "Population Policies and the American Political System," *Political Science in Population Studies*, edited by Richard L. Clinton, W.S. Flash and R.K. Godwin, (Lexington: Lexington Books, 1972), pp. 25–53.
45. Theodore J. Lowi, "Introduction," of *Private Life and Public Order* (New York: W.W. Norton & Co., 1968), p. xiv.
46. Theodore J. Lowi, "Population Policies . . . ," p. 31.
47. Theodore J. Lowi, "Decision Making vs. Policy Making: Toward an Antidote for Technocracy," *Public Administration Review*, 30 (1970), p. 320.
48. Lowi, "Population Policies . . . ," p. 36 and 37.
49. United Nations, ECLA, "Population Trends and Policy Alternatives in Latin America," Conference Document E/CN/12/874 (Santiago de Chile: ECLA, 1971).
50. Anne Marie Dourlen-Rollier, *Le Planning Familial dans le Monde* (Paris: Payot, 1969), p. 227.
51. Bernard Berelson, "Beyond Family Planning," p. 4.
52. Theodore J. Lowi, "Population Policies . . . ," p. 42.
53. Richard L. Clinton and R. Kenneth Godwin, "Political Science in Population Studies: Reasons for the Late Start," in *Political Science in Population Studies*, p. 144.

Chapter Thirteen

The Politics of Family Planning in the Dominican Republic: Public Policy and the Political Process*

Howard J. Wiarda

Population policy in Latin America is a controversial subject area. It evokes strongly-held moral, religious, and ideological passions. Perhaps no other policy area has so many confirmed "true believers" on the one hand and so many bitter foes on the other. Politically it is an issue of great sensitivity.

The literature dramatically sets forth the consequences for which unchecked, spiralling population growth rates in poor countries like the Domincan Republic are at least partially responsible: continued poverty, illiteracy, and underdevelopment; widespread illegitimacy, abandoned children, malnutrition, disease; low life expectancy; illegal and frequently dangerous abortion; accelerating social problems and economic dislocations; discontent, political eruptions, and perhaps even governmental breakdowns.[1] Surely public policy programs aimed at resolving some of the underlying causes of these ills are to be encouraged. At the same time, the argument that family planning provides women and families with more alternative choices and with greater control over their own lives is persuasive.

On the other hand, it seems equally clear that a program of family planning and/or population control is not *the* determining factor in Dominican

---

*This chapter has been prepared originally for this volume. This material is part of a larger study being undertaken with Dr. Iêda Siqueira Wiarda, who is also a contributor to this volume, dealing with the comparative aspects of population policy formulation and implementation in Latin America. The analysis in the present chapter is derived from three main sources: an exploration of virtually all newspapers, magazines, journals, etc.; access to a wide variety of private documents, memos, studies, etc., issued by United States and Dominican population agencies; and interviews with United States and Dominican population officials and with a broad spectrum of other Dominican leaders and government officials. Research was conducted in the Dominican Republic on this subject area in 1969 and 1970 when Wiarda was a post-doctoral fellow at the Mershon Center, Ohio State University, and in 1972 under a grant from the Center for Population Research of the National Institute of Child Health and Human Development.

underdevelopment—and may not even be of first-rank importance.[2] Family planning must thus be kept in perspective; it is, in Sanders words, a *feature* of modern society and a *concomitant* of a sound development program, but only a feature and concomitant. Family planning may be part of a national development effort; it cannot be a substitute for such development.[3] Viewed in this light population policy is not the cure-all that some of the popular literature would lead us to believe, and there is much doubt among demographers whether official programs to limit births can have much effect. In the Dominican case, furthermore, there is considerable uncertainty and flux in defining the "population problem" or determining its precise dimensions. Nor are the moral and ethical arguments so clearly one-sided. The "genocide" and "imperialism" arguments as put forward frequently by the extreme Left are unconvincing, but the fact is that in the Dominican Republic population policy has been carried through largely by foreign technicians, often with little sensitivity to or understanding of Dominican customs, traditions, or socio-historical conditions. Dominicans resent this interference—and the corruption and arrogance that frequently go with it. In their own list of priorities, Dominican government and population officials have assigned family-planning policy to a secondary level of importance, and this may well be a more realistic view than that of the foreign agencies pushing a more extensive program. The Dominicans tend to see other problems as both more immediate and more crucial, and they view the payoffs from family planning—if it is to have any payoff—to be so marginal and distant as to be almost insignificant. On this score they may also be correct.

Having noted these qualifications, it should also be said that population policy is a fascinating and critical area of public policy, one that reveals a great deal about the Dominican Republic and its political process. Encompassed in this question are important and exciting issues of national values and political culture, of dependence and interdependence, of conflict among both domestic and external political forces, and of the interaction of private individuals and public agencies. Though current policies would seem to offer but limited hope in terms of reducing the population growth rate, the family-planning program nevertheless provides a remarkable case study of the workings of Dominican politics, of the policy role of the United States, of the nature of executive power and of bureaucratic behavior, and finally, of the way things get done, don't get done, or get partially done for mixed and varied reasons in an increasingly complex, nationalistic, and developing system.[4]

THE DOMINICAN CONTEXT

The Population Problem

It is difficult to define the Dominican "population problem" with much certainty. During the 1960's the Dominican Republic's rate of population growth was put at 3.5 or 3.6 percent annually and was touted by population experts and in popular accounts, not without a certain perverse sense of national pride, as among the highest in Latin America and in the world. These figures were based on the 1960 census, however, conducted by dictator Trujillo and purposely inflated both for purposes of national power and prestige, and to qualify for greater foreign assistance funds computed on a per capita basis. Using the 1960 census as base point, estimates in the succeeding decade continued to show an incredibly high population growth rate, until the 1970 census revealed that for those intervening ten years the growth rate was only 2.96 percent rather than the expected 3.5 or 3.6 percent. Another reason why the estimates were so inflated was that census officials, in the absence of hard figures, underestimated the amount of emigration, chiefly to Puerto Rico and New York, where many Dominicans went—often without proper papers—in search of higher wages. Emigration during the 1960's had come to serve as a major outlet for surplus population. An overall growth rate of 2.96 percent is still high, of course, with the natural growth rate even higher than it seems due to out migration. Nevertheless, the lower figure has taken some of the steam out of the argument for population control in the Dominican Republic and made it incumbent upon population officials that they talk in the lower key of population "growth" rather than the more dramatic "explosion."[5]

Nor does the "economically ruinous burden" argument regarding population any longer carry so much weight. At the time a population control strategy for the Dominican Republic was formulated in the mid-1960's, the country was devastated by the revolution, civil war, and the United States intervention of 1965 and 1966. The economy was in ruins, on the verge of complete collapse. The economic arguments for the control of population growth appeared to make eminently good sense. Now, however, with massive infusions of foreign aid, a breathing period of political stability under Balaguer, and renewed confidence on the part of many Dominicans, the economy has not only recovered but boomed ahead at growth rates of 6 to 8 percent per year for the last several years. This obviously is not to say that immense poverty and inequality do not remain or that the economy is no longer weak and shaky. But as Dominican population experts themselves agree, with economic growth now far outstripping population growth for the first time in a tortuous, unstable decade, the economic argument for population control is no longer quite so powerful.[6]

Many Dominicans in and out of government do not see their country as notably overpopulated. With a density (1970 figures) of approximately 83 persons per square kilometer, it is crowded compared to the mainland countries but not in comparison with other Antillean islands.[7] Like many Latin American countries, the Dominican Republic still has large areas of unused arable lands and also a great deal of land that could be used far more effectively. While much of this land is now being swallowed up by private entrepreneurs, the government still retains title to the bulk of the vast, former-Trujillo estates, designated for distribution to peasants under a major agrarian reform program. Thus, although the issue is not settled, many Dominican scholars and public officials (and not just those of the Left) believe that the population issue has been greatly exaggerated in their country; that the characteristics and rate of growth of their population are not necessarily dysfunctional given *Dominican* social mores and the nature of their social mechanisms and economic requirements; that more hands in the fields and numerous children to care for the parents in old age are sound and rational arguments; and that the problems lie in the distribution of the population and in the structure and underdevelopment of the society, economy, and polity and not in the fact of population growth. In addition, one must bear in mind the historical conditions of an underpopulated, near-empty country in the nineteenth and early twentieth centuries and because of that, a situation of retarded development, repeated Haitian invasions, and national impotence and vulnerability, inviting foreign interference. Dominican population officials, it should be noted, are not necessarily in disagreement with the thrust of some of these arguments.

But if the rate of growth has been exaggerated, if the "economically ruinous burden" argument no longer carries so much weight, and if it is agreed the problems are largely "structural" rather than due to population overcrowding, wherein lies the "population problem"? The answer is that it lies in what most Dominicans still conceive to be rather marginal and secondary problem areas. It lies, for example, in the high rates of unwanted and abandoned children, of illegitimacy, and of abortion. It lies also in the high rate of illiteracy (60 percent), and the inadequate health and nutritional conditions of the bulk of the population. It lies at the heart of successive governments' often well-meaning but inadequate efforts to provide housing, education, water supplies, health and medical facilities to their people. It lies in the fact that almost half (47 percent) of the population is under 15 years of age with no possibility whatsoever that the economy will be able to absorb them all, or that the government can provide them with the minimum of services concomitant with their rising demands. And it lies in the Malthusian prospect of a population nearly three times its present size by the year 2000 and with it the prospect for social, economic, and political chaos. Indeed, from whatever direction one approaches the problems of the landless peasants and the restless slum dweller, where social ills and the dilemmas of over-large families are most acute, one finds the spiralling population increase to be at the heart of the matter.[8]

All this, in the eyes of informed population experts, together with the still residual arguments regarding high growth rates, the economic consequences of unchecked population increase, and overcrowded conditions, add up to a major "population problem" or even "crisis." Nevertheless, among Dominicans—and particularly among government officials wrestling with not one but a whole gamut of complex, virtually unresolvable dilemmas—the "population problem" has low priority. As compared with the overriding need to establish political and administrative stability, to stimulate economic growth, and to secure Dominican sovereignty over its own affairs, the population problem is of secondary importance. In fact, without these higher order prerequisites, it makes little sense to speak even of a population policy. This is why, incredible as it may seem to American observers and population experts, the Dominicans are probably correct in assigning the population program a marginal priority. Even granting the population problem's "crisis" dimensions but also taking into account the total context and not just one part of it, these other and even more critical concerns must and do receive first consideration.

The Political Framework

It is not necessary in this essay to discuss all the Dominican Republic's often sorry history: the Trujillo dictatorship, the revolution and intervention of the mid-1960's, the vicious circles of underdevelopment in which the country is locked.[9] Suffice it here to mention only those more salient features that seem to bear directly on the population problem.

> First, and perhaps most striking to the observer, is the instability of Dominican politics. There have been twelve governments in the last twelve years (a fact disguised by Balaguer's longevity in office) and an even greater turnover of ministers, agency heads, programs and policies. The first priority in Dominican politics, therefore, is merely to survive, to establish one's place and position, and hope to hang on. As a result, policy implementation—of any policy— is often of necessity relegated to a back burner.[10]
> Second, and related to the first, is the almost totally uninstitutionalized character of the Dominican system. Even more than most Latin American countries, the Dominican Republic lacks the funds, the resources, the personnel, the planning, the administration for an effective, institutionalized, modern system and with it the capacity for effective policy planning and implementation.
> Third, as a result, government policies tend to be tentative, ephemeral, ineffective, temporary. Each change of government requires a complete change of personnel and programs. There is little coherent, sustained development strategy; programs have little effect on those they are designed to benefit; seemingly paradoxically, Dominicans expect both much and nothing at all from government.
> Fourth, and related to these others, the Dominican Republic is a highly centralized system. Again, more than in, say, Venezuela, all power and all the levers of patronage and decision-making are concentrated in the president's office; no cabinet official would make even a minor administrative decision without clearing it at

the top. For a population program located in the Ministry of Health and Public Welfare, this has powerful implications.

Fifth, one must bear in mind the underdeveloped nature of the Dominican system—socially, economically, politically, indeed in all aspects. In comparison with other Latin American countries, the Dominican Republic simply lacks the requisite money, men, material, and resources. It is a poor country with inadequate hospitals, doctors, nurses, health care. This also is reflected in the prospects for effective population policy implementation.

Sixth, in keeping with its underdeveloped, uninstitutionalized character, traditional influences and institutions remain powerful. For our purposes this implies not only the strong cultural influence of *machismo,* the role of women, Catholicism, etc., [11] it also means that disability insurance, social security, old-age retirement, etc., which in a modern secular society are the function of the state, in the Dominican Republic remain the function of large families.

Seventh, the Dominican Republic has become a conflict society. It is characterized by the overlap of traditional and modern, a crazy-quilt pattern of old and new, a mosaic of discord and conflict. Because of the experiences of the 1960's, ideological passions run high and frequently boil over in violent confrontations. Social and political cleavages are deep and bitter; mutual distrust is widespread; the possibilities for a rightist coup, a leftist revolution, and/or total societal breakdown are still strong.

Eighth, at the same time, the Dominican people have become increasingly nationalistic. There is a new sense of pride in Dominican power and accomplishments and a resentment of foreign influences. Among the traditional Right, this often takes the form of a desire for a greater population to offset that of next-door (and black) Haiti; among the Left this leads to hostility and suspicion regarding all things North American.

Ninth, then, one must bear in mind the overwhelming presence of the United States in Dominican life and the dependency pattern that this implies. Although the United States public presence is now diminished, at the time the official population program in the Dominican Republic was initiated in 1966 and 1967, it was omnipresent in all areas of Dominican life. The question arises as to whether programs such as those in the area of population are United States or Dominican programs, or represent some shifting, overlapping mixture of both.[12]

Clearly, these propositions merely hint at some of the more obvious aspects of what is a complex socio-political system. Equally clearly, however, anyone doing research in the Dominican Republic in the population or any other area must understand and come to grips with this entire national milieu, must understand the dynamics of the whole system before any parts of it will begin to make sense. Having at least provided a summary overview, we can now try to comprehend the Dominican population program.

TOWARD A FAMILY-PLANNING PROGRAM

There are numerous, although not often readily accessible, accounts of the origins of the Dominican population program.[13] Seldom in any of these accounts is adequate attention given to the overwhelming role of the United States in founding and sustaining the program. Although even in its early stages there was some Dominican input, which has since become considerable, basically the population program was—and remains to an important extent— a United States operation.

Origins and Evolution

The history of family planning and population control efforts in the Dominican Republic is long, complex, and colorful; not all the details can be recounted here. In the 1920's the Dominican Republic's first woman doctor did post-graduate studies in Europe and returned to the country to urge, with little success, a halt to population increase; in the 1940's another Dominican doctor did work with the American pioneer Margaret Sanger. By the 1950's an increasing number of Dominican doctors had received specialized training in Europe and the United States where they too were exposed to the newer currents of population control and the latest contraceptive techniques. But in Trujillo's strongly nationalistic and pro-natalist regime, they had no possibilities of beginning any national campaign of population control and could only use what they had learned in private practice. Ironically, one of the strongest public defenders of Trujillo's pro-natalist policies was Joaquín Balaguer, a puppet president under him, who is again serving as president (this time "constitutional") and under whose aegis and blessing the public population program was begun and gained momentum.[14]

By the early 1960's access to and the use of contraceptive devices had become fairly widespread among upper-middle and upper class women of Santo Domingo, through private physicians and pharmacies. For lower-middle and lower class women, however, prohibitive costs often ruled out consultation with private physicians, and traditional techniques of avoiding too many children or no techniques at all remained the rule.

The impetus for a program to begin reaching these women came chiefly from the efforts of the many North Americans who came to the country in the early 1960's to help make the post-Trujillo Dominican Republic a showcase for the Alliance for Progress. The Reverend Donald Dod and his wife, affiliated with the Protestant social action arm, Church World Services, made brief trips to the Dominican Republic in 1962 and 1963 to evaluate the program there; they urged and began a small family-planning program which resulted eventually in a long-term Dominican assignment for the Dods beginning in late 1964. In early 1964 another group of non-Dominican Evangelical women began a birth control program in their churches' child-care clinics; a number of United States Embassy wives and the wife of the then Peace Corps director also became involved.[15]

In 1964 and early 1965, the family-planning program began on a more organized basis. The Pathfinder Fund provided contraceptive foam and pills to the Evangelical clinics. A number of small meetings took place. In December, 1964, the Board for Social Action of the Dominican Evangelical Church and the interested women of the clinics sponsored a conference. Friends of the Dods from the Puerto Rican Family Planning Association, Drs. Adelaide Satterthwaite (a medical missionary) and Samuel Lugo, came to the Dominican Republic and spoke to the medical association as well as to interested social workers and Evangelical Church people. A number of Dominican doctors were trained in the use of IUD's. An ad hoc committee was formed called the "Friends of Family Planning", and in April, 1965, the Association for Family Planning was organized with Dr. Antonio Herrera Báez, a dentist, as president. Now there were both a program and an organization.

The revolution and intervention of 1965 interrupted and set back these developments. The Association ceased to function. And because for much of the time the downtown areas of Santo Domingo were cut off, the Dods reopened their clinic in the poor Los Minas section on the east side of the Ozama River. This was the first institution to be dedicated exclusively to family-planning activities in all of Dominican history. Later that year as the country returned to something resembling normalcy, expanded activities were begun in Santo Domingo, San Pedro de Macorís, and San Juan de la Maguana.

By early 1966 the demand for family-planning services had far outstripped the capacity of a handful of private individuals to provide them. Hence, in March, the original "Friends" group reconstituted itself as the Asociación Dominicana Pro-Bienestar de la Familia (ADPBF). ADPBF lost no time in soliciting modest ($14,000 for 1966, $40,000 in 1967) support from USAID and also joined the International Planned Parenthood Federation. Initially ADPBF took over the running of the Los Minas clinic and helped support the programs in other parts of the country. It acquired an office and small staff. The organization of ADPBF also enabled those interested in family planning to broaden interest in and support of their program, and to pave the way for eventual separation from Evangelical sponsorship.[16]

It should be recalled that up to this point there was no official Dominican government policy regarding population, only private efforts. Interim President Héctor García-Godoy was persuaded of the merits of a family-planning program, but his regime in the immediate post-revolutionary period was so shaky and preoccupied with sheer survival that it could not begin any effective programs. Nor up to this time had there been much official United States action. A USAID Alliance for Progress officer had met with the ad hoc committee in early 1965, and late that year, after the most violent phase of the revolution had ended, there were other meetings. But United States assistance even of a modest amount did not begin until 1966. On the Dominican side, Reverend Dod gleefully recalls his visits to successive ministers of health to fill them in on the activities of the private Association and he found them consistently dumbfounded to discover that such a program existed without their knowledge. Relations between the Association and the government thus remained, as Segal puts it, cordial but distant. Treading carefully so as not to provoke an outcry of opposition before the program was well established, the Association moved cautiously and quietly. Fearing reactions from the Church and the Left, the government also took little active role. It allowed Church World Services to import contraceptives duty-free by labeling them "religious-educational materials," and it permitted birth control information to be made available in public clinics and hospitals on request, but the government itself took no direct role. It had not even officially acknowledged the existence of a population problem. The period up through 1966 to 1967 might be considered one of neutrality and laissez faire so far as any official action was concerned.[17]

Despite some modest expansion and successes, the private activities of the ad hoc group and ADPBF had produced exceedingly limited results. ADPBF still lacked group, institutional, and governmental support. The new Balaguer regime, inaugurated in 1966, was also inclined to allow private activities but not the use of public facilities; indeed, to some extent, external financing was used as a means to avoid any national commitment.[18] ADPBF thus struggled on, without official sanction. Outside of Santo Domingo it had to rely on private physicians whom it could not pay, and in the capital it depended on volunteers. Although its clientele continued to grow, it had made no dent whatsoever in the national population problem. The laissez faire role of the government was matched by the near invisibility of the private efforts.

In the aftermath of the revolution, however, the United States presence grew enormously in 1966-67 in an effort to reconstruct the shattered nation. Replacing military intervention, as Susanne Bodenheimer has dubbed it, a civilian takeover began.[19] During these years United States assistance per capita, which was the highest for any country in the world, virtually kept the Dominican Republic afloat. There were United States counterpart officials and technicians advising, and frequently running, almost every important office in the Dominican government. This was also the time when President Johnson, Robert McNamara of the World Bank, the foundations, the lending agencies, the media, and the popular imagination all became preoccupied with population growth.

In Santo Domingo, given its historic dependency and its particular vulnerability to United States influence at this point, the new emphasis on population control to solve problems of underdevelopment inevitably had a powerful impact. Already in late 1965, visiting USAID officials had begun expressing to the Dominican Family Welfare Association the official concern of their government with the population issue. In the Association and in the group of doctors now commited to population control, the United States had a ready-made structure and nucleus for carrying out a population policy; and while one should not understate the impact of these pioneering Dominicans, it was not until the official United States involvement that the program began to assume a significant national scale. By 1966-67 the stream of United States officials had become a virtual flood. Population control was the new panacea, comparable to agrarian reform in the early days of the Alliance for Progress. But in the haste to start a program, relatively little consideration was given to the special nature of the Dominican situation. One cannot help echoing Thomas G. Sanders' comment regarding the origins of family planning in Chile: "My guess is," he writes "that officials in Washington are so eager to get birth control programs under way in Latin America that they lose little sleep over the subtleties of how best to do it."[20]

In April, 1966, Dr. Clifford Pease of the Population Council's Technical Assistance Division visited the country to advise the USAID mission and ADPBF as to future steps. Professor J. Mayone Stycos, Director of the International Population Program at Cornell, perhaps the leading scholar in the field, and Senior Consultant on Latin America for the Population Council, accompanied Pease.[21] Other experts and advisers followed, some announced, others quietly. The report Pease presented to the Population Council and to USAID, derived from conversations with both USAID officials in Santo Domingo and Dominicans already active in the population field, was a key turning point. It helped serve as the basis for a series of discussions in Santo Domingo and New York that in late 1967 became the master plan for a major effort to be undertaken in the Dominican Republic. Under this plan, the private Association would continue running the model clinic at Los Minas, engage in educational and propaganda activities, and seek further outside assistance. But the plan also called for the initiation of a public program under a semi-autonomous government agency, hopefully immune from politics. This plan remained almost exclusively a United States concept and operation. Notwithstanding significant Dominican imput in terms of ideas and organizing concepts, it was the initiative, commitment, financial support, and basic orienting principles of United States agencies that were critical.[22]

There remained the problem of selling the program to a skeptical Dominican government. For although Balaguer had by this time alluded to the population problem in several public utterances, most notably at the Punta del Este meeting of American heads of state in April, 1967 (a speech which served as a powerful impetus for foreign and Dominican population officials to go forward with their plans), he still saw it as a problem to be solved through economic development, not fertility control. Meanwhile, ADPBF continued to expand its activities, including plans for a pilot public health center in Santo Domingo staffed with a full-time doctor, nurse, and social worker. Although the government again put no obsracles in the way of USAID support for this project, it still showed little interest in a government program.

Then the Association and various North American public and private agencies began what Segal calls a sustained and intensive campaign among politicians, government workers, and other influentials which would focus on the relationship between population growth and economic development.[23] There was as yet no great public debate on population policy; instead the campaign went forward quietly in a series of small meetings and face-to-face contacts that eventually resulted in a number of prominent Dominicans from various walks of life using their influence to raise consciousness about population issues. They and United States officials worked on Balaguer, convincing him that his plans for economic growth, political stabilization, and the expansion of education, health, housing, and other facilities would never succeed unless population growth were checked. In this campaign the local USAID director played a key role, especially in helping win over Fernando Alvarez Bogaert, an ex-cabinet minister and budding *Balaguerista* politician, who helped put the program over with the government.

Balaguer, keeping his own political survival as the top priority, was finally persuaded to at least acquiesce and give some verbal support to the population program. And, although the details of the final *quid pro quo* remain murky, arrangements for the establishment of the official program were in the end facilitated by a $7 million loan to the health ministry which Balaguer used in part for political patronage purposes and to advance his own pet projects and prestige. The loan carried with it (probably as a condition) the establishment of an official family-planning program and the appointment of a public health minister supportive of family planning. At the end of 1967, therefore, the government agreed to incorporate family-planning services into the maternal child health care units of the public hospitals, and by decree law in February, 1968, it established the Consejo Nacional de Población y Familia to administer the program.[24]

The Consejo Nacional de Pobalción y Familia

Although the Council was formally established in February, 1968, it was not until eight months later that it actually began functioning. In the meantime, a group of Peace Corps volunteers trained in family planning promotion had already arrived in the country and had been sent out into the field. With the Council not yet operating, the Association having financial problems, and no administrative structure existent in the health ministry, the Peace Corps stepped into the vacuum and helped establish an on-going program.[25] Once again it was United States agencies that were instrumental in this development, organizing a system of local clinics in the interior towns staffed by interested local physicians and auxiliary personnel. Although the United States role was disguised and downplayed, the Peace Corps provided the drive, the supervision, and even much of the technical assistance, while USAID and the population agencies provided the materials. The ministry of health and upwards to the president's office, still not fully committed to implementing the program now formally in existence but gradually pushed along by the growing activity, operated as ponderous, slow-moving, and often reluctant vehicles through which requests for materials, equipment, and decisions passed.

By the fall of 1968 the Council had come into actual existence and was beginning to carry out its prescribed functions. Early in 1969 it formally began administration of the clinics already being manned with Peace Corps assistance. Establishment of the Council, together with the beginning of an on-going program, marked a significant change from the laissez faire of previous years. By now the Balaguer administration had become committed to an explicit policy of population control encompassing the following key points:

1. The Dominican government formally recognized the existence of a population problem retarding the social and economic growth of the country.
2. The government recognized its responsibility to act in the area of population control just as it did in the areas of education or health.
3. The implementation of a policy of population control was to be considered a necessary condition, but not a sufficient one, for national socio-economic development. Methods of population control, such as family planning, were not to be considered substitutes for government action in other areas.
4. The official family-planning program was required to respect individual free choice in selecting the number and spacing of the children. Under no circumstances was population control to be imposed or made compulsory.[26]

This was clearly a sweeping mandate, but it also implied certain limitations which, as we shall see, have since become issues of considerable sensitivity and conflict. The Consejo Nacional de Población y Familia (CNPF) was the instrument designed by the Balaguer government and the foreign population experts to formulate and carry out the new population policy. According to the decree (No. 2091) establishing the Council, it had as its principal objectives the study, investigation, and analysis of all matters relating to the country's population growth, mobility, and future projections, and the dissemination of that information. It was charged with planning, investigation, and offering technical advice and assistance with regard to maternal-child health programs, elaborating a plan for population control, and administering the official family-planning program.[27]

The structure of the Council is dual: an executive secretary to handle the daily administration of the program and a medical supervisor with chief responsibility for the medical activities in the clinics. The Council itself consists of the Minister of Health, as chairman, and representatives from the agricultural, labor, and education ministries; from the private family-planning Association (ADPBF); from the Technical Secretariat of the Presidency; and, since 1970, from the maternal-child health care division of the health ministry. The executive secretary also sits as a Council member. The Council offices are physically located in the Ministry of Public Health and Social Assistance, although it has still not been fully integrated into that unit or even into the division of maternal-child health care. In fact, there is a great deal of delicacy and much ill will regarding this issue. The very autonomy by which the designers of the Council plan sought to divorce it from politics has also served to keep it isolated from the very ministry and division to which it must rationally and logically be linked.[28]

The men chosen, chiefly on the advice of USAID and population experts, to lead the Council in these early formative years have been remarkably able. Significantly, however, in this new era of rising Dominican nationalism, even those pre-selected by the United States for what was an essentially United States program harbor sometimes strong nationalistic sentiments and frequently feel resentment at the interference and lack of sensitivity of the North Americans working in the population field. In executive secretaries Lic. Manuel Rodríguez-Casado and Lic. Luis González Fabra, the Council has had some very impressive leadership—young, smart, dedicated, well-trained, politically sensitive, pragmatic, realistic. The same characteristics apply to the medical supervisor, Dr. Bienvenido A. Delgado Billini, a former Minister of Health in the government of Donald Reid Cabral.

The Council has moved astutely in getting the population program off the ground. Its initial goals were:

1. To consolidate its political and organizational base by moving slowly, cautiously, and inconspicuously. The Council leadership recognized the sensitivity of the issue, both in a moral and political sense, and, recognizing also the tentative and ephemeral nature of most Dominican governments and policies, determined to push ahead quietly and without provoking a public debate and outcry. They saw that a major confrontation could result in the cancellation of the entire program; they were also determined to consolidate strongly enough their position so that even if the government collapsed or were overthrown, the program would survive. This strategy was

followed against the advice of numerous American advisers who wanted more rapid results. In retrospect, the Dominicans followed the proper and perhaps only acceptable course.
2. To create a series of clinics throughout the interior, building upon the earlier activities of the private family-planning Association, that would be well-run, well-administered, well-staffed, carefully supervised, and with a strong infrastructure. The emphasis initially was to be on quality rather than quantity. On this point the Council has been far less successful than on point 1, as the performance in the interior clinics has been decidedly uneven and supervision has been spotty.
3. To establish a model clinic in the capital which would be a showcase of performance and accomplishment. This clinic was founded in September, 1968, in the Dr. Francisco E. Moscoso Puello Hospital.[29]

To further these goals the Council lost no time in preparing a national five-year plan for the family planning programs, encompassing the years 1969 through 1973.[30] The plan set forth the goal of reaching 5 percent of the women of child-bearing age (given as 15 to 49) during the first year, with 5 percent increments in each succeeding year. Though at this point clinics had been established in only eight municipalities plus the capital city, these included the most populous areas of the country, and the plan was to open new clinics in other populous centers as quickly as feasible. The necessity to make such an immediate quantitative impact thus came in conflict with the desire to establish only quality services and was one key reason for the uneven results mentioned in point 2 above. With 5 percent increases each year for five years, the aim was to reduce the birth rate to 37 per 1,000 inhabitants by the end of 1973, representing a drop in the population growth rate to 2.7 percent. As the 1970 census indicates, this rate may well be reached, though if it is, it will be due more to mistaken estimates, emigration, and other dynamic social changes rather than to the efforts of the family-planning program.

The effects of the Council's program are difficult to assess with certainty. It has shown steady growth, but has by no means reached the targets in the five-year plan.[31] From nine clinics at the beginning of 1969, the program expanded to 37 clinics by mid-1971 with plans for opening a dozen more. Five of the clinics were located in the capital city, there were two each in Santiago and La Romana, and virtually all of the country's provincial capitals and secondary towns (between 10,000 and 40,000 population) had a clinic. At least two of the clinics had been closed in 1971, however, and there was considerable doubt as to whether new ones would continue to be opened so rapidly. In addition, many of the clinics function only part time and sometimes not at all.

In terms of the number of those who have "accepted" family planning (that is, who agreed to the insertion of an IUD or to the use of contraceptive foam or pills), the program has also registered steady gains, rising from 4,200 clients at the end of 1968 to 46,000 at the end of 1971.[32] These figures tell us nothing, however, about how many "acceptors" continued to use contraceptive materials. The Council has no effective means of ascertaining this, although privately Council officials estimate the figure may be as low as 30 to 40 percent of those who initially "accepted", or roughly 15,000 to 20,000 women of a total of some 900,000 of child-bearing age.

The Asociación Dominicana Pro-Bienestar de la Familia

While CNPF has, since its organization in 1968, been carrying out the official family-planning program, matters of education, propaganda, and training have remained largely in the hands of the private Asociación Dominicana Pro-Bienestar de la Familia. In addition, ADPBF continues to administer the original model clinic at Los Minas and collaborates with the Council in the Moscoso Puello Hospital clinic.

From the beginning of the official program, CNPF and the Association have worked closely together. They have collaborated in training nurses, doctors, *promotores,* and auxiliary personnel for family planning, have worked hand-in-hand in holding conferences and seminars, and have sought together to further public acceptance of the family-planning program. The formal division between their functions also makes sense, in that the private Association can engage in a variety of propaganda and public relations activities which the Council, as a public agency, cannot. At the same time, the Council's autonomous position in the health ministry gives it protection, freedom, and official status for carrying out the government program. There is, of course, some friction between the Council and the Association due to the fact that their functions overlap and that they have not entirely separated out their respective roles; but generally the two organizations have complemented each other nicely.[33]

Like the Council, the Association, particularly at the highest levels, has had remarkably able leadership during these early, formative years. It continues to work quietly and unobtrusively to influence Dominican leaders and opinion-molders. Its director, Dr. Orestes Cucurullo, has given numerous addresses to, and held countless meetings with, military officers, students, nurses, doctors, journalists, businessmen, and government officials.[34] These efforts have paid off not only in terms of fomenting understanding of family planning in relation to Dominican underdevelopment and social problems, but also in recruiting a number of key leaders into support roles for the Association.

Nor has the Association shied away from a more public campaign. Although the early emphasis was low profile, once the official program was established the Association began to make its case to a broader forum. Its officials have appeared on numerous radio and television discussions and panels, and have given hundreds of speeches and interviews. The Association has provided press releases and promoted feature and news stories; it keeps files of newspaper clippings dating back to the earliest days of the family planning program. To the general public it distributes pamphlets and comic books (prepared by USAID, IPPF, and the Population Council) extolling the virtues of planned parenthood and small families, and seeking to demonstrate the disadvantages of *machismo* and uncontrolled procreation. It shows popular films on the same theme, holds open, public meetings, and has sponsored an extensive radio campaign of spot commercials and longer discussions. The special courses it conducts are oriented not only toward the training of doctors, nurses, and other aides, but also toward the orientation of leaders and the general population. In addition, it is the Association that has been involved in most of the public controversy regarding the population program.

THE POLITICS OF FAMILY PLANNING

Although both the Association and the Council have sought to work inconspicuously so as to avoid the public and/or partisan outcry that might destroy the fledgling program, they have not been entirely successful. Indeed, from the beginning, the population program has been intimately involved in politics and controversy.

Organized Opposition

Organized opposition to family planning was probably most vigorous in 1968, at the time the official program was initiated. During that year the country went through one of its periodic "great debates" with strong positions being taken on all sides. Since then the opposition has been less vocal, but there remains a great deal of latent suspicion and hostility toward the program.

On what has often been mistakenly called the "conservative nationalist" or "traditional right," the opposition to family-planning centers organizationally in the Committee for the Defense of the Frontiers and, more broadly, in the widespread Dominican fear and resentment of the next-door Haitians. Remembering the long nineteenth century history of repeated Haitian invasions, the Committee for the Defense of the Frontiers urges a strengthening of Dominican settlements in the border areas and the preservation of the Dominican Republic's white, western, Hispanic culture.[35] The fact that Haiti's population still outnumbers that of the Dominican Republic by a ratio of about 3:2, that masses of Haitian laborers are brought in every year to cut cane and seldom return to Haiti, and that the total Dominican population is now estimated to be at least 10 percent Haitian give special urgency to the Committee's appeal. Although its approach is frankly racist as well as nationalistic, and although its leaders have muted their criticism in recent years, even indicating their willingness to accept family planning, the Committee's influence remains considerable. For one thing, its channels reach directly into President Balaguer's office. For another, the nationalistic, anti-Haitian, even pronatalist positions for which it stands are often shared not only by middle and upper class Dominicans but also by the lower class.

On the Left, the situation is somewhat analagous. Given the birth control programs in the Soviet Union, China, and Cuba, the Communists have waxed hot and cold on the Dominican family-planning program, usually framing their criticisms in terms of "genocide" and "imperialism." But the extreme Left in the Dominican Republic is badly fragmented. Its leadership is gone (dead, exiled, in jail) and its organization almost non-existent. It simply does not count for much. That is why the luring of the prominent Marxist Pedro Mir to the family-planning cause, a fact which population officials cite with great pride, has little other than symbolic importance. It rings of the familiar "house Communist" tactic.[36]

Far more important than the Communist Left is the nationalist Left, led by Juan Bosch, his Dominican Revolutionary Party, and the students at the Autonomous University of Santo Domingo. In his celebrated thesis on "Dictatorship with Popular Support,"[37] and in subsequent writings by Bosch, and in statements by the Party and its sympathizers, particularly in the University and the newspaper *El Nacional,* the criticism has contained two main themes: first, that population policy is "imperialistic," another lever in the seemingly endless arsenal used by the United States to control and manipulate the Dominican Republic; and second, that population control does not get at the underlying problems of poverty and underdevelopment, which, in Bosch's view, lie in the maldistribution of land, wealth, power, educational opportunities, and the like.

At least two points should be noted with regard to this position. The first is simply to admit that Bosch and his followers are essentially correct—a position with which *all* Dominican population officials interviewed agreed. Their response, however, to the first point is that it is naive to cast the United States in a uni-dimensional straightjacket, and that so long as some interests dovetail and the United States is willing to supply the money and materials, the Dominicans should take maximum advantage of this assistance. Moreover, they maintain that while the funds come from abroad, responsibility for the administration, planning, and programming of family planning rests exclusively in Dominican hands. Dominican population experts also agree that family planning is not a cure-all for their country's underdevelopment, but they argue that a sound population policy does make sense as one part of a broadscale national development program.

The second point that should be noted regarding Bosch's arguments is that Bosch has not criticized the population program and family planning head-on, but only indirectly. In private, Bosch agrees there is a problem. In all likelihood he would continue the population program in some form should his movement ever come to power. It should be noted that there are strong Bosch and PRD supporters within both the health establishment and the population program.[38] Nevertheless, the nationalist Left remains skeptical and vaguely opposed to the population program. It is still bitterly hostile toward the United States, resentful of its interference, and unconvinced of its altruism. In general, the Left is not entirely convinced that a population policy will help solve any of the nation's problems, nor that the Dominican Republic even has a population problem. Among students and university intellectuals especially, despite a number of "confrontations" organized by population officials, these suspicions and resentments remain strong, though seldom now so openly expressed. Thus, population control remains a touchy, unresolved issue on the Left.[39]

Opposition has also been strong at times within the Dominican Medical Association. There have been many heated debates among Dominican doctors over the issue; to the opposing arguments discussed above some doctors have added the possible harmful effects of the pill and intrauterine devices. Although many doctors are convinced of the merits of the program and are working with the Council and Association, or prescribing contraceptives in their private practices, the Medical Association itself has not taken an official stand. This is due not just to the political, medical, or ideological reasons already mentioned, however, but frequently springs from immediate self-interest. Many doctors have lucrative private abortion practices which they see threatened by the broadscale, free dispensation of contraceptives.[40]

The Church, as elsewhere in Latin America, has been ambivalent—but with some special twists. Clerics and the hierarchy are, of course, obligated to abide publicly by the Church's official opposition to "artificial" methods. Many priests and nuns remain unalterably opposed to any family-planning program. On the other hand, a number of leading clerics have recognized the problems of uncontrolled fertility, urging "responsible parenthood" as the solution. They have resolved the moral issue by arguing that illegitimacy, abortion, inhumane living conditions, and so forth constitute greater moral evils than birth control. With these and other interpretations possible, there are nearly as many Catholic positions as there are clerics. Some priests, especially the younger, foreign-born, are openly collaborating with the program. Others are working with the Instituto Nacional de Educación Sexual, a Catholic organization that has collaborated with ADPBF. The Movimiento Familiar Cristiano, at first somewhat suspicious of the entire concept, is another Catholic group that has begun to deal with family-planning themes. The Revolutionary Social Christian Party has spoken out against population control, but in favor of responsible family planning. In addition, it should be noted that because of its past history, the institutional Church in the Dominican Republic is in such a precarious position that the hierarchy is reluctant to interfere officially in questions that might cast the Church in an unpopular light. As a result, the Church was persuaded to refrain from publicly criticizing the official family-planning program so long as no "irreversible" methods were used and the government kept it a voluntary and not a compulsory program.[41]

A complicating factor arises from the fact that in the Dominican Republic the shortage of nurses is such that Catholic nuns administer and staff many of the public hospitals precisely where the family-planning clinics are located. Again, though many nuns see the problem, they find it morally offensive to work in institutions openly and manifestly in violation of the Church's strictures. Some have communicated their outrage to the Dominican bishops who, in turn, in a confidential letter to President Balaguer in December, 1970, threatened to pull the nuns out of all the public hospitals where family planning was practiced.[42] This threat provided the first real challenge to Balaguer on the issue, and demonstrated where family planning was on the President's list of priorities. Rather than risking the open hostility of the Church and thus undermining the structure of authority he had gradually and carefully built up, Balaguer knuckled under, closing two clinics where the nuns had been most adamant. This provoked a crisis within the population program that has not been resolved to this day. The opening of new clinics was postponed, the question of how to deal with the nuns remains unresolved, and Balaguer has made it clear he will permit a population policy just so long as it does not interfere with his own higher priorities.[43]

There is other organized opposition to family planning in the Dominican Republic, centered within the government and among wealthy, landed, conservative interests more generally. The chief opposition, however, is not organized. It lies in apathy and indifference, in cultural and social norms that place strong emphasis on *machismo* and large families, and, some five years after the initiation of the program and despite all its publicity, in the almost complete lack of knowledge among the overwhelming bulk of the population as to what family planning means and the methods available to limit family size. When all is said and done, this factor may be far more critical in restricting the population program to but limited advances than all the organized opposition previously analyzed.[44]

The Government's Position

Mention has already been made of the fact that in the executive-dominated, highly centralized Dominican Republic, President Balaguer has consigned population policy to a low level on his list of priorities. The question may be raised as to why the adept Balaguer, who weighs all his moves with care, has any interest in the population issue at all. First, it seems clear that the President is personally genuinely convinced of the need for family planning, and is committed to a limited program.[45] Second, Balaguer sees his own development programs in housing, education, and other areas as threatened by uncontrolled fertility. When queried as to Balaguer's motives for supporting family planning, this was the response most government and population officials gave: that the president's political interests will be served by the successful completion of various socio-economic programs, all of which promise to make no dent whatsoever unless population is held in check.

Third, there was a manifest political deal, not only in the form of the $7 million USAID health loan but also in the provision for a number of patronage positions, sinecures, and political payoffs that were conditions of the establishment of the program. Fourth, there is in the population program an element of letting the Americans do "their thing." Through the succession of agrarian reform, community development, and other United States-inspired programs, Dominican governments have learned that it is often best to let the Americans have at least one pet panacea to work with, so long as they leave the Dominican officials alone to follow the pursuits of concern to them. The population program helps fill that function for Balaguer—a relatively "safe" project (again, so long as it does not get out of hand or threaten powerful vested interests) that helps keep the Americans content, while the President himself handles the important issues of money, patronage, and power. As with all programs, thus, the motives are mixed and the final result reflective of a series of compromises, but it is probably safe to say that so long as Balaguer remains in power, the population program will continue, albeit on a limited basis. What happens if and when he goes—and one cannot assume stability of regimes or programs in the Dominican Republic—is another question.

Elsewhere in government, opinion varies. Some in Balaguer's entourage are in favor, others are against. Within the technical secretariat of the presidency, population issues are not often taken into consideration, but then this is not where power lies anyhow. On the other hand, in Balaguer's prestigious and influential National Development Commission, where crucial policy issues *are* considered, the population question has received a thorough hearing. Recent ministers of health have been supporters, not surprisingly since this has been one of the a priori qualifications for office. And even though the program still rests uncomfortably within the public health administration, the new dynamism in the field of public health and the new funds available to the health ministry have also served to provide a climate conducive to the growth of family planning. Among government agencies, the National Social Security Institute has worked closely with the Council, but other logical collaborators, such as the education, agriculture, and labor ministries do not. Both within the health ministry and within the governmental system as a whole, the family-planning program is still only weakly institutionalized.

The Role of the United States

Allusion has already been made on numerous occasions to the heavy—and sometimes heavy-handed—United States role. It was almost wholly due to the initiative of the United States that the Dominican population program began and has been sustained. Although there have been some attempts at multilateralization of assistance (Great Britain, Sweden) the overwhelming bulk of sustaining funds come from the same United States sources, either directly through USAID, or indirectly through such private agencies as the Pathfinder Fund, the International Planned Parenthood Federation, and the Population Council. USAID and the Population Council have underwritten virtually all of the administrative costs and salaries of the Consejo Nacional de Población y Familia. United States materials are used in the program, and United States advice, frequently inappropriate in the Dominican situation, is omnipresent. In addition, an entire cadre of Dominicans, who have worked with North American agencies for so long in one capacity or another that they are almost professional "Americans," have now tied themselves into the population program.

Historically Dominicans have never been certain whether the powerful United States presence in their country was for good or ill. Although nationalistic sentiment has always been strong, the country has for so long been so dependent on the United States that a peculiar love-hate syndrome exists: admiration of the United States for its wealth, democracy, accomplishments, and foreign assistance, and resentment for its interference in Dominican affairs. My own reading of the situation indicates that the balance has now tipped toward the latter viewpoint. Significantly, this sentiment has become stronger as the United States presence and assistance have been reduced in the 1970's. The Dominicans have come to recognize that they do very well on their own without North American funds and technicians.[46]

Much of the resentment toward the population program on the part of Dominican young people and the Left is due not to the merits or demerits of the program, but simply because it is North American. Part of this reasoning is, of course, irrational; but part of it stems also from a genuine resentment of United States arrogance and dominance in this area, and the fear that they are the victims of a foreign-directed experiment into unknown and perhaps dangerous areas; that they are again being manipulated; and that somehow their culture and way of life are being tampered with by those who neither understand nor sympathize with it. Informed Dominicans, for example, are perfectly aware that USAID and the Population Council did not intend to stop with a small-scale family-planning program but were using this as a base to prepare the way for experimentation with, and perhaps a program of, sterilization and other irreversible methods.[47]

That the Left and the students should harbor these suspicions is not surprising; what is interesting is how widely they are shared among Dominican doctors, professionals, and even those working in the population program. Dominican population officials feel that North American technicians do not adequately understand the local problems and socio-cultural milieu; nor do they feel the experience of Puerto Rico, where so many population people received their early training, is relevant to the Dominican Republic. Such strong sentiments as these are perhaps one of the most significant—and surprising—findings of the interviewing: namely the degree of resentment, often camouflaged by Dominican politeness, cordiality, and good taste, that even family-planning personnel feel regarding American interference, the wrong-headedness of many of the American schemes, the sheer stupidity of promoting a sterilization campaign at this time, and the general lack of empathy and understanding on the part of Americans for Dominican culture and mores.

Internal Dynamics

All of the above considerations have come to a head in the present crisis of family planning program of the Dominican Republic. The Church issue and the problem with the nuns; the facts that USAID stopped most of its assistance in 1971, that the Population Council wishes to use its funds in other ways, and that the Dominicanization of the financing would undoubtedly politicize the program to an unacceptable degree; the fact that Balaguer's commitment had cooled and that the program had expanded about as far as it can within present institutional and financial confines; the fact that the five-year plan came to an end in 1973 with a number of the key goals unaccomplished—problems such as these combined to provoke in mid-1972 a series of meetings and high-level discussions to chart new and future developments for the program. In addition to the dilemmas already discussed, the program is beset by numerous other problems: shortages of trained personnel, inadequate record-keeping, frequently poor program-client relations, withdrawal of Peace Corps from the program, doctors whose time and commitment to the program is limited, and clinics that still exist largely on paper.

In March, 1972, a meeting was held in Santo Domingo of all the sponsoring organizations (USAID, Population Council, I.P.P.F., Pathfinder, United Nations, Pan American Health Organization, and others) to discuss the financial and administrative crisis. One result of the meeting was a decision to seek greater UN involvement as a means both of increasing the funds already available, and of making the Dominican Republic eligible for aid from other sources. To that end, further, efforts are being made to present the Dominican experience as a model program or showcase, for it is, after all, one of the few countries with an official program. In June, 1972, a large UN mission arrived in Santo Domingo to explore such possibilities. As a condition of their continued assistance, the other sponsoring agencies forced the Dominicans to define their program more explicitly and draw up concrete plans for implementation. Another outcome of the March meeting, hence, was the establishment of a series of work-groups, consisting chiefly of family planning officials and friends of the program, to evaluate the program and draw up a new master plan for the next four years.

AN ASSESSMENT

The Dominican family planning program has, to the point of this writing, been in existence nearly five years—too short a time, really, to offer any definitive assessments and conclusions. Although the program has shown steady growth in terms of the number of clinics established, doctors, nurses, and *promotores* trained, clients served, and even perhaps in its degree of public and official acceptance, its impact has been almost insignificant. It is a weak, vacillating, and still largely ineffectual program. In terms of the individual women and families assisted, the program has undoubtedly performed a beneficial service, but in terms of the national population figures, the results have been infinitesimal.[48] Perhaps no more should be expected at this stage.

An equally important question is whether the program is building a base for future results. Here there have been some important, if not quantifiable, developments. The Council and especially the Association have been quite successful in pushing their cause, reaching out, and gaining support among Dominican influentials and opinion-molders, both in and out of government. Much of this success can be attributed to the quiet, efficient, unemotional, and professionally competent and convincing way the leadership has worked, and to the logic, documentation, and careful marshalling of the case it sought to present. Although the Left remains suspicious, the Church hostile, and the issue itself still combustible, the opposition is no longer as vocal against the program as it once was, and it may be that the Association has at least part way succeeded in defusing the issue and providing a climate of greater acceptability. It is also working on the other centers of opposition.[49]

In addition, for all its limited accomplishments, the apathy and indifference it faces, and the problems it confronts, the population program is a part of, and perhaps helping effect, a quiet revolution currently underway in the Dominican Republic. This revolution is related to a variety of other changes in Dominican life: the new educational and health services available, the new wealth being generated and the opportunities for advancement that go with it, the change in public mood from pessimism and despair to greater optimism and hope, the new sense of pride in Dominican accomplishments, the strong commitment to national development, and so forth. These changes have all been of a gradual and piecemeal sort, and many Dominicans feel that under Balaguer reform is not going forward fast enough. But of the fact that things are changing in the Dominican Republic there can be little doubt. As regards population policy, the payoff will likely be small and many years away, and there is some doubt as to how much the change is due to the population program's efforts and how much to other causes. But there seems also to be emerging a change in the climate regarding family structures in the country; a new consciousness seems to be emerging, and the results, among other things, may well include more modest family sizes and a reduced rate of population growth. Judging from the 1970 census, some of this seems already to be occurring.[50]

The Dominican population program, allowing for some overlap, has gone through three distinct stages.[51] In the first stage, from the first stirrings in 1962 until 1965, the program was wholly private, carried out through the private efforts of dedicated pioneers, without official sanction or support. These individuals took it upon themselves to raise the level of popular consciousness regarding family planning, opened clinics, and began advocating a family-planning program. In the second stage, roughly 1965 to 1967, there was a growth in the demand for such services, private agencies and the United States government became involved, new allies were recruited, and pressure was placed on the Dominican government to establish an official program. In the third stage, 1967 to 1971, the government established an official program, its activities and services expanded, funding was obtained, and the program actually got off the ground. This was still a period of initial, tentative efforts, however, of feeling out the routes and terrain, and of seeking a firmer foundation. It may be that in 1973-74 the program will enter another and more institutionalized stage, but that depends on the results of the reevaluation begun in 1972.

In seeking to explain the nature and growth of the Dominican family planning program, one need not correlate a battery of socio-economic and demographic indicators. The answer is quite simple: the United States. The Dominican Republic is a country where the United States presence has been historically strong. In 1966-67 when the population program was established, the Dominican Republic was particularly vulnerable and in no condition to resist or even significantly modify the policy proposals of the United States. This is not to say, however, that a program of population control was *imposed* on an unwilling Dominican Republic, for as we have seen, many Dominican doctors and public officials share a concern for the consequences of unchecked population growth, and many Dominican women do wish to limit family size. But it is to say that U.S. initiative, commitment, support, money, planning, organization, and ideas were critical at every important phase of the program, and that without the U.S. there would probably be no public program.[52] As in other policy areas, the Dominicans went along, hoping to take advantage of what at least some doctors and officials felt was a sound program, and seeking to make as much input as they could into its planning and execution. Thus, the very weakness of the Dominican Republic and its underdeveloped, uninstitutionalized condition are precisely what have accounted for its population program being among the most advanced in Latin America. In this vacuum, the United States was—up until recently—able to carry out its population program virtually unfettered.

There are other important variables. Surely the skill, tact, dedication, and hard work of the family-planning program officials in the Dominican

Republic have been crucial. So has the stance of President Balaguer—and the fact that under him the Dominican Republic has enjoyed a period of remarkable governmental stability and program continuity. That advantage, however, cannot be taken for granted in a country as potentially volatile as the Dominican Republic.

Although the Dominican Republic has one of the most "developed" population programs in Latin America, it remains uncertain whether it could withstand a change of regimes. Though the demand on the part of Dominican women is growing, though the number of doctors and nurses trained to do the work is increasing, and though the program has considerable governmental and private support, it is not yet firmly enough institutionalized in its own right to survive in the face of an adverse administration. This weakness makes the efforts to elevate the Dominican program into a model program questionable at best. Dominican population program officials recognize the tentative and ephemeral nature of their organization far more than do outsiders, they see that the Council could be swept away (or rendered just another in a considerable list of chiefly paper agencies), that the Association could be dissolved or rendered impotent, that their channels to authority could also disappear, and that they themselves might well lose their positions. But they are also convinced that even if all this should happen in the unstable, shifting currents of Dominican politics, the population program itself—in one form or another—would continue.[53]

In the final analysis, of course, no population program can be successful if it runs counter to the mainstreams of national political culture and ideology, or if it is divorced from other changes taking place within the system. Nor can population policy be considered as an alternative to national development or elevated to an importance which it does not have. However, in the present-day Dominican Republic, these are precisely the areas where change is occurring: development is going forward, the political culture reflects a new mood of hope and possibilities for achievement, and social mores and customs are gradually being altered. Although we do not know the precise relationship between all the variables, there is no doubt that some socio-political restructuring is taking place in the Dominican Republic, and that along with this, some considerable demographic changes are under way. There will be no quick and dramatic successes and it is unlikely the family-planning program will ever do more than provide a slight push and nudge. But it may be that in the Dominican Republic the era of population "explosion" has already passed and an era of more restrained growth begun. For some, even the present rates of increase are too high, and doubtless such a case can be made. But it seems unlikely that very much more can be expected from the program as presently constituted, and, in any case, one senses that if the growth rate is to fall further, it will be a long-term process accompanied by other long-term alterations in the socio-economic and political-cultural structure.

NOTES TO CHAPTER 13

1. For the statistics see Rafael Lancer "Tendencias actuales y perspectivas de la situación socio-demográfica de la República Dominicana" (Santo Domingo: Consejo Nacional de Población y Familia, Secretaria de Estado de Salud Pública y Assistencia Social, June, 1969); and Juan Ulises Garcia Bonnelly, *Sobrepopulación, subdesarrollo y sus consecuencias socio-económicas: Ensayo de biogeografía dominicana* (Santo Domingo: Ed. Cultura, 1971).
2. In formulating these ideas the author has been persuaded by some of the arguments in the great debates between Peterson, Berelson, Hauser, Davis, Driver, Blake, Schultz, Stycos, and others. In the Dominican context the debate has swirled especially in the pages of *Ahora* and *El Nacional*.
3. Thomas G. Sanders, *Family Planning in Chile: The Public Program*, West Coast South American Series, American Universities Field Staff, XIV (December, 1967), p. 63.
4. For a fuller analysis of the policy process in the Dominican Republic, see the discussion in Howard J. Wiarda, *The Dominican Republic: Nation in Transition* (New York: Praeger, 1969), chap. XII; as well as the case studies analyzed in the author's more recent major study of the Dominican political system, tentatively entitled *Dictatorship, Development, and Disintegration: The Political System of the Dominican Republic* (forthcoming).
5. Notwithstanding Trujillo's earlier manipulations, the Dominican census office is among the best anywhere. Especially useful is the *República Dominicana en cifras* compilations. The census office has also published numerous specialized studies, and students of population will find the papers written in conjunction with the analysis of the 1970 census useful. On the flow of emigration see Nancie L. González "Peasants Progress: Dominicans in New York" *Caribbean Studies*, X (October, 1970), pp. 154–171.
6. See the data in the United States Embassy's semi-annual "Economic Trends;" the reports of the Dominican Planning Office; and Howard J. Wiarda "Dominican Republic" in Charles Perkins, ed., *Latin America and the West Indies Up to Date* (Rutherford, N.J.: Scholarly Resources Co., 1973). Based also on interviews with Dominican population officials.
7. Donald R. Dyer, "Distribution of Population on Hispaniola," *Economic Geography*, XXX (October, 1954), pp. 337–346; John P. Augelli, "The Dominican Republic," *Focus*, X (February, 1960), pp. 1–6; and R.H. Fitzgibbon, "Political Implications of Population Growth in Latin America," *Sociological Review Monograph II* (February, 1967), esp. p. 29.
8. These arguments are all analyzed at great length in the *Boletín* of the Dominican Family Welfare Association, as well as in lectures, analyses, and press releases of Association officials. See also some of

the news stories written at the U.S. suggestion to help publicize the problem, e.g. in *New York Times,* October 29, 1969; and the AP dispatch of November 20, 1969.

9. These are discussed extensively in the items mentioned in note 4, as well as in the general literature.
10. These and succeeding propositions are derived from the conclusions in the author's *Dictatorship, Development, and Disintegration.*
11. See Centro de Investigaciones, Universidad Nacional Pedro Henríquez Ureña, *Informe final del estudio sobre valores y actitudes de los jefes de familia respecto al mejoramiento de los niveles de vida en la República Dominicana* (Santo Domingo, 1971). See also Gregorio Lanz, S.J., "Apuntes sobre machismo en República Dominicana," *Estudios Sociales,* III (July–September, 1970), pp. 135–157.
12. Abraham F. Lowenthal, "The United States and the Dominican Republic to 1965: Background to Intervention," *Caribbean Studies,* X (July, 1970), pp. 30–55.
13. Manuel M. Ortega, "Políticas de control de población en República Dominicana," *Estudios Sociales,* IV (April–June, 1971) pp. 62–99; Jack Harewood, "Recent Population Trends and Family Planning Acitivity in the Caribbean," *Demography,* (V (1968) esp. pp. 882–883; Aaron Segal, *Politics and Population in the Caribbean* (Río Piedras, Puerto Rico: Institute of Caribbean Studies, University of Puerto Rico, 1969); and Donald D. Dod, "History of the Family Planning Association in the Dominican Republic" (Unpublished: typed carbon copy, 1965). The present director of the Asociación Dominicana Pro-Bienestar de la Familia, Dr. Orestes Cucurullo, is also working on a history, and Frank Hale's Ph.D. dissertation at Syracuse University, entitled "Fertility Control Policy in the Dominican Republic" 10 (1972) contains much useful information.
14. See Balaguer's *La realidad dominicana: Semblanza de un país y de una régimen* (Buenos Aires: Imp. Ferrari Hermanos, 1947), chap. II.
15. This account relies on Dod, "History of the Family Planning Association ..."
16. Segal, *Politics and Population in the Caribbean.*
17. *Ibid;* and Ortega, "Políticas de control de población ..."
18. Segal, *Politics and Population in the Caribbean,* pp. 10, 13, 128.
19. Susanne Bodenheimer, "The Hidden Invaders: Our Civilian Takeover of the Dominican Republic," *Liberation,* XI (February, 1967), pp. 12–17; and Howard J. Wiarda, "The Dominican Fuse," *The Nation* (February 11, 1968), pp. 238–241.
20. *Family Planning in Chile Part II: The Catholic Position,* West Coast South America Series, American Universities Field Staff, XIV, (December, 1967), p. 4.
21. Stycos' thinking at about this time is outlined in his "Politics and Population Control in Latin America," *World Politics,* XX, No. 1 (October, 1967), pp. 66–82. (see Chapter 1 of this volume) Among other things, Stycos urged that "family planning" be disassociated from "population control." As a tactic, this emphasis would enable

people in their own minds to distinguish between allowing information to be disseminated and making it compulsory, it would emphasize free choice and responsible parenthood as opposed to an imposed obligation, and it would thereby mute and blunt the opposition of the Left, the Right, and the Church. If implemented adequately, a "family-planning" program would slow population growth but in such a way that the coercive aspects implied in the term "population control" need not arise. It seemed likely, therefore, that an approach that used the family planning rationale—concern for the health and well-being of the family, together with the stress on the basic human right of free choice in size of family—would find the least opposition. This, of course, is precisely the approach used in the Dominican Republic and elsewhere in Latin America. It would be wrong to ascribe to Stycos the role of *eminence grise* behind the Dominican and Latin American population programs, but of his considerable influence there can be little doubt. See Chapter 1 of this volume.

22. See the letter sent by Pease to Alex Firfer, Director of USAID in the Dominican Republic, dated May 16, 1966. Based also on interviews with Stycos and with a variety of USAID, Population Council, ADPBF, and Council officials in 1969, 1970, and 1972.
23. See, for example, Rafael Lancer, "Planificación familiar: Un instrumento para el desarrollo dominicano" (Santo Domingo: ADPBF, 1969).
24. See Agency for International Development, *Population Program Assistance* (Washington: GPO, 1971) pp. 150-151. Based also on interviews.
25. The Peace Corps role during this period was a fascinating one, and the volunteers who served in the program are a rich but as yet untapped source. My own knowledge of this period stems from working with a Peace Corps training group designated for the family planning program, from access to numerous Peace Corps reports and memos regarding the program, and from interviews with volunteers who worked in the program.
26. Ortega, "Políticas de control de población . . .", p. 69. See also the Council's published communique in *Listín Diario,* August 15, 1968, p. 12.
27. The decree has been reprinted in numerous documents. An English translation may be found in the Appendix to Alfred D. Sollins, "Family Planning in the Dominican Republic" (Report for the Population Council, March, 1970).
28. Symptomatic of the problem faced by the Council is the fact that the salary of its executive director is higher than that of the health minister under whom the director serves; this and a variety of other sticky personal, professional, and political problems have kept the relations between the Council and the health ministry rather touchy.
29. Based on interviews with Council officials as well as 1968 USAID and Peace Corps documents dealing with the issue.
30. CNPF, *Proyecto del programa de planificación de la familia, 1969-1973* (Santo Domingo, 1968). See also the report of Dr. José de Js.

Alvarez Perello, "Planificación familiar—Acción oficial" (Santo Domingo: 1968).
31. The best source for tracing the statistical growth of the program is the semi-annual reports of the Council. See also the UPI dispatch by Miguel Guerrero as published in *El Mundo* (San Juan, Puerto Rico), January 5, 1971.
32. *Ibid.* See also the report in *El Sol,* June 20, 1972, II, in which Council director González Fabra updated these figures to 60,000 clients being served in 48 clinics.
33. In cases of disagreement, the Association and Council tend to confront each other bureaucratically and indirectly through intermediaries, such as Population Council representatives.
34. These activities are reported in detail in the Association's *Boletín.*
35. See, for example, a letter in *El Caribe,* February 8, 1968; and an article in *El Nacional,* August 1, 1968.
36. On the Dominican Communist movement and the way it has been used by a succession of Dominican administrations see Chapter XX of Wiarda, *Dictatorship, Development, and Disintegration.*
37. Santo Domingo: Publ. Ahora, 1968.
38. Based on interviews with PRD and population officials. See also the article in the PRD's new theoretical journal: Enrique Ruíz García, "La hipótesis capitalista del control de la natalidad," *Política,* I (June, 1972), pp. 33–43.
39. See especially the discussion in *El Nacional* and *Ahora,* 1968 to the present; see also the articles by Juan José Ayuso in *La Información.*
40. Based on personal interviews. See also the reports of the Barahona meeting where many of these disputes were aired, in *Boletín,* III (April, 1971).
41. Ortega, "Políticas de control de población . . .", pp. 73–74. Ortega, an ex-Jesuit, is particularly detailed on this matter. See also the volume published by the Archbishop's office containing the papers and commentaries offered in the 1968 Church-sponsored Seminar on "Development, Population, and Family."
42. Eventually word of the Church's stand was leaked; see *El Nacional* January 16, 1971, p. 1.
43. Based on interviews with population officials and officials within the President's technical secretariat and development commission.
44. See not only the elaborate and expensive report of the Centro de Investigaciones, *Informe Final . . .,* but also the results of the "informal survey" in *El Caribe,* March 16, 1968, p. 16-A.
45. Balaguer's speeches at Punta del Este, before the 1968 Church-sponsored seminar, to the assembled population establishment in March, 1972, and on a variety of other occasions, both public and private, seem to make this clear.
46. The material in this and the following section is derived from the interviews and field work in the Dominican Republic during the summer of 1972.

47. There was a great uproar among Dominicans of all political persuasions when it was revealed that the Ford Foundation was contemplating an experimental sterilization campaign in the Dominican Republic; see virtually any Dominican newspaper or magazine for mid-February, 1971. This announcement was also an important factor in goading the Church into opposition, for it implied the violation of the understanding prohibiting irreversible and involuntary methods of population control. Notwithstanding these clear expressions of national opinion and the disavowal of Dominican population officials of such a program, plans are currently still going forward for a large-scale campaign of vasectomies among rural farm workers. (Based on information provided by Population Council officials.)
48. In assessing the most recent census figures, the Family Planning Association's director said in January, 1972, that the government program had not as yet contributed to reduce the birthrate. See his statement in *El Caribe,* January 28, 1972, p. 1.
49. These strategies and tactics are discussed at greater length in the larger comparative study on which Dr. Iêda Siqueira Wiarda and the author are now working.
50. See Arpad von Lazar and John C. Hammock, *The Agony of Existence: Case Studies of Community Development in the Dominican Republic* (Unpublished ms.: Fletcher School of Law and Diplomacy, 1970) pp. 39–41; and John C. Belcher and Pablo B. Vázquez Calcerrada, "Diferenciales del tamano ideal de la familia en la República Dominicana," *Estudios Sociales,* V (January–March, 1972), pp. 35–45.
51. Segal, *Politics and Population in the Caribbean;* and Carl E. Taylor, "Five Stages in a Practical Population Policy," *International Development Review,* X (December, 1968), pp. 2–7.
52. One high-ranking Dominican population official, when queried politely as an opening question as to the origins of the program, replied with refreshing candor: "It was the United States. No one else. They wrote the program, told us the money was available, and we took advantage of the offer." When I next assured this official that his remarks could be considered off-the-record and not for direct attribution, he responded, "No! Put it on the record, because it's the truth!"
53. Based on interviews with Association and Council officials.

Chapter Fourteen

Approaches and Strategies of Population Policy-Making in a Democratic Context: The Case of Venezuela*

Iêda Siqueira Wiarda

Little is known about how population policies are formulated and the strategies that eventually lead to their implementation. Although there has been considerable progress on the *medical* means of controlling conception, the *political* means of effecting a policy of population control have been generally ignored. And yet, as most of those involved in the actual operation of population and/or family-planning programs are acutely aware, the *political* variable is crucial to the very existence of their activities. The very paucity of research into the political variable is sufficient to recommend this area to today's social scientist.[1]

Given the gaps in our knowledge concerning the population policy process, this study will offer an analysis of the process of population policy formulation and implementation, more specifically of the approaches and strategies employed by the three major Venezuelan organizations presently involved in population policy. It will highlight distinct aspects of the Venezuelan policy milieu, for it is our contention that population policy cannot be considered in isolation, apart from the social, psychological, economic, and political constraints operating in the particular system under study.[2]

With the existence and even progress of the family-planning cause in a country in which the official governmental attitude toward population con-

---

*This chapter has been prepared originally for this volume. An earlier version of this paper was delivered at the III National Meeting of the Latin American Studies Association, Austin, Texas, December, 1971. The author wishes to thank the Mershon Center, Ohio State University, for its support at the initial stage of this project. The paper profitted from sixty formal interviews in Venezuela in 1970 and 1971 and also from those who volunteered information on a not-for-attribution basis. Helpful comments were presented by Professors Howard J. Wiarda, University of Massachusetts; Thomas G. Sanders, American Universities Field Staff; and Terry McCoy, Ohio State University. The author is solely responsible, however, for whatever views and information are presented herein.

323

trol has been at least ambiguous and possibly even hostile, we are compelled to seek explanations for this seeming inconsistency at this stage of population policy, not only among population policy actors but also among actors in the overall political process. In this sense, we view population policy as a policy issue area within the Venezuelan political process. As in other policy areas, we would argue that an examination of the total national context is itself as crucial for an understanding of the strategies and approaches used toward policy formulation as is a consideration of the strategies and approaches themselves. By the same token, strategies and approaches may well appear meaningless if one does not take into account the rationale that prompted them in the first place. Further, by pointing out the unique aspects of the population policy process in Venezuela, we also shed some light on how that same policy process is likely to take place elsewhere. The analysis presented here proceeds from the general context of policy-making in Venezuela, to a survey of this process in relation to population, and, finally, attempts to offer some implications for population policy-making in any democratic setting.

THE GENERAL CONTEXT OF POLICY-MAKING IN VENEZUELA

For nearly a decade and a half, Venezuela has been one of the brighter spots in the Latin American political panorama. Those who have studied the country extensively are virtually unanimous in this appraisal.[3] Gains have been registered in just about every index of modernization and development. Moreover, these gains have taken place within a relatively free, open, and democratic context.

Democratic development was not achieved rapidly nor easily, and democracy is not yet firmly established in that country. To achieve her present enviable position, Venezuela had to overcome a turbulent past, which saw the enactment of more constitutions than any other Latin American country, along with a steady succession of dictators. Yet, since 1958 Venezuela has demonstrated that modernity and traditionalism can coexist in a dynamic symbiosis, and that democracy, albeit with a particularly Latin American style and structure, can be made to function effectively.[4]

In 1958 a crucial turning point was reached in the history of Venezuelan development. In spite of its vast potential and the considerable economic growth that had occurred, Venezuela was still in many ways socially and politically underdeveloped. A decade of economic prosperity had benefitted relatively few with most of the wealth concentrated in Caracas and a few of the provincial capitals. The nation's economy had become almost totally dependent on petroleum revenues, which tied Venezuela's fate to the fluctuations of a world market over which it had little control. Agriculture, traditionally the mainstay of the economy, had steadily declined to the point that

Venezuela became ever more dependent on the importation of food staples. Industry, in spite of high tariff walls, was still incipient. Plans for large-scale exploration of the country's rich iron and bauxite deposits had been formulated but remained mostly on the drawing boards. Education continued to follow the classic mold, to stress rote learning and to reach only a few. While the population continued to grow at the rate of well above 3 percent per annum, the government failed to develop an educational system that would provide opportunities and skills for the nation's youth. Rapid population growth added new burdens to the unemployment situation while the progressive migration of the peasants spelled a massive housing shortage in the big citites. Social problems multiplied, and once the dictatorial controls were thrown off in 1958, urban unrest and rural restlessness became commonplace.

That Venezuela was able to break out of the web of interlocking vicious circles in which it was entrapped, and "take off"—socially, economically, and politically—was due to a number of rather fortuitous circumstances, including above all, the natural riches which the country enjoyed. Petroleum insured a steady flow of capital that made possible the initiation of many of the programs promised by civilian reformers in 1958. Thus, in starting to move Venezuela toward self-sustained economic growth based on greater utilization and diversification of the nation's resources, the newly elected democratic leaders did not have the problem of insufficient capital. They could use the revenues from petroleum to diversify the economy and thus reduce the country's dependence on one product. The Venezuelans called this "sowing the petroleum." Oil revenues were used to establish new industries, to attract new investments, and in general to launch the major development and reform efforts that would make Venezuela a more modern nation.[5]

Although political parties often quarrel over specific policies, both the dominant Acción Democrática and the Social Christian Party (COPEI) parties, as well as most other political groups, generally agree that Venezuela should develop its resources for the maximum benefit of the largest number of its citizens. This consensus, often embraced under the concept of a "development society," has come to serve as a bond between Venezuelans of different ideological persuasions and of different socio-economic status.[6] Given Venezuela's abundant natural resources, plus the skilled manpower and technical capabilities to exploit these resources efficiently and the drive that its dynamic, development-oriented ideology provides, there is considerable reason to be optimistic regarding the prospects for Venezuelan development.[7]

This is all the more significant because Venezuela has been able to fulfill many of the demands of its rapidly growing population through an increasingly institutionalized democratic system of policy-making. A whole spectrum of developmental programs in such policy areas as agrarian reform, education, industrialization, and health is being implemented through a gradual but democratic process in which various intermediate institutions such as political parties and interest groups play prominent roles.[8] Priorities set by the central government after consultation with group leaders guide the formation of public policy. Elitism and mass participation coexist in the formulation and implementation of policy.[9] A deep sense of nationalism does not deter the government from reaching out to gather the opinions and to profit from the research of foreign scholars in various policy fields.[10] Yet, at the same time, policy emerges through existing political and societal channels in a way that conforms with a Venezuelan concept of policy-making, a concept which is generally pluralistic and democratic in character.[11] If the recent past is any precedent then, it is plausible that in other, newer policy areas such as population, broad consultation will take place with government taking into consideration the views of public health officials, doctors, other interested parties, and even public opinion revealed through research on the popular perceptions of the demographic conditions in the country.

APPROACHES AND STRATEGIES TOWARD POPULATION POLICY FORMULATION

The Population Problem

With an annual natural increase of approximately 3.4 percent, Venezuela has one of the highest population growth rates in Latin America.[12] Besides its high rate of growth, the estimated 11 million Venezuelans are unevenly distributed, highly mobile, mestizo, and highly urban.[13] With rapid and massive urbanization, the family structure has been severely strained. Even though based more on custom than on formal-legal or -religious arrangements, family ties in the countryside are fairly stable. This is not true in the frequently alien environment of the burgeoning cities, however, where family ties have proved to be far less durable.[14] At the same time, the traditional fecundity of the *campesino* seems unabated when he moves to the city.[15] Better sanitary conditions and the greater availability of medical assistance ensure that more pregnancies run their full course in the cities than is true in the countryside. But, because in the cities family ties are tenuous, an important result is the rapid increase in the number of fatherless families along with abandoned children, now conservatively estimated at roughly one-half million.[16]

Tenuous family ties, irresponsible parenthood, and abandoned children all make up the picutre of what Venezuelans label the "disorderly" character of population growth in their country.[17] These factors define the "population problem" for those engaged in actual family planning activities in that country, such as the privately-financed Venezuelan Family Planning Association (AVPF).[18] Other groups, more concerned with the overall context which precipitates this "disorderliness," have sought through in-depth research to isolate the variables that would have to be taken into account in the eventual designing of a population policy tailored to the Venezuelan situation.[19] These groups have coalesced around the Venezuelan Center of Population and Family (CEVEPOF). A third position, mixing family planning activities with social and medical research, best characterizes the approach of the team working at the Concepción Palacios Maternity Hospital in Caracas.[20] These three positions imply different rationales, different personnel, different strategies on the part of the three major organizations involved, with different impacts on population policy formulation and implementation. Since those engaged primarily in actual family-planning activities are presently the best financed and most visible actors in the population policy arena, they will also receive the greater portion of our attention.

Service and Research: The Concepción Palacios Maternity Hospital Team and the Venezuelan Center of Population and Family (CEVEPOF)

Family-planning activities had a slow, late, and modest start in Venezuela. Even though the country for years had an excellent cadre of economic planners and a number of internationally recognized physicians in its extensive public health system, the population question, either as an economic or as a health issue, did not seem to have directly intruded into the considerations of either the Central Planning Agency (CORDIPLAN)—possibly the best organized, best staffed, and most powerful planning agency in Latin America [21]—or the public health service which had existed since 1936. The various national and sectoral plans emanating from CORDIPLAN took into consideration the persistently high annual birth rate of 46 per thousand of population, the declining death rate of 10 per thousand of population, and the country's skewed population curve.[22] But it does not appear, however, that the popultion increases, the fact that over half of the population was under 20 years of age, and the growing contingent of abandoned minors were viewed as constituting problems whose unbearable strains hampered the eventual attainment of a modern, developed society.

With its rich natural resources and governmental programs both to develop the agricultural and industrial bases of the economy and to carry out far-reaching reforms, Venezuelan per capita income (the highest in Latin America, estimated at $1,100 for 1972), continued to rise in spite of the population growth. The gross domestic product has been moving upward at an even faster pace than the population while a vast range of welfare measures and social programs reach increasing numbers of Venezuelans. The very fact that the government has at least partially implemented some of its many development-oriented programs has meant that the pressures of its high birth rate have so far been less than acutely felt.

Since the economy and governmental social services expanded

faster than the population, the question as to whether there might be problems deriving from the high birth rate within the context of an unstable and disorderly family situation was seldom raised. When it was raised, it was answered with the reassertions that about one-half of Venezuela's national territory was practically uninhabited and the economy was healthy enough to absorb whatever population increases did occur.[23]

In this context, it is easy to understand why the National Health Program in 1965-1968 made no mention of family planning, concentrating instead on the need to expand mother-child care.[24] A subsequent publication of the CORDIPLAN Health Sector did show concern over the increase in abortions, especially in the Caracas area, and recommended that "an efficient study of family planning and birth control be undertaken."[25] This study was later commissioned to the Venezuelan Center of Population and Family (CEVEPOF). The overwhelming concern at the CORDIPLAN Health Sector, however, has not been with abortion or other health-related population problems but rather with speeding up the exceedingly complex process of establishing a health service with nationwide standards and facilities under one centralized agency, possibly the Ministry of Health and Welfare, MSAS. One of the major justifications for this plan is that it will enable the public health ministry to better serve the Venezuelan population, even if it continues to grow at the present rate.[26]

Outside of CORDIPLAN or MSAS, interest in family planning began to pick up during the 1960's. The pioneers in this movement were Venezuelan doctors who, in various cities throughout the country, began to meet with other similarly-interested physicians to discuss the possibility of providing birth control information whenever so desired or demanded by their clients. Most of these doctors worked full- or part-time in the public health system; most were gynecologists and obstetricians, although some considered themselves nutritionists, pediatricians, and otherwise specialized.[27]

Some of these doctors were instrumental in starting the first family-planning clinic in the out-patient department of a public hospital in La Guaira, just outside Caracas, in 1962. But it was not until the following year that a dynamic group of gynecologists began discussing family-planning methods with their clients as well as training other medical personnel in birth control procedures in the Concepción Palacios Maternity Hospital in Caracas.[28]

Working at one of the world's largest maternity hospitals, these doctors soon established a distinguished team directly interested in promoting information among other professionals on health-related population problems and on ways of controlling such problems. With the support of the International Planned Parenthood Federation (IPPF), the Population Council, the Ford Foundation and, for a time, the United States Agency for International Development (USAID), that team had, by the end of 1971, treated without charge nearly 40,000 women at the Maternity family-planning clinic. The impact of the services and training at this clinic can hardly be underestimated. The Maternity Hospital is affiliated with the Central University Medical School and most of the doctors now working for the Asociación Venezolana de Planificíon Familiar received their training there. Others, trained elsewhere, received additional specialization there. A total of 158 physicians and 397 paramedical personnel were trained in family-planning techniques in two years of operation—1968 to 1970. Eleven physicians and a score of sociologists, nurses, psychologists, social workers, aides and clerks made up its staff in 1971.

The collaboration of psychologists and sociologists has been particularly useful in devising motivational and educational techniques for the clinic staff. They have also helped in client acceptance of family planning as well as in client continuation of these services. Whenever problems outside of the clinic's domain are uncovered during patient orientation sessions, referral is made to appropriate agencies within the government welfare system. In this task the clinic is greatly aided by its connections with the School of Social Work at the Central University. In turn, students of that school have taken courses in family-planning orientation at the clinic, while nurses and nurses' aides routinely receive training concerning how to deal with patients, especially those to whom pregnancies are particularly risky because of their previous medical histories.[29]

All these activities, combined with the quality of its services and its affiliation with the country's largest medical school, have made the clinic well known in professional and popular circles. There has been a steady and increasing demand for its services and, in contrast to its earlier years of operation, the clinic in 1970 served more younger women (75.7 percent were between 14.8 and 26.7 years of age) and more women with fewer children (74.8 percent had less than 5 living children) than had previously been the case. In 1965 the distributions were 46.2 percent under 30 years of age and 68.1 percent had more than 5 living children. It was thus felt that more women were now coming to the clinic out of a desire for family planning rather than from sheer desperation over the number of an already large brood.[30]

Doctors actively involved in the running of the clinic were primarily responsible for the establishment of a Population Division within the Ministry of Health and Welfare in 1965. Interview information indicates that the establishment and subsequent staffing of the Division came largely through personal contacts, the personal inclination of the health minister at the time, as well as the expertise and interest of the physicians involved. The same combination of factors holds for the establishment and evolution of the family planning/postpartum clinic at the Concepción Palacios Maternity Hospital itself. There, while training and research have gone hand in hand, the uppermost concern has been for fulfilling a "medical service" function rather than a "purely research" need. Given the tremendous load at the Maternity (120 births daily), its clinic provides large numbers of the women with an exhaustive postpartum examination. Family planning is closely linked to postpartum care at the clinic.[31]

The clinic's creation nearly a decade ago, its daily operation, and general orientation are more "native" than "foreign." Most of its personnel received all of their training in Venezuela. They are well established and confident enough in their own field of expertise that they have not blindly followed an American or any other "model" of family-planning procedure. The clinic operates largely independent of foreign contributions.[32] Rather, its operation depends primarily on a delicate but apparently workable relationship—based more on personal contacts than on ideological principles or formal bureaucratic structure—between clinic personnel, the hospital administration, and the municipal government which sponsors the Maternity. A considerable portion of the financial support for the clinic comes from governmental sources, and it benefits by being physically located in a public hospital complex. A key person in its establishment, operation, and financing was a former director of the hospital and president of the Caracas municipal council.

Greater concern for research dominates CEVEPOF. Founded in 1965, the same year that saw the formation of the Population Division within MSAS, the Venezuelan Center of Population and Family was established first to conduct research and then to stimulate action programs as well. In the Center's own words, "research and study [constitute] the stepping stones towards the establishment of a population policy."[33] Staffed mainly by sociologists, but also by psychologists, economists, and social workers on a consulting basis, CEVEPOF is closely associated with the Andrés Bello Catholic University. In gathering material for several studies on population, CEVEPOF has used students of the University as interviewers and University professors as advisers. Dr. Aristide Calvani, its director and one of its founders, is a prominent member of the Social Christian Party and was appointed Minister of Foreign Affairs in 1969 with COPEI in power.

Calvani and the CEVEPOF staff view their organization as being primarily concerned with *research* rather than *action* on population questions, though they realize the close relationship that exists between data collection and policy formulation and implementation. "Before establishing a demographic policy, it is indispensable to know the values and attitudes of our people" is its guiding motto.[34] CEVEPOF's activities have thus been limited almost exlusively to research, but its possible impact on policy formulation cannot be discounted, especially if one considers its strategic links with certain key figures within COPEI and within the Social Christian Caldera government.

Experiments in Action: The Venezuelan Family Planning Association (AVPF)

The III Venezuelan Congress on Public Health, held in March, 1966, marked a turning point in health care and population policy. Among the topics discussed at the Congress were the relations between population and health.[35] A group of participants decided that the time had arrived to establish a family-planning association.

The private, nonprofit Venezuelan Family Planning Association (AVPF) was formally established in August, 1966. Its statutes list the Association's goals as the promotion of family planning, creation of family planning clinics, publication of studies, establishment of contacts with national and international organizations, collaboration with private and governmental entities interested in family planning, and the fight against illegal abortions.[36] Instrumental in AVPF's creation were gynecologists and other physicians, including those working for the Population Division of MSAS, all of whom had for years shown interest in family planning. Dr. Pablo Liendo Coll, a professor at the Central University Medical School, was chosen as the executive director.

Once established, AVPF launched an ambitious program to train doctors in contraceptive techniques in order to make family-planning services available to a growing number of women. In its training program, AVPF worked closely with the Concepción Palacios Maternity Hospital Clinic which serves as the training center. By December, 1971, AVPF-trained doctors staffed 54 clinics throughout the country under the direct sponsorship of the Association. In addition, 24 other clinics cooperated with AVPF by accepting materials and orientation but not direct financing. An unspecified number of individual doctors also received free contraceptive materials from AVPF on an irregular basis. Overall, it was estimated that in 1970, through both its regular clinics and individual doctors, some 100,000 women received AVPF family-planning advice and contraceptives. Most of the women used IUDs, while a few used oral pills and a negligible proportion opted for "other methods."[37] No sterilizations are performed in AVPF clinics, although they can be obtained at the Concepción Palacios Maternity Clinic.

Due to the peculiarities of Venezuelan health care, AVPF has been from the beginning intimately, if informally, linked with the overall government-sponsored health and welfare system. This system traditionally has placed both initiative and execution of preventive and curative medical activities under national control through the Ministry of Health and Welfare (plus some 80 other smaller public agencies). Most doctors in Venezuela (about 75 percent) work full- or part-time for the public health system, although they may also maintain private practices. Medical and paramedical services reach most of the country through an elaborate network of public hospitals, clinics, and other types of medical stations.[38]

An extensive public health system can be a great asset in the establishment of family-planning services, [39] and AVPF has indeed utilized the network of public health facilities to further its own activities. But just as significant as this public health system has been the existence of personal contacts between the AVPF and those already working within that system. All the clinics have been established through informal arrangements, usually resulting from personal and professional contacts between AVPF executives and hospital administrators and frequently utilizing a sympathetic doctor already affiliated with the particular health unit. There are no formal contracts, but there is an unwritten agreement that the hospital will allow the AVPF clinic to occupy one or two rooms within the hospital free of charge and that it will be provided with the necessary utilities and supplies, while AVPF will pay for the doctor, the *motivadora* (motivating aide), and the nurse. It is evident that the government is aware of these informal arrangements, yet it has not made any moves to either encourage or discourage them. These arrangements have continued to operate through changes both in the government and in the hospital administration.[40]

Since AVPF envisages extending family-planning services to reach all levels of the public health system, it recently stepped up its efforts to train rural medical and paramedical personnel. The Association is optimistic about this project because family-planning services have had an encouraging reception in the rural sectors, so much so that some limited cooperation between AVPF and agrarian reform personnel has been established. The training courses are well publicized in medical circles, the doctors do not incur any extra expenses while attending them, and in some cases state and local officials have lent the prestige of their presence at the inaugural or the graduation ceremonies. The Pathfinder Fund financed some of these courses and the state health administration has occasionally been a sponsor. In a parallel project, AVPF plans to intensify the training of medical dispensary personnel so that nurses and simplified medicine aides [41] may become qualified to refer patients to the *medicatura rural* (rural medical station) for family-planning guidance, or will themselves provide such guidance when referral to the *medicatura* is not feasible.[42]

Financing for all these AVPF activities, which accounted for an annual budget of approximately $600,000 in 1971, comes from contributions from IPPF, the Population Council, the Pathfinder Fund, the Ford Foundation, USAID, and a number of private Venezuelan sources. Pharmaceutical companies have also contributed in kind and/or in cash, while for a time some materials were allowed to enter duty free through the United States Embassy. It must also be remembered that though no estimates of the amounts are given, the Ministry of Health and Welfare makes a substantial contribution by the simple fact that almost all of the AVPF clinics are operated within MSAS facilities, with the rooms, the basic furniture, and utilities furnished free of charge.[43]

Direct United States government financial assistance for AVPF activities virtually ceased after 1969, even though Embassy and Association personnel often exchange views on projects. There is no longer a USAID Population Office at the Caracas Embassy, although an Embassy official handles population matters on a part-time basis. While never a major actor behind family planning in Venezuela, the United States government does not now provide any direct funds to AVPF. "As low key as possible" was the way its efforts were characterized in 1969, and if anything these efforts have become even more discreet since.[44]

THE SEARCH FOR POLITICAL ALLIES AND SPONSORS IN THE POLICY PROCESS

The reluctance of the United States government to openly support AVPF is matched by the attitude of the Venezuelan government itself towards AVPF and more generally towards the whole population issue. At the level of the President, the Cabinet, and CORDIPLAN there have not been any clear policy statements. Unofficially it is known that some influential government figures favor the idea, while other influentials are totally opposed to family planning or any policy that might be characterized as antinatalist. Among the latter is former Minister of Interior Lorenzo Fernández, President Caldera's choice as successor in the 1973 elections.[45] Given this split within the government, it is not coincidental that the most ambitious publishing venture of AVPF, a book justifying its existence and promoting its cause, was obviously tailored to the particular government context and was explicitly intended for distribution among Venezuelan "influentials" and "governing personnel."[46]

A genuine interest in family-planning services has been evident in the Ministry of Health and Welfare at the middle-range, divisional level. These services were a recurring discussion topic during 1965–1968, especially within the Population Division which issued a memorandum recognizing that family planning constitutes an integral part of public health and as such should be available just like any other health service.[47] Although this memorandum was laudable for bringing the population issue into the open and for stimulating discussion at the ministry level, its actual impact was negligible. The Division practically disappeared in 1969 with the appointment of a minister not particularly interested in the family-planning cause. The Division was reorganized and the family planning-oriented staff was replaced by demographers and demography-oriented doctors. The aims of the 1968 memorandum have not been repudiated, but neither have they been implemented.

Within the Ministry as a whole, the impression one gets is that while there is concern over abortion and other family-related problems, they are viewed primarily as *health,* not *population* problems. MSAS officials at high levels (Director of Public Health, Director of Maternal and Child Health, and Director of Social Welfare) appear convinced that family planning should be part of the overall services provided by MSAS and routinely offered to all who utilize the public health system. These officials show an increasingly open interest in adding responsible parenthood orientation to their programs and to formalizing the relationship between MSAS and family-planning clinics.[48]

With the possibility of the establishment of sex education courses in the school curriculum, Ministry of Education personnel have now become more directly involved in questions of family planning and overall population policy. Educators, along with members of the Concepción Palacios Clinic and of the Association for Family and Sexual Orientation (AVOFYS),[49] have participated in sex education courses, at AVPF headquarters. The expectation is that sex education courses, which would include lectures on family planning, will start operating on a nationwide basis in the near future. It is of interest to note that this ambitious plan has received a measure of support from Catholic leaders who view this as a chance to inculcate a greater sense of parental responsibility and moral values among Venezuelan youth.[50]

Interest in population questions has been growing within the national planning agency, CORDIPLAN. Half of the budget for CEVEPOF (about $150,000 in 1971) was provided by CORDIPLAN. The significance lies not in the sum involved, but in the centralized and strategic location of CORDIPLAN itself, which is intimately linked to the central government structure, of great prestige within governmental circles, and crucial in overall government planning and budgetary decisions. Present CEVEPOF research efforts dealing with abortion, fertility, and the interrelation between economics and demography are all partially sponsored by CORDIPLAN and are likely to have an impact on that organization. CEVEPOF personnel, for their part, do not view their research as primarily aimed at pressuring the government toward a population policy, but rather as raising certain areas of concern and possible government action based on the results of extensive studies.[51] These studies, in turn, have relied greatly on the scholarly efforts and advice of students and faculty of the Catholic University Andrés Bello in Caracas.

For its part, AVPF has concentrated on securing the support, or at least the neutrality, of the Catholic hierarchy. This has some justification for, after all, the cultural and religious as well as the political influence exerted by Spain for nearly three centuries made Venezuela overwhelmingly Catholic. Traditionally, however, Venezuelans have practiced a type of Catholicism that is generally characterized by its laxity and its assimilation of many Indian and African beliefs. Few attend church regularly or strictly adhere to Catholic precepts, and the level of general knowledge for basic tenets of the faith among the population is generally low.[52]

Preliminary findings of CEVEPOF surveys indicate that the overwhelming majority of the women interviewed did not know the Church's position in relation to birth control (only 9 percent demonstrated such a knowledge),[53] while all AVPF doctors interviewed by the author affirmed that in not a single case had religion been a barrier to a patient's acceptance of family-planning services. Other interviewees, in discussing the Venezuelan Church's posture, concluded that since the majority of family-planning clients were not married in a religious ceremony to begin with, the Church was reluctant to condemn the prescription of birth control devices, reasoning that without such devices, the result would be another generation of illegitimate children. It is thus possible that the Church viewed the evils of illegitimacy—often accompanied by the subsequent abandonment of children—as being at least as great as the evils of birth control.

A pastoral letter issued by the Venezuelan bishops in November, 1969, was considered so liberal in its interpretation of the individual's ability to decide for himself on the question of family planning that AVPF reprinted it and made it available to its personnel and the public at large.[54] Individual priests who have written articles critical of family planning have received personal letters from the AVPF leadership clarifying the Association's position and activities. Finally, the AVPF leadership has taken great pains to show that it seeks the same moral and ethical basis of procreation as advocated by the Church, and that thus there is no conflict between the Encyclical *Humanae Vitae* and AVPF's own statutes and activities. Like the Encyclical, AVPF has worked against "disorderly and extramarital procreation"—not against procreation itself.[55]

Prominent Catholic leaders have been invited to participate in the Association's lecture series. The director of the Social Science Faculty of the Catholic University was among the participants in the AVPF "I Family Planning Information Course for Journalists" held in March, 1971.[56] This *cursillo* marked a high point in the increasing coverage that family-planning activities and topics were receiving in the media. Association meetings, lectures by the Concepción Palacios Maternity team, and announcements of population-related publications and debates are now fully reported by the major periodicals, including those in the interior. This fact is another indication of a distinct change in the handling of such topics. Only a few years ago these issues were seldom, if ever, reported or discussed in the papers; they are now given full, and often prominent, front-page coverage. Advertisements for contraceptives and for physicians trained in contraceptive techniques appear routinely. Given this new media openness, AVPF is now considering the possibility of placing "spot" announcements advertising its services and/or family-planning concepts on radio and on television.

In addition to their work with the Church and the media, AVPF executives devote a great deal of time and effort in securing invitations to serve as participants, lecturers, or discussants in meetings sponsored by the major business and economic groups. On such occasions, they have stressed the economic drag resultant from disorganized and unplanned reproduction, the instability brought on by large numbers of unemployed, and the cumulative and corrosive effects of large numbers of abandoned children and youth on the future of democratic development in Venezuela. This education of businessmen appears to be paying off. Topics such as family planning and the demographic explosion have frequently been included in the agenda of business meetings. Dividendo Voluntario para la Comunidad, a foundation with wide business support, has given some financial help to AVPF, as have other private business concerns.[57]

In 1971, a group of businessmen created the Fundación Paternidad Responsable (Responsible Parenthood Foundation) to finance AVPF services, to support population-related research, and to provide greater support for family planning at the governmental level as well as within individual industries.[58] The promoters of this foundation each contributed 25,000 Bs (approximately $5,500) and established as their initial goal the sum of $150,000 for the Foundation. These business leaders proposed to the United States Ambassador that he use his good offices to obtain a matching sum from an American foundation. Although not publicized, the Ambassador was instrumental in obtaining a $305,000 grant from the Pathfinder Fund for 40 new clinics. With it, and support from the Foundation, the AVPF working budget for 1972-1973 would be approximately $1 million for the operation of nearly 100 clinics.

The similarity between the Foundation's support of AVPF and the Victor-Bostrum Fund's support of IPPF is striking and probably not coincidental. On the other hand, there are a number of private, philanthropic foundations in Venezuela through which businessmen and others support a particular cause. Thus the Fundación Paternidad Responsable is not unique. The businessmen involved are Venezuelans who openly admit that one of their major goals is to pressure the government into taking a positive stand in relation to family planning. Further, they are optimistic that, given their financial and moral backing for AVPF, the government might find it embarrassing and counter-productive to curtail already established AVPF clinics. Finally, these businessmen envision themselves as missionaries for the family-planning cause among other businessmen and they intend to serve as examples by adding family planning to the medical services given to their own workers.[59] If the experience of the crucial role played by businessmen in other policy areas is any indication,[60] the relationship developed between the Foundation and AVPF will more than compensate for all the Association's effort to build support among the economic elite of Venezuela.

There is little information on the various political parties' attitudes towards population issues. When interviewed, party personnel were extremely vague in their responses and at best felt that population was not an issue in Venezuela. In fact, most *políticos*—whether for or against—feel there are few votes in the population issue. Some Social Christian literature has explicitly opposed birth control, but the Party itself has not officially come out against family planning.[61] Acción Democrática, the other major party in the country, has had an attitude that may be better described as one of "passive neutrality." This attitude may now be changing. The AD presidential candidate for the 1973 elections, Andrés Pérez, has made statements favoring the availability of family planning advice to all who may seek such advice. However, the possibility of a nationwide network of family-planning clinics has not been raised.

AVPF did distribute an essay on population by former presidential candidate and intellectual-economist Arturo Uslar Pietri. He has also been speaker at some of the Association's public meetings.[62] Dr. Martín Vegas, AVPF president, is president of the Frente Nacional Democrático, a small party. The Communists, much splintered and demoralized, have had little time or energy to deal with the topic of family-planning activities as this is hardly a "live" issue in Venezuela. Communist Congresswoman Argelia Laya, a member of the Juvenile Delinquency Commission, has devoted many of her efforts to trying to implement existing laws that guarantee family protection and day care centers by business firms.[63]

Although AVPF has not sought the endorsement of the political parties for its activities, it has established personal contacts with several congressmen and senators, who in turn have participated in some of the Association's meetings. These contacts were largely instrumental in the December, 1971, congressional appropriation of 1,600,000 Bs (approximately $363,000), in the national budget to AVPF through the Consejo Venezolano del Niño, an "autonomous" but semi-official agency for child care and protection. This congressional appropriation, though not hailed as an official embrace of the family-planning cause, certainly comes very close to effectively linking AVPF and the government. It is in keeping with the government's reluctance to give its official blessing to the cause, however, that the appropriation was not the result of governmental or even Social Christian pressure in Congress. Rather, it was achieved through the lobbying of the Fundación Paternidad Responsable and Senator Enrique Tejera París. Tejera París, an economist with ties to Acción Democrática (he was considered a possible AD presidential candidate), had been directly involved in the creation of CORDIPLAN and, more recently, was the Venezuelan ambassador in Washington. His wife worked for the Foundation for some time and continued to be deeply involved in various efforts to promote the family-planning cause in Venezuela. Both are well known socially and politically, and Tejera París is recognized as the father of overall national planning in Venezuela.[64]

Even though there is practically no information available on the attitude of organized labor towards AVPF or towards family planning, it is noteworthy that in a union-operated hospital there is an AVPF clinic in which the hospital even pays the salaries of the nurse and the *motivadora*. Realizing that if it hopes to become an effective organization it must obtain the support of organized labor, now a significant element in the society and a powerful contender in political affairs, AVPF is undertaking to reach labor leaders.[65] The goal is to get an agreement to use union halls as promotional centers for family-planning literature and, eventually, services. Interviews with labor leaders, however, indicate indifference to population topics. Recently split among political factions and further weakened by not having an openly pro-labor government, labor is in a state of flux at the moment with little time, funds, or inclination to deal with anything beyond what it considers the "vital" and "pressing" interests of the labor class.[66]

AVPF has been instrumental in the design of a pamphlet on sex education and responsible parenthood that the Armed Forces plan to use in their regular courses for new recruits. This decision on the part of the military was the direct outcome of an address by the AVPF executive director to a group of over 400 high-ranking officers. Given the crucial role that the military has played throughout Venezuelan history, plus the fact that military service is compulsory, the desire of military officers to better understand and actively participate in a program designed to promote responsible parenthood may well presage a greater governmental role in family planning.[67]

AVPF has also taken care to establish itself as a bona fide "medical" entity that dispenses professional services. Besides its many tracts on this point, [68] AVPF subsidizes the specialization of its medical and paramedical personnel in well-established, recognized professional centers. In addition, the Association has maintained informal links both with the Colegio de Médicos and the National Academy of Medicine. The Colegio, similar to the American Medical Association, has so far refrained from taking any position toward family-planning services.[69] The VIII Congress of Medical Sciences, on the other hand, adopted a resolution in favor of the establishment of family-planning services as part of the services rendered by the national health system.[70] Meanwhile, a large group of individual doctors, some of whom are prominent in professional and/or political circles, have publicly stated their support of such a service.[71]

This is another indication that the cautious but steady, and so far largely successful, approach by AVPF to key groups and individuals will eventually lead to the establishment of the indispensable link between the government—which is overwhelmingly dominant in the health field—and the Association itself. By spreading its base through approaching various groups and political agencies, hoping thus to use them as bridges to the government. AVPF is operating within the present rules of the Venezuelan political game. At least in the short run, it appears likely that the Venezuelan system will continue to respond to pressures emanating from powerful socio-economic and political groups, from elite elements and popular leaders, and from genuinely popular demands.[72]

In order to have some chance of being enacted, any policy must, in the eyes of the national leadership, contribute to the overall goals of a development-oriented society. Viewed in context, the concern over the abandoned child as a strategic justification for family planning activities is a logical one for an action-oriented organization such as AVPF to take. The high birth rate has not noticeably slowed Venezuela's efforts to attain her goals of a democratic, developed society, but a disorganized, prolific population expansion in the context of a persistently unstable family situation is beginning to take its toll in the form of bands of children and youth living largely on their own, outside of the law and social control. Their situation and antisocial behavior take on a class nature when one also realizes that these children are largely the products of the lowest economic rungs and the most affected by the uneven distribution of wealth. AVPF's focusing of its promotional campaign on the "abandoned child" theme has been a wise strategy, paying rich dividends in muting the opposition that would likely appear if the campaign were directed, for example, at a more blatantly "population control" theme or on the "economically ruinous burden" issue. Neither of these themes seem to apply to present-day Venezuela. Given the continued prosperity, population per se is not an overriding issue in the minds of governmental or political leaders or even scholars concerned with demographic questions. It is thus understandable why AVPF has chosen to downplay population control and has instead opted to promote a voluntary appeal to family planning as a means to achieve a more stable and satisfying family situation in Venezuela, a country where population growth is largely "disorderly" because it takes place outside a stable family situation. By the same token, in its appeal for private support of its activities and in its efforts to influence government, AVPF has forgone a simple economic explanation of the benefits of a lower birth rate.[73] It has instead concentrated on the damaging and cumulative effects of an abandoned child problem on the whole society. Not sheer economic growth, but illegitimacy, a growing abortion problem, and the ills that go with them are of increasing concern in Venezuela. With the number of abandoned children growing at the rate of 100,000 a year, this is one facet of the "population problem" that has received considerable public attention, for the abandoned child seems to present a blemish on an otherwise promising picture of democratic development.[74]

In contrast to AVPF's elaborate strategy, those of both the Concepción Palacios Maternity Hospital team and CEVEPOF are relatively simple. The Concepción Palacios team perceived its functions primarily as those of a medical nature, with research and policy aspects being accorded a secondary place. The team existed to fulfill fairly well-defined roles: to attend patients who pass through the Maternity, and to provide medical and paramedical personnel an opportunity to obtain further training and experience in dealing with problems of conception and family life. Its affiliation with the Central University Medical School has ensured a constant and qualified staff, while its location in a government-financed institution has provided a steady source of minimum support. The functions it performs and the demand for its services ensure it an unemcumbered, if restricted, existence. Fully 70.1 percent of all deliveries in Caracas and approximately 10 percent in the whole country take place at the Maternity, and through June, 1971, some 30,000 of these former Maternity patients had benefitted from the services provided by the Maternity family-planning clinic.[75] Further, by providing specialized training and orientation to physicians and other professionals, the Concepción Palacios Maternity team has clearly had a far greater impact than its own services to patients would indicate. Finally, by cooperating with the Ministry of Health and Welfare and by serving as the locus for much of CEVEPOF research, the clinic team has extended its influence into governmental and research areas it might not have been able to reach by itself.

CEVEPOF's strategy and impact have been greatly facilitated by the research and political context in which it has operated. By eschewing a more "action" orientation and by concentrating instead on an "apolitical" research stance, CEVEPOF has less need to justify its own existence than has been the case with AVPF. CEVEPOF can approach the population question from a seemingly detached vantage point. Its existence is justified by the function it fulfills—essentially long-range research—while AVPF must justify itself at every step and proclaim its own role as one that mitigates an already pressing problem, that of irresponsible parenthood and the concomitant abandonment of children. CEVEPOF can still affirm that its role is not to promote a population policy, but rather to analyze the preconditions for such a polity; AVPF must wrap its own actions in the population field by giving them an orientation and a label that will win the Association more friends and disarm its potential enemies. AVPF has thus purposely used the appeal of the "abandoned child" issue and has proclaimed its services as consonant with those that promote the democratic development of Venezuela.

In terms of staff, budget, and visibility, AVPF easily overshadows both CEVEPOF and the Concepción Palacios team. But the presently limited nature of CEVEPOF should not mislead us into underestimating its potential influence on the population policy-making process now going on in Venezuela. Because of CEVEPOF's links with the Social Christian government, its research findings were given a sympathetic hearing by the centrally-located government planning office, CORDIPLAN, as well as by highly placed and influential Social Christian leaders. CEVEPOF was thus able effectively to bypass the intermediaries, on whom AVPF has so far relied so heavily to bring its message across in higher governmental circles. In a similar vein, because CEVEPOF concentrated on research and because it enjoyed the coveted *visto bueno* of the Social Christian government, it could openly receive United States aid for its activities.[76] Further, on its own and through help from CORDIPLAN and presumably also from the United States government, CEVEPOF has been negotiating more formal research and exhange ties with North American universities interested in population questions. If the full range of activities contemplated in these negotiations are consummated—and some preliminary arrangements have already been completed—CEVEPOF would have the financial and academic prestige that accrues from international collaboration. Finally, because from its inception CEVEPOF has been linked with the Catholic University, it can present itself as a genuine research institution with a bona fide academic standing at the same time that it benefits from its informal, though significant contacts with Catholic officials and lay leadership.

Perhaps because CEVEPOF feels it enjoys all these advantages over AVPF, there has been little coordination between the efforts of the two organizations. They exchange publications and keep each other informed on their respective activities, but there is little more in the way of cooperation. That CEVEPOF has at times worked in close association with the Concepción Palacios Maternity team has been more coincidental than representatives of a real effort to cooperate and coordinate in the population area. With the Maternity and CEVEPOF located in Caracas, and with the Maternity team heading the most medically advanced and largest family-planning clinic in the capital, it is only natural that CEVEPOF utilize its facilities to undertake some of its research.

SOME IMPLICATIONS FOR POPULATION POLICY-MAKING IN A DEMOCRATIC CONTEXT

Even though it would be premature to say that the three organizations considered are building a loose coalition in favor of family planning and a governmental population policy, we find some rough similarities in their styles and modes of operation as well as in the stage in population policy development to which these pertain. For this purpose, we may conveniently utilize Segal's three-stage pattern in the evolution of population policies.[77] In Segal's first stage, dedicated pioneers and private individuals take the initiative in raising the level of popular consciousness concerning the advantages of family planning, opening clinics or dispensaries for contraceptive devices, and beginning education programs. In the second stage, there is a growth in popular demand for such services, private philanthropic and other groups become involved, and population becomes a "live" political issue. It is at this stage that international organizations become involved, allies are recruited and foes disarmed, and the pressures on government begin. In the final stage, the government may openly adopt a population policy and provide family planning on a large scale; it may follow a policy of general laissez faire, or it may reject any positive policy altogether. Venezuela has clearly passed through the first stage and is now deeply into the second stage, except that population has not become a "live" political issue.

Given the tentativeness with which the government has so far responded to pressures for a population policy (aptly described as a stance of "surreptitious encouragement"),[78] AVPF has refrained from forcing the issue and trying prematurely to move into Segal's third stage. It has avoided overreaching and overextending itself by rejecting, for now at least, a vigorous national promotional campaign for family planning at a stage in which it is not yet financially and organizationally prepared to operate a fully nationwide family-planning program. In the words of its executive director, AVPF "works from day to day, trying to lessen the ills of irresponsible parenthood and to diminish the number of illegitimate and abandoned children and not as though it could single-handedly solve the population problem or dictate the population policy for Venezuela."[79] Similarly, CEVEPOF has avoided the pitfalls of trying to design a blueprint for a far-reaching population policy. It has instead opted to feed its research results on the population-related problems and desires of Venezuelans into the established machinery of governmental policy-making. Again, given the structure of this policy-making machinery, CEVEPOF has directed its influence, not at the lower levels of bureaucracy, but where it is likely to count: at the level of the presidential agency CORDIPLAN, which is responsible for overall and nationwide policy planning. Access to CORDIPLAN has been gained through informal channels by means of face-to-face contacts and personal connections.

The strategies followed by the population organizations have thus been cautious, incrementalist and gradualist, in the classic style of problem-solving in Latin America.[80] They have not followed a "grand design" but have involved a long "journey toward progress."[81] This type of strategy in policy-making has been cogently described by Lindblom as that of a "disjointed incrementalist variety." Lindblom explains:

> Those decisions effecting small or incremental change and not guided by a high level of understanding are the decisions typical of ordinary political life—even if they rarely *solve* problems but merely stave them off or nibble at them. . . . It is decision-making through small or incremental moves on particular problems rather than through a comprehensive reform program. It is also endless; it takes the form of an indefinite sequence of policy moves. Moreover, it is exploratory in that the goals of policy-making continue to change as new experience with policy throws new light on what is possible and desirable. In this sense, it is also moving *away* from social ills rather than *toward* a known or relatively stable goal.[82]

By linking their efforts with the overall goals of a democratic, development-oriented society, by carefully choosing their allies and their channels of communication in the policy process, by rejecting purely economic arguments that carry little weight in the Venezuelan context, and by perceiving that population policy is still a largely uncharted field, AVPF and CEVEPOF have taken a series of limited, though significant steps towards the enactment and implementation of a sound family-planning program and overall population policy. The strategies followed and the decisions made have been thoroughly pragmatic, incrementalist, and appropriately gradualistic. The approach has been one of "piecemeal engineering" [83] —in which strategies are adapted to the nature of desired social reform and in which the ends are adjusted to the means through repeated reappraisals of objectives.

The leadership of the population organizations in Venezuela has likewise understood the *ambiente* in which all policy-making takes place. These leaders have operated as political actors who recognized the crucial importance of pursuing a frankly political strategy in promoting a population policy within a system that has been ambiguous or indifferent to the whole population issue. They have understood that even in such "apolitical" areas as public health [84] and research, the political aspects are so crucial that in order to be enacted and implemented successfully, any policy (establishment of family-planning clinics in public hospitals, sponsorship of medical and social research on abortion, and so forth), must take into account the political and organizational patterns familiar and peculiar to the people in the particular community.[85] No policy can be devised or promoted according to an ideal organizational model, no matter how sound such a model may be in theory or however much it may appeal to program planners. Rather, the policy and program must be adapted to existing local needs if they are to have any chance of success.

In an article on comparative policy analysis, Anderson gives us an imaginative scheme for categorizing the style and mode employed by the Venezuelan organizations according to their strategies and daily operations to date. He raises the question as to why certain policy approaches appear in some systems while not in others. His answer points out that the selection of approaches is not wholly coincidental. Canons of legitimacy and constitutional conventions provide limits on the range of possible approaches selected. On the other hand, since policy-making depends so much on habitual responses to problems, historical precedent or the adaptation of means that have evolved from previous problem-solving situations can also be delimiting factors. Finally, extant power and group relations circumscribe the range of alternatives that will be considered appropriate responses to a given problem.[86]

Applying Anderson's suggestion, we can say that in Venezuela ideology, tradition, and constitutional convention have placed the locus for policy decision-making, execution, and implementation in the central government.[87] It is thus not accidental that all three population organizations have emerged, survived, and expanded by the good will, or at the very minimum, the benevolent indifference of the central government. The strategy employed by AVPF gives us a clear example of its aiming toward an eventual response by the central government. Since AVPF's ultimate goal is the establishment of clinics on a national basis, and since it is the government that has a virtual monopoly on health care, it has concentrated its long-range efforts on influencing the government, hoping thereby to secure the eventual promotion of family-planning services throughout the extensive public health system.

These long-range efforts have taken several forms, but they have consistently been within the context of existent national goals. Since 1958 most programs devised and implemented by the government have been promoted as a means toward achieving a democratic, development-oriented society. This ideological goal, which is usually linked with the glories of the country's past history, [88] as well as the more efficient and socially-just utilization of its abundant resources, has been embraced by the vast majority of the country's leaders. At the same time, it has acquired meaning to many sectors of the general population through its translation into such programs as agrarian reform, education, and welfare—programs that are already reaching down and benefitting many of the country's citizens.

In pursuing the Anderson scheme further, we see that the "habitual response" or way of dealing with problems has been largely personalistic in the Venezuelan context.[89] For example, family-planning clinics are established in public hospitals not so much out of an explicit policy on this issue by the central government as out of personal and professional relations between family-planning advocates and hospital administrations. It is this same characteristic of personalism that helps explain why in all three agencies certain individuals have, from their inceptions, held leadership positions, and these same leaders are often regarded as the personification of their organizations.

Finally, the Venezuelan context is such that the alternative responses considered appropriate in the population field are also restricted. The questions of abandoned children and, increasingly, of abortion, rather than of the birth rate, overpopulation, or the economic implications of rapid population growth, are perceived as salient facets of the population problem. We may again turn to Anderson by quoting his dictum that "the country that does not adopt a policy innovation from abroad may just not have the same problem as that which led to the creation of a particular policy technique."[90] Since abandoned children are perceived as potentially having a detrimental effect upon the achievement of a democratic, developed society, this issue has been used effectively by AVPF as a rallying cry for the promotion of its activities. By the same token, because research has been accorded such a prominent role in the overall planning efforts of CORDIPLAN,[91] it is also logical to see that central governmental agency reaching out and supporting the scholarly endeavors of the private CEVEPOF. Similarly, the "medical service" orientation of the Concepción Palacios Maternity Clinic team has been in accord with the existing ideology and operation of the whole public health system.

Once the population question was translated in terms of an already recognized problem of societal implications, the organizations involved in population control made judicial use of groups and individuals who have direct access to the governmental machinery. This is a mode of operation common to other Venezuelan organizations, many of which have already made an impact in such policy areas as agrarian reform, education, and the like.

In a society which to a considerable extent is organized in a corporate and elitist manner, with certain key groups in the society playing a decisive role in policy-making and implementation, one must necessarily work through these groups to reach the apex of the socio-political pyramid—the government itself. Only in this fashion can a group or an association hope to see its particular interest articulated, enacted, and implemented into national policy.[92]

Thus viewed, the very uniqueness of the Venezuelan case in relation to policy-making in general does have implications that extend beyond its borders and that transcend the peculiar political realities of that country. The overall implication to be derived is that the politics of population, in Venezuela as elsewhere, must be tailored to the particular arena in which the policy process takes place. While techniques and methods may be and often are useful irrespective of national boundaries, the particular choice of strategies of policy-making used to promote a population program and have it become part and parcel of an overall government effort are dictated not so much by their abstract "rationality" as by their congruence with the traditional and habitual patterns of political culture and of policy-making.

NOTES TO CHAPTER 14

1. Edwin D. Driver, "Summary of the Social Sciences and Population Policy: A Survey," *Demography*, VII (August, 1970), pp. 379–392.
2. In support of this contention, see, among others, Henry M. Raulet, "Family Planning and Population Control in Developing Countries," *Demography*, VII (May, 1970), pp. 211–234; Philip M. Hauser, "Family Planning and Population Programs, A Book Review Article," *Demography*, IV, No. 1 (1967), pp. 397–414; Margaret Bright, *Measures, Policies and Programmes Affecting Fertility, with Particular Reference to National Family Planning Programmes* (New York: United Nations, 1972); Steven Polgar, ed., *Culture and Population: A Collection of Current Studies* (Chapel Hill, N.C.: Carolina Population Center, 1971).
3. Robert J. Alexander, *The Venezuelan Democratic Revolution* (New Brunswick, N.J.: Rutgers University Press, 1964); Philip B. Taylor, Jr., ed., *Venezuela 1969: Analysis of Progress* (Houston: University of Houston, Latin American Studies, 1971). For appraisals which concede development but decry its orientation, see D.F. Maza Zavala, *Venezuela: Una economía dependiente* (Caracas: Universidad Central de Venezuela, 1964); and José A. Silva Michelena, *The Illusion of Democracy in Dependent Nations* (Cambridge, Mass.: M.I.T. Press, 1971).
4. John D. Powell, "Peasant Society and Clientelist Politics," *The American Political Science Review*, LXIV (June, 1970), pp. 411–425.
5. Fred D. Levy, Jr., *Economic Planning in Venezuela* (New York: Praeger, 1968), pp. 5–28.

6. John Friedmann, *Venezuela: From Doctrine to Dialogue* (Syracuse, N.Y.: Syracuse University Press, 1965), pp. 18-30.
7. Daniel J. Lerner, "Conflict and Consensus in Guayana," *A Strategy for Research on Social Policy* edited by Bonilla and José A. Silva Michelena. (Cambridge, Mass.: M.I.T. Press, 1967), pp. 317-332; Lisa R. Peattie, *The View From the Barrio* (Ann Arbor, Michigan: University of Michigan Press, 1968).
8. Acción Democrática, *Acción Democrática: Doctrina y programa* (Caracas: Secretaria Nacional de Propaganda, 1962); *Venezuela: La realidad nacional, 1968. Ideas para la elaboración de un programa de gobierno* (Caracas: Publicaciones del Programa Extraordinario, 1968).
9. John D. Powell, *Political Mobilization of the Venezuelan Peasant* (Cambridge, Mass.: Harvard University Press, 1971).
10. Lloyd Rodwin and Associates, eds., *Planning Urban Growth and Regional Development* (Cambridge, Mass.: M.I.T. Press, 1969).
11. Powell, *Political Mobilization...*, and Taylor, *Venezuela 1969...*, especially pp. 1-12 and pp. 249-259.
12. Ramón A. Tovar, *La población de Venezuela* (Caracas: Universidad Central de Venezuela, 1968); Agency for International Development, *Population Program Assistance* (Washington, D.C.: AID, 1971), p. 166.
13. Levi Marrero, *Venezuela y sus recursos* (Caracas: Cultural Venezolana, S.A., 1964), chap. VIII.
14. Eduardo E. Arriaga, "Some Aspects of Family Composition in Venezuela," *Eugenics Quarterly*, XV (September, 1968), pp. 177-190.
15. José Eliseo López, *Tendencias recientes de la población venezolana* (Mérida: Universidad de Los Andes, 1968), especially pp. 22-23.
16. Estimates of abandoned children vary widely, from a conservative 400,000 to a high of 2 million or nearly one in every five Venezuelans. J.L. Salcedo-Bastardo, *Historia fundamental de Venezuela* (Caracas: Universidad Central de Venezuela, 1970), p. 707; Carlos Acedo Mendoza, *Venezuela: Ruta y destino* (Barcelona, Spain: Ediciones Ariel, 1966), II, pp. 85-90. Estimates of illegitimacy show less variation and involve around 50 percent of all *registered* births.
17. Acedo Mendoza, *Venezuela...*, II, chap. IX.
18. Pablo Liendo Coll, *Contenido de un programa de planificación familiar* (Caracas: AVPF, 1970).
19. CEVEPOF, *Lo que piensa y hace el Centro Venezolano de Población y Familia* (Caracas: CEVEPOF, n.d.), n.p.
20. Ela Bergher de Bacalao, "Postpartum Family-Planning Program at Concepción Palacios Maternity Hospital, Caracas, Venezuela," paper presented at the VI International Congress of Gynecology and Obstetrics, New York, April 14, 1970. Other organizations, such as the Instituto Venezolano del Consumidor, may eventually take positions on a population policy, but they are either too small or too recent to merit our attention here. The Venezuela Association for Family and Sexual Orientation (AVOFYS) formed in May,

1970 is a small entity that may show greater potential than its size indicates. It recently received a $100,000 grant for research and training in family life education; see *Ford Foundation Annual Report, 1971* (New York: Ford Foundation, 1971), p. 75.
21. Levy, *Economic Planning* . . .; Friedmann, *Venezuela* . . . .
22. Acedo Mendoza, *Venezuela* . . ., I, pp. 153–159; Population Reference Bureau, *1971 World Population Data Sheet* (Washington, D.C.: PRB, 1971).
23. Marrero, *Venezuela y sus recursos*.
24. Oficina Central de Coordinación y Planficación, *Plan de la Nación, 1965–1968, Programa salud* (Caracas: CORDIPLAN, 1965), pp. 127–134.
25. Oficina Central de Coordinación y Planificación, Sector Salud, *Resumen de los puntos de agenda tratados en el Comité Coordinador de la Salud entre los dias 20-4-66 y 18-12-68* (Caracas: CORDIPLAN, 1969), p. 26.
26. *Ibid.*, pp. 31–32. Interview with Dr. Angeles Sotillo de Gooden, Director, CORDIPLAN Health Sector, Caracas, January 15, 1970; CORDIPLAN, *IV Plan de la Nación, 1970–1974, Version preliminar, II, El desarrollo social y cultural* (CORDIPLAN, n.d.), chap. IX-6.
27. Interviews with Dr. José Limongi, AVPF Education and Information Director, Caracas, January, 1970, and May–June, 1971.
28. Interviews with the Concepción Palacios Maternity Hospital clinic team, Caracas, May–June, 1971.
29. Ela Bergher de Bacalao, "Maternidad Concepción Palacios: Family Planning Clinic-Caracas," (n.d., mimeo). Interviews with social work professor, Dr. Frescia Rubilar, Caracas, May–June, 1971.
30. Bacalao, "Postpartum Family Planning . . ."
31. Susan Evans, "Urbanization and Fertility in Latin America: A Comparison of Caracas and Mexico City" (M.A. thesis, Latin American Studies, University of California at Los Angeles, 1970).
32. Greater budgetary information can be found in Iêda Siqueira Wiarda, *Family Planning Activities in a Democratic Context: The Case of Venezuela* (Columbus, Ohio: Mershon Center, 1970).
33. CEVEPOF, "Lo que piensa y hace . . .; "see also "La primera investigación de CEVEPOF," *Boletín CEVEPOF,* I, (April, 1971), p. 2.
34. *Ibid.;* "Editorial", *Boletín CEVEPOF,* I (April, 1971), p. 1; interviews with Dr. Marisela Paúl Bello, CEVEPOF executive secretary, Caracas, May 26, 1971, and with CEVEPOF sociologist Milagros Pérez, Caracas, May 31, 1971.
35. Dr. Luis Domínguez, *et. al., Población y educación* (Caracas: III Congreso Venezolano de Salud Pública, ponencia no. 1, 1966); *Acta Final del Congreso, Ponencia I: Población.* The latter concludes that "in view of the real demand for advice and services about the medico-social problems of fertility, the official [public] health services must be able to offer such help and advice and the practical means to all those who spontaneously solicit them."

36. Family planning is understood as a socio-medical system which encompasses the functions of birth control, promotion of fertility, detection of pathological processes, and medical-social education, with the view of regulating the number of children and promoting family welfare. AVPF, *Informe que presenta la Asociación Venezolana de Planificación Familiar ante la reunion anual del Consejo Regional y el Comité Médico Regional de la I.P.P.F.* (Cuernavaca, Mexico: October, 1969), "Anexo," p. 1.
37. For details, see Wiarda, *Family Planning Activities...;* AVPF, *Directorio de servicios de planificación familiar* (Caracas, n.d.). Interviews with Drs. José Limongi, A. Lugo, and Ali Jorgez, AVPF, 1970-1971.
38. "Many Tasks Fall on Ministry of Health," *Venezuela Up-to-Date,* XII (Spring, 1967), p. 9.
39. Goran Ohlin, *Population Control and Economic Development* (Paris: Development Centre of the Organization for Economic Co-Operation and Development, 1967), p. 103-104.
40. Wiarda, *Family Planning Activities...,* pp. 93-95.
41. The simplified medicine system is one of the most imaginative uses of paramedical personnel in rural Venezuela. See Ministerio de Sanidad y Asistencia Social, *Manual normativo de enfermería y otro personal voluntario* (6th ed.; Caracas: MSAS, 1968).
42. Pablo Liendo Coll, *Programa de la Asociación Venezolana de Planificación Familiar del 1° de julio al 31 de diciembre de 1969* (Caracas: AVPF, 1970); "Cursos para Medicos Rurales," *Boletín,* I (August, 1969), p. 2.
43. For details, see Wiarda, *Family Planning Activities...,* especially pp. 99-100.
44. U.S., Congress, House, Committee on Government Operations, *USAID Operations in Latin America under the Alliance for Progress, Hearings, before a Subcommittee of the Committee on Government Operations,* House of Representatives, 90th Cong., 2nd session (Washington, D.C.: Government Printing Office, 1969), p. 790.
45. J.E. Rivera Oviedo, *Los Social Cristianos en Venezuela* (Caracas: Impresos "Helmar," 1970), pp. 111-116. Fernandez lost the election.
46. Pablo Liendo Coll, *Contenido de un programa...,* p. ii.
47. AVPF, *Informe...,* p. 12.
48. Interviews with MSAS personnel, Caracas, January, 1970 and May-June, 1971.
49. *Ford Foundation Annual Report, 1971,* p. 75. AVOFYS, formed in 1970, is still exerting a relatively circumscribed influence compared with either AVPF or CEVEPOF. Its publications and advertisements indicate an orientation similar to that of the Masters-Johnson team in the United States.
50. Interviews with participants of these discussions on sex education, Caracas, May-June, 1971.
51. Interviews with CEVEPOF personnel, May-June, 1971.

52. Isidoro Alonso, et al., *La Iglesia en Venezuela y Ecuador* (Bogotá: Oficina Internacional de Investigaciones FERES, 1962); Leroy C. Hoinacki, "Religion's Political Dimensions in Venezuela," (M.A. thesis, Latin American Studies, University of California at Los Angeles, 1969); Evans, *Urbanization and Fertility* . . ., pp. 69–72.
53. CEVEPOF, *La mujer venezolana y regulación de nacimientos* (Caracas: CEVEPOF, 1970), pp. 38–39, 59, 115–116.
54. *Carta pastoral de los obispos venezolanos sobre planificación familiar*, reprinted from *La Religión,* November 23, 1969.
55. Liendo Coll, *Contenido de un programa* . . ., p. 11.
56. "I Curso de Información de Planificación Familiar para Periodistas," (Caracas: AVPF, 1971, mimeo). The *cursillo* received full and wide coverage in several newspapers, such as in *El Nacional* and *El Universal,* March 9, 1971.
57. The speech of the AVPF executive director before the "Dividendo" was subsequently reprinted and distributed by that group, as well as published as "La crisis de la familia y la procreación irregular en Venezuela," *El Farol,* April–June, 1969, pp. 34–37.
58. "Reporte de paises: Venezuela," *Fomento Economico, FIPF/RHO,* I (Spring, 1971), p. 2.
59. Interviews with and communications from Caracas businessmen, May–June, 1971; Spring, 1972.
60. Levy, *Economic Planning* . . .; Friedmann, *Venezuela* . . .; Acedo Mendoza, *Venezuela* . . ., II, pp. 236–242.
61. Rivera Oviedo, *Los Social Cristianos* . . ., pp. 111–112.
62. Arturo Uslar Pietri, "Población" (mimeo).
63. For Laya's role in the Communist Party, see Eleazar Díaz Rangel, *Como se dividio el P.C.V.* (Caracas: Editorial Domingo Fuentes, 1971). pp. 26, 80.
64. Friedmann, *Venezuela* . . ., pp. 14, 35–37, 76.
65. Powell, *Political Mobilization* . . .; Robert J. Alexander, *Organized Labor in Latin America* (New York: Free Press, 1969), pp. 3–24, 142–152.
66. Interview with Magdalena de Becerra, CTV (Confederation of Venezuelan Workers) Feminine Director, Caracas, June 1, 1971; and also her *La mujer y el trabajo* (Caracas: Imprenta del Congreso de la República, 1971).
67. AVPF, *Informe* . . ., p. 17.
68. Ali Jorgez, *et. al., Planificación familiar, comunicación preliminar* (Caracas: January, 1971); and Pablo Liendo Coll, *Planificación familiar* (Caracas: October, 1970). The latter was first presented to the National Academy of Medicine.
69. There has been a dispute between the Colegio and AVPF over the latter's contracts with doctors. Outside observers see it as essentially a labor dispute.
70. "Las convicciones religiosas de los gobernantes no deben interferir la planificación familiar," *El Nacional,* February 7, 1971.

71. "Iglesia y médicos: Posiciones contrarias frente al control de la natalidad," *El Universal,* April 14, 1971.
72. Powell, *Political mobilization...;* Friedmann, *Venezuela....*
73. Stephen Enke, "The Economic Aspects of Slowing Population Growth," *Economic Journal,* LXXXVI (March, 1966), pp. 45-56; T. Paul Schultz, *Demographic Conditions of Development in Latin America* (Santa Monica, Calif.: The RAND Corp., 1968), pp. 33-36.
74. "En Venezuela cada año quedan 100,000 abandonados," *El Nacional* May 18, 1969; and Rafael Caldera, "La familia y el derecho," *Sociología Jurídica,* II (Caracas: Universidad Católica Andrés Bello, 1960).
75. Bacalao, "Postpartum Family Planning..."
76. U.S., Congress, *USAID Operations...,* p. 167.
77. Aaron Segal, *Politics of Population in the Caribbean* (Rio Piedras, P.R.: Institute of Caribbean Studies, University of Puerto Rico, 1969). Compare to Aníbal Faundes and Ellen Hardy, "El proceso de acceptación nacional de la planificación familiar en América Latina," Comunicación al II Laboratorio Nacional de Planificación Familiar, Manizales, Colombia, 1967.
78. Private communication from Susan Evans, October 10, 1969.
79. Interview with Dr. Pablo Liendo Coll, Caracas, January 19, 1970.
80. Charles W. Anderson, *Politics and Economic Change in Latin America* (Princeton, N.J.: D. Van Nostrand, 1967), pp. 68-86; Powell, *Political Mobilization...,* especially Part II.
81. Albert O. Hirschman, *Journeys Toward Progress* (New York: Doubleday, 1965), pp. 299-384.
82. David Braybrooke and Charles E. Lindblom, *A Strategy of Decision* (New York: Free Press, 1963), p. 71; italics in the original. Prominent Venezuelans, in describing the policy process in their country have specifically pointed out its similarity to the Lindblom model. See Hector Hurtado, a former CORDIPLAN director, in Taylor, *Venezuela 1969...,* pp. 254-255.
83. Karl Popper, *The Open Society and its Enemies,* I (London: George Routledge, 1945), pp. 138-144.
84. For comparison see Polgar, *Culture and Population...;* Oscar Lewis, "Medicine and Politics in a Mexican Village," (ed.) Benjamin D. Paul, *Health, Culture and Community* (New York: Russell Sage Foundation, 1955), pp. 403-434.
85. Pablo Liendo Coll, *Políticas de Población* (Caracas: AVPF, 1971).
86. Charles W. Anderson, "Comparative Policy Analysis: The Design of Measures," *Comparative Politics,* IV (October, 1971), pp. 117-131.
87. Leo B. Lott, "Venezuelan Federalism: A Case Study in Frustration," (Ph.D. dissertation, Political Science, University of Wisconsin, 1954).
88. J.L. Salcedo-Bastardo, *Visión y revisión de Bolívar* (Buenos Aires: Imprenta López. 1957).

89. Powell, *Political Mobilization* . . ., especially chap. VIII.
90. Anderson, "Comparative Policy Analysis . . .," p. 130.
91. Levy, *Economic Planning* . . .; Friedmann, *Venezuela* . . . .
92. Powell, *Political Mobilization* . . . ; Taylor, *Venezuela 1969* . . . .

   Prospects for such a "national policy" may be increasing. Newly-inaugurated President Carlos Andres Pérez and some of his close associates are considered sympathetic to family planning by AVPF personnel, who have often expressed the view that his Acción Democrátic Party has been more pragmatic and open on this subject that COPEI. It was during an AD administration that both AVPF and the Population Division in the Ministry of Health got their starts.

Chapter Fifteen

The Context of Population Policy Formation in Peru*

Richard Lee Clinton

Peru offers a seemingly archetypal case of a country in which the question of population policy has failed to emerge from the nebulous state of the nondecision. Noted for its seignorial and Catholic traditions, Peru as recently as 1962 was one of only four Latin American countries to vote against the inclusion in a United Nations resolution of an innocuous proposal which stipulated that the "United Nations give technical assistance, as requested by Governments, for national projects and programs dealing with the problems of population."[1] In spite of the complications created by its 3.1 percent per annum rate of population increase and exacerbated by heavy rural-urban migration, the Peruvian government has taken no steps toward meeting the challenge of population growth at its source.[2] In a country where the commitment to economic and social development has been explicit and fairly consistently implemented since at least the early part of the 1960's, how is it possible that the interactions between rapid population growth and developmental problems have been so ignored?[3] Perhaps the concept of "the mobilization of bias," broadly interpreted so as to include the entire value orientation of the culture in addition to the suppression of conflictive issues by elites, might contribute to an understanding of this apparent anomaly.[4] Elsewhere I have described the pervasive psychology of underpopulation that is almost universally encountered in Latin America.[5] This mind set stems from historical and geographical factors such as the fear of being overwhelmed by Indian hoards during the Colonial Period, and the feelings common even today of almost infinite potential fostered by the sheer vastness of the continent and the illusion of its unparallelled natural resources. Given such an outlook, it is not likely that population growth, even very rapid population growth, will be

*This chapter has been originally prepared for this volume.

viewed with alarm, particularly in a region where the mechanisms and implications of population change are seldom taught even in major universities.[6]

Some efforts, albeit extra-official ones, have been made to initiate family planning activities in Lima, Peru's capital and largest city, and in its nearby port of Callao.[7] A modicum of success was being achieved in enlisting government support for such efforts, at least within the Ministry of Public Health, when the military coup d'etat of October 3, 1968, overthrew the largely ineffectual constitutional regime of Fernando Belaúnde Terry.[8] Almost immediately the few family-planning facilities that had recently been opened in government clinics under the individual responsibility of a middle-level Ministry of Health official were discontinued, and since that time family-planning programs in Peru have been confined to those of unofficial, mostly foreign-supported groups with an interest in promoting responsible parenthood.[9]

In view of the traditional conservatism of Latin American military governments, which in their frequent interventions in national politics have seldom distinguished themselves as champions of change, the results of the 1968 coup were not surprising. After all, the military as a social institution has persistently demonstrated a pronatalist bias throughout history, since its strength and survival depend so directly on the continuous replenishing of its ranks with young men. In Latin America, moreover, the military has historically aligned itself with the landholding interests and the Church, both bastions of the status quo, and both concerned with encouraging large families.[10] Although the modern military establishment in Latin America has widened its base and has become, in effect, middle class, the reactionary tendencies of that amorphous sector have served to maintain military aversion toward radical changes.[11] For reasons largely unique to Peru, however, the military regime of October 3, 1968, evidenced from the outset an altered outlook toward changes in the basic structures of society.[12] By no means was it determined to make a socialist republic of the country, as most foreign businessmen frantically asserted, but the ruling officers had clearly decided to replace Peru's archaic form of unbridled capitalism and abject dependence with a closely regulated system of mixed state and private enterprise and a national sovereignty that had substance as well as form.

How the advent of such a regime may affect Peru's official stance vis-à-vis population policy will be touched upon in the conclusion. At this point, however, let us turn to the principal tasks of this paper, a review of the present state of population activities in that country and how they came about.

CURRENT STATUS OF POPULATION ACTIVITIES

Population matters in Twentieth Century Peru began receiving systematic attention in 1940 when the first national census since 1876 was carried out under the direction of Dr. Alberto Arca Parró. Dr. Arca Parró, who later served for 23 years in the Peruvian Congress and is today one of his country's few widely respected former legislators, traces his interest in population to his study of economics at the University of Indiana between 1921 and 1923 and to the experience in 1931 of organizing Peru's first formal voter registration.[13] In 1942, as Peru's delegate to the first Inter-American Conference on Population, Dr. Arca Parró pushed for the adoption of common procedures and definitions in conducting censuses throughout Latin America in order to improve their comparability, and from 1947 to 1948 he served as the first president of the United Nations Population Commission. In recognition of his labors in behalf of a better understanding of population dynamics, he was named the first president of Peru's Centro de Estudios de Población y Desarrollo (CEPD) when that organization was formed by Supreme Decree No. 244 of December 4, 1964.

One might think that as the findings of the 1940 census began to appear, demonstrating that Peru's population had more than doubled since the previous census—from 2.7 million to 6.2 million in 64 years—some concern for the country's population growth rate might have been stirred.[14] But, it seems that Dr. Arca Parró was largely alone in his call for greater attention to the demographic variables and their implications for Peru's development. Even as late as 1960, he recalls that he was attacked by *La Prensa,* one of Lima's two principal dailies, for having "invented the problem of Peru's population growth" as a pretext for justifying an increase in the national budget.[15]

In 1961 Peru's second census involving modern procedures and techniques was carried out, thus laying the basis for a more meaningful comparative analysis of demographic data than had theretofore been possible. Such a study was made by the Peruvian demographer Eduardo Mostajo Turner, but it ventured little further than a brief description of the intercensal changes that had taken place in the demographic characteristics of the different departments of Peru.[16] In commenting on the data on literacy of the population 15 years of age or older, for instance, Dr. Mostajo dealt only with percentages.[17] That the literate portion of the Peruvian population had increased from 42.5 percent in 1942 to 61.1 percent in 1961 is indeed an index of that country's substantial efforts and expenditures on education. But to fail to point out that in spite of these efforts and expenditures there were nearly two hundred thousand more illiterates in Peru in 1961 than there had been in 1940 is to overlook some of the major implications of the figures. It is difficult not to suspect that such an oversight resulted from a conscious intent to present the data in the most favorable light possible. Given Dr. Mostajo's position in the Oficina Nacional de Estadística y Censos, he may well have been subject to such pressures. It is possible, however, that the negative impact of Peru's rapid population increase between 1940 and 1961 was not, in fact, thoroughly recognized, simply because the values prevalent among local observers conditioned them to define population growth exclusively in positive terms.

The Centro de Estudio de Población y Dessarrollo (CEPD)

The story of exactly how President Fernando Belaúnde Terry was persuaded to create CEPD should provide an enterprising historian with many hours of engrossing investigation, for Belaúnde Terry seems to share[18] many of the pronatalist ideas of his distinguished uncle, the late Víctor Andrés Belaúnde, who, while Peru's delegate to the United Nations, inveighed against the involvement of that organization in population matters.[19] When the full story is known, however, certainly much of the credit will go to Dr. Carlos Muñoz Torcello and Dr. Javier Arias Stella, both of whom were prominent members of President Belaúnde's shadow cabinet (*"los carlistas"*), and both of whom are widely recognized as exponents of the need for improved understanding of population dynamics in Peru.[20]

The 60 percent increase in Peru's population between the 1940 and 1961 censuses –from 6.2 million to 9.9 million–was perceived by a few Peruvians as serious enough a phenomenon to warrant more systematic study. It seems likely that the substantiation of Peru's increasingly rapid population growth which was offered by the results of the 1961 census was an important weapon in the arsenal of those who were attempting to establish the need for a center for population studies, for shortly after the census data began appearing, the initiatives of Drs. Arca Parró, Arias Stella, and Muñoz Torcello bore fruit, and CEPD was formed. Although it is difficult to assess without access to the files of a number of organizations, considerable credit must also be given to the efforts of non-Peruvians representing such groups as the United States Agency for International Development (USAID), the Ford Foundation, the International Planned Parenthood Federation (IPPF), and the Population Council, whose influence on the above-named individuals was probably substantial and who were quick to provide CEPD with grants and technical assistance.[21]

The avowed aim of CEPD was to study the interrelations between demographic variables and economic development in order, as one observer has phrased it, "to provide through research and publications, the intellectual infrastructure for confronting Peru's population problems."[22] Rather than risk incurring the animosity of other research associations in Peru by appearing as a competitor, CEPD cautiously commenced its operations by identifying already existing research organizations, motivating them to build a population component into their research interests, and offering funding for projects with a population emphasis. Such an approach was astute, given both the vulnerability of a new paragovernmental agency such as CEPD and the pervasive tendency toward aggressive defense of vested interests—be they financial or intellectual—in an environment of relative scarcity. The necessity for such a circumspect beginning, however, meant that many needed studies and potentially useful pilot projects were not undertaken until four years or more after CEPD was created.

While in Chile heavy reliance has been placed on the economic and human costs of the high rate of induced abortion as a major justification for an official family-planning program, and Venezuelans interested in promoting family planning have emphasized the unconscionable level of child abandonment in their country, Peruvians seem to have concentrated on demonstrating the existence of a felt-need for family-planning services.[24] By mid-1968, CEPD had sponsored four KAP-type (knowledge, attitudes, and practice of contraception) surveys in the Lima area and one in the provincial mining town of Cerro de Pasco.[25] A pilot family-planning project, begun in 1967 in the barriada of Pamplona Alta, was a departure in CEPD activities and was carried out with the same circumspection which had characterized the organization's initial phase of existence. The Pamplona Alta clinic was primarily oriented toward maternal and child health, with family planning a natural adjunct to these wider services. The experience gained in the all-too-typical slum environment of Pamplona Alta will doubtlessly be invaluable in structuring future family planning programs in what are now referred to in Peru by the optimistic euphemism "Pueblos Jóvenes," for as Sanders has observed:

> Eventual implementation of family planning in Peru will have to resolve many of the problems confronted in Pamplona Alta: a migrant population that comes predominantly from the *sierra;* substantial rates of illiteracy, especially among women; prevalence of Indian languages rather than Spanish; extreme poverty; and high fertility rates (57 percent of the population is less than fourteen years old).[26]

As CEPD broadened its activities to include direct involvement in family planning, albeit only to the limited extent of an experimental pilot project, two principles were rigidly adhered to: (1) all family-planning services must be provided within the context of maternal and child health and sexual and family education programs, and (2) only recognized and widely respected institutions such as medical schools or the public health services are to be used as delivery mechanisms for CEPD-sponsored family-planning services.[27] Obviously, these principles placed rather severe constraints on the development of family planning programs by CEPD, and the organization has consequently been criticized for its less-than-optimal contribution to the advancement of family planning in Peru as well as for its almost paranoic fear of government suppression. The freedom with which private family-planning activities are carried out in Peru is cited by some critics as evidence of its exaggerated cautiousness. Other strictures allude to CEPD's reluctance to undertake forthright studies of the parameters of the contribution to economic development which might be made by official programs promoting family planning, of the costs and feasibility of such programs, and of their pay-off in comparison with alternative measures. One of the subjects interviewed in this study who had occupied a high post in the former administration, for instance, lamented that CEPD had not supplied him with the hard, cold facts and figures he needed in order to argue forcefully the case for a population policy before the Cabinet.

While these criticisms of CEPD may have some validity, there are extenuating circumstances which should not be overlooked. In the first place, CEPD was not created to promote family-planning programs. Nor is there any direct analogy between the freedom with which private family planning groups are able to operate and the ease with which CEPD might carry out a wider spectrum of family planning-related activities. CEPD, although a *para*governmental agency and only partially funded by the Peruvian Government,[28] is nevertheless intimately linked to the government through the Ministries of Labor and Health, representatives of which are members of its board of directors.[29] Moreover, during the period 1970-1972 there seemed to be a possibility of CEPD's being combined with the Instituto Nacional de Planificación to form a separate Ministry of Planning. Consequently, it is natural that the government would be much more sensitive to the activities sponsored by CEPD than to those carried out by strictly private organizations.

In sum, then, there is little doubt that CEPD could have been a more aggressive champion of both family planning and of the need for population limitation in Peru. Whether such a course of action would have been more successful in furthering these causes, however, is highly debatable, since a more aggressive approach might well have elicited a more rigid reaction on the part of the government, a more concerted *anti-controlista* campaign from those interests opposed to interfering with Peru's population growth, or, indeed, it might have emasculated the effectiveness of CEPD or even brought about its early demise. Unquestionably CEPD has made a positive contribution towards the development of a population policy in Peru through the research, publications, seminars, fellowships, educational programs, and pilot projects it has sponsored. Given the very real constraints of being connected with a pronatalist government and of being funded principally from foreign sources, it seems unfair to criticize it too harshly for not having launched an all-out frontal assault on the population problem in Peru, even if some of this prudence results from a self-interested concern for its own institutional viability.

Church World Service (CWS)

Chronologically, the family-planning efforts of Church World Service, a Protestant social action group, preceded by a year the formation of

CEPD, but these efforts have remained limited and peripheral to the main activities of CWS (relief work, community development, distribution of food, clothing, and medicine, and so forth). Since 1963, however, this organization has been importing and distributing contraceptives and informational brochures concerning their use and the advantages of family planning. The relative importance of this segment of CWS activities has varied in direct proportion to the degree of concern with population problems of its director.[30]

It would be a tedious enterprise to attempt to assess with any accuracy the impact that CWS has had in promoting family planning in Peru. Doubtless its influence has been insignificant if measured in terms of its effect on the country's population growth rate or even as the percentage of the target population reached. It has certainly been far from negligible in other respects, however, for it has performed an invaluable service for the several thousands of couples who have learned of family planning and the existence of modern contraceptives through CWS efforts.[31] By providing provincial physicians with IUD's and literature regarding their use, moreover, CWS has probably helped to fill a hiatus in the education of many of these general practitioners, as such materials have only recently begun to appear in the curricula of many Peruvian medical schools.[32]

A fascinating line of inquiry, albeit more amenable to anthropological techniques than to those of political science, would be to attempt to determine whether those who have adopted family planning through the efforts of CWS have had a significant "demonstration effect" within their communities. The difference between the Protestant world view and that fostered by Hispano-Catholic traditions could scarcely find clearer expression than in the individual-instrumental attitudes of the former as opposed to the institutional-fatalistic *Weltanschauung* of the latter, and these two contrasting patterns of belief could, in turn, hardly be better represented than by the attitude toward whether or not to admit the possibility of and to engage in the planning of the number and spacing of one's children. One potentially fruitful outcome of research into this area would be to add an empirical dimension to the argument over whether the pay-off of family planning is a long-term or a short-term one. It is frequently argued that a principal obstacle to the development of positive population policies in Latin America and other regions as well is that such measures must necessarily be of lower priority for policy makers than measures which would yield more immediate economic benefits. This argument is particularly emphasized when the political system under discussion is democratic in form, since elected officials must propose programs which can be quickly perceived as helpful by their constituents in order to assure their continued popularity and re-election. While it is true that even the most successful national family-planning program could not expect to yield significant benefits to the economy for many years—only after 10 to 20 years in most cases—the individual perspective seems to offer a quite different appearance. After all, a woman who might normally expect to have another baby every two years or so would probably be very much aware of the fact that this painful, dangerous, debilitating, and expensive (if not in actual monetary outlays, then in terms of energy-drain and time-loss, and thus in the lessening of the returns from remunerative pursuits) process was not taking place. Certainly the realization of the benefits of this situation would not be long in coming to the woman's husband as well, as her contributions to the well-being of the family continued uninterrupted and the increased demands of a larger number of children did not materialize.

Instituto Marcelino (IM)

What is now the largest single family-planning clinic in Peru, the Instituto Marcelino sprang from the efforts of four concerned individuals: Dr. Steban Kesserü, Dr. Alfredo Larrañaga, and Ing. Fernando Graña Elizalde and his Swedish wife. Whether the primary impetus originated with the physicians or with the Grañas, I was not able to determine with certainty, but in 1966 these young doctors opened a small clinic on the Graña's hacienda (Huando) to make modern means of family planning available to the hacienda workers. In spite of some allegedly Communist-inspired opposition from the workers' union,[33] the success of the clinic among the women not only of the hacienda but of the surrounding area prompted the group to establish a larger, more permanent clinic in Lima with facilities for more comprehensive gynecological services. With a grant from USAID and additional support from the Schering Pharmaceutical Company, this well-equipped clinic was opened in 1967 in the centrally located Barrios Altos section of downtown Lima within a block of the nation's largest maternity hospital. The demand that quickly developed for the clinic's services was little short of phenomenal and has convinced the doctors involved that family planning is already a felt-need among a large proportion of Peru's poor.[34] Some 3,700 women per year receive the services of the Instituto Marcelino, which by 1972 could claim approximately 7,000 steady contraceptors.[35]

The physicians who have invested so much of their time and energy in making the Instituto a going concern impress one as intelligent, dedicated, hardworking, socially conscious, and sincerely concerned individuals. Unintentionally, however, and perhaps unavoidably, they have provided opponents of family planning with some of their most effective weapons for attacking such activities in Peru. In the first place, IM's connection with the Graña name, a prominent one among those generally included on a list of Peru's "oligarchy," assured leftist opposition to the project from the outset. (In addition, Dr. Larrañaga himself might be considered by some to hold oligarchic credentials, since he is the grandson of the late President Augusto B. Leguía.) Beginning the operations on an hacienda, moreover, provided a basis for lurid rumors of forced sterilization of workers as a means for reducing costs. Since haciendas are normally rather self-contained units where food, housing, recreation, and varying levels of other amenities are supplied to the workers and their families by the hacienda itself, any reduction in the number of workers' dependents would indeed lower the operating expenses of the hacienda and increase its profits. Furthermore, medieval abuses of ignorant workers by conscienceless *hacendados,* in addition to being a favorite theme of Peruvian literature,[36] have been common occurrences in isolated regions of the Peruvian sierra until quite recent times. Hence, the grisly tales were not, on their face, improbable, and, in fact, they found fairly wide acceptance. (I was given slightly varying versions by several different people.) Although Huando, located on the coast a short drive from Lima, was an unusually modernized hacienda dedicated principally to citrus growing, the mere fact that it was an hacienda sufficed to lend credence to the vicious stories circulated by left-wing opponents of any form of population limitation in Peru. That the bulk of IM's financing was derived from USAID was another boon to these leftist elements, since it enabled them to point out the apparent community of interests which exists between the "imperialist center" and its "collaborators on the periphery— the exploiting native ruling classes."[37]

The most glittering of the golden opportunities for discrediting family-planning activities provided by the Instituto Marcelino, however, was its arrangement with Schering to carry out clinical testing of a new contraceptive called Noristerat, which is administered once every three months by injection. Although the product was said to have been extensively tested with animals for several years before it was approved for clinical testing with human beings, the implication was unavoidable that indigent Third World women were being used as guinea pigs by a capitalist enterprise from an industrialized nation, in this case Germany. There is certainly much validity to the argument that the slight and carefully monitored risk incurred in taking a still not completely tested contraceptive is far less than the known dangers involved in pregnancy, provoked abortion, and childbirth under primitive conditions. But, given the forces of nationalism, the sensationalism of the press—particularly in Peru— and the emotion-laden area of anything involving wives and mothers, such a highly rational defense of such activities rarely receives the attention given to the repugnant aspects of carrying out potentially dangerous experiments on poverty-stricken human beings.

Toward the end of 1970 Schering discontinued use of Noristerat in humans as a result of toxic skin reactions in rats injected with very large quantities of the drug.[38] In one sense this reconfirms the circumspection exercised by the company in testing this product, yet it also serves to reinforce the case of those attacking IM. It is too early to assess what the overall effect of this unfortunate congeries of factors will be, but the whole situation points up the extremely complex and delicate nature of the task confronting those who would try to do something about the population problem in Peru at present levels of knowledge—both scientific and public.

Movimiento Familiar Cristiano (MFC)

All treatments of MFC invariably contain in their opening paragraph such phrases as the "most unusual" or "the most enigmatic" of family-planning organizations in Peru.[39] Given the anomaly of this organization's connection with the Peruvian Catholic Church and its activities involving distribution of "the pill," such superlatives are not entirely unwarranted.

The Peruvian MFC was organized in 1966 by a North American physician, Dr. Joseph Kerrins.[40] Since the original MFC began its activities in France more than 20 years ago, these Catholic-lay groups have sprung up in many countries throughout the world. Basically they exist to promote Catholic family values, and thus they have usually been middle-class organizations, since as Sanders so accurately observed:

> The distance between Catholic norms and the Latin American reality [give] the MFC an image of moralism and linkage with the classes whose culture, financial status, and concern for respectability enabled them to fulfill the norms with greater ease than the lower class.[41]

Probably due to the interests of Dr. Kerrins, who had come to Peru with the Cardinal Cushing Project to do voluntary medical work among the poor, the Peruvian MFC became oriented toward the less privileged classes, where family instability and its accompanying problems are most severe.[42] The effects of unregulated fertility in exacerbating these problems could not long go unnoticed, hence the Peruvian MFC had to grapple with the thorny issue of fertility regulation as it sought to promote more responsible parenthood.

MFC's theological consultant, a Peruvian Jesuit, Father Enrique Bartra, resolved the dilemma posed by the group's concern for advancing the cause of responsible parenthood among the poor and the Roman Catholic Church's stand against artificial means of contraception. Father Bartra, drawing on the thinking of a Colombian priest, Father Gustavo Pérez Ramírez, noted that a biological defense mechanism operates to prevent fecundity while a mother is lactating, thus assuring that she will have time to attend to her newborn infant and to recoup her strength before the strains of another pregnancy begin. Due to the demands of poverty, however, many poor women have to cease nursing in order to work, or, because of malnutrition or illness, they cease lactating prematurely. In either case, they are exposed to the risk of conceiving before they would be strong enough to bear the process safely. Under these circumstances, Father Bartra argues, an anovulent could legitimately be taken to insure that the mother's fecundity would not return for the approximately two years that she would normally have been lactating and thus naturally infecund.[43]

On the basis of this consummate example of casuistical reasoning, MFC allows the use of anovulent pills for two years *post partum* by married women enrolled in its family education programs. During the series of classes, which both husband and wife must attend, the officially sanctioned "rhythm" method of contraception is taught and its moral superiority extolled, on the assumption that it will be employed when provision of the pills ceases.

In addition to its main offices in the center of Lima, MFC has some 14 branch offices in different parts of the barriadas surrounding the city.[44] Apparently these branches are opened only at the request of the local parish priest, hence their location follows no pattern, and their coverage is correspondingly uneven.

Toward the end of 1970, one of the most dedicated directors of the Peruvian MFC, Sr. Pedro Pazos, launched a companion effort called the Programa de la Asociación de Trabajo Laico Familiar (PALF) as a vehicle for extending MFC's family education and responsible parenthood programs into the provinces.[45]

It should be obvious that these organizations lead a rather precarious existence. Although much of their financial support comes from CEPD, they are intimately tied to the Church and are thus understandably sensitive about journalistic reports of their activities which discount the principal thrust of their program—responsible parenthood—and focus exclusively on their involvement in what is invariably labelled "birth control."[46] In spite of the limitations of the MFC and PALF programs—only married women, only with the husband's permission and cooperation, only two years, only *post partum*—both the efforts and the orientation of these two organizations have established helpful precedents, particularly as regards the involvement of the Roman Catholic Church in family planning.[47] Moreover, the fact that, except for Dr. Kerrins' seminal role, these groups are exclusively Peruvian makes their experience of special interest.

Asociacion Peruana de Protección Familiar (APPF)

Although slow in getting started, APPF after 1969 rapidly assumed a major role in Peruvian family-planning efforts. It was loosely organized in 1967 by a group of physicians whose experience had sensitized them to the need for providing sexual education, family planning information, and responsible parenthood counseling to the disadvantaged inhabitants of Lima and its surrounding barriadas.[48] Little was done other than to discuss the problem, however, until 1969, after it had become clear that the Ministry of Health under the military government would not support the Lima-Callao project of maternal-child health *cum* family-planning services.[49] In March, 1969, a new directorate took over and requested funds from USAID in order to set up an active program which would include family-planning promotion.[50]

The reorientation and activation of APPF seems to have been largely due to the social concern and ogranizational expertise of a North American businessman, Mr. Daniel Carter, a resident of Peru for over 20 years, and his vivacious Peruvian wife. Together they were responsible for attracting Dr. Carlos Alfaro, a career officer of the Ministry of Public Health and holder of a Master of Public Health degree from the United States, as the APPF's new Executive Director and Ing. Fernando Graña Elizalde as its first president.[51]

Affiliation with IPPF was finally consummated, and with funding from that source and from USAID, APPF set up its administrative offices and began consolidating the sponsorship of various on-going family-planning clinics in sections of greater Lima and in the provincial towns of Ica, Huancayo, and Chimbote.[52] By the end of 1972, APPF had assumed part of the financial responsibility for the Instituto Marcelino, and was serving over 7,000 steady contraceptors through 11 Family Protection Centers—8 in metropolitan Lima and 3 in the provinces mentioned above.[53]

Like CEPD and MFC, APPF emphasizes a multifaceted approach to the problems of the Peruvian family, eschewing the narrow label of a birth control center which is so often attributed to it by the press.[54] Dr. Alfaro describes APPF's program as designed to meet the multiple needs for elementary sexual education, instruction in family health measures, prevention of provoked abortions, cancer detection, and marital sterility problems as well as for family planning, *per se*.[55] APPF's activities include the organization of study groups for both laymen and medical personnel, maintenance of a library, holding exhibitions, showing films, and publishing a newsletter with articles of related interest in addition to provision of gynecological examinations and counseling on family planning.[56]

Although still far from being as aggressive an organization as Venezuela's Asociación Venezolana de Planificación Familiar,[57] or as active as some of the other IPPF affiliates in Latin America, APPF seems to provide Peru the most potentially effective private vehicle currently available for mounting a concerted attack on the myriad population-related problems of the Peruvian family. It is, after all, a secular organization, unrestrained by government ties, increasingly financed through IPPF rather than directly from USAID, and is under the direction of Peruvians. On the negative side of the ledger, the connection with the wealthy classes through the Carters and the Grañas provides grounds for criticism from those on the Left who oppose any form of population limitation.[58] In addition, for most of the critics of family-planning activities, no amount of rechanneling can ever entirely "sanitize" USAID funds, and it is common knowledge that a sizeable portion of the funding of the IPPF derives from this source. Yet another problem arises from the potentially powerful opposition of the many Peruvian doctors who derive a lucrative tax-free income from the illegal abortions they perform. Finally, there is also to be considered what might be called a certain institutional timidity resulting from job insecurity—an all-too-understandable phenomenon in an environment where good jobs are in very short supply.

On balance, the assets of APPF may well outweigh its liabilities. What is essential to the realization of APPF's potential, however, is dedicated leadership willing to speak out in public and in the halls of power in favor of an enlightened approach to population matters and to forthrightly answer those who challenge such an approach. To date, the most serious weakness of the cause of population limitation in Peru has been precisely this lack of an outspoken champion and of effective liaison between the enlightened few, on the one hand, and the wielders of power and the general public, on the other. APPF seems to hold forth more promise than any other organization for fulfilling these needs, but the promise remains unfulfilled.

Other Organizations Involved with Population

While the five groups discussed above are the only ones in Peru directly interested in family planning at present, there are several others whose activities are relevant to population change. They are likely to play important roles in any future movement toward the formation of a national population policy.

Perhaps the most obvious such organization is the official entity responsible for planning, conducting, and analyzing periodic censuses of the Peruvian population, the Oficina Nacional de Estadística y Censos (ONEC), which was formerly the Dirección Nacional de Estadística y Censos. Well-staffed with demographers, statisticians, and secretarial help, ONEC, nevertheless suffers from its status as an appendage of the Government, both in the sense that it is vulnerable to official pressures in the interpretation of its data and as regards the productivity problems endemic to the Peruvian bureaucratic establishment.

Within the Ministry of Labor, the Servicio de Recursos Humanos (SERH) is officially charged, *inter alia,* with studying the evolving relationship between the size, age distribution, and skills of the population and the country's employment opportunities and requirements.[59] Given the importance of the relationship between population growth and the supply of and demand for labor, SERH should be in a position to provide invaluable inputs into the population policy formation process. Associated with both SERH and the Ministry of Labor is a sophisticated survey research center, the Centro de Investigaciones de Mano de Obra (CIMO), which was formerly the Centro de Investigaciones Sociales por Muestreo (CISM). Set up in 1964 with the assistance of USAID and the University of Michigan's Survey Research Center, CIMO has carried out a number of KAP-type surveys in both Lima and the provinces and is said to have amassed some of the most reliable data of this nature in Latin America.[60] The importance of such information for policy makers can scarcely be overstated.

The Instituto Nacional de Planificación (INP), an extremely influential group within the present government, has perforce confronted the interplay of Peru's rapid rate of population growth and its realistic possibilities for economic development and has unequivocally stated the need for a national population policy as a fundamental component of the country's developmental plans.[61] Unfortunately, however, the Population Unit which functioned within the INP during 1971 was dissolved in 1972.

An Instituto de Estudios de Población was formed by interested faculty members at the Universidad Peruana Cayetano Heredia (UPCH) in 1969.[62] In spite of the encouragement of the Population Council, however, the Institute has remained largely a "paper" organization.[63] This is the more regrettable in this case, for the exceptionally professional atmosphere of this particular university and its outstanding array of available talent would seem to have assured the success of such an institute. Another university group with significant potential for contributing to the informational base as well as to recommendations necessary for the formulation of a population policy congruent with the needs of Peru is the Centro de Investigaciones Sociales, Económicas, Políticas, y Antropológicas (CISEPA), the social science research arm of Lima's Universidad Católica. Although only minimal specific interest in population presently exists at CISEPA, its impressive complement of competent social scientists and its commitment to modern research techniques augur well for the contributions it could make once such an interest were evolved.[64]

There are other groups with currently tenuous or nonexistent connections to population change in Peru which may eventually participate in the formulation of a national population policy. They include such governmental agencies as:

1. The Oficina Nacional de Desarrollo de los Pueblos Jovenes (Sistema Nacional de Apoyo a la Movilización Social).
2. The Oficina Nacional de Desarrollo de Cooperativas (Sistema Nacional de Apoyo a la Movilización Social).
3. The Oficina Sectorial de Planificación Agraria (Ministerio de Agricultura).
4. The Dirección General de Asistencia Social (Ministerio de Salud).
5. The Dirección General de Servicios Integrados de Salud (Ministerio de Salud).
6. The Oficina de Planeamiento Sectorial (Ministerio de Educación).

In addition, such private organizations as Acción Comunitaria del Perú, Acción para el Desarrollo, Centro de Estudios y Promoción del Desarrollo

(DESCO), Instituto de Estudios Peruanos, El Colegio de Abogados, El Colegio de Economistas, and El Colegio Médico should not be overlooked as possible contributors to a future population policy in Peru.

CONCLUSIONS

The organizational infrastructure for population policy formation in Peru, while rudimentary, is far from nonexistent. In fact, in spite of their haphazard and completely uncoordinated beginnings, it would seem that the organizations just described have been reasonably successful in laying a solid foundation upon which the initial stage of a viable population policy could now be erected. The information they have generated and diffused; the interest and concern for population matters they have stirred up; and the special skills they have helped to develop are all indispensable to the formulation and implementation of an adequate population policy. What still is lacking, however, is a person or group which can provide overall leadership in a concerted drive for the adoption of an explicit population policy by the Peruvian Government. Such leadership, to be optimally effective, would almost certainly have to come from Peruvians untainted by excessive contact with either the United States or the local oligarchy. Preferably it should emanate from professionals whose competence and relative disinterestedness are widely acknowledged. Ideally it would come from someone or some group whose patriotism and concern for the Peruvian masses are beyond question. It would, moreover, have to be aggressive and tenacious in advancing and defending the cause of the state's obligation to insure every couple's right to access to family planning; yet its efforts would probably be counterproductive were it not discreet and pliant in its approach. These exacting requirements make it clear why such leadership is not readily forthcoming, but in its absence it does not seem likely that the potential of the organizational infrastructure that has been so laboriously developed can be realized.

Another missing prerequisite for the formulation of a Peruvian population policy with any pretentions to comprehensiveness is the active support of a "critical mass" of local elites, particularly those within such key agencies as the Instituto Nacional de Planificación. As has been shown in other developing areas, the adoption of a national population policy depends in no small way on the extent to which the country's demographic conditions are perceived by influential experts as negatively associated with economic development.[65] If the sample of 81 Peruvian influentials that I studied was at all representative, such perceptions are neither very clearly nor very strongly held by Peru's *clases dirigentes*. [66]

In a general way, the uneven and often imperceptible movement toward the formulation of an official population policy in Peru has followed what seems to be the usual path. As improved censuses provide a better picture of the country's demographic realities, a few important individuals begin to question the conventional wisdom that population growth is an unqualified good. Contact with these influentials is quickly established by representatives of foreign and international agencies interested in promoting family planning and improved understanding of population dynamics. Both by familiarizing these individuals with the processes and implications of population dynamics through participation in international conferences, seminars, and workshops and by assuring them that financial support will be forthcoming if they create institutionalized mechanisms for employing it in population-related activities, these external agencies significantly shorten the lag time between the initial recognition of the problematic aspects of population growth and the establishment of formal means for dealing with population-related problems. Because the individuals who first become sensitized to population-related problems are often medical doctors and because the thrust of most external agencies is toward family planning, the first organizations in the population field are likely to be private family-planning clinics, usually encapsulated in a health-oriented program. Soon, however, the need for a broader approach and for more information on the interrelations between population and other socio-economic variables in the particular context at hand gives rise to the formation of a study or research group with the specific responsibility of investigating the effects of the country's demographic circumstances on national goals. Again the availability of external funds can be assumed to play a catalytic role in bringing such groups into being. It is not unlikely, moreover, that external diplomatic pressures also contribute to the creation of such organizations, which usually are to some extent or another official entities. On the basis of the country-specific information generated by these local study groups and the increase in expertise fostered by their fellowship and exchange programs, the possibilities for devising realistic population policy measures are heightened. Moreover, the political feasibility of such measures is enhanced by the educational and publicity activities of these official or semi-official groups as well as by the public and media response to the private action programs already in existence. Eventually the most influential advisers of the government, who in most cases are the economic planners, explicitly recognize the advantages for achieving economic development goals inherent in lower rates of population increase. At that point forthright adoption of population-influencing policies becomes primarily a question of the government's perception of the strength of its position *vis-à-vis* other power contenders within the political system, a perception which clearly depends on a host of system-specific considerations, such as the extent to which public support really matters to the regime, the nature of previous statements by the regime on population issues, the position of opposition groups on population questions, the nature and number of other issues pressing for attention, the state of relations with foreign powers with which population limitation programs are closely associated in the public eye, etc.

Peru's passage along this general trajectory of population policy development in Latin America seems to have been stymied at the point where the government's advisers add their weight to the case being advanced by private or semi-official groups for reduction in the rate of population increase, although, as the information reported in this chapter indicates, the case against unrestrained population growth is being only weakly made in Peru even by private and semi-official groups. It is clear, however, that some of the government's advisers are aware in a general way of the problematic implications of the country's rapid population growth,[67] although few of them seem cognizant of the intimacy of the interplay between demographic variables and the process of development, and none has displayed any sense of urgency regarding the need for fertility reduction as a vital aspect of the country's development program. This lack of insight into the importance of the population limitation component of developmental efforts, in combination with the sheer immensity of the task which the Peruvian military have set for themselves, helps to explain why nothing has yet been done at an official level to meet the population challenge in Peru.

In addition to these intellectual and practical obstacles to action on the part of the Peruvian government to reduce population growth rates, there are, of course, several strictly political constraints. The military are extremely anxious to avoid open invitations to conflict with either the far right or the far left,[68] both of which oppose the idea of population limitation, albeit for widely differing reasons. The ruling officers want the cooperation of these elements wherever possible and thus are unwilling to antagonize them (or to offer them a rallying point about which their warring factions might unite) unless the issue involved is deemed of central importance to "the revolution." Similarly Peru's military leaders are highly sensitive to the possibility that any involvement in fertility control programs on their part might be construed as acquiescence to pressures from the United States. Given the regime's firmly nationalistic stance, heightened by the strained relations between Lima and Washington over the expropriation of the International Petroleum Company and the fining of North American boats fishing in Peruvian coastal waters, any charges that Peru might be going along with the United States designs to limit the populations of Third World countries would be profoundly embarrassing if not severely damaging to the regime. Finally it bears pointing out that, faced with the unavoidable necessity of choosing only a limited number of priorities from amongst the bewildering array of matters vying for their attention, the military rulers, like their civilian predecessors, respond preferentially to the best organized and most strongly formulated demands. As it has been the object of this chapter to show, the cause of population policy lacks a determined and outspoken champion in Peru, hence it has yet to reach a priority status on the generals' agenda.

As Peru's economic situation becomes tighter (which it seems sure to do, at least for the next year or two), as relations with the United States become strained (which they recurrently do, *inter alia*, because of our refusal to recognize Peru's claims to 200 miles of territorial waters), and as more and more demands compete for scarce government resources (which, alas, is inherent in the process of economic development), the political obstacles to the adoption of an official population policy in Peru can hardly be expected to disappear.

Academic and ideological debates persist as to whether Peru's ruling military government is reformist or revolutionary, bent on modernizing an inefficient capitalist system or on radically restructuring it. The spokesmen for the regime have repeatedly insisted that their objective is to promote their country's development pragmatically, imitating neither communist nor capitalist models but adhering to Christian ideals and Western humanistic values. Obviously the regime is not as revolutionary as its rhetoric, but the actions, policies, and programs of the past three years have amply demonstrated that whatever its shortcomings, it is genuinely oriented toward improving the lot of the Peruvian masses. This being so, the incorporation of family planning into official maternal-child health programs—one small component of an explicit population policy—would seem eminently congruent with the regime's resolve to widen the scope of the individual's control over his or her life. That this has not yet been done attests to the profound degree to which population considerations have been and continue to be the missing dimension in Third World analyses of the *problematique* of development.

NOTES TO CHAPTER 15

1. J. Mayone Stycos, *Human Fertility in Latin America: Sociological Perspectives* (Ithaca, N.Y.: Cornell University Press, 1968), pp. 53-54.
2. Growth rate from Population Reference Bureau, Inc., 1972 World Population Data Sheet. For analyses of internal migration see Hector Martínez, "Las migraciones internas en el Perú," *Estudios de Población y Desarrollo* (Lima), 2, No. 1 (1968); an expanded version of which may be found in *Aportes* (Paris), No. 10 (October, 1968), pp. 136-160; J. Oscar Alers and Richard P. Appelbaum, "La migración en el Perú: un inventario de proposiciones," *Estudios de Población y Desarrollo* (Lima), Vol. 1, No. 4 (1968); and Stella Lowder, "Lima's Population Growth and the Consequences for Peru," pp. 21-34 cited in Bryan Roberts and Stella Lowder, *Urban Population Growth and Migration in Latin America: Two Case Studies* (Liverpool: Center for Latin American Studies, Monograph Series No. 2, 1970). A significant indirect measure was the creation of a study group, the Centro de Estudios de Población y Desarrollo, by the Belaúnde administration in December of 1964. See José Donayre, "Research Planned by the Center of Studies of Population and Development in Peru," *The Milbank Memorial Fund Quarterly*, XLVI, No. 3, Part 2 (July, 1968), pp. 155-163.

3. See Carlos A. Astiz, *Pressure Groups and Power Elites in Peruvian Politics* (Ithaca and London: Cornell University Press, 1969), pp. 113-114.
4. See Chapter IV, "The Displacement of Conflicts," in E.E. Schattschneider, *The Semisovereign People: A Realist's View of Democracy in America* (New York: Holt, Rinehart and Winston, 1960).
5. See "Opposition to Population Limitation in Latin America: Some Implications for U.S. Policy," chapt. 5 of Richard L. Clinton and R. Kenneth Godwin, eds., *Research in the Politics of Population* (Lexington, Mass.: D.C. Heath & Company, 1972), pp. 99-100.
6. Council on Higher Education in the American Republics, *Demography and the University: The State of Population Studies in Latin America* (New York: Institute of International Education, 1969), pp. 3, 4, 16-17.
7. Suzanne Aurelius and Ulf Borell, *Family Planning in Latin America,* Swedish International Development Agency Field Tour Report (1969), mention the Asociación Peruana de Protección Familiar, El Instituto Marcelino and the Christian Family Movement. See the excellent description of current efforts by Thomas G. Sanders, "Family Planning in Peru," American Universities Field Staff Reports, West Coast South America Series, XVII, No. 6 (April, 1970), p. 5, who notes in addition to the above groups the informal and peripheral family planning activities of the Church World Service. The present study will deal with these groups in some detail below.
8. Interview with Dr. John V.D. Saunders, Professor of Sociology at the University of Florida and formerly with the Ford Foundation in Lima, in Gainesville, Florida, on December 30, 1969. Interview with Mr. Clifford Belcher, USAID official in Lima, Peru, May 5, 1970. Interview with Dr. Félix Pérez Lagos, Ministry of Health official, in Lima, Peru, May 18, 1970.
9. Letter to the author from J.V.D. Saunders dated November 17, 1969. See also Aurelius and Borell, *Family Planning . . .,* pp. 39-42.
10. The Peruvian military's role as "defender of upper-class interests," particularly during the Twentieth Century, is emphasized by Liisa North, *Civil-Military Relations in Argentina, Chile, and Peru* (Berkeley, Cal.: Institute of International Studies, University of California, 1966), p. 24.
11. José Nun, "The Middle-Class Military Coup," pp. 66-118 in Claudio Véliz, ed., *The Politics of Conformity in Latin America* (London: Oxford University Press, 1967), provides the most perceptive analysis of the changed complexion of the Latin American military to appear to date. See also Eric A. Nordlinger, "Soldiers in Mufti: The Impact of Military Rule Upon Economic and Social Change in the Non-Western States," *American Political Science Review,* LXIV, No. 4 (December, 1970), pp. 1131-1148.
12. For a discussion of the conditions which gave rise to this altered outlook toward change and a tentative analysis of the character of this regime,

see my "The Modernizing Military: The Case of Peru," *Inter-American Economic Affairs*, 24, No. 4 (Spring, 1971), pp. 43-66. For a contrary interpretation from the Marxist perspective see Aníbal Quijano, "Nationalism and Capitalism in Peru: A Study in Neo-Imperialism," *Monthly Review*, 23, No. 3 (July-August, 1971), pp. 1-122.

13. Interview with Dr. Alberto Arca Parró in Lima, Peru, on June 2, 1970.
14. Leonel Alvarez Leiva, "Proyecciones de la población peruana," *I-Seminario Nacional de Población y Desarrollo, Paracas, Diciembre 5-11, 1965, Documentos*, p. 99.
15. Interview with Dr. Alberto Arca Parró in Lima, Peru, on July 27, 1970. A brief but insightful analysis of the positions and clientele of Lima's major newspapers is given by Christopher Roper, "Peru's Longstanding Problems," *The World Today* (London) 25, No. 6 (June, 1969), pp. 249-250.
16. "Evolución de la población en el período intercensal 1940-1961," *I-Seminario : . .*, pp. 67-96.
17. *Ibid.*, pp. 69 and 79.
18. Personal communication from former President Fernando Belaúnde Terry, May 8, 1969.
19. See report of the United Nations Population Commission, December 18, 1962 (mimeo), excerpts of which appear in Stycos, *Human Fertility . . .*, pp. 39-40 and 46.
20. In addition to Dr. Muñoz Torcello, who served as Vice President of CEPD's board of directors during its crucial first year and subsequently as its President, and to Dr. Arias Stella, Minister of Health and Social Assistance under Belaúnde, Dr. Arca Parró mentioned Frank Griffiths Escardó, Minister of Labor and Indian Affairs under Belaúnde, as one of the prime movers in CEPD's creation. In fact, he states that Arias Stella and Griffiths Escardó were responsible for inviting knowledgeable persons to draft the document which later served as the basis for the decree which created CEPD. Alberto Arca Parró, "Discurso del Presidente del Centro de Estudios de Población y Desarrollo," *I-Seminario . . .*, p. xii.
21. Dr. Arias Stella, for instance, attended a conference on the IUD in New York in 1964 under the auspices of The Population Council, and Dr. Orfelia Mendoza of IPPF was deeply involved with the efforts to bring CEPD into being. John W. Morse, the USAID population officer in Lima at that time, also worked long and hard in getting CEPD under way. The Ford Foundation was the original source of funding for CEPD. (Interview with Dr. Clifford Pease of The Population Council, formerly a USAID official in Peru, in Chapel Hill, N.C., on March 18, 1971). See also the summary review of family planning activities in Peru by Deborah Larned, "Birth Control in Peru—A Quiet Revolution," *Andean Air Mail and Peruvian Times* (Lima), February 26, 1971, p. 7.
22. Sanders, "Family Planning in Peru," p. 2.

23. Donayre, "Research Planned . . .," p. 157.
24. For Chile see Drs. Rolando Armijo and Tegualda Monreal, "Factores asociados a las complicaciones del aborto provocado," *Revista Chilena de Obstetricia y Ginecología,* XCI (April, 1963); "Epidemiología del aborto en Santiago," *Revista Medica Panamericana,* X, (August, 1963), pp. 221-224, an expanded version of which appears in English as "Epidemiology of Provoked Abortion in Santiago, Chile," *Journal of Sex Research,* 1, No. 5 (July, 1965), pp. 143-159; and "The Problem of Induced Abortion in Chile," *The Milbank Memorial Fund Quarterly,* XLIII, No. 4, Part 2 (October, 1965), pp. 263-280. Iêda Siqueira Wiarda, *Family Planning Activities in a Democratic Context: The Case of Venezuela* (n.p., published privately, December, 1970), p. 149; Chapter 14 in the present volume documents the Venezuelan experience.
25. Donayre, "Research Planned . . .," p. 158.
26. Sanders, "Family Planning in Peru," p. 2.
27. Donayre, "Research Planned . . .," p. 161.
28. According to Deborah Larned, "Birth Control in Peru . . .," p. 10, CEPD received 20 percent of its funds from the Peruvian Government, with 40 percent coming from USAID and 40 percent from the Ford Foundation. The proportions vary, of course, from one fiscal year to another, and in 1973 it is hoped that the United Nations Fund for Population Activities (UNFPA) will begin to provide the bulk of CEPD's financing.
29. Donayre, "Research Planned . . .," p. 156.
30. Interview with Mr. Richard Frohmader, director of CWS, in Lima, Peru, on May 22, 1970.
31. Sanders, "Family Planning in Peru," p. 5, gives the present CWS director's estimate of approximately 5,000 women currently using CWS-provided contraceptives.
32. Interview with Dr. Jorge Campos Rey de Castro in Lima, Peru, on July 21, 1970. Dr. Campos was largely responsible for the successful organization of a new medical school within the Universidad Nacional Mayor de San Marcos after that faculty was torn asunder by the university strife of 1961.
33. Interview with Dr. Steban Kesserü in Lima, Peru, on May 21, 1970.
34. Interview with Dr. Alfredo Larrañaga in Lima, Peru, on May 28, 1970.
35. Letter to the author from Dr. Carlos Alfaro-Alvarez, Executive Director, Asociación Peruana de Protección Familiar, dated December 20, 1972.
36. See, for example, Clorinda Matto de Turner, *Aves sin nido* (Cuzco: Universidad Nacional de Cuzco, 1948); Enrique López Albújar, *Cuentos andinos* (Lima: Librería-Editorial Juan Mejía Baca, 1965); and Ciro Alegría, *El mundo es ancho y ajeno* (Santiago: Ediciones Ercilla, 1941).
37. A recent and all-too-typical statement of the leftist view of the rationale for capitalist sponsorship of population limitation appeared in the

Lima daily *Expreso* on August 6, 1972, under the signature of a respected young law professor, Luís Pásara:

> ... the interest of these "generous donors" in such programs is as clear as water. The high rate of population increase in the underdeveloped countries helps to demonstrate that the real situation of most of these countries within the capitalist orbit is not one of development as we are told but of increasing underdevelopment.... Fertility control, while not resolving the exploitation which causes this underdevelopment, at least is seen as a way of keeping the situation from becoming uncontainable.

38. Larned, "Birth Control in Peru ...," p. 8.
39. Sanders, "Family Planning in Peru," p. 3, and Larned, "Birth Control in Peru ...," p. 8.
40. Interview with Dr. Guillermo Tagliebue of MFC in Lima, Peru, on June 1, 1970.
41. Sanders, "Family Planning in Peru," p. 4.
42 Interview with Dr. Clifford Pease of The Population Council and formerly of USAID in Peru in Chapel Hill, N.C., on March 18, 1971.
43. Interview with Father Enrique Bartra in Lima, Peru, on July 11, 1970.
44. Agostino Bono, "Birth Control in Peru I," *Latinamerica Press* (Lima), 1, No. 77 (December 19, 1969), p. 2A; Larned, "Birth Control in Peru ...," p. 10.
45. Larned, *op. cit.*, p. 10.
46. For two examples of this sort of reporting see Bono, "Birth Control in Peru I," and Larned, "Birth Control in Peru ..."
47. It was repeatedly pointed out to me that the Cardinal Archbishop himself is favorably inclined toward the work of MFC, and Monsignor Luis Bambarén, "the Bishop of the Barriadas", also is known to approve thoroughly of MFC.
48. Interview with Dr. Carlos Alfaro, Executive Director of APPF, in Lima, Peru, on May 25, 1970.
49. Sanders, "Family Planning in Peru," p. 3.
50. Alfaro, interview of May 25, 1970.
51. Pease, interview of March 18, 1971.
52. For the first two years of its existence, APPF had not met IPPF requirements as a national organization. Aurelius and Borell, "Family Planning in Latin America," p. 41. USAID gave $30,000 from July to December, 1969, and $160,000 for 1970, according to Dr. Alfaro and confirmed by Clifford Belcher of USAID-Peru, interviews of May 25, 1970, and May 5, 1970, respectively.
53. Alfaro, letter dated December 20, 1972.
54. See, for example, Bono, "Birth Control in Peru I," and Larned, "Birth Control in Peru ..."
55. Alfaro, interview of May 25, 1970.
56. See *APPF* (Lima), No. 3 (diciembre de 1970), pp. 1–8.
57. Wiarda, *Family Planning Activities ...*, pp. 58–124.
58. Ing. Graña resigned the presidency of APPF in late 1970 but was succeeded by another prominent man, Dr. Genaro Ferreyros Falen. Daniel

Carter, a North American and a businessman, and his wife, a member of one of Peru's most distinguished and well-to-do families, continue to play important roles in APPF through their positions on its Board of Directors. Interview with Mr. and Mrs. Daniel Carter in Lima, Peru, on June 21, 1970.
59. Interviews with Sr. Alberto Insúa, Director General of SERH, and with Sr. Francisco Codina, Assistant Director of SERH, in Lima, Peru, on June 9, 1970.
60. Interview with Dr. Albert M. Marckwardt, Chief of Party, USAID-University of Michigan Sample Survey Project, in Lima, Peru, on June 9, 1970, and letter to the author from Dr. Donald P. Warwick, Department of Social Relations, Harvard University, formerly of USAID in Peru, dated November 10, 1969.
61. Interview with Dr. Carlos Delgado, Social Science Coordinator, INP, in Lima, Peru, on June 23, 1970. See Instituto Nacional de Planificación, "Lineamientos básicos de política de desarrollo a mediano plazo," March, 1970, (mimeo). Pages 15-18 of this 96-page document deal with population. There was, however, a distinct toning down of certain statements and phrasings relative to population in the final version approved by the cabinet. In describing Peru's rate of population growth, for instance, the word *acelerado* was substituted for *explosivo* and, in general, the sense of urgency regarding the need for a population policy which was explicit in the original draft was absent in the final form of the document. I am grateful to Dr. Abraham F. Lowenthal, Acting Representative of the Ford Foundation in Peru, for alerting me to these suggestive differences. See Gregory F. Treverton, Ford Foundation Inter-Office memorandum dated May 22, 1970.
62. Interview with Dr. Carlos López Cre, Director, Hospital Rimac (the hospital of the UPCH Medical School), in Lima, Peru, on May 20, 1970, and with Dr. Leopoldo Chiappo, Vice Rector and Chairman of the Department of Humanities and Social Sciences of the UPCH, in Lima, Peru, on July 14, 1970.
63. Pease, interview of March 18, 1971.
64. Interview with Dr. Jorge Capriata, Director of CISEPA, in Lima, Peru, on June 15, 1970.
65. See, for instance, Gayl D. Ness and Hirofumi Ando, "The Politics of Population Planning in Malaysia and the Philippines," *Journal of Comparative Administration,* 3, No. 3 (November, 1971), pp. 296-329.
66. Richard Lee Clinton, *Problems of Population Policy Formation in Peru* (Chapel Hill: Carolina Population Center Population Program and Policy Design Series: No. 4, 1971), pp. 113-115.
67. Carlos Delgado and Leopoldo Chiappo, for example.
68. Interview with General Oscar Vargas Prieto, Contralador General de la República, in Lima, Peru, on July 24, 1972.

Chapter Sixteen

A Paradigmatic Analysis of Mexican Population Policy*

Terry L. McCoy

The purpose of this undertaking is to describe and analyze Mexican public policy regarding fertility and population growth. Neither the policy nor the organized interests associated with it differ on the surface from their counterparts in other Latin American countries. In the early 1970's there was a change in national policy that apparently reflected growing antinatalist pressures. However, instead of quietly abandoning traditional policy in favor of discreet public support for limited family-planning and related measures, the Mexican government abruptly reversed its adamant pronatalist position in favor of a comprehensive national family-planning effort with demographic objectives. Careful comparison of the facts of population policy-making with general models or paradigms of Mexican politics suggests a plausible explanation for this dramatic "flip-flop." It also tends to confirm one particular paradigm.[1] The findings of this case study are relevant to understanding not only Mexican policy-making but also the population policies of other countries with similar political characteristics, namely Peru and Brazil, which have not yet abandoned pronatalism.

ENVIRONMENT, POLICY, AND PROCESS

The Problem

Due to declining mortality and relatively stable fertility, Mexico's annual average rate of population growth jumped from 1.7 percent in 1930-

---

*This chapter has been prepared originally for this volume. Financial assistance from the Mershon Center of The Ohio State University enabled the author to conduct field research in Mexico City during Summer 1971. While there he benefitted from the cooperation of numerous individuals and institutions. In addition, the reactions of Eli Bergman, Robert Bezdek, David Chaplin, William Liddle, Susan Purcell, and Philip Stewart to an earlier draft were helpful in the preparation of this version for which the author alone is responsible.

1940 to 3.4 percent in 1960-1970.[2] Accompanying the "population explosion" was an "implosion" of massive rural-to-urban migration.

Aside from the fact that its rate of growth has been slightly higher than the Latin American average,[3] the Mexican situation has attracted special attention for three reasons. First, with 50 million people Mexico is a large country, the second most populous in Latin America, of potential world significance. Its current growth rate could produce a total population of 200 million in less than fifty years. Secondly, observers are interested in the interplay between Mexico's population growth and its economic growth. For over two decades it has sustained a rate of economic expansion unique in Latin America. It may be that the Mexican "economic miracle" diverted attention from the Mexican population explosion. Recently, however, the economic situation has ceased to appear so rosy. A 1971 decline in the rate of overall economic growth resulted in little growth in per capita income, when combined with population growth, and increasing attention is focused on the uneven distribution of wealth in Mexico.[4] Finally, there is interest in how a country which has undergone a major revolution copes with rapid population growth.

The History of Mexican Population Policy

Modern Mexican political history begins in 1917 with the adoption of a new constitution, an event signaling the triumph of the revolution which had begun in 1910. After 1917 politics and public policy centered on "institutionalization" of the Mexican Revolution, one of the genuine socio-economic upheavals of this century. Early in the institutional phase of the revolution, the government permitted the initiation of private family-plannning centers. Under President Calles in the 1920's, private clinics opened with government approval.[5] But shortly thereafter official attitudes shifted so that by the 1930's pronatalism was the guiding principle of national policy. Several factors help explain this emphasis, which held sway until 1972. The violence of the revolution, lasting almost a decade, had taken a tremendous toll in human lives, and general mortality rates in the 1920's remained rather high, thus holding overall growth down. Mortality began to drop rapidly after 1930,[6] but its negative implications did not occur to Mexican demographers and government officials until some three decades later. Furthermore, in the pre-World War II period population growth was almost universally perceived as an asset, not a liability, to development. Virtually by definition a growing population was part and parcel of national development. Therefore, when Mexican policy-makers became aware of their country's rapid population growth, they were not alarmed but gratified. In addition, nationalism nurtured the notion that Mexico must be large to be great. This feeling was given special urgency by proximity to and the history of stormy relations with the United States. During the 1920's and 1930's, the country's leading demographer argued that rapid population growth was necessary to protect Mexico from external threats, particularly those to its sparsely populated north.[7]

The above combination of factors combined to create a pronatalist bias in the institutional revolutionary regime. What were the specific instruments of its policy? In 1947 the government passed the General Law of Population which called for accelerated population growth through a combination of natural means and immigration and which enumerated various measures designed to encourage population growth.[8] Beyond this general codification of government policy, there were other measures of a positive nature. Although pronatalism may not have been its original motivation, Article 123 of the 1917 Constitution provides for certain substantive rights regarding salaries and family allowances that were in practice interpreted to reward large families.[9] On the negative side, the government used the Sanitary Code and laws governing the manufacture and distribution of drugs to restrict the use of artificial contraceptives and discourage family planning. Into the 1970's birth control devices could not be purchased without a prescription—a regulation violated by those with the knowledge and money to afford them—nor could family-planning services be advertised. Combined with the general commitment to accelerate population growth, then, the Mexican policy sought to deter individual couples from limiting the size of their families. As is typically the case in Latin America, this policy most strongly affected lower class couples who could not satisfy their needs with the commercially available oral contraceptives that inevitably creeped on to the Mexican market in the 1960's despite existing legal restrictions.

Throughout the 1960's as pressures grew on developing nations to do something about their exploding populations, the Mexican government aggressively defended its pronatalism and refused to sanction or sponsor organized family planning. The successful presidential candidate of the revolutionary coalition in 1970 rejected the need to control the rate of population growth. Then in April, 1972, it was announced that his government would undertake a national "responsible parenthood" campaign, the essence of which is the massive diffusion of family-planning services throughout the nation with an underlying objective of slowing growth. We shall examine this new policy in more detail later; first we must equip ourselves to understand its sudden, unexpected appearance.

Paradigms of Mexican Politics

In one sense students of Mexican public policy are fortunate, since widespread interest in the revolution (combined with proximity to the United States) has resulted in numerous descriptions of the political process, some even formulated in terms of policy analysis.[10] But these studies do not always agree on the basic character of Mexican politics. Consequently, in interpreting a specific policy or set of decisions, the researcher must choose among the competing paradigms to structure his analysis and fill in the empirical gaps with theoretical probabilities. At the current stage of development in the study of Mexican politics, most of the literature falls into two general paradigms—the pluralist and the authoritarian—that, while not mutually exclusive, still characterize the same political system differently.[11]

All serious observers recognize the gap between the democratic ideals of the 1917 Constitution and the actual operation of government in which certain institutions and individuals, namely PRI (Institutional Revolutionary Party) and the president play disproportionately influential roles. Nevertheless, scholars such as Scott and Padgett characterize Mexican politics as increasingly responsive to a plurality of organized interest.[12] Instead of policy being shaped by the open competition of parties and interest groups through elections and legislative lobbying, interest articulation and aggregation take place within PRI and, most importantly, the presidency. Their point is that allowing for the peculiar institutional arrangement, a variety of interest group pluralism exists in Mexico. Organized interests not only exist, but they also successfully intervene in policy-making. Padgett summarizes the process as follows: "The President, and recently the Institutionalized Office of the President, must balance the competing demands coming from these various sources and develop overall policies generally acceptable to the articulate elements of the system."[13] Scott's central thesis is that Mexico is evolving a Western-style democratic pluralism.

> Despite obvious weaknesses in this governing system [at this stage in its evolution], it does seem to take into account all of the principal and most active interest groups and associations when the highest public officers are being selected and when major policy questions are decided. Moreover, the political system is flexible enough to permit access of new groups and associations representing developing interests which grow out of changes in the social and economic environment.[14]

While no one, except official propagandists, characterize the present Mexican political system as pluralist and democratic, there is a school that sees such a system emerging. Furthermore, during the transitional phase, autonomous interest groups do interact with each other, the PRI, and the presidency to effectively influence policy. According to this paradigm, then, a shift in population policy would result primarily from the interaction of organized interests.

Recently a number of works have appeared in English and Spanish to challenge the notions that the revolutionary regime is either democratic in its process or progressive in its policies.[15] They join a growing body of literature which rejects the conclusion that Latin American political development is inevitably moving toward democracy.[16] Revisionist authors look at contemporary Latin America and see a pluralist facade covering an authoritarian core. Johnson charges that the "esoteric" democracy of Mexico is in fact an authoritarian process manipulated by a privileged elite. He refers to the PRI as an "organized dominant class"—in pursuit of narrow self interests.[17] Hansen warns that the apparent plurality of interests is misleading since:

> The official party is used by the Revolutionary Coalition to control Mexican politics at two levels. At the first level the PRI is used as a mechanism to attain majorities in . . . elections.
> At the second it is used to control the various sectors of the party itself; the PRI structure provides access to large organized groups which can furnish the party with electoral majorities without granting those groups anything that could be reasonably labeled effective representation.[18]

At the same time political participation has been extended, it has been carefully controlled. The revolutionary regime is even willing to resort to repression, as it did in 1968 before the Olympic Games and again in 1971, to maintain control over a political process that, in contrast to the rhetoric of the revolution, has enriched the few and ignored the many. In summary, then, the Mexican system is authoritarian with no evidence of countervailing trends.

Susan Kaufman Purcell has elaborated on the authoritarian paradigm of Mexican politics as applied to policy analysis. Her model originates with Juan Linz who argues that authoritarianism is more than just a gradation of totalitarianism or democracy. Authoritarian regimes are distinct with distinctive ways of performing the functions common to all political systems.[19] Purcell asserts that the institutional revolutionary regime satisfies the basic elements of authoritarianism. First, there is *limited political pluralism* in which organized interest groups exist but they are more tied to and dependent on the regime than under democracy. Even those groups not functionally part of PRI, which is also governed by the dynamics of limited pluralism, are not really independent of the regime according to Purcell's model. Secondly, Mexican politics feature *low subject mobilization* with participation limited to demonstrations of support for the regime. Certainly serious opposition is not tolerated. The PRI rarely receives less than 80 percent of the vote in national elections, and, between 1935 and 1961, an average of 84 percent of all legislative bills sent to the Chamber of Deputies by the executive received unanimous approval.[20] Thirdly, the Mexican president stands at the apex of a modern variation of *patrimonial rulership*. He is the benevolent patron who takes care of his people and who is beyond criticism. Fourthly, although not a prerequisite of authoritarian regimes, Mexico does have a high degree of *elite consensus* centering on glorification of the institutional revolution. Its specific themes include nationalism, constitutionalism, economic development, and social justice.[21]

The authoritarian paradigm does not exclude organized interests. Rather it defines their role differently, putting emphasis on the indirect nature of their influence and their mobilization in support of regime decisions. Specifically, according to this model, we would expect population policy to reflect an erratic relationship between official decisions and group demands because of limited pluralism and the low level of explicit demands; absence of horizontal alliances among groups and of direct confrontation due to patrimonial rulership; yet somewhat innovative decisions because of the "revolutionary" aspect of the elite consensus.[22]

We shall now examine the facts of the population case in light of the two paradigms. Our analysis must be regarded as tentative and demanding of subsequent confirmation since information on policy decisions is not readily accessible.[23] Nevertheless, it seems worth undertaking in order both to explain the dynamics of population policy in Latin America's second largest country and to evaluate competing interpretations of Mexican policy-making. In regard to this latter task the point has been made elsewhere that advancement of our general understanding will come from turning to "intensive examination of limited aspects of Mexican politics, selected for their strategic linkage with already existing theory."[24] What we are particularly interested in here is the role of interest groups and their interaction with the presidency in the making of population policy.

THE INTEREST GROUP SUBSYSTEM

Support for the pluralist paradigm appears in the form of a full spectrum of population-related interest groups, not unlike those found in other countries. Here we want to survey the interest group subsystem, paying particular attention to how its component parts behave in the Mexican context and the impact of their actions.

Private Family Planning Associations

Our inventory begins with consideration of the advocates of family planning and population control, since they are typically better organized than the opponents. Crucial to the antinatalist effort in virtually every Latin American nation are private family-planning associations, those organizations which have as their main purpose the advocacy of public programs of voluntary fertility control.[25] In addition to serving as the organizational umbrella for the supporters of family planning, local associations usually initiate a wide variety of services designed to meet existing needs and generate pressure for government action. Mexico has two private family-planning associations. The differences between them is instructive of how interest groups must adjust to the peculiar rules of Mexican politics in order to be effective.

The Maternal Health Association (Asociación Pro-Salud Maternal) was founded in 1959 as one of the first private family-planning groups in

Latin America, and for several years the only organization providing contraceptive and related services in Mexico. At its peak in the mid-1960's, the Association had one large and five small clinics in Mexico City, plus a clinic in Monterrey and four rural centers.[26] Beyond offering family-planning services to the public, it pioneered medical research on oral contraceptives, building up a very good longitudinal data set.[27] Its staff presented papers at professional conferences all over the world, while pharmaceutical companies sought out the Association for contract research. Between 1965 and 1970, the Association trained over 500 medical and paramedical personnel who are today active in population/family planning throughout Latin America.[28] As the first to raise the banner of family planning, the Association suffered a great deal of abuse from the opponents of anything suggesting population control. The government even closed its clinics at one point.[29]

No one can deny the Association's contribution as a trailblazer; yet it was never accepted as a legitimate participant in policy-making. By the end of 1970 it was clearly in decline. Due to vanishing foundation support and the necessity of relying almost totally on contracted research, the Association was forced to consolidate its activities into one clinic and abolish its courses.[30]

Possible explanations for the Association's relatively low efficacy all relate to the fact that it did not play by the rules of Mexican politics. In the first place, it was foreign, founded by a North American doctor who came to Mexico to do research on oral contraceptives. Although she and her top assistants are by now long-time residents, they are still not Mexicans, and central to the revolutionary consensus is an explicit rejection of external intervention in Mexican affairs. In addition, to its strong foreign ties, the Association violated another rule by overtly challenging the government on the population issue.[31] After 1965, the Association saw its leadership in family planning gradually eroded by the newly created Foundation for Population Studies (Fundación para Estudios de la Población).

Despite its name, the Foundation is a lobby for family planning, affiliated with the International Planned Parenthood Federation (IPPF). It eclipsed the Association as the principal repository for outside money and organizational umbrella for the family-planning cause with a carefully cultivated strategy based upon an acute appreciation of Mexican politics. The Foundation's directive council is made up of influential Mexicans from business, finance, journalism, academia, and government.[a] The only foreigner on the board is Norman Borlaug, winner of the Nobel Peace Prize for his work in Mexico on the

---

[a]A key link between the Foundation and the regime was the late Gilberto Loyo, an economist-turned-demographer, former Minister of State, and long time PRI spokesman on population matters. At one time an outspoken opponent of population control in Mexico, Loyo became a supporter of family planning and joined the Foundation's directive council. PRI congressmen are also members of the council. For a resume of Loyo's views see Chapter 10 in this volume.

"miracle" grains of the Green Revolution.[32] To buttress its Mexican image, the Foundation actively solicits financial donations from local sources even though, as is the case with other Latin American family-planning associations, most of its income comes from IPPF, foreign foundation grants, and patient fees.[33] It resolutely rejected even indirect financial support from United States government agencies up until the change in government policy in 1972. Beyond simply establishing its identity as a Mexican organization, the Foundation studiously avoids any appearance of criticizing government policy or questioning the regime consensus. Rather it attempts to demonstrate how its position is compatible with both. Thus, prior to the change in government policy, it carefully stressed that "family planning" was not the same as "birth control" nor the solution to underdevelopment but the human right of determining one's own destiny.[34] The Foundation engaged in the variety of activities typical of IPPF affiliates with particular attention devoted to courses on population and family planning for opinion leaders and clinical services. In 1970 its 48 clinics received over 155,000 visits.[35]

The articulated purpose of Foundation's clinical services, some offered through public hospitals, was to reach those unable to satisfy these needs through commercial channels. The Foundation also admitted ulterior motives. "The socio-economic, demographic, and medical information which is collected in them [the clinics] will undoubtedly be a solid basis for the future planning of a state program."[36] Foundation spokesmen never denied that their organization was dedicated to achieving the enactment of public family planning, but its tactics were consciously geared to local political mores.

The Foundation encountered occasional governmental resistance. For instance, officials delayed renewing the tax exempt status of contributions to it in 1971, the same year that the Foundation was forced to close its clinic in a large state maternity hospital.[37] Generally, however, its strategy of working quietly to build support for family planning among both users and elites, while avoiding direct confrontation with the Mexican government, appears to have led to the Foundation's emergence as a leading defender of the family-planning cause. When the government decided to enact its own program it enlisted the cooperation of the Foundation, which enthusiastically accepted a reactive-supportive role.[38] Without commenting on the extent of its policy influence, which remains to be evaluated, the behavior of the Foundation seems to indicate a perception of limited pluralism in Mexico on behalf of its leadership.

Academic, Research, and Professional Groups

University, research, and professional groups constitute another source of inputs usually important in population policy-making in Latin America. Together they generate the intellectual pressure and justification for policy decisions. Mexico is no exception, though once again we find differences apparently dictated by the political process. One organization, the Colegio de México, has been particularly important in building the demographic case for government action to slow population growth. Before analyzing its role, let us briefly review some of the other groups in this category.

Unlike the situation in other countries, the Mexican medical profession did not lead the fight for family planning. Nevertheless, because of its size, prestige, and important research in reproductive physiology, it and its representative organizations contributed to the raising of population-related issues for public discussion and official consideration. For example, in 1965 the Mexican Association of Gynecology and Endocrinology sponsored a conference on contraceptives at which Dr. John Rock issued a strong appeal for a total attack on uncontrolled reproduction.[39] Other professional associations provided forums for discussion of population-related issues, and private physicians, encouraged by drug manufacturers, liberally prescribe contraceptives. Individual physicians also worked inside and outside of the government to further the cause of family planning. (There is some speculation that President Echeverría's brother, who is a doctor, may have influenced the decision to begin government family planning.)

In terms of numbers, most social scientists in Mexico are probably employed by the gigantic National Autonomous University (UNAM); yet the important social science research in population studies takes place in other institutions, a fact reflecting the lower quality of social science research at UNAM and the controversial nature of the population issue among Latin American intellectuals, many of whom are of leftist political persuasions. While UNAM now has a small population center, led by a prominent Mexican demographer, the most important research is carried out in the more insulated settings of the Mexican Institute for Social Studies or IMES (Instituto Mexicano de Estudios Sociales) and the Colegio de México. Founded in 1960, IMES is a private, nonprofit organization engaged in applied social science research. In recent years with substantial assistance from the Ford Foundation, it has focused on population-related topics, giving special attention to the family and the church.[40] Although a small organization, IMES has contributed to the population debate through its publications.[41] It carefully skirts direct policy questions, however, so as not to "destroy its credibility."[42]

The Colegio, the leading social science research and graduate training institute in Mexico, is highly respected throughout Latin America. It is also a favored recipient of grants from foreign foundations. The Colegio got into population-related research in 1964 with the creation of the Center for Economic and Demographic Studies (Centro de Estudios Económicos y Demográficos) that has as one of its objectives to "assist in the systemization of the knowledge on Mexican demography."[43] In part because of valid intellectual convictions but also because of the Colegio's special juridicial status, its directors have maintained a scrupulously nonpartisan public posture on questions of government population policy. Although it is legally autonomous, even more so than the National University, the Colegio receives substantial financial support from the government, support that the government is apparently not hesitant to reduce should the Colegio step out of line.[44] Consequently, it is very discreet about exerting influence. Nevertheless, the Colegio, through the work of the Center, affects the path of national policy in several ways. First, recipients of the Center's masters degree in demography find employment in public agencies. Second, the Colegio has increasingly stressed demographic variables in its general economic research for the government.[45] Third, the Center sponsors noncontract research and publications on population topics. As of 1971, no one on the Center's staff was doing strictly policy research although the Colegio had recently helped form a consortium of Latin American institutions to undertake such research. It publishes the journal *Demografía y Economía,* and its book, *Dinámica de la población de México,* won a national annual award in 1971 as the best book on development.[46] The book's expressed purpose was to present the facts on Mexico population since, "These are factors with important implications for those with public or private responsibility in determining ... the economic and social development of the country."[47] Fourth, the Colegio engages in a variety of miscellaneous activities that keep population in the public arena. In 1970 it co-sponsored and co-hosted a Latin American conference on population.[48] Its president, the well-known Mexican economist Victor Urquidi, is frequently quoted in the Mexican papers on population-related topics.[49] In summary, then, the influence of the Colegio is low-key but extensive. Of particular importance are the personal ties of Urquidi and others to the revolutionary coalition.

The Drug Industry

Another conceivable source of pressure for the expansion of family planning through government sponsorship is the local pharmaceutical industry. Throughout most of Latin America, oral contraceptives are widely available in pharmacies, even though legally they are to be sold only under prescription. Thus women can practice artificial contraception without going to a physician. Mexican drug manufacturers "detail" pharmacists just as they do doctors. Other somewhat unique characteristics of the Mexican pharmaceutical industry might render it particularly influential in policy-making.

Mexico is the world's leading producer of the steroids used in birth control pills, with exports to over 30 countries. Investments, overwhelmingly foreign, in their extraction and processing grew from $101.2 million in 1962 to $229 million in 1967 for total sales of $215 million 1969.[50] Peasants cultivating the root from which the steroid is extracted earn 30 pesos per day versus ten to twelve for those in the same area growing traditional crops.[51] Even though most of the product is exported, Mexican drug interests stand to benefit from the expanded local use of oral contraceptives. In point of fact, limited local consumption came early as some of the pioneer research on "orals" took place in Mexico, and, because of minimal regulations governing the testing of new drugs, especially compared with those in the United States, widespread experimentation with new contraceptives continues. The Maternal Health Association got its start testing "orals" among lower-class Mexicans and exists today largely through similar contract research.

Pressures to expand local markets are intensified by the competitive nature of the drug industry in Mexico. In contrast to the regulations governing investment in other industries, there are no a priori limitations on foreign ownership. Large foreign firms have bought into the local market to the extent that 80 percent of private sales are accounted for by four affiliates of foreign companies, but local drug firms, aided by nonexistent patent laws and contracts for supplying generic drugs to state institutions, keep the market very competitive.[52] The advantage of the large foreign companies lies in their ability to detail physicians and pharmacists with free samples and subsidized clinical tests. One of the less charitable interpretations of the movement toward population control in Latin America is that it represents a conspiracy by multinational drug manufacturers to swell their profits by pushing the "pill." While we cannot document the existence of a conspiracy, the drug industry in Mexico uses every means available to it within locally acceptable norms to promote its birth control products. The local Searle affiliate went so far as to enlist the participation of other companies in a multifaceted campaign to promote family planning in general. The impact of this on public policy is hard to measure. We do know, however, that use of artificial contraceptives grew rapidly during the 1960's. According to one estimate in 1971 roughly ten percent of all fertile women in Mexico used birth control devices, with commercial channels supplying the majority and the Association and Foundation clinics servicing the remainder.[53] That same year a public health official called for a national effort to educate women in the use of contraceptives, since he estimated that some 500,000 women in Mexico City alone already used the pill but only a small percentage of them had medical supervision.[54] Throughout its drive to increase the local use of birth control devices, however, the drug industry was careful not to push the government too hard.[55] Even the foreign companies learned to live with Mexican political practices.

External Linkage Groups

In Chapter 4 of this book I have attempted to demonstrate the central role played by external organizations in the evolution of antinatalist population policies in Latin America. The Mexican Revolution was fought in a large measure to free Mexico from foreign domination. External linkage groups are at work in the population field, but they carefully avoid any appearance of direct involvement in politics. Indirectly, of course, they do affect policy.

Most noticeable by its absence is official United States government assistance for population-family planning activities. Given the bitterness in United States-Mexican relations up to World War II, the institutional revolutionary regime has been careful to demonstrate independence from its neighbor to the north. It has accepted only token foreign aid from the United States. There is no Agency for International Development (USAID) mission nor any Peace Corps volunteers in Mexico. Because of nationalism, the negative connotations of foreign aid, the fact that population control is very sensitive internally, and attitudes like the following, expressed in a 1965 newspaper column just after President Johnson announced his support for population control, the Mexican government adamantly refused bilateral population assistance from the United States government, even to private groups.

> Mania—speaking frankly, which is how one ought to speak, I do not find a rational justification nor an excuse which is worthy explanation for the attitude with characteristics of mania adopted by persons and groups in the United States who, without the pretext of promoting the social welfare and preventing the grave risks threatening the world, have become something like universal propagandists or ecumenical 'apostles' for what they call 'family planning' or 'birth control' and which, particularly with reference to some of the means that they proposed, ought to be called debasement of moral law, a crime against nature, and threat to life.[56]

In the late 1960's USAID officials considered the possibility of channeling funds to the two family-planning associations through IPPF, the Population Council, and the Pathfinder Fund, but this tactic was rejected out of fear that it would be discovered and publicized in Mexico.[57]

Up to 1972 external population assistance came from safe, ostensibly nonpolitical private organizations such as IPPF, the Population Council, the Ford and Rockefeller Foundations, and the Pathfinder Fund. Together they made a variety of inputs into both private and public population-related activities. In fact, virtually every population-related activity in Mexico received significant foreign support. (See Table 16-1) Foreign participation increased with the shift in government policy. Missions from United Nations Agencies and the Pan American Health Organization helped prepare the new program after the basic policy decision was taken.

Even without direct assistance from the United States government, external linkages, ranging from the modest yet timely efforts of the Friends Service Committee to the considerable financial assistance of the Ford Foundation, have been prominent in Mexican population activities. Their influence on policy-making was not so much in the form of overt demands and supports as through the seeding and backstopping of local activities which con-

Table 16-1. External Assistance for Population-Related Activities in Mexico (Cumulative, January, 1973)

Recipient	Donor
I. Private	
A. Maternal Health Association	1. Pathfinder Fund
	2. Friends Service Committee
	3. Southwest Foundation
	4. Clayton Fund
	5. McAshan Educational Charitable Trust
	6. Contract Research
	7. Individual donations
B. Foundation for Population Studies	1. IPPF
	2. Population Council
	3. Ford Foundation
	4. Oxfam of Canada
	5. United Nations
C. Colegio de México	1. Population Council
	2. Ford Foundation
	3. Rockefeller Foundation
D. Mexican Institute for Social Studies	1. Ford Foundation
	2. Contract Research
E. American-British Hospital	1. Population Council
F. Inter-American Regional Workers Organization	1. Pathfinder Fund
G. Individual Training Fellowships	1. Population Council
	2. Pan American Health Organization
	3. USAID
H. Family Planning Services	1. Church World Service
II. Public	
A. National Autonomous University	1. Population Council
	2. Ford Foundation
B. Hospital de la Mujer	1. Ford Foundation
C. National Institute of Nutrition	1. Ford Foundation
D. Mexican Institute of Social Security	1. Ford Foundation
E. Mexican Government	1. United Nations
	2. Pan American Health Organization

Sources: USAID, Bureau for Technical Assistance, Office of Population *Population Program Assistance* (Washington, D.C.: Agency for International Development, 1971), p. 160; *1969 Annual Report* of the Maternal Health Association; documents of the Pan American Health Organization; *1971 Annual Report* of the Pathfinder Fund; and personal interviews.

stituted both indirect pressure on the government and the potential infrastructure of a public program. The continued availability of outside money facilitates acceptance of the new policy by minimizing the drain on scarce local sources. It appears, however, that the government will still not accept direct bilateral aid from the United States although indirect assistance is now possible.

Opponents of Family Planning and Population Control

Opposition to government population policy and family-planning programs does not come from secondary groups organized for that purpose. There are no pronatalist equivalents of the local family-planning associations. Rather, the principal obstacles are more likely to be social norms, elite attitudes, and existing policy. Initiation of activities by organizations favorable to population control and family planning in Mexico in the 1960's did, however, bring the latent hostility of existing groups to the surface. Reading through the Mexican newspapers of the period, one finds a public dialogue in which pronatalist spokesmen deny that rapid population is a problem or that it even exists. These challenges were often directed at the assertions of foreigners like President Johnson or Robert McNamara of the World Bank.[58] Occasionally there were direct attacks on the work of local family-planning groups. For instance, in 1970 a group known as the Unión de Mujeres Intelectuales y de Negocios (Union of Intellectual and Business Women) charged that the family-planning clinic in a large, public maternity hospital sterilized poor women without their consent.[59] The presence of such charges in the press undoubtedly had the ironical impact of raising public awareness of birth control techniques and services. Now women knew that the large maternity hospital offered family planning.

Because of its rejection of artificial contraception, the Catholic Church is perceived as the major obstacle to government population control efforts in Latin America. The position of the Church in Mexico is somewhat unique, however. As a result of the revolution's strong anti-clerical content, it lost its traditionally privileged place in Mexican society. The 1917 Constitution secularizes education, deprives the Church of the right to own property, and provides for formal separation of Church and State, at the same time subjecting the Church to close government control. According to Vallier, "The Church is separate from the State but does not possess full independence to direct and develop its own affairs."[60] Beyond the constitutional limitations governing it, the Church's policy influence is circumscribed further by its political position. Even though overt anti-clerical sentiments are seldom displayed in contemporary Mexico, the Church is not and could not be an integral part of the revolutionary coalition headed by the PRI. This would violate the programmatic consensus of the institutional revolution. Clerical interests are represented by the leading minority party but heretofore ineffective National Action Party (PAN) and the discredited Sinarchista movement.[61] There is only fragmentary evidence that either organization has taken an active stand on the population issue.[62]

In keeping with its general political caution, the Church has not actively attempted to pressure the government on the population issue. On the contrary, it has always found it possible to agree with the government, even after the flip-flop in policy.

From the early 1960's until Pope Paul's encyclical *Humanae Vitae* on birth control in mid-1968, the Mexican Church betrayed the uncertainty of not knowing what the Pope would decide. The Pope selected a Mexican family to help represent Latin American lay attitudes in the Pontiff's well-publicized reconsideration of the birth control issue.[63] In the face of uncertainty it was hard for the local Church and its allies to take a stand on the practice of family-planning and government population control programs. There was much public vacillation. In early 1965, for example, it was reported that the local hierarchy and the Christian Family Movement, an important lay group, had approved the practice of artificial contraception to avoid economic stress and marriage difficulties caused by too many children.[64] Shortly thereafter, however, a group of Jesuit priests denied that use of the pill by Catholic women was now acceptable to the Church.[65] As the declarations and counter declarations became more confusing, Catholic leaders retreated into refusing to go on record until the Pope issued his encyclical. In an interview in 1967, the head of the Christian Family Movement stated that family planning in general was not a matter that should concern the state and that individual Catholics must await the Pope's decision.[66]

Along with the effect of weakening the Church's potential impact on public policy, the extended period of indecision and public debate undoubtedly accelerated growing public awareness of artificial birth control techniques without clarifying the Catholic position on them. With the publication of *Humanae Vitae* the local hierarchy quickly fell into line. In instructions to priests the Mexican Episcopate declared that, "All we Catholics are obligated to receive this teaching of the Pope . . . as certain and definitive."[67] The impact of its position was at best contradictory. There is evidence that its new found opposition did not significantly offset the growing popularity of family planning among the population, a trend reinforced by the Church's earlier ambiguity. A survey of women in three large cities found that the publication of *Humanae Vitae* and local instructions to obey it did not affect the increasing use of artificial contraceptives.[68] On the other hand, as we shall see, the encyclical came at a crucial time in the struggle between opponents and proponents of family planning within the Mexican government. In spite of the formal separation of church and state, the encyclical probably made it more difficult for those favoring government action. Most importantly, it kept the Church in line with official policy.

Despite the encyclical, the local Church's opposition did not last. In late 1972, the Mexican Episcopate gave qualified support to the government's newly announced family planning program. Justifying their "reinterpretation" of *Humanae Vitae* with reference to the emergency situations confronting Mexico, the bishops condoned artificial birth control which is adopted after clear examination of parental conscience.[69] The significance of this announcement lies not only in its substance but also in its timing. That it followed rather than preceded the change in government policy indicates the essentially reactive role of the Church in Mexican politics. It managed to side with the government even when official policy contradicted Catholic doctrine. In general, then, the Church's role in population policy-making underlines the extent to which it has been co-opted into the corporate structure of Mexican politics.

Interest Groups and Population Policy: Preliminary Conclusions

Thus far, our examination of the population-related interest groups suggests their awareness both of vulnerability to a variety of official sanctions and, as a result of the necessity of working in a quiet, nonantagonistic way to effect policy changes. Rather than forming coalitions to mount public campaigns and confront each other in the policy-making arena, as say the opponents and proponents of legalized abortion do in the United States, interested Mexican groups did not challenge each other or the government directly, but worked in a number of unobtrusive ways to demonstrate that their objectives were compatible with the programmatic consensus of the regime. The pressures that were applied were done so behind the scenes at the elite level. The actual impact of this indirect strategy—of providing officials with updated "technical" advice so that they can make the right decisions— will momentarily receive more attention as we move to the inner sanctums of policy-making. Failure to take this approach was costly for the Maternal Health Association, however. Interested parties do not publicly demonstrate unless they are supportive. After the basic decision to change policy was made in 1972, those groups actively in favor of it were called upon to contribute to the details of its implementation and the others were expected to declare their support or keep quiet.[70]

Organizations central to Mexican politics have been missing from our analysis up to this point. What about the semi-official interests represented by the Institutional Revolutionary Party? The labor, peasant, and popular sectors of PRI all might have logically pushed for the expansion of family planning as something benefiting their constituencies. On the contrary, however, there is little evidence of such action, and, where it did occur, it was quickly abandoned when higher-ups in the revolutionary coalition indicated their displeasure. In 1969, the Mexican Labor Confederation, one of the pillars of PRI, let it be known that it wanted to initiate family-planning services for its considerable membership. Such a move probably indicates that the Confederation had been working within PRI for national family planning and, because of certain moves made in that direction, felt that it could go ahead on its own with at least the tacit approval of regime leadership. However, shortly after the PRI candidate for the 1970 presidential election began attacking proponents of population control, the Confederation dropped its program without a word of public protest or explanation.[71] Subsequent lobbying, if any, was carried on quietly within the confines of the party. The behavior of semi-official interest groups conforms to the authoritarian paradigm and emphasizes their corporate, rather than pluralist, character. The same pattern holds for powerful industrial and commercial interests in Mexico who showed little public interest in population except *ex post facto* support of the government's decision to change its policy.

Public opinion and the press are two other potential sources of policy inputs. The profile of Mexican public opinion on population matters does not differ significantly from those of other Latin American nations. KAP (Knowledge, Attitudes, and Practices) studies and other survey research uncover relatively widespread latent support for family planning. A 1964 survey by the United States Information Agency found that slightly over one-half of the Argentine, Mexican, and Brazilian respondents approved of helping people to learn to limit the number of their children.[72] In a study of contemporary Mexican women using survey data, a Mexican sociologist concludes that they are no longer disposed to accept family size as beyond their control, but instead increasingly consider the use of scientifically developed birth control devices as both licit and necessary.[73] The policy consequences of such attitudes are questionable, however. The most politically active segments of the population satisfy their family-planning needs through commercial channels while the lower classes showed no active desire to transform their private needs into public demands. Family planning and population control were not public issues in Mexico any more than in the rest of Latin America, until the government declared them so. Had they been, then there might have been serious obstacles to the transformation of public demands into official policy.

An assessment of the media, especially newspapers, indicates that their role was essentially passive. Editorial coverage of the population issue included representatives both in favor of and against government family-planning efforts.[74] The prestigious Mexico City dailies took cautiously pro-family-planning positions while the provincial and conservatives *El Sol* chain along with mildly leftist *El Dia,* tended to be anti-family planning.[75] But our survey of newspaper coverage fails to uncover any sustained criticism of official policy.[76] This is not to say that the media did not affect policy; rather it is to call attention to the indirect nature of its influence. It seems reasonable to expect that the widespread coverage given the population explosion and related developments during the 1960's affected the knowledge, attitudes, and practices of the *attentive* public, making it at least receptive to a shift in government population policy. When it came to direct comment on government policy, the media exercised self-restraint unless its position was favorable.

Despite the existence of a plurality of organized interests, group behavior seemed to be more in keeping with the authoritarian model of Mexican politics. Instead of openly lobbying for a change in government policy using the techniques associated with interest group politics in the United States and other developed democratic systems, the advocates of family planning and population control worked quietly to erode the rationale for traditional policy and build justification for a new policy. Once the government decided to change policy, these groups were quick in offering their congratulations and support while the opponents of family planning caved in to the new policy. The basic policy decision, however, was made well within the confines of the institutional revolutionary regime. It is to this process that we now turn.

POLICY-MAKING WITHIN THE REGIME

Since Mexican population policy cannot be explained solely, or even primarily, in terms of interest group interaction, we must now direct our attention to the regime itself. Unfortunately from the researcher's perspective, it is not easy to penetrate the "black box" of Mexican policy-making. Policy decisions do not emerge from readily observable steps. Rather they tend to appear abruptly and mysteriously from the inner sanctum of the revolutionary coalition. Nevertheless, there is enough information available to allow us to trace and tentatively analyze the evolution of population policy up through its sudden reversal in 1972.

Population as an Issue

The Mexican government could not indefinitely escape facing the issue of rapid population growth. While perhaps authoritarian in nature, the political system of Mexico is not impenetrable. The government could not prohibit discussion of the issue entirely; what it could do was structure the terms and level of the debate. By reaffirming its traditional pronatalist policy throughout the 1960's and into the 1970's, the government effectively discouraged public cries for a new policy. Behind the scenes, however, a debate developed within the governing coalition that produced some deviation in policy implementation at the lower levels of the bureaucracy and eventually led to a new policy. While we cannot definitely say what caused this reversal, it seems linked to the fact that the coalition ultimately came to perceive uncontrolled population growth and the denial of public family-planning services as threats to the very existence of the institutional revolutionary regime. Even though the decision to change policy came at a time of growing organized antinatalist activities, it did not occur directly in response to them.

Discussion of the population issue within the ruling coalition began sometime in the early 1960's under the administration of President Adolfo López Mateos (1958-1964). As early as 1957 there were calls in the press for the government to at least pay attention to national demographic trends,[77] but official responses to local and external suggestions for government action did not appear publicly until the early 1960's. In 1962 the Secretary of Public Health rejected birth control as being antithetical to Mexican religious and social values.[78] A year later in opening the National Congress of Gynecology and Obstetrics, the Secretary of Public Health enunciated the government's standard defense of its pronatalism. What the Mexican Revolution stood for was not birth control, he said, but a just distribution of wealth that could support a growing population.[79] In addition to the growing world debate on population and the development of oral contraceptives, two things may have helped catch official attention in the early 1960's: the 1960 census, which confirmed the nation's rapid rate of demographic growth; and President Lopez Mateos' state visit to India, a country with much publicized population-related problems.[80]

During the presidency of Gustavo Díaz Ordaz (1964-1970), governmental consideration of the population issue intensified and some tentative steps were taken toward a change in national policy. Díaz Ordaz took power during a period of growing world concern about the population explosion. Local developments also tended to focus attention on population. The previous administration had allowed pharmaceutical companies to begin producing and marketing oral contraceptives locally and the first private family-planning association was already functioning. Other groups, usually with external support, initiated the various population-related activities referred to earlier during the mid 1960's so that the new government faced an atmosphere in which family planning and population control were increasingly on the minds of the attentive public.

The Erosion of Traditional Policy

During Díaz Ordaz's administration, a group within the ruling coalition began quietly pushing for the introduction of public family-planning services. Publicly, government officials continued to reject the necessity of population control in Mexico. In 1966 a spokesman for the Department of Public Health stated that, ". . . the government considers that population growth, rather than posing serious economic problems, is a factor conducive to national progress." [81] There was some ambiguity in the public position of the government on the right of individuals to practice birth control, however. According to another statement in 1966 made by several PRI congressmen, the government not only respected the right of individual couples to plan their family but it also provided family-planning services for those unable to purchase them commercially.[82] And, in fact, public family-planning services did become available under Díaz Ordaz, who was reputedly a dedicated Catholic and clearly associated with the more conservative wing of the revolutionary coalition.[83] Government family-planning services began quietly, probably without an explicit presidential mandate. Although never justified in terms of limiting population growth, they may have reflected a growing fear, fed by domestic unrest, that the government would not be able to cope with such a rapidly increasing population. To admit this, however, would have been to admit the failure of the institutional revolution. In fact the government kept its venture into family planning fairly quiet.

The actual extent of government family planning under Díaz Ordaz and his predecessor is broader than was commonly realized, though it never reached major proportions. The best known clinic was in the largest maternity hospital in Mexico City (Hospital de la Mujer). Originally set up in the mid-1960's to provide family-planning counseling and devices to women admitted for post abortion complications, it extended these services to others and began training medical personnel in family planning.[84] The Mexican Social Security Institute, which operates the most extensive public health program in the country, dispensed family-planning services in some of its hospitals and clinics, once again in the name of controlling illegal abortion. It, along with the National Institute of Nutrition, also undertook population-related research projects during the mid-1960's.[85] But beyond these relatively well-known instances of family-planning activities, other government institutions, such as the Federal Employees Institute and Armed Forces hospitals, supplied their clientele with artificial contraceptives as part of normal health care. Thus, by the mid-1960's, one drug company estimated that government purchases accounted for around 15 percent of its local contraceptives sales, a percentage probably characteristic of other companies.[86]

Policy Reversal: Paternidad Responsable

The gradual, some felt inevitable, movement toward announcement of a national family-planning program came to an abrupt halt in the last year of the Díaz Ordaz administration, triggered by the nomination of a successor to the presidency. As is well-known, the only candidate who counts in Mexico is the PRI nominee. The final selection process for the 1970 election narrowed the field down to two "pre-candidates." On the issue of population and family planning, which was hardly a deciding factor, the two men differed. One, who served as Secretary to the Presidency under Díaz Ordaz and who had a brother directing the development of the Social Security Institute's family-planning activities, favored continuation, even expansion, of ongoing programs. The other, Luis Echeverría Alvarez, advocated the traditional pronatalist stance. Once he gained the PRI nomination and his position on population became clear, the family-planning activities of the outgoing administration stopped.

During his campaign, candidate Echeverría periodically reiterated his contention that Mexico needed more people. In January, 1970, he declared, "I do not know, perhaps those present do, if the pill is effective or not." But, he added, "I do know that we need to populate our country, that we need to have faith in our young people . . ."[87] We can only speculate as to why he took this position. It was not for religion since Echeverría is a professed agnostic. His political roots are in the left wing of the revolutionary coalition, and he has the reputation of being an intellectual. Perhaps his pronatalism reflected nationalism or leftist intellectual feelings; perhaps it was campaign posturing designed to appeal to the Left, which was very disenchanted with the government and PRI by 1970. Whatever the reasons, the effects illustrate the extent to which the President dominates Mexican politics and policymaking. Even before his election and inauguration, government policy reflected Echeverría's position. Plans for expanding government services in cooperation with the Fundación para Estudios de la Población were scrapped.[88] As we have already seen, the Mexican Labor Confederation abandoned its familyplanning proposal. On taking office, he continued to take a pronatalist line, reiterating his campaign promise of no birth control programs during his administration.[89] He not only replaced the architect of the Social Security Institute's family-planning program (and brother of his former competitor for the PRI candidacy) as director of the Institute, but also forced him out of his civil service position.[90] Reacting to these cues, lower level bureaucrats began to roll back steps taken under the previous administration. The new director of the Hospital de la Mujer closed its family-planning clinic while Ministry of Finance officials held up approving a tax exempt status for contributions to the Fundación para Estudios de la Población.[91]

The offensive against organized family planning continued well into 1971 when indications of a weakening in the President's hard line began to appear. For instance, in May after an interview with the chief executive, the head of the Mexican Gynecological and Obstetrics Association reported that President Echeverría was studying the population problem and considering the possibility of birth control for medical reasons.[92] Then, with little further warning, in April of 1972 the government announced to a rather surprised world and Mexican citizenry that it was about to institute a comprehensive national family-planning program.

The central theme of the new policy is "responsible parenthood" (*paternidad responsable*). In selecting this slogan, Mexican authorities choose to play down macro-demographic planning and dispell any notions of compulsory birth control in favor of an emphasis on broadening the options open to individual couples. According to an official publication:

> Mexico's demographic policy is closely tied to policies applied in other areas. It in no way infringes on family decisions, but is based on persuasion and the use of essentially educational and health measures. It does not seek to place an arbitrary curb on population growth but to ensure higher living standards. Neither

does it attempt to resolve economic problems through population control.[93]

This description of the new policy stresses that "Family planning and responsible parenthood are very different concepts from compulsory birth control."[94]

Even though official explanations describe the new policy as one directed at serving individual families, there is convincing evidence that it was also motivated by a desire to curb population growth. The means selected for accomplishing this objective was a national family-planning program with its simultaneous emphasis on voluntarism and public education, an approach typical of Latin America. Organizationally the Mexican program is located in the Ministry of Health as part of an integrated mother-child care effort (in the General Office for Mother-Child Medical Attention which was set up in 1971) and in the Social Security Institute as part of its medical services. Other government agencies, such as the Social Security Institute for Federal Workers, are also initiating family-planning services under the Paternidad Responsable campaign.[95] Projected policy actions include:

1. technical and professional personnel training;
2. midwife training;
3. information for the medical corps and general public;
4. services;
5. research;
6. evaluation.[96]

The demographic intentions of the new program are not far beneath the surface. For instance, an official description of it begins with statements relating Mexico's rapid rate of population growth ("one of the highest in the world") to the struggle for national development.[97] In describing the objectives of his organization's participation in "paternidad responsable," an official of the federal employees social security institute mentioned lowering fertility along with extending family planning as a human right and preventing illegal abortions.[98] Finally, the government has proposed a new "General Population Law" with the stated purpose of lowering the population growth rate.

By 1973 it was clear that the Mexican government had abruptly abandoned its traditional pronatalism for a new population policy to slow growth through a national family-planning program. This radical transition was symbolized internationally by the selection of a number in good standing of the revolutionary coalition—Antonio Carrillo Flores, a former holder of the Finance and Foreign Affairs portfolios—to be Secretary General of the 1974 World Population Conference.[99]

CONCLUSIONS

In spite of the presence of a variety of organized interests, the population policy decision does not appear to support the pluralist model of Mexican policy-making. Rather it appears to confirm the authoritarian paradigm in that the decision was taken at the highest levels of the government independent of *direct* outside pressures. The level of demands made on the regime were relatively low, and its decision reflected an erratic relationship between it and them. It emerged during a period of declining interest group activity to the surprise of virtually everyone rather than at the climax of national debate and public bargaining over the population issue. The President and his close advisers apparently made the decision; certainly they announced the new program and took full credit for it. Thus, even in this second-level policy area, the status of the president as patrimonial leader is confirmed.[100] Finally, in keeping with regime's "revolutionary" consensus, the responsible parenthood campaign turned out to be a bit more daring and extensive than most other Latin American family-planning programs. As a new element in the revolutionary consensus, Mexicans were expected to, and did, rally in support of it.[101]

Why did the President and his advisers change their minds on the population issue? Attempting to answer this question should help isolate the factors that might influence the Brazilian or Peruvian regimes to reverse their population policies since their political systems approximate the authoritarian model.

The tentative explanation offered here for the Mexican flip-flop is that the top leadership of the ruling coalition finally came to see population control as of possible relevance to its primary goal of perpetuating the institutional revolutionary regime. What evidence is there to support this hypothesis? First of all, there is the circumstantial evidence of President Echeverría taking power in late 1970, at a time of rising domestic discontent with the revolutionary establishment as evidenced in the 1968 riots. In June of 1971 violence broke out again in the streets of Mexico City as right-wing thugs attacked students and guerrilla activities accelerated in the countryside. Secondly, and again using circumstantial evidence, 1971 was a bad year economically for Mexico. In Echeverría's first year in office, Mexico suffered its worst economic performance in over a decade. The Mexican economic miracle was threatened. [102] To a certain extent the slowdown reflected government policy aimed at curbing inflation, but any Mexican president must be concerned about national economic growth since it has been central to the success of the regime. Finally, there are the president's own public declarations in which he indicated that he too had come to see uncontrolled population growth as a threat. Speaking to the United Nations Conference on Trade and Development in Santiago in April, 1972, he recognized that rapid population growth posed a problem for the developing nations in attendance.[103] Then in his Second State of the Union Address in September of that same year, President Echeverría made a number of references to uncontrolled demographic developments in Mexico. For example, he pointed out the enormous growth of Mexico City,[b] the lack of employment opportunities, and the pressures of demographic expansion on agricultural land, and he stressed that:

> Mexico cannot call a halt when halfway along the road. It has no right to either indecision or conformism. Population growth could win out over economic development. Failure to make an intense, sustained effort could condemn the country to frustration and dependency.[104]

After a year and one-half in office, facing the frustrations of problems which did not disappear, the President and his advisors decided to gamble on a new approach. They, in effect, broadened the revolutionary consensus to encompass a previously rejected policy in the hopes that it would contribute to the maintenance of the regime itself. Although baptized with the vague, unthreatening title of "responsible parenthood," the new policy is aimed at protecting interests at the very core of the institutional revolutionary regime. Therefore, the new Mexican policy is tied more directly to the all-important process of national development than is the case in countries like Chile or Costa Rica since the Mexican regime feels that it must have no stone unturned to maintain rapid economic growth and increasingly broaden the benefits of this growth in order to calm the unrest of recent years.[105]

If our analysis of the Mexican experience is valid, we would hypothesize that the Brazilian and Peruvian governments will revise their demographic policies, not in response to organized pressures, but when they see population control as relevant to their essential interests. Both countries feature increasingly institutionalized, semi-corporate, authoritarian regimes which base their *raison d'etre* on the ability to deliver rapid, sustained economic development. One, of course, should not overlook differences between the two military regimes. The Peruvian government puts more emphasis on redistribution of wealth, for example, but both publicly identify themselves with national development above all else. One frequently hears talk today of the Brazilian economic miracle, for instance. According to our hypothesis, we would expect the Brazil-

---

[b]The President's brother, who is an MD, was named to head the fight to control air pollution in Mexico City, where the municipal government had already set up an office to analyze demographic developments. *Newsweek* magazine featured an article (August 27, 1973) on pollution in Mexico City. It claimed that Mexico's capital was the world's most polluted city and that the problem was aggravated by the population explosion. Mexico City is one of the fastest growing urban areas in the world, although much of it comes from migration.

ian and Peruvian government to turn to national family-planning programs should their countries experience a year or two of economic slowdown. In other words, what we are predicting is that in neither instance is the change in policy likely to be gradual and unobtrusive, as it has been throughout Latin America, except perhaps in Colombia which also has a semi-authoritarian regime, but rather abrupt and fullblown as in Mexico. And, once the basic policy decision is made at the highest level of government, organized interests from the Church down will be expected to forget previous policy and declare their support for family planning and population control.

Returning to a general concern of this paper, the facts of the population policy case, as they are available to us, seem to best fit—and in a limited sense confirm—the authoritarian paradigm of Mexican politics.[106] However, they also emphasize that, while Mexico is not democratic, neither is it totalitarian. There is a plurality of organized interests that do influence public policy.[107] That the extent and nature of their influence is different than the pluralist paradigm implies should not lead to the conclusion that they are unimportant. Even though the basic policy decision was taken at the highest levels of the revolutionary regime, it was stimulated and informed by interested groups and individuals. Mexican scholars and research institutions provided the intellectual rationale for moving to control population growth,[108] while the availability of external financial assistance provided the means. The final decision was that of the President and his closest confidants, however, and only indirectly representative of other interests since, in contemporary Mexico, interest groups have neither the capabilities nor inclination to directly challenge the institutional revolutionary regime.

NOTES TO CHAPTER 16

1. "In its simplest terms a paradigm is just a pattern or framework that gives organization and direction to a given area of scientific investigation." Robert T. Holt and John M. Richardson, Jr., "Competing Paradigms in Comparative Politics" in *The Methodology of Comparative Research,* edited by Robert T. Holt and John E. Turner (New York: The Free Press, 1970), p. 23. In this paper we shall speak of paradigms of Mexican politics in the sense that one would refer to the pluralist or elitist paradigms of American politics, that is, generalizations emphasizing different variables and relationships of the political system.

2. El Colegio de México, Centro de Estudios Económicos y Demográficos, *Dinámica de la población de México* (México, D.F.: El Colegio de México, 1970), p. 5. While the death rate dropped dramatically, the crude birth rate registered only a slight decrease from 50.8 births per 1,000 people in 1930 to 44.0 per 1,000 people in 1930 to 44.0 per 1,000 in 1970, p. 48.

3. Mexico City had the highest birth rate of a sample of major Latin cities. *Ibid.*, p. 70. However, there is some evidence from the 1970 census that the national growth rate has declined.
4. For examples, *Ibid.*, and Roger D. Hansen, *The Politics of Mexican Development* (Baltimore: Johns Hopkins Press, 1971). A study by the UN Economic Commission for Latin America reported in *Excelsior*, September 5, 1972, p. 16A, that, of four Latin American nations representing regional types, Mexico had the most skewed income distribution.
5. Calman J. Cohen, "Mexico Lays Base for Nationwide Family Planning Program," *Population Dynamics Quarterly*, 1, No. 1 (Winter 1973), p. 2.
6. Eduardo E. Arriaga, *Mortality Decline and Its Demographic Effects in Latin America*, Population Monograph Series No. 6 (Berkeley: Institute of International Studies, University of California, 1970), p. 35.
7. Giberto Loyo, "Algunos problemas demográficos de México y América Latina," *Cuadernos Americanos*, CL, No. 2 (January–February, 1967), p. 9 (of reprint issued by the Fundación para Estudios de la Población).
8. Ma. del Carmen Elu de Leñero, *Mujeres que hablan*, (México, D.F.: Instituto de Estudios Sociales, A.C., 1971), pp. 32–33.
9. *Ibid.*, p. 33.
10. See Susan Kaufman Purcell, "Decision-Making in an Authoritarian Regime: Theoretical Implications from a Mexican Case Study," *World Politics*, XXVI, No. 1 (October, 1973), for example. Robert Scott in *Mexican Government in Transition* (Urbana, Illinois: University of Illinois Press, 1964) also deals with the policy implications of his interpretation of Mexican politics, although not as systematically as Purcell.
11. For an interpretative summary of the literature in English on Mexican politics up to 1969 see Carolyn Needleman and Martin Needleman, "Who Rules Mexico? A Critique of Some Current Views on the Mexican Political Process," *The Journal of Politics*, 31, No. 4 (November, 1969), pp. 1011–1034. In this piece the authors distinguish "four basic positions on the issues of the distribution of political power and the locus of decision making," p. 1014. All four concern the role of the president.
12. Scott, *Mexican Government in Transition* and L. Vincent Padgett, *The Mexican Political System* (Boston: Houghton Mifflin Company, 1966).
13. Padgett, *The Mexican Political System*, p. 158.
14. Scott, *Mexican Government in Transition*, p. 300.
15. Pablo González Casanova, *La democracia en México* (México: ERA, 1965); Hansen, *The Politics of Mexican Development*; Kenneth F. Johnson, *Mexican Democracy: A Critical View* (Boston: Allyn

and Bacon, Inc., 1971); and Richard R. Fagen and William S. Tuohy, *Politics and Prestige in a Mexican City* (Stanford: Stanford University Press, 1972). Frank Brandenburg in *The Making of Modern Mexico* (Englewood Cliffs, N.J.: Prentice-Hall, 1964) presented an earlier version of this interpretation.
16. For example, see Howard J. Wiarda, "Toward a Framework for the Study of Political Change in the Iberic-Latin Tradition: The Corporate Model," *World Politics,* 25 (January, 1973), pp. 206-236, and James M. Malloy, "Authoritarianism, Corporatism and Mobilization in Peru" (unpublished paper, April, 1973).
17. Johnson, *Mexican Democracy,* p. 60.
18. Hansen, *The Politics of Mexican Development,* p. 122.
19. Juan Linz, "An Authoritarian Regime: Spain," *Cleavages, Ideologies, and Party Systems: Contributions to Comparative Political Sociology,* edited by Erik Allardt and Yrjo Littunen (Helsinki: The Academic Bookstore, 1964), pp. 293-295.
20. González Casanova cited in Purcell, "Decision-Making in an Authoritarian Regime," p. 8.
21. *Ibid.,* pp. 3-11.
22. *Ibid.,* pp. 12-13.
23. The information used here comes primarily from printed sources available in the United States and Mexico. The newspaper clipping files of the International Population Program at Cornell University and Foundation for Population Studies in Mexico City were particularly valuable. In addition, the author interviewed persons knowledgeable on population and family planning, although he was not able to talk with government officials while in Mexico in the summer of 1971.
24. Needleman and Needleman, "Who Rules Mexico?", p. 1034.
25. Colville Deverell, "The International Planned Parenthood Federation: Its Role in Developing Countries," *Demography,* 5, No. 2, p. 574. Colville refers specifically to IPPF affiliates.
26. The Mexico City *News,* May 15, 1966.
27. From annual reports of the Association and interviews with knowledgeable observers in August, 1971.
28. From 1968 and 1969 annual reports.
29. In 1961 according to information obtained in a confidential interview.
30. Interviews with Association staff in August, 1971.
31. For example, in a 1966 interview the Association's founder declared that the Mexican government must eventually play an active role in family planning. The *News,* October 2, 1966.
32. *IPPF News,* No. 213 (December, 1971).
33. According to an interview with a Foundation official, **IPPF** supplied from 50 to 60 percent of the yearly income for a budget of around $1,000,000 in 1971 while patient fees provide another 20 to 30

percent with the remainder coming from foundation grants and local donations.
34. F.E.P.A.C., *La Fundación para Estudios de la Población* (México: F.E.P.-A.C., 1970), pp. 6-10.
35. Horacio F. Gutiérrez, "Las actividades médicas y clínicas en siete asociaciones miembros de la Federación Internacional de Planificación de la Familia, Región del Hemisferio Occidental, durante 1970" (paper presented at IPPF seminar, Managua, Nicaragua, July 5-10, 1971).
36. "La Fundación para Estudios de la Población" (mimeo, n.d.), p. 15.
37. The tax exempt status was eventually renewed. One explanation for the forced closing of the clinic in the Hospital de la Mujer was that it was attracting too much publicity. Interview with Foundation official and *IPPF News*, No. 208 (July, 1971).
38. After the government had announced its new program, the fact that the "head of a private clinic" was warned by officials not to speak to reporters indicates that discretion in the reactive role is expected. *New York Times*, June 22, 1972. Change in government policy allowed the Foundation to accept external aid from a wider variety of sources, most importantly from the UN Fund for Population Activities.
39. *Excelsior*, February 13, 1965.
40. In 1972 the Ford Foundation gave IMES a three year grant of $200,000 to supplement its earlier support for research, training, publications, and public information. *Ford Foundation Letter*, 3, No. 6 (September, 1972), p. 7. The rest of its income is generated by contract research. IMES research has three foci: (1) the family and population, (2) socio-economic topics, and (3) socio-cultural topics which include the church. "IMES, a.c.: Objetivos, organización, proyectos, publicaciones, 1970-72" (brochure, n.d.).
41. Examples of its publications include: Enrique Brito Velázquez, *¿Quién escucha al Papa?* (1971); Ma. del Carmen Elu de Leñero, *¿Hacia dónde va la mujer mexicana?* (1969); Luis Leñero Otero, *Población, Iglesia y cultura* (1970); and Oscar Maldonado P., *Los Católicos y la planeación familiar* (1969).
42. Interview with IMES official.
43. *Dinámica de la población de México*, pp. 1-2.
44. Interview with Colegio official, who gave the example of the Colegio's alleged involvement in the 1968 student riots as generating great governmental disfavor and warnings to refrain from assisting and sheltering the dissident students.
45. *Ibid*.
46. *Actividades del CEED*, No. 14 (abril-mayo-y junio de 1971).
47. *Dinámica de la población de México*, p. 3.
48. The Colegio also published a two volume set of the proceedings of the conference. See Unión Internacional para el Estudio Científico

de la Población, *Conferencia regional latinoamericana de población, Actas* (Mexico: Colegio de Mexico, 1972).
49. See for example the article "México genera una fuerza laboral que no podría absorber" in *Excelsior,* July 4, 1971, which is an interview with Urquidi and the director of the Center in which they discuss various aspects of Mexican population dynamics in relation to its economic growth.
50. "México y la píldora," *Expansión,* I, No. 7 (April 23, 1970).
51. *Ibid.*
52. Information on the drug industry and its role in the diffusion of family planning came from an interview with a former executive of a large foreign-owned pharmaceutical company.
53. Interview with former drug company executive. His estimates were based on private market surveys plus published figures of family-planning associations.
54. *El Día,* June 14, 1971.
55. For instance, the drug companies backed away from the more aggressive aspects of the Searle proposal, including plans for an "educational" television show.
56. *Excelsior,* February 18, 1965.
57. From official USAID files. For 1969 United States officials agreed to quietly encourage the Mexican government to act on population without involving the United States government.
58. The rejection to McNamara's periodic warnings on population growth was particularly vehement. See *El Sol* (chain of provincial papers), December 8, 1969, and *El Día,* September 24, 1970.
59. Story carried in *El Día,* August 26, 1970, and several other papers. The hospital administration replied that its clinic offered family-planning services on a voluntary basis and performed sterilizations only for reasons of health.
60. Ivan Vallier, *Catholicism, Social Control, and Modernization in Latin America* (Englewood Cliffs, N.J.: Prentice-Hall, Inc., 1970), p. 35.
61. *Ibid.,* pp. 129–130.
62. A letter to *Hispania,* 54, No. 3 (September, 1971), p. 585, reported that priests in Zacatecas with financial support from "the militant rightist Sinarchista" group forced a local family-planning center to close.
63. *Ovaciones,* March 30, 1965.
64. *El Norte,* January 29, 1965.
65. *Novedades,* February 28, 1965.
66. *La Prensa,* March 16, 1967.
67. Cited in Brito Velázquez, *¿ Quién escucha al Papa?,* p. 18.
68. *Ibid,* p. 63 and pp. 83–84. The percentage of the sample using pills grew from 13.7 percent in 1966 to 33.3 percent in 1969 while a corresponding drop in the use of the rhythm method occurred from 86.3 percent in 1966 to 66.7 percent in 1961.

69. Report of story in *Excelsior,* December 14, 1972, from UPI wire-service report of December 16, 1972.
70. Purcell, in "Decision-Making in an Authoritarian Regime," and Fagen and Tuohy, in *Politics and Privilege in a Mexican City,* stress that interest groups are aware that the policy process opens up to broader participation once the basic principle is decided.
71. Reconstruction of the incident done with information from confidential files and interviews.
72. From USIA, World Survey II (1964), question No. 9. Data processed by the Roper Center. The actual distribution of positive responses was: 59.77% for Argentina, 53.27% for Mexico; and 51.07% for Brazil. For a more recent comparative study see Leñero (ed.), *Población, Iglesia y cultura.* The findings presented in the latter work indicate that Mexican public opinion is somewhat less receptive to family planning than public opinion in Brazil, Chile, Colombia, and Venezuela.
73. Ma. del Carmen Elu de Leñero, ¿ *Hacia dónde va la mujer mexicana?,* p. 102.
74. Assessment based upon review of clippings on population in Mexican newspapers assembled by the International Population Program at Cornell University and by the Fundación para Estudios de la Población. The two clipping files cover the period from 1956 to 1971.
75. Categorization suggested by informed observer and review of clippings. The publisher of *Novedades,* a leading Mexico City paper, is on the board of directors of the Fundación para Estudios de la Población.
76. Survey does not include newspaper coverage after the shift in policy. In a personal communication with the author, Robert Bezdek points out that there were limited attacks on the President's policy, most notably those in *Excelsior* by Abel Quezada, an editorial cartoonist.
77. See articles by Gonzálo Blanco, an agronomist, in *El Nacional,* June 4, 1957, June 19, 1958, October 9, 1958, and November 13, 1958.
78. *La Prensa,* August 16, 1962. He implied that he spoke with the President's endorsement.
79. *Excelsior,* June 10, 1963.
80. Impact of Indian trip suggested in interview with observer of population developments in Mexico.
81. *Novedades,* March 5, 1966.
82. *Novedades,* March 29, 1966
83. Confidential interview. Díaz Ordaz's conservative inclinations were revealed in the 1968 confrontation with Mexican students. See Johnson, *Mexican Democracy: A Critical View,* pp. 148–164.
84. *El Día,* August 26, 1970 and personal interviews.
85. Confidential interviews.

86. Information provided by a former official of Searle's Mexican affiliate. According to this source, the government added birth control pills to its list of standard approved medicines (*Cuadro Básico*) in the early 1960's. First pills were prescribed to remedy certain "female problems" and later as contraceptives.
87. *Excelsior,* January, 1970.
88. Confidential interview.
89. See, for example, *El Heraldo,* April 19, 1970.
90. Confidential interview.
91. *IPPF News,* No. 208 (July, 1971) reports a prolonged debate taking place within the government over the tax exemption question and indicates that some governmental officials were using it to harass the Foundation. Other sources confirm this interpretation.
92. From clipping from Mexican newspaper in file of the Fundación para Estudios de la Población. The exact date and title of the paper were not discernible.
93. Republic of Mexico, Office of the President, *Mexican Newsletter,* No. 21 (November 30, 1972), p. 8.
94. *Ibid.,* p. 9.
95. For a complete list of cooperating organizations see Dirección General de Atención Médico Materno Infantil, *Paternidad Responsible-Planificacion familiar una tesis de projección social,* (México, D. 4: Editorial Pax-México, Libería Carolos Césarman, S.A., 1973).
96. Republic of Mexico, Office of the President, *Mexican Newsletter,* No. 21 (November 30, 1972), p. 9.
97. *Ibid.,* p. 8.
98. Dr. Andres G. de Wit in *El Informador* (Guadalajara), June 30, 1973.
99. *Population Crisis,* VIII, No. 3 (November, 1972), In the past Mexico had on occasion worked to block actions by international bodies which it considered to be antinatalist in nature. According to a foundation official resident in Mexico, Carrillo Flores, among others, is pressing President Echeverría to say something specific about the demographic goals of the new program. Personal correspondence to the author, July 10, 1973.
100. "Once the Mexican president and his advisors are in agreement regarding the wisdom of making the decision, the president publicly associates himself with it. All important decisions are formally initiated by the president and the president both claims and receives full credit for the decision." Purcell, "Decision-Making in an Authoritarian Regime," p. 27.
101. In a cartoon poking fun at the regime's insistence on cloaking its actions in the mystique of the revolution, Abel Quezada traces the evolution of the recently announced "Health Revolution," which includes family planning, to the founding of the *Institutional* Revolutionary Health Party." *Excelsior,* July 19, 1973.
102. See the *New York Times* end of the year economic review for Latin

America, January 28, 1972. The title of the article on Mexico is "Mexico: No More Miracle."
103. República de México, Oficina de la Presidencia, *Carta de México,* No. 6 (April 19, 1972).
104. *Mexican Newsletter,* No. 8 (September, 1972).
105. While aggregate economic growth rates have recovered since 1971, the Echeverría administration is preoccupied with expanding participation in the economic miracle, according to several feature articles in the *Christian Science Monitor* by James Nelson Goodsell (July 31, 1973). It also faces severe inflation.
106. See Arend Lijphardt, "Comparative Politics and the Comparative Method," *The American Political Science Review,* 65, No. 3 (September, 1971), p. 692, for a discussion of the "theory-confirming" case study.
107. Philip D. Stewart challenges the notion that organized interests are *absent* in a totalitarian system in "Soviet Interest Groups and the Policy Process: The Repeal of Production Education," *World Politics,* XXII, No. 1, (October, 1969), pp. 29–50. The nature of organized interests and legitimate policy actions are much more restrained than in Mexico.
108. For recent work by distinguished Mexican scholars on the relationship between population growth and economic development, see Victor Urquidi in *Dinámica de la población de México,* especially p. 227, and Raúl Benítez Zenteno, "Política de población," in *El perfil de México en 1980,* Vol. 3 (Mexico, D.F.: Siglo Veintiuno Editores, S.A., 1972), pp. 557–580.

Biographical Notes on Contributing Authors

J. Mayone Stycos is a Professor of Sociology and the Director of International Population Program at Cornell University. He is the author of numerous works on Latin American population topics.

Thomas G. Sanders, who has a Ph.D. in religion, is currently a faculty associate of the American Universities Field Staff specializing in Latin American population matters.

Axel Mundigo, member of the faculty at Rensselaer Polytechnic Institute, is a consultant to the Population Council. He was formerly associated with the International Population Program at Cornell University, from which he received his doctorate in Sociology.

Benjamín Viel, long active in the Chilean family-planning movement is currently Director General of the Western Hemisphere Region of the International Planned Parenthood Federation.

Jorge Iván Hubner Gallo is a Professor of the Facultad de Ciencias Jurídicas y Sociales of the University of Chile.

José Consuegra is a Columbian economist.

The late *Gilberto Loyo* was a Mexican economist, Minister of State, and demographic spokesman for the PRI (Partido Revolucionario Institucional).

Vivian Epstein-Orlowski is currently Social Science Bibliographer at Yale University Library. She is also a candidate for the Ph.D. in Political Science at the University of Wisconsin where she is completing a dissertation on "Family Planning Programs and the Dynamics of Agenda-Building in Costa Rica and Chile" under the supervision of Professor Charles W. Anderson.

Germán A. Bravo is currently on leave from his post as Director of the Socio-Demographic Division of the Department of National Planning of Columbia in order to work on his Ph.D. in Sociology at the University of North Carolina, Chapel Hill. In his native country, he has also served as Technical Secretary of the National Population Council and has worked and published on Columbian population problems since graduation from the Catholic University of Louvain, Belgium, in 1966.

Howard J. Wiarda is a professor of Political Science at the University of Massachusetts in Amherst. He has written extensively on Latin American topics, especially on politics and development in the Dominican Republic and Brazil.

Iêda Siqueira Wiarda is a post-doctoral research associate in the Department of Political Science at the University of Massachusetts in Amherst and is presently engaged in a long-term project involving a comparative study of the population policy process in Latin America under a grant from the National Insitute of Health.

Richard Clinton is an assistant professor of Political Science at the University of North Carolina at Chapel Hill and a research associate at the Carolina Population Center. He has written extensively on politics and population, including a Ph.D. dissertation on Peruvian population policy for which he conducted field research.

About the Editor

Terry L. McCoy is a member of the Political Science Department and research associate of the Mershon Center at the Ohio State University. Since receiving his Ph.D. in Political Science from the University of Wisconsin-Madison in 1969, his main teaching and research interests have been in the analysis of public policy, particularly in Latin American. He has conducted research and published on the political dynamics of agrarian reform in Latin America and has most recently been engaged in research on Latin American population policies. In addition to his publications in the field of political demography, Prof. McCoy served as a consultant to the 1972 Summer Workshop for Curriculum Development in Demography at Cornell University and as a faculty member of the 1973 NSF Summer Institute in Social Demography and Population Policy at Lawrence University.